T

FOR REFERENCE
Do Not Take From This Room

ENCYCLOPEDIA OF GERMAN~AMERICAN GENEALOGICAL RESEARCH

ENCYCLOPEDIA OF GERMAN~AMERICAN GENEALOGICAL RESEARCH

CLIFFORD NEAL SMITH
and
ANNA PISZCZAN-CZAJA SMITH

Originally published: New York, 1976
Reprinted 2003 by Genealogical Publishing Co., Inc.
1001 N. Calvert St., Baltimore, MD 21202
Copyright © 1976 by Clifford Neal Smith
All Rights Reserved
Library of Congress Catalogue Card Number
International Standard Book Number 0-8063-1742-6
Made in the United States of America

To four distinguished Europeans
in the shadow of the
Holy Roman Empire German Nation

Count Charles-Henri de Pourtalès

Countess Ruth de Pourtalès
geb. v. Kleist-Retzow

Erich Pogorzelski

Jan Samuel François van Hoogstraten

CONTENTS

PREFACE

The primary purpose of this *Encyclopedia of German-American Genealogical Research* is to survey the material available to the genealogist seeking to link American lineages with their origins in German-speaking Europe.

Since German-American genealogical research has not been systematically studied heretofore, the writers hope this Encyclopedia will serve as an inventory of both the known and the unknown and a spur to the fashioning of new research tools. As examples, we hope the vast emigration lists assembled at Hamburg and practically unknown in the United States can be translated and ordered in such manner as to make them readily available to American researchers. Another project would be to reissue the lists of emigrants that have appeared in various German publications, few of which are accessible in America.

A further purpose of the Encyclopedia is to provide American researchers with background material on German customs, sociological stratification, governmental organization, and ethnographic considerations having a bearing upon immigrant ancestors. Since the teaching of history and literature in the United States is primarily devoted to the British background, very few Americans have much knowledge of the widely divergent conditions within the Holy Roman Empire German Nation, despite the fact that so many Americans are of German descent.

At the outset it had been hoped that a listing of all known emigration files in German archives could be included in this Encyclopedia, but, upon completion of the list, it was found to be far too large for inclusion, and so it is to be published separately under the title *American Genealogical Resources in German Archives (AGRIGA)*. When it appears, researchers will want to consider its contents in their research. Subject matter too detailed to be included in either this Encyclopedia or in *AGRIGA* but too lengthy for journal articles—for example, the large collection of muster rolls of German mercenaries who fought in the American Revolution—will be found in a newly instituted series entitled *German-American Genealogical Research Monographs*

(Westland Publications). Journal articles resulting from our research in German-American genealogy appear in the *National Genealogical Society Quarterly,* especially if dealing with material before 1800, and in the *Illinois State Genealogical Society Quarterly,* when pertaining to material after that date.

DEFINING GERMANDOM

It is not easy to say who is a German. To begin with, there is the problem of what comprises the German language. Usually, one thinks of *Hochdeutsch* (High German), the language of educated speakers, but to confine the scope of this Encyclopedia to such speakers, or to areas where High German was indigenously spoken, would be highly artificial. All along the *Wasserkante* (water's edge) from Holland to the Baltic lands, *Plattdeutsch* (Low German) was spoken, and these speakers certainly must be included. However, the Low-German-speaking Netherlanders are not included, because Dutch history and social organization have independent origins, and the corpus of their manuscript collections is distinct and worthy of separate treatment.

Within central Germany itself, the Jews comprised a special group speaking *Jüdisch* (Yiddish), a venerable Middle High German dialect spoken until the beginning of the nineteenth century among the Jews of Germany and into present times in Slavic lands. Records of Jewish immigrants to America have been included in this Encyclopedia because, when extant, they are to be found commingled with other records in Germany, and because we feel a particular obligation to contribute to the reconstruction of information largely destroyed during the Holocaust of the Third Reich period.

For southern and southwestern Germany it has been especially difficult to delineate the scope of this Encyclopedia. Should one include the records of German-speaking Austria and Switzerland and those of the enclaves of Germans in Slavic Europe? Where possible, we have done so, but there has been no systematic attempt to include them all, simply because most of the bibliographic information is at least fifty years old, fragmentary, and possibly no longer accurate.

A second problem in defining the scope of this Encyclopedia is a historical one: Which borders ought one to use for Germany? If one were to use the shifting limits of the Holy Roman Empire German Nation, the official title from 962 to 1806, one would ignore important German-speaking areas, principally in the Alsace, Lorraine, and the old archbishopric of Lüttich (Liège), which in the minds of earlier immigrants to America were "German" regardless of the flags which flew. One is left with a central truth about German history: Germany is an ideal in the hearts of men which has never, in a thousand years, corresponded to the shifting political boundaries. Always there have been German-speaking areas of Europe not subject even theoretically to a German central administration. One can say only that most of the material covered in this Encyclopedia pertains to the core of Germany with particular emphasis on southwestern Germany, Baden-Württemberg, Hessen, and Rheinland-Pfalz in modern parlance, from whence a large portion of the immigrants to America came.

GERMAN-AMERICAN GENEALOGY

There probably are more Americans of German descent than of English. Certainly in the period 1820–1957 German immigrants to America far outnumbered those from Great Britain.[1] The fact that the official language of the United States is English, rather than German, is a matter of historical accident, wherein English-speaking immigrants established the patterns of government and society under the British Empire before the arrival of the main body of Germans. After the American Revolution, English immigration, though a steady stream, rarely exceeded the flood of German immigration. In 1882, the peak year of German immigration, 250,630 Germans entered the United States; during the same year, only 102,991 emigrants from Great Britain arrived. Today, it would be quite impossible to determine the precise size of either group in the American population, but certainly it can be said that German-American genealogical research is not merely "ethnic," carrying the connotation that it is a specialty of interest only to a few scholars.

In the future, American genealogical research may be as concerned with German ancestry as it currently is with English. Despite the large German component in the population, American genealogical literature has been overwhelmingly devoted to Anglo-Saxon Protestant origins. German-Americans have shown less interest in their lineages, even though genealogy, as a study, is perhaps more avidly pursued in Germany than in America.[2] There are at least three reasons for this lack of interest on the part of German-Americans. For one thing, many German ancestors emigrated to the new world with sentiments of bitterness toward the old; they turned their backs on Germany; they frequently refused to tell their American descendants much about their pasts. The residue of this bitterness often lingers on in their descendants in the form of disinterestedness.

Probably an even more important cause for the failure of German-American genealogy to develop as fully as that of Anglo-American genealogy has been the traumatic experiences of two world wars. German-speaking groups in America abruptly ceased speaking the language of their ancestors during the first world war and many of their newspapers were discontinued. When forced to choose between two cultures, German-Americans had little choice but to take on the American; the old German clubs and schools were closed. Being German-American—during wartime a considerable danger —became in peacetime something of an embarrassment. The writers hope that enmity between Germany and the United States is now at an end for all time, and that Americans of German descent will find in their ancestry the same pride that Anglo-Americans take in theirs.

A third, quite overwhelming, reason for the failure of German-American genealogy to develop has to do with the language barrier and the inaccessibility of the primary research materials. To this difficulty, this Encyclopedia particularly addresses itself.

SUBJECT MATTER INCLUDED IN THIS ENCYCLOPEDIA

The problem of what subject matter should be included in this Encyclopedia has proved to be an

---

[1] U.S. Department of Commerce. Bureau of the Census. *Historical Statistics of the United States, Colonial Times to 1957* (Washington, D.C.: Government Printing Office, 1960), pp. 56–57.

[2] For example, the *Archiv für Sippenforschung*, Germany's largest genealogical periodical, has a subscription list of over 7,000; the *National Genealogical Society Quarterly*, by way of contrast, has only 3,300.

extremely difficult one. The American genealogical researcher has little familiarity with German administrative history *(Verfassungsgeschichte),* yet without such knowledge the administrative procedures to which would-be emigrants were subjected becomes almost unintelligible. As a consequence, the Encyclopedia contains information, otherwise unconventional in a genealogical reference work, which a German researcher might find self-evident, but which for the American user is quite outside the realm of research experience. For example, land ownership and tenancy in western Germany is strikingly different from that of eastern Germany. The German researcher is likely to have this in mind almost subconsciously when planning a research strategy; the American researcher, accustomed to a very different system of land ownership, would miss a valuable insight into the motivations for ancestor migration without this knowledge. So, likewise, with the varying regional confessional differences—a German researcher would know, for example, that some cities in southwestern Germany are predominantly Protestant, whereas their immediate environs are mainly Catholic, but an American researcher would not even be aware of the historical reasons for these differences within the confines of a very small area, now submerged within the borders of the modern states.

In general, then, the Encyclopedia presents "background" information selected for its relevance to the circumstances and motivations of emigration and the cultural baggage the immigrants brought with them to America. The exclusion of specific material has been the most difficult decision to make. Should one, for example, include the lists of German mercenary-deserter immigrants of the American revolution, thus converting the Encyclopedia into a supplement to Strassburger's and Hinke's great work on early Pennsylvania-German settlers? The writers have elected, after much hesitation, to exclude such material, confining their discussion to a general essay setting forth the whereabouts of such deserter lists. The lists, themselves, are more appropriately the subect of journal articles and of monographs.

So, likewise, in the matter of published articles: Over the last fifty years several extraordinary bibliographies of printed material on German-American culture and genealogy have appeared. We have relied heavily of these bibliographies in fashioning our essays but wish in no way to supplant them. When possible, findings published in obscure, inaccessible German publications have been included in the essays in the conviction that, unless special effort is made to bring these findings to the attention of American researchers, they are unlikely ever to receive attention in the United States. Less emphasis has been placed on the more readily available English-language publications, for qualified researchers will know how to discover them for themselves.

BIBLIOGRAPHIC ESSAY

This essay deals mainly with those published works which, because of their great inclusiveness, can truly be called research tools. Throughout this Encyclopedia, bibliographic references have been kept to a minimum in order not to duplicate materials which can easily be found in these reference tools.

CASTING THE NET WIDELY

Researching the lineages in America of persons of German descent is no different from that of any other American--one uses the census data, land and probate records, ship entry lists, and the like, tracing backward from the present to the original immigrant. When the outlines of descent have been established, only the beginnings of a family history have been made. Placing one's ancestors in the context of their times and surroundings brings them to life; their actions become explicable; perhaps, even, it leads to hypotheses regarding the trajectories of the investigator's own life and those who come after him. Knowledge of the times and immediate surroundings in which one's ancestors lived implies study of the local history, religious customs and beliefs, and the day-to-day occurrences which affected them. Hereinafter follows an annotated list of the reference tools giving access to these areas of study.

To begin with, the genealogical researcher should survey the literature to determine what has already been written about the immediate group of persons surrounding his ancestor. If the ancestor belonged to a religious group, this certainly will lead to numerous published studies, either general as to the sect and its history, or specific as to the congregation in which he was a participant. If the ancestor was a member of a colony of settlers, this, too, may have been studied. If he participated in a political movement, a social club, or founded a business, the fact is probably noted somewhere in published form. For German-Americans there is a vast literature over and above the usual county and local histories. To find this published material, there are two useful guides:

¶ If the lineage dates from colonial times in America, Emil Meynen's *Bibliography on German Settlements in Colonial North America, Especially on the Pennsylvania Germans and Their Descendants, 1683-1933* will open fascinating new areas of study.

¶ If the lineages descends from a German immigrant after the American Revolution, Pochmann's and Schultz's *Bibliography of German Culture in America to 1940* will contain nearly all references, aside from those which may be found in general local history books not specifically German-American in subject matter.

In addition, the researcher should look for German-language newspapers and periodicals which might have reported salient events in the lives of his ancestors. To do so, one refers to Arndt's and Olson's great bibliography entitled *German-American Newspapers and Periodicals, 1732-1955*. These three bibliographic works are described in some detail hereinafter.

Meynen, Emil. *Bibliography on German Settlements in Colonial North America, Especially on the Pennsylvania Germans and Their Descendants,*

1683-1933. Leipzig, 1937; reprint ed., Detroit: Gale Research Co., 1966.

This work was prepared in Germany during the Third Reich period, in which it was the stated policy of the government to reacquaint Germans settled abroad with their European origins. It remains the standard work on the subject and contains references to 7,858 publications, both in German and English, many of which are quite obscure. Since the emphasis is on the Pennsylvania-Germans, there is considerably less material on later German immigration to the United States.

The citations are arranged by areas in the United States (and some in Canada), as for example, "German Settlements in New England," by religious denominations, by local historiography (usually arranged by county), and an extremely valuable section on family histories and biographies. The index is thorough.

Pochmann, Henry August, and Schultz, Arthur R. *Bibliography of German Culture in America to 1940*. Madison, Wisconsin: University of Wisconsin Press, 1953.

The work includes about 12,000 citations, alphabetically arranged by author, to books, periodical articles, theses, etc. This is the leading bibliography in the field. A good deal of water has passed under the bridge since 1940, however, and the bibliography is gravely in need of a supplement covering the many publications which have appeared in the intervening 35 years.

Genealogical researchers would be wise to read the introduction, giving particular attention to its footnotes. In them will be found many valuable leads to collections of German-Americana heretofore unpublicized. Some of the collections mentioned therein have since been described in the *National Union Catalog of Manuscript Collections*, described hereinafter, but others remain unlisted, neglected because they have never had the attention of trained archivists and librarians.

Arndt, Karl J. R., and Olson, May E. *German-American Newspapers and Periodicals, 1732-1955: History and Bibliography*. Heidelberg: Quelle & Meyer, 1961 (distributed in the United States by Clark University Press).

_____, and _____. *German-American Newspapers and Periodicals, 1732-1955: History and Bibliography*. 2d. rev. ed. New York: Johnson Reprint Corp., [1965].

This is a reprint of the 1961 edition with the addition of an appendix, pages 796-810, chiefly listing refugee and prisoner-of-war camp publications of the second world war.

_____, and _____. *The German Language Press of the Americas*. Munich-Pullach: Verlag Dokumentation, 1973.

This latter work is a supplement (often called volume 2) to the above two titles with the additions for Latin America and an extensive section on newly-found American periodicals and newspapers in German.

Newspapers can be an extremely useful aid to genealogical research. Birth and death notices in local newspapers often contain information available in no other source. And, if one asserts--as do these writers--that genealogy should have as its ultimate goal the construction of ancestral biographies, as well as the usual lineage charts, use of newspapers becomes of utmost importance.

The Arndt bibliographies give access to every known periodical published in the German language in the United States. There were hundreds of them, dating from the earliest immigrants in the American colonies down to modern times. Each entry gives information on dates of publication and the repositories in which copies will be found.

Arrangement of the work is by place of publication, which is only partially helpful to the genealogist, because place is not always a good indicator of the newspaper's readership and reportage. For example, under Inman, Kansas, is listed the *Wahrheitsfreund* (friend of truth), published by the Crimean Mennonite Brethren, a small band of immigrants closely related among themselves, who settled in various places in the Middle West, not entirely on farms around the town of Inman. In like manner, under Breda, Iowa, is listed the *Ostfriesen Zeitung: Heimatblatt der Ostfriesen in Amerika* (newspaper for immigrants from East Friesland), which may contain information on specific immigrants from northern Germany. Similarly, the *Luxemburger Zeitung* (newspaper for Luxemburg immigrants) was published in Chicago, and the *Schwäbische Wochenblatt* (Swabian weekly news) and *Der Schweizer* (the Swiss newspaper) were published in New York, each likely to contain information on specific immigrants to the United States from these German-speaking areas of Europe, regardless of the immigrants' places of residence in America. Of special interest are the newspapers serving well-defined religious groups; the Catholics, Lutherans, and Mennonites all had periodicals covering wider areas than congregations or parishes in the cities and towns in which they were published. There were also numerous social club, political, and other interest group periodicals, usually meant for a readership over regional or national areas.

One can over-emphasize the regional, rather than the local, character of many of the

German-language periodicals. In fact, a great many of them were the "home-town" newspapers which contain so much data for the researcher. Certainly, one of the best indicators of vigorous Germanic cultural growth in America was the existence of such local publications; a list of the towns and cities in which they were published is, correspondingly, a list of the major German settlements in the United States.

Thus it is that the genealogical researcher should spend considerable time with the Arndt bibliography, perhaps reading it page by page, in order to discover periodicals of interest to his research, if location and title indexes do not identify them for him. What is needed now is a special index to the principal

areas of reportage and readership covered by these periodicals; with such a tool in hand it would have been a simple matter to identify, for example, the publication of the Crimean Brethren, thereby gaining access to whatever genealogical information may be found in their newspaper. As the Arndt bibliography now stands, only random discovery or diligent search will turn up the existence of such publications, and even then only imperfectly.

Hereinafter follows a list of the towns and cities in the United States in which German-language periodicals were published. Not all states are listed, because no newspaper in German was published in them.

AMERICAN TOWNS AND CITIES IN WHICH
GERMAN-LANGUAGE PERIODICALS HAVE BEEN PUBLISHED

Alabama

Birmingham
Cullman
Mobile
Warrior

Arizona

St. Michaels

Arkansas

Fort Smith
Little Rock
St. Joe

California

Anaheim
Fresno
Lodi
Los Angeles
Oakland
Petaluma
Sacramento
San Diego
San Francisco
San Jose
Santa Barbara
Stockton

Colorado

Denver
Greeley
Leadville
Pueblo

Connecticut

Bridgeport

Hartford
Meriden
New Haven
Norwich
Rockville
Southbury
Waterbury

Delaware

Wilmington

District of Columbia

Washington

Florida

Jacksonville
Miami
Pensacola
San Antonio

Georgia

Atlanta
Savannah

Idaho

Cottonwood

Illinois

Addison
Alton
Apple River
Arlington Heights
Aurora
Beardstown
Beecher
Belleville

Bloomington
Brookfield
Cairo
Carlinville
Carlyle
Carmi
Centralia
Champaign
Chester
Chicago
Danville
Decatur
Dundee
East St. Louis
Edwardsville
Effingham
Elgin
Forest Park
Freeport
Galena
German Valley
Hawthorne
Highland
Hoyleton
Joliet
Kankakee
Kewanee
LaSalle
Lensburg
Leonore
Lincoln
Litchfield
McHenry
Mascoutah
Mattoon
Mendota
Mundelein
Mt. Olive
Naperville
Nashville
Nauvoo
Nokomis

Okawville
Ottawa
Pekin
Peoria
Peru
Quincy
Ravenswood
Red Bud
Rock Island
Rockford
Shermerville (Techny)
Springfield
Staunton
Sterling
Streator
Techny
Urbana
Warsaw
Waterloo
Wheaton
Woodstock

Indiana

Anderson
Batesville
Berne
Bowling Green
Brazil
Brookville
Collegeville
Crown Point
Elkhart
Evansville
Fort Wayne
Goshen
Hamburg
Hammond
Huntingburg
Indianapolis
Jeffersonville
Lafayette

SEARCHING FOR PRIMARY SOURCE MATERIAL

Genealogy, as it nears the twenty-first century, is a very different discipline than it was a hundred years ago. The old family histories, based upon inadequate sources, are nearly always found to be inaccurate when compared with newly-discovered data; they can be corrected only by reassessment and the use of primary source materials. The older researchers did not have facilities to enter the archival remains that we have today--and, indeed, researchers of the future will be in an even better position than we--because these remains, both in America and Germany, are now being brought into proper focus by union cataloging;

AMERICAN TOWNS AND CITIES IN WHICH

GERMAN-LANGUAGE PERIODICALS HAVE BEEN PUBLISHED--*Continued*

LaPorte
Logansport
Michigan City
Mount Vernon
New Albany
Richmond
Rockport
St. Meinrad
Seymour
South Bend
Tell City
Terre Haute
Vincennes

Iowa

Ackley
Andrews
Boone
Breda
Burlington
Carroll
Cascade
Cedar Bluffs
Cedar Rapids
Charles City
Clinton
Council Bluffs
Davenport
Decatur
Denison
Des Moines
Dubuque
Dumont
Dysart
Earling
Elkader
Essex
Fort Dodge
Grundy Center
Guttenberg
Holstein
Ida Grove
Independence
Iowa City
Keokuk
Lansing
LeMars
Lyons
Manning

Maquoketa
Marshalltown
Monticello
Muscatine
New Hampton
Newton
Osage
Ottumwa
Postville
Reinbeck
Remsen
Rock Rapids
Rockford
Schleswig
Sigourney
Sioux City
Spirit Lake
Sumner
Tama City
Toledo
Vinto
Walcott
Waterloo
Waverly
Wellsburg
Wheatland

Kansas

Atchison
Atwood
Burrton
Canada
Ellinwood
Emporia
Fort Scott
Great Bend
Halstead
Hays
Hillsboro
Hutchinson
Inman
Kansas City
Kingman
Kinsley
Lacrosse
Lawrence
Leavenworth
Lehigh
Lindsborg

McPherson
Marion
Marysville
Newton
Pittsburg
Russell
Topeka
Wichita
Winfield
Wyandotte

Kentucky

Berea
Covington
Louisville
Newport
Stanford

Louisiana

Lafayette
New Orleans

Maryland

Baltimore
Fredericktown
Hagerstown
New Windsor

Massachusetts

Boston
Clinton
Fitchburg
Greenfield
Holyoke
Lawrence
Lowell
Springfield
West Roxbury

Michigan

Adrian
Ann Arbor
Au Gres
Battle Creek
Bay City

Coldwater
Detroit
East Saginaw
Grand Rapids
Jackson
Lansing
Manistee
Marquette
Menominee
Monroe
Muskegon
Port Huron
Saginaw
Sebewaing
Sturgis
West Bay City

Minnesota

Carver
Chaska
Duluth
Fairmont
Freeport
Glencoe
Jordan
Lake City
Little Falls
Mankato
Melrose
Minneapolis
Mountain Lake
New Ulm
Owatonna
Perham
Red Wing
Rochester
St. Cloud
St. Paul
Shakopee
Springfield
Stillwater
Wabasha
Waconia
Winona
Wykoff

Missouri

Boonville

that is to say, the related holdings of various archives are juxtaposed in one composite index. The instrument which accomplishes this in the United States is the *National Union Catalog of Manuscript Collections*, commonly abbreviated to NUCMC, a project of the Library of Congress, which every genealogical researcher should be mindful of, whether he is interested in German-American genealogy or in any other facet of the genealogical research process.

In Germany, the Deutsche Gesellschaft für Amerika Studien (German Society for America Studies) at the University of Cologne brought to fruition a project of great importance to

---

AMERICAN TOWNS AND CITIES IN WHICH
GERMAN-LANGUAGE PERIODICALS HAVE BEEN PUBLISHED--*Continued*

California
Cape Girardeau
Centreton
Chamois
Clayton
Clyde
Concordia
Festus
Franklin
Fulton
Hannibal
Hermann
Higginsville
Jackson
Jefferson City
Joplin
Kansas City
Lexington
Marthasville
Moberly
O'Fallon
St. Charles
St. Joseph
St. Louis
Ste. Genevieve
Sedalia
Springfield
Starkenburg
Stewartsville
Warrenton
Washington
Westphalia

Montana

Butte
Great Falls
Helena
Plevna

Nebraska

Deshler
Fairbury
Falls City
Fremont
Grand Island
Hartington
Hastings
Jansen
Leigh

Lincoln
Meadow Grove
Nebraska City
Norfolk
Omaha
Schuyler
Seward
Steinauer
Sterling
Sutton
West Point
York

Nevada

Virginia City

New Hampshire

Manchester

New Jersey

Atlantic City
Bayonne
Bound Brook
Camden
Carlstadt
Egg Harbor
Elizabeth
Fairview
Hoboken
Irvington
Jersey City
Newark
New Brunswick
Orange
Passaic
Paterson
Sea-Isle City
Town of Union
Trenton
Union
Union City

New York

Albany
Amsterdam
Auburn
Bardonia

Brooklyn
Buffalo
College Point
East New York
Elmhurst
Elmira
Forest Hills, L.I.
Haverstraw
Hicksville
Huntington
Ithaca
Jamaica
Kingston (Rondout)
Liberty
Lockport
Long Island City
Mount Vernon
Newburgh
Newtown
New York
Poughkeepsie
Rochester
Schenectady
Sea Cliff
Staten Island
Syracuse
Tonawanda
Troy
Utica
Williamsburgh
Yonkers

North Carolina

Goldsboro

North Dakota

Arthur
Ashley
Berwick
Beulah
Bismarck
Dickinson
Fargo
Fessenden
Golden Valley
Harvey
Havelock
Hebron
Jamestown

Linton
McClusky
Mannhaven
Medina
Minot
New Salem
Richarton
Rugby
Stanton
Wahpeton
Wishek
Zap

Ohio

Akron
Baltic
Bellaire
Berea
Bluffton
Bowling Green
Bridgeport
Bucyrus
Canton
Carthagena
Celina
Chillicothe
Cincinnati
Cleveland
Columbiana
Columbus
Coshocton
Dayton
Defiance
Delphos
East Liverpool
Elyria
Findlay
Fremont
Germantown
Greenville
Hamilton
Ironton
Kenton
Kingsville
Lancaster
Lima
Lisbon
Lorain
Mansfield
Marietta

American genealogists and historians in 1967. Graduate students and collaborators of the Society analyzed the holdings of hundreds of archives in western Germany, from the national to the village level, to discover items having to do with German-American subjects--diplomatic relations, emigration, wills and estates, military and historical subjects. The result was an eleven-volume typescript, never published but available on microfilm or photocopied, entitled *Americana in deutschen Sammlungen* . . . (Americana in German collections). From this catalog, these writers have gleaned the entries which seem most likely to contain genealogical information, particularly regarding emigration from Germany to the United States, and have

---

AMERICAN TOWNS AND CITIES IN WHICH
GERMAN-LANGUAGE PERIODICALS HAVE BEEN PUBLISHED--*Continued*

Marion
Massilon
Millersburg
Minster
Morrow
Napoleon
New Bremen
New Philadelphia
Newark
Norwalk
Oak Harbor
Osnaburgh
Ottawa
Paulding
Perrysburg
Piqua
Pomeroy
Port Clinton
Portsmouth
Sandusky
Sidney
Springfield
Steubenville
Tiffin
Toledo
Upper Sandusky
Wapakoneta
Waterloo
Weinberg
Woodsfield
Woodville
Wooster
Xenia
Youngstown
Zanesville
Zoar

Oklahoma

Bessie
El Reno
Enid
Guthrie
Kingfisher
Medford
Okeene
Oklahoma City
Perry

Oregon

Astoria
Bend
Portland
St. Benedict
Salem

Pennsylvania

Aaronsburg
Abbottstown
Allegheny
Allenton
Altoona
Bath
Berwick
Bethlehem
Boyertown
Carlisle
Cattawissa
Chambersburg
Chestnut Hill
Columbia
Danville
Doylestown
Easton
Economy
Ephrata
Erie
Gap
Germantown
Gettysburg
Greenburg
Hamburg
Hanover
Harrisburg
Hazleton
Hellertown
Herman
Honesdale
Huntingdon
Jefferson
Johnstown
Kutztown
Lancaster
Lansdale
Lebanon

McKeesport
Mansfield
Marietta
Mauchchunk
Meadville
Mercerburg
Meyerstown
Middleburg
Mifflintown
Milford Square
Millheim
Nazareth
New Berlin
Norristown
Orwigsburg
Pennsburg
Perkasie
Philadelphia
Philipsburg
Pittsburgh
Pottstown
Pottsville
Quakertown
Reading
Schellsburg
Scottdale
Scranton
Selinsgrove
Sharpsburg
Skippack
Somerset
Souderton
Strassburg
Sumneytown
Telford
Thurlow
Weissport
West Chester
Wilkes-Barre
Williamsport
Womelsdorf
York
Zieglerville

Rhode Island

Providence

South Carolina

Charleston

South Dakota

Aberdeen
Herreid
Java
Mitchell
Olivet
Orient
Parkston
Pierre
Redfield
Sioux Falls
Watertown
Yankton

Tennessee

Chattanooga
Columbia
Hohenwald
Memphis
Nashville
Robbins

Texas

Austin
Bastrop
Bellville
Boerne
Brenham
Castroville
Comfort
Cuero
Dallas
Denison
Fort Worth
Franklin
Fredericksburg
Gainesville
Galveston
Giddings
Gonzales
Hallettsville

translated the entries into English in a companion work to this Encyclopedia, entitled *American Genealogical Resources in German Archives*, known by its acronym AGRIGA. Use of NUCMC and AGRIGA will make it possible for the investigator to find a great deal of information not heretofore available to him.

U.S. Library of Congress. Descriptive Cataloging Division. *National Union Catalog of Manuscript Collections*. Annual volumes beginning in 1959 (various publishers, dates, and places of publication).

As an illustration of the vast scale of NUCMC, as the catalog is commonly called, the first two volumes alone contain descriptions of more than 12,000 manuscript collections in over 400 archives in the United States. The entries are published as they are received from the archives; some entries give more detail than others. The copious indexing provided by the Library of Congress makes it possible to find related material now dispersed in widely separated collections, a significant aid to investigators.

Genealogical researchers should particularly check the annual indexes under the subject heading "Genealogy;" therein will be found the collections of private persons which have found their ways into public archives. Check likewise under the appropriate geographic headings and for the records of religious congregations; there are many listed in the various volumes of the catalog.

The most important fact to remember about NUCMC is that it includes only the holdings of non-governmental archives. The failure to include the holdings of governmental archives leaves a gap of potentially serious consequence to the unwary investigator. For example, among the holdings of the Illinois Historical Survey at the University of Illinois, described in NUCMC, is an important collection of late eighteenth-century documents pertaining to French settlements in Illinois. Missing from NUCMC are the companion and successor collections which are among the holdings of the Illinois State Archives, Springfield, and of one of the original Illinois counties. These latter collections are not described in NUCMC, because they are in governmental archives.

AMERICAN TOWNS AND CITIES IN WHICH

GERMAN-LANGUAGE PERIODICALS HAVE BEEN PUBLISHED--*Continued*

Houston	Washington	Dorchester	Milwaukee
Independence		Durand	Monroe
LaGrange	Bellingham	Eagle	Neillsville
Lockart	Everett	Eau Claire	New Glarus
Marlin	Ritzville	Fond du Lac	Oshkosh
Meyersville	Seattle	Fort Atkinson	Phillips
New Braunfels	South Bend	Fountain City	Platteville
Rosebud	Spokane	Glidden	Plymouth
San Antonio	Tacoma	Grand Rapids	Port Washington
Schulenberg	Walla Walla	Green Bay	Portage
Seguin		Hamburg	Princeton
Shiner	West Virginia	Horicon	Racine
Taylor		Janesville	Reedsburg
Temple	Wheeling	Jefferson	Ripon
Victoria		Juneau	St. Francis
Waco	Wisconsin	Kaukauna	St. Nazianz
Windthorst		Kenosha	Sauk City
	Antigo	Kewaunee	Schlesingerville
Utah	Appleton	Kiel	(now Slinger)
	Arcadia	LaCrosse	Shawano
Logan	Ashland	Lomira	Sheboygan
Salt Lake City	Athens	Madison	Stevens Point
	Beaver Dam	Manitowoc	Stockbridge
Virginia	Beloit	Marathon	Superior
	Burlington	Marinette	Theresa
Alexandria	Cedarburg	Marshfield	Watertown
Bridgewater	Chilton	Mauston	West Bend
New Market	Chippewa Falls	Mayville	Weyauwega
Norfolk	Clintonville	Menasha	
Richmond	Cochrane	Menominie	Wyoming
Staunton	Columbus	Merrill	
Winchester	Cumberland	Merrimack	Laramie

There is currently no way to remedy this defect. True, most governmental archives have guides to their holdings, but the number of libraries which have extensive collections of these guides is not large, and they are rarely kept together for ready reference.

Smith, Clifford Neal, and Smith Anna *geb.* Piszczan-Czaja. *American Genealogical Resources in German Archives.* DeKalb, Ill.: Westland Publications, forthcoming.

AGRIGA surveys the primary source materials in German archives having to do with Germans who came to, or were associated with, America. The entries therein have been selected and translated from the unpublished typescript catalog compiled by the Deutsche Gesellschaft für Amerika Studien (German Society for America Studies) entitled *Americana in deutschen Sammlungen (ADS): Ein Verzeichnis von Materialien zur Geschichte der Vereinigten Staaten von Amerika in Archiven und Bibliotheken der Bundesrepublik Deutschland und West-Berlins* (Americana in German collections (ADS): A list of materials on the history of the United States of America in archives and libraries of the German Federal Republic and West Berlin).

It should be noted that, despite its size, there were scores of small, mainly *Gemeinde* (communal), collections which were not catalogued, so that the listing of holdings of genealogical interest in Germany is hardly complete. A good many of these holdings have been microfilmed for the Genealogical Society of The Church of Jesus Christ of Latter-day Saints and can be consulted in Salt Lake City.

AGRIGA is divided into three indexed sections, as follows:

¶ Surname Index. Where the archival materials pertain to specific persons in America, or having some association with persons in America, they are listed by surname. These materials have mainly to do with probate matters in which there were heirs in one country entitled to, or claiming, an estate in the other country, thus setting up genealogical links of interest to researchers. The cases of former wards of the German state--welfare, orphan, or convict--in which the ward was sent off to America are also listed under surname.

¶ Geographic Index. The majority of the immigrants from Germany are not listed by name in AGRIGA, because they are to be found only in emigration lists prepared in the various administrative districts of Germany. Files containing these lists are indexed in AGRIGA under the name of the district or village. It remains a major task of the specialist in German-American genealogy to publish these lists, as time permits, making the names of the emigrants accessible to researchers.

¶ Subject Index. Military records and the files of religious denominations and of missionaries are frequent entries in this index.

Some of the materials now in the archives of western Germany pertain to former provinces of the German Reich now in the German Democratic Republic, Poland, or the USSR. These files have also been listed in AGRIGA. Hereinafter, are listed the cities and towns in Germany having primary source materials in their archives pertaining to German-Americans. The type of archive in which these materials are now deposited is coded as follows:

C   Communal (*Gemeinde*) or administrative district (*Kreis*) archive

C/M Combined rural administrative district (*Landkreis*) and municipal archive

E-I Estate archive of the higher nobility

E-II Estate archive of the lower nobility

F   Federal archive

M   Municipal (*Stadt*) archive

P   Collection of a private person

R-I Archive of a religious order, bishopric, or superintendency at the regional or national level

R-II Archive of a religious order, congregation, cloister, etc., at the local level

S   State (*Staat*) archive

Soc Society or firm archive

GERMAN ARCHIVES WITH PRIMARY SOURCE MATERIALS ON GERMAN-AMERICANS, AS LISTED IN AGRIGA

Baden-Württemberg

Aalen C/M	Biberach C/M	Donaueschingen E-I	Eberbach C/M

SOME NOTABLE RESEARCH TOOLS
IN THE GERMAN LANGUAGE

A vast literature is available to the researcher who can read German, for genealogical research has been practiced in Germany for centuries; indeed, until the fall of the monarchy in 1918 wide circles of German society can be said to have been congealed by the strictures of genealogical considerations enjoined upon them by law.

Certainly, a most useful German genealogical handbook remains Eduard Heydenreich's *Handbuch der praktischen Genealogie* (handbook of practical genealogy) published in 1913. His bibliographies of the older literature are still valuable today, despite the skewing of his interests toward the genealogies of noble houses, then regnant. Heydenreich's efforts have now been supplemented by Rudolph Dimpfel's *Biographische Nachschlagewerke: Adelslexika, Wappenbücher* (biographical reference works:

GERMAN ARCHIVES WITH PRIMARY SOURCE MATERIALS

ON GERMAN-AMERICANS, AS LISTED IN AGRIGA--*Continued*

Esslingen M
Freiburg/Breisgau
  S; C/M
Freudenstadt C
Göppingen C/M
Karlsruhe S
Langenstein E-II
Leonberg C/M
Ludwigsburg S; C/M
Nürtingen C; M
Oberndorf C/M
Reutlingen C/M; P
Rottweil C/M
Schwenningen C/M;
  Soc
Sigmaringen S
Singen C/M
Sinsheim Soc
Stuttgart S; C/M
Wimpfen C/M

Bavaria

Amberg S
Amorbach E-I
Ansbach Soc
Augsburg C/M
Bamberg S; R-I
Coburg S
Dinkelsbühl C/M
Erlangen C/M
Fürth C/M
Gars/Inn R-II
Greding C/M
Gunzenhausen C/M
Herrieden C/M
Kempten C/M
Kulmbach C/M
Landshut S; C/M
Lauingen C/M
München S; C/M
Neuburg S
Nördlingen C/M
Nürnberg S; Soc
Pöttmes E-II
Regensburg C/M
Roth C

Rotheburg ob d.
  Tauber C/M
Schwabach C/M
Weissenburg C/M
Windsheim C/M
Wunsiedel C/M
Würzburg S

Berlin

Dahlem S

Bremen

Bremen (city) S

Hamburg

Altona S
Hamburg S; C;
  R-I; R-II; Soc
Harburg S; C/M
Horn R-II

Hessen

Astheim C
Bauschheim C
Berkach C
Biebesheim C
Biedenkopf C/M
Bischofsheim C
Braunfels E-I
Büdingen E-I
Büttelborn C
Butzbach C/M
Crumstädt C
Darmstadt S; C/M
Dornheim C
Erfelden C
Frankfurt/Main
  S; C/M
Fulda C/M; R-I
Geinsheim C
Gernsheim C
Ginsheim-Gustav-
  burg C

Goddelau C
Gross-Gerau C/M
Hungen M
Ilbenstadt M
Kelsterbach C
Klein-Gerau C
Klein-Rohrheim C
Korbach M
Leeheim C
Mörfelden C
Nauheim C
Ortenberg M
Raunheim C
Rüsselsheim C
Sachsenhausen M
Seligenhausen M
Trebur C
Ulrichstein M
Viernheim M
Wallau M
Walldorf C
Wallerstädten C
Weilburg/Lahn M
Wetzlar Soc
Worfelden C

Niedersachsen

Aurich S
Barterode R-II
Becksted Soc
Bockel E-II
Braunschweig C/M
Bremerhaven C/M
Bremervörde C
Bücken C
Buxtehude Soc
Celle C/M
Clausthal-Zeller-
  feld C/M; Soc
Daverden/Kreis
  Vechta R-II
Dissen R-II
Dransfeld C/M
Einbeck C/M
Emden C/M
Eschershausen C/M

Gifhorn C
Göttingen S
Grasdorf/Leine
  R-II
Hannover S; M
Harpstedt C
Hattorf R-II
Helmstedt C/M
Hildesheim C/M
Hohnsen R-II
Holdenstedt P
Hornburg C/M
Iber R-II
Idensen R-II
Imbshausen R-II
Jacobidrebber
  R-II
Jörk Soc
Leer C/M
Lenne R-II
Lüchow C/M
Lüneburg C/M
Melle C/M
Northeim C/M
Oldenburg S
Oldershausen
  E-II
Osnabrück S
Otterndorf C
Pyrmont C/M
Riessen R-I
Rinteln Soc
Salzuflen C/M
Schoeningen C/M
Schüttorf C/M
Springe C/M
Stade S; C
Ueffeln R-II
Winsen/Luhe C/M
Wolfenbüttel S
Wunstorf C/M
Zeven C

Nordrhein-Westfalen

Altena M
Bergisch Gladbach
  M

lexica of the nobility and works on armorial bearings) published in 1969, and by Eckart Henning's and Wolfgang Ribbe's *Handbuch der Genealogie* which appeared in 1972. Using the Heydenreich, Dimpfel, and Henning-Ribbe bibliographies together will give the researcher command over nearly all the important genealogical reference works in the German language.

There are several other powerful tools at the hand of the researcher: one of these is *Der Schlüssel* (the key), an index to all articles in German genealogical publications during the first sixty years of the twentieth century. There are a number of bibliographies dealing with church records, of which two recent ones are of distinct interest to German-American researchers: Hermann Franz's *Die Kirchenbücher in Baden* (parish records in Baden) and Marie-Joseph Bopp's *Die evangelischen Gemeinden und Hohenschulen in Elsass und Lothringen* (Lutheran congregations and secondary schools in the Alsace and Lorraine). Finally, there is a contribution prepared by the Swiss federal government, the *Familiennamenbuch der Schweiz* (surname book of Switzerland), which sets forth the movements, both inside and outside the country, of Swiss nationals from at least the beginning of the nineteenth century and frequently earlier.

Heydenreich, Eduard. *Handbuch der praktischen Genealogie* [handbook of practical genealogy]

2 vols. Leipzig, 1913; reprint ed., Neustadt an der Aisch: Verlag Degener & Co., 1971.

Despite its age, and also because of it, this handbook remains without peer. Heydenreich's main interest was in primary and secondary source materials; research presentation was of only minor concern. His bibliographies of the older literature are exhaustive; his descriptions of the contents, in 1913, of archives now inaccessible to the western genealogist for political reasons are a promise of the treaures which await investigation when these archives are again opened. Information from his handbook has been liberally quoted in this Encyclopedia in the article on genealogy in Germany.

Dimpfel, Rudolph. *Biographische Nachschlagewerke: Adelslexika, Wappenbücher* [biographical reference works: lexica of the nobility and books on heraldry] 2d. ed. Wiesbaden: Dr. Martin Saendig oHG, 1969.

The first edition of this work was published in 1921, but the second edition does not include new material. It is of considerable usefulness, however. The work was intended as a systematic compilation for historians and genealogists. The following subject matter is covered:

¶ General biographical reference works

GERMAN ARCHIVES WITH PRIMARY SOURCE MATERIALS

ON GERMAN-AMERICANS, AS LISTED IN AGRIGA--*Continued*

Berleburg E-I	Schwerte C/M	Odernheim a. Gl. C	Lübeck S; P
Bethel bei Bielefeld Soc	Siegburg C/M	Simmern C	Lunden R-II
Bielefeld M	Siegen R-II	Speyer S; C/M; R-I	Mehlbek/Kr. Steinburg E-II
Blomberg C/M	Solingen C/M	Wachenheim C/M	Meldorf Soc
Bonn F; M	Wattenscheid C/M	Weierhof/Pfalz Soc	Norderwöhrden/Kr. Norderdithmarschen R-II
Detmold S; C/M	Wesel C/M		
Düsseldorf S; R-I	Wuppertal P	Schleswig-Holstein	
Duisburg C/M			Oldenburg C/M
Gevelsberg C/M	Rheinland-Pfalz	Albersdorf R-II	Panker E-II
Hallenberg C/M		Büsum R-II	Pellworm C
Kamen C/M	Andernach C/M	Burg auf Fehmarn C/M	Ratzeburg C; M; R-I
Köln C/M	Annweiler C/M	Delve/Kr. Norderdithmarschen R-II	Rendsburg C/M
Krefeld C/M	Bad Dürkheim C/M	Eckernförde C/M	Schleswig S
Lage C/M	Diez C/M	Flensburg C/M	Süderhastedt/Kr. Süderdithmarschen R-II
Mark über Tecklenburg E-II	Kaiserslautern S	Hedwigenkoog C	
Meckenheim C/M	Koblenz F; S; R-I	Heide C; R-II	Tönning C/M
Münster S	Kusel C	Heiligenhafen C/M	Weddingstedt/Kr. Norderdithmarschen R-II
Neheim-Hüsten C/M	Landau/Pfalz C/M	Hemme R-II	
Obermarsberg R-II	Landstuhl C/M	Henne/Kr. Norderdithmarschen R-II	Wesselburg/same Kr. R-II
Rietberg	Mainz C/M	Husum C; M	
Sassenberg/Kr. Warendorf P	Mörzheim C	Kiel S; C/M; R-I	Wilster/Kr. Steinburg C/M
Schwalenberg C/M	Montabaur C/M	Kropp bei Schleswig R-I	Wyk auf Föhr C
Schwarzenau R-I	Neustadt/Weinstrasse C/M		
	Neuwied E-I		

¶ Registers of the nobility and books on heraldry

¶ Genealogical and heraldry periodicals

¶ Selected bibliographies

¶ Librarians and booksellers

¶ Poets, professors, teachers, authors

¶ Jews

¶ Artists

¶ Physicians and natural scientists

¶ Military

¶ Theologians

¶ Local history reference tools

Henning, Eckart, and Ribbe, Wolfgang. *Handbuch der Genealogie* [handbook of genealogy] Neustadt an d. Aisch: Verlag Degener & Co., 1972.

This handbook is excellent. Of particular significance is the bibliography of publications, pages 255–293, covering the following subject matter:

1. Bibliographical reference works

2. *Überregionale* (country-wide) periodicals and series

3. Genealogical tables

4. The nobility (lists, lexica, etc.)

5. Biographical reference works

6. Textbooks on genealogy

7. Genealogy as a *Begriff* (concept)

8. History of genealogy

9. The two basic genealogical ideas--ascendancy and descendancy

10. Consanguinity, affinity, and lists

11. Implex (lineage extinction)

12. Agnation, cognation, filiation

13. Methods of numbering and the tables in genealogical publications

14. Genealogy and the computer

15. Library aids

16. Archival aids

17. Church source materials

18. Civil registries

19. Military source materials

20. Judicial decisions and files

21. Financial and business source materials

22. Lists of persons and similar sources

23. Personal memoirs

24. Monuments and inscriptions

25. Diplomatic records

26. Chronologies

27. Heraldry

28. *Spragistik* (study of seals)

29. *Vexillogie* (study of flags)

30. Historical *Metrologie* (study of weights, measurements, etc.)

31. Numismatics

32. Cartography

33. Genealogy and art history

34. *Namenkunde* (study of names)

35. Family and society

36. Elites

37. Specific racial and social groups (Masons, religious orders, etc.)

38. Professional groups

39. Migrations

40. Law

41. Human genetics

42. *Familienpflege* (anthropology, structures)

43. Family organizations

Der Schlüssel: Gesamtinhaltsverzeichnisse mit Ortsquellennachweis für genealogische, heraldische und historische Zeitschriftenreihen [the key: comprehensive index, including place names, to genealogical, heraldic, and historical periodical series] 5 vols. Göttingen: Heinz Reise Verlag, 1950–1965.

This publication is indispensable for entry into the periodical literature on genealogy in German. Literature to the second world war period is indexed in the first four volumes, and that of the Federal Republic of Germany for ther period 1945-60 is indexed in the fifth volume. Place names, subject matter, and surnames appearing in article titles are separately indexed. Citations to articles containing many names, such as transcriptions of ship lists, are noted with an asterisk, a very helpful device for the researcher.

Despite the title, the publications indexed are exclusively of a genealogical and heraldic nature; publications of the major local and provincial history societies, which often contain material of genealogical use, are not included in *Der Schlüssel*. Presumably, there will be further volumes from time to time indexing articles appearing after the 1960 cut-off date. Genealogical periodicals indexed in *Der Schlüssel* are listed below. Not all of them are available in the United States, however.

GERMAN GENEALOGICAL PERIODICALS
INDEXED IN *DER SCHLÜSSEL*

	Period Indexed	In Der Schlüssel volume
General genealogical publications		
Archiv für Sippenforschung [archive for family research] including its predecessor *Kultur und Leben* [culture and life]	1924–44	1
Ekkehard: Mitteilungsblatt deutscher genealogischer Abende [Ekkehard: reports on German genealogical evenings]	1925–41	1
Familie, Sippe, Volk [family, tribe, people]	1935–44	4
Familie und Volk [family and people]	1952–60	5
Der Familienforscher [the family researcher]	1924–28	4
Familiengeschichtliche Blätter [family history notes]	1903–44 1955–60	1 5
Familienkundliche Nachrichten [family history news]	1956–60	5
Mitteilungen der Arbeitsgemeinschaft für Familienkunde in Kulturkreis Siemens [reports of the working party for family history within the Siemens cultural circle]	1957–60	5
Praktische Forschungshilfe [practical aid in (family) research]	1956–60	5
Der Sippenforscher [the family researcher]	1934–39	4
Heraldry and genealogy		
Archiv für Stamm- und Wappenkunde [archive for genealogy and heraldry]	1900–21	2
Genealogie und Heraldik [genealogy and heraldry]	1948–51	5
Der deutsche Herold: Zeitschrift für Wappen-, Siegel- und Familienkunde: Monatschrift des Herold zu Berlin [the German herald: periodical for armorial bearings, seals, and genealogy: monthly magazine of the Herold of Berlin]		3
Der Herold für Geschlechter-, Wappen- und Siegelkunde [the herald for genealogy, heraldry, and seals]	1939–43	4
Mitteilungen des Herold [reports of the herald]	1949–58	5

Franz, Hermann. *Die Kirchenbücher in Baden* [parish registers in Baden] 3d. ed. Karlsruhe: Verlag G. Braun, 1957.

Lists, by village, every congregation and gives its beginning date. Also cites articles and studies which have been published thereon. Includes Mennonite, *Altkatholische* (Old Catholic), Walloon, Huguenot, and Waldensian registers, in addition to the remaining Jewish ones. Also mentions military church books (chaplaincies) and gives much information on church registers in neighboring regions--Württemberg, Hessen, Switzerland, Alsace, Hohenzollern, and the Bavarian Palatinate. Particularly valuable are the author's comments on emigration and immigration of congregations to and from the territory of Baden. This is an extremely useful reference tool for German-American genealogical researchers.

GERMAN GENEALOGICAL PERIODICALS

INDEXED IN *DER SCHLÜSSEL*--Continued

	Period Indexed	In Der Schlüssel volume
Der Herold [the herald]	1959-60	5
Mitteilungen des Heraldischen Vereins "Zum Kleeblatt" in Hannover [reports of the Heraldry Club "Zum Kleeblatt" in Hannover]	1890-1921	2
Der deutsche Roland [the German Roland]	1913-42	4
Mitteilungen des Roland [reports of the Roland]	1916-43	4
Vierteljahrsschrift für Wappen-, Siegel und Familienkunde (des Vereins "Herold") [quarterly for armorial bearings, seals, and genealogy of the "Herold" Society]	1872-1931	4

Baden-Württemberg

	Period Indexed	In Der Schlüssel volume
Blätter für württembergische Familienkunde [notes on Württemberg genealogy]	1921-44	5
Südwestdeutsche Blätter für Familien- und Wappenkunde [southwest German notes on genealogy and heraldry]	1949-60	5
Badische Familienkunde [genealogy in Baden]	1958-60	5

Bavaria, Franconia, Swabia

	Period Indexed	In Der Schlüssel volume
Blätter des Bayerischen Landesvereins für Familienkunde [notes from the Bavarian Genealogical Society]	1923-42; 1958-60	5 5
Der Familienforscher in Bayern, Franken und Schwaben [the genealogical researcher in Bavaria, Franconia, and Swabia]	1950-57	5
Blätter für fränkische Familienkunde [notes on Franconian genealogy]	1926-44; 1957-60	5 5

Eastern and Central Germany

	Period Indexed	In Der Schlüssel volume
Altpreussische Geschlechterkunde [Old Prussian family research]	1927-43; 1953-60	2 5
Mansfelder Blätter [notes from the Mansfeld region]	1887-1944	4
Mansfelder Sippenkunde [genealogy of the Mansfeld region]	1933-41	4

Bopp, Marie-Joseph. *Die evangelischen gemeinden und Hohenschulen in Elsass und Lothringen* [Evangelical Lutheran congregations and secondary schools in the Alsace and Lorraine] Landgeschichtliche Publikationen der Zentralstelle für deutsche Personen- und Familiengeschichte, volume 5. Neustadt an d. Aisch: Verlag Degener & Co., 1963.

Gives concise information on every estate and territory within the Alsace and Lorraine systematically. Lists date when the congregations changed from Catholic to Lutheran (often vacilating) and gives histories of the estates and the owners thereof. This work is especially useful for genealogical researchers of Pennsylvania-German families.

GERMAN GENEALOGICAL PERIODICALS
INDEXED IN *DER SCHLÜSSEL*--Continued

	Period Indexed	In Der Schlüssel volume
Die Sippe der Nordmark [family groups of the Nordmark]	1937–42	4
Archiv ostdeutscher Familienforscher [archive for East German genealogists]	1952–63	5
Ostdeutsche Familienkunde [East German genealogy]	1953–60	5
Familiengeschichtliche Mitteilungen der Pommerschen Vereinigung für Stamm- und Wappenkunde--Sedina Archiv [genealogical reports from the Pomeranian Society for Genealogy and Heraldry--the Sedina Archive]	1955–60	5
Die Thüringer Sippe [Thuringian family groups]	1935–44	2
Deutsche wissenschaftliche Zeitschrift im Wartheland [German scientific news in the Wartheland]	1940–43	2
Mitteilungen des Westpreussischen Geschichtsvereins [reports from the West Prussian History Society]	1902–36	2
Zeitschrift des Westpreussischen Geschichtsvereins [periodical of the West Prussian History Society]	1880–1941	2

Silesia, Poland, East Prussia, and the Baltic Area

	Period Indexed	In Der Schlüssel volume
Schlesische Geschichtsblätter [Silesian historical notes]	1908–43	2
Der schlesische Familienforscher [the Silesian genealogist]	1930–44	4
Deutsche wissenschaftliche Zeitschrift für Polen [German scientific news for Poland]	1923–39	2
Deutsche Blätter in Polen [German notes in Poland]	1924–31	2
Weichselland [the Vistula region]	1937–43	2
Elbinger Jahrbuch [yearbook of the city of Elbing]	1920–41	2
Danziger familiengeschichtliche Beiträge [contributions to Danzig genealogy]	1929–43	2
Baltische familiengeschichtliche Mitteilungen [Baltic genealogical reports]	1951–53	5
Baltische familiengeschichtliche Nachrichten [Baltic genealogical news]	1954–60	5

Familiennamenbuch der Schweiz [surname book of Switzerland] 2d. ed., 6 vols. Zürich: Polygraphischer Verlag A.G., 1968.

When searching for the origins of early immigrants to the United States, it is wise to consider the possibility that such persons may have come from Switzerland, perhaps via the Palatinate or the Alsace. The above-cited work is of unique construction and usefulness in such research. It was prepared by the Swiss Federal Statistical Office, Bern, from the citizenship (*Bürgerrecht*) records of the various communes (townships) of the Swiss cantons. In Switzerland the granting of citizenship is a jealously guarded prerogative of the communes

---

GERMAN GENEALOGICAL PERIODICALS

INDEXED IN *DER SCHLÜSSEL—Continued*

	Period Indexed	In Der Schlüssel volume
Baltische Ahnen- und Stammtafeln [Baltic lineage charts]	1957–60	5

Hessen, Frankfurt/Main, Nassau, and Waldeck

	Period Indexed	In Der Schlüssel volume
Mitteilungen der Hessischen Familiengeschichtlichen Vereinigung in Darmstadt [reports of the Hessian Genealogical Society in Darmstadt]	1925–53	2
Frankfürter Blätter für Familiengeschichte [notes on Frankfurt genealogy]	1908–14	1
Veröffentlichungen der Zentralstelle für Frankfurter Familienforschung [publications of the Central Office for Frankfurt Genealogical Research]	1914–19	1
Hessische Familienkunde [Hessian genealogy]	1948–60	5
Der hessische Familienforscher [the Hessian genealogical researcher]	1948–52	5
Nachrichten der Gesellschaft für Familienkunde in Kurhessen und Waldeck [news from the Society for Genealogy in Electoral Hessen and Waldeck]	1925–41	1
Der Uhrturm: Mitteilungen der Nassauischen Familiengeschichtlichen Vereinigung Wiesbaden [the clock tower: reports from the Nassau Genealogical Society, Wiesbaden]	1929–41	1
Rheinische Sippen und Rhein-Mainische Sippen [Rhenish family groups and Rheno-Main family groups]	1937–43	1

Lower Saxony

Publications of the Braunschweiger genealogischen Abends zu Braunschweig [the Braunschweiger Genealogical Evening, Brunswick]:

	Period Indexed	In Der Schlüssel volume
a. *Braunschweiger genealogischer Blätter* [Brunswick genealogical notes]	1926–27	4
b. *Quellen und Hilfsmittel zur braunschweigischen Familiengeschichtsforschung* [sources and aids in Brunswick genealogical research]	1927	4

and their records go back to the early nineteenth century, if not before. In this work
are listed the surnames (but not the given
names) of persons who obtained citizenship in
the various communes or who emigrated abroad.
In order to condense a large amount of data,
the entries are exceptionally cryptic. Here,
for example, are the entries for the distinguished family of De Pourtalès, originally of
Canton Neuchâtel:

The Entry	*Interpretation*
de Pourtalès GE Genève 1961 (Neuchâtel)	A member of this family became a citizen of Canton Geneva, registering in the city of Geneva in 1961, being a Swiss national transferring citizenship from Neuchâtel

---

GERMAN GENEALOGICAL PERIODICALS

INDEXED IN *DER SCHLÜSSEL*--Continued

	Period Indexed	*In Der Schlüssel volume*
Publications of the "Maus" Gesellschaft für Familienforschung in Bremen ["Maus" Society for Genealogy, Bremen]:		
a. *Die Blätter der "Maus"* ["Maus" notes]	1925–35	4
b. *Die Mitteilungensblätter der "Maus"* [report sheets from the "Maus"]	1929–37	4
c. *Sippenforschung in Nordwestdeutschland* [genealogical research in Northwest Germany]	1937–39	4
Publications of the Geschichtsverein für Göttingen und Umgebung [Historical Society for Göttingen und Surrounding Region]:		
a. *Protokolle* [protocols]	1892–1907	4
b. *Jahrbuch* [yearbook]	1908–12	4
c. *Göttinger Blätter für Geschichte und Heimatkunde in Südhannover und seiner Nachbarschaft* [Göttinger notes on history and local history in southern Hannover and surroundings]	1914–19	4
d. *Göttinger Blätter für Geschichte und Heimatkunde in Südhannover* [Göttinger notes on history and local history of southern Hannover]	1935–39	4
e. *Der Wanderer in Cheruskerland* [wanderer in the land of the Cheruskans]	1922	4
f. *Neues Göttinger Jahrbuch* [new Göttinger yearbook]	1928–34	4
g. *Gaben des Geschichtsvereins für Göttingen und Umgebung* [contributions of the Historical Society for Göttingen and Surrounding Region]	1937–41	4
Göttinger Mitteilungen [Göttinger reports]	1948–51	5
Das Hannoversche Magazin [the Hannover magazine]	1925–37	4
Publications of the Verein für Niedersächsische Familienforschung [Society for Genealogical Research in Lower Saxony]:		
a. *Der Weserbote* [Weser messenger]	1912–13	4

The Entry--Cont.	Interpretation	The Entry--Cont.	Interpretation
de Pourtalès BE Bern 1815 (Neuchâtel)	A member of this family became a citizen of Canton Bern, registering in the city of Bern, being a Swiss national transferring citizenship from Neuchatel	F + Le Ponts-de-Martel a (Neuchâtel)	from France in 1729; a member, or members, of the family transferred citizenship to LeLocle in 1808 from Neuchâtel
NE Fleurier a (Neuchâtel) + LeLocle 1808 (Neuchâtel) + Neuchâtel 1729	This family was flourishing in Canton Neuchâtel, village of Fleurier, and at Les Ponts-de-Martel before 1800, having come	de Pourtalès-Marcet BE Bern 1815 (Neuchâtel) NE Neuchâtel 1729 F	Another branch of the family, de Pourtales-Marcet, came to canton Neuchâtel, city of Neuchâtel in 1729 from France, transferring citizenship to Bern 1815

GERMAN GENEALOGICAL PERIODICALS

INDEXED IN *DER SCHLÜSSEL*--Continued

	Period Indexed	In Der Schlüssel volume
b. *Niedersächsische Familienarchiv* [Lower Saxon family archive]		4
Zeitschrift der Zentralstelle für niedersächsische Familienkunde [periodical of the Central Office for Lower Saxon Genealogy]	1919-41	1
Zeitschrift für niedersächsische Familienkunde [periodical for Lower Saxon genealogy]	1949-60	5
Heimatblätter (des Museumsvereins für Northeim und Umgebung) [local history notes of the Museum Society for Northeim and Surrounding Region]	1925-39	4
Oldenburger Jahrbuch [Oldenburger yearbook]	1892-1950	2
Quellen zur Oldenburgischen Familienforschung [sources for Oldenburger genealogical research]	1936-57	5
Oldenburgische Quellen zur Familiengeschichte [Oldenburger sources of family history]	1951-58	5
Familienkundliche Beiträge [in] *Oldenburger Beiträge zur Familien- und Bevölkerungskunde* [genealogical contributions in Oldenburger contributions to family history and population studies]	1955-60	5
Oldenburgische Familienkunde [Oldenburger genealogy]	1959-60	5

North Germany (East Friesland, Schleswig-Holstein)

Norddeutsche Familienkunde [North German genealogy]	1952-60	5
Ostfriesische Familienforschung [East Frisian family research]	1950-55	5
Quellen und Forschungen zur ostfriesischen Familien- und Wappenkunde [sources and research on East Frisian genealogy and heraldry]	1952-60	5
Ostfriesische Familienkunde [East Frisian genealogy]	1960	5

PRIMARY SOURCE MATERIALS ON
THE REFUGEES FROM THE EAST

During the eighteenth century, when the first Germans were immigrating to America, an even mightier stream was pouring out of the war-plagued areas of western Germany into eastern and southeastern Europe. There they were to prosper among Hungarian, Romanian, and Slavic neighbors until the upheaval of the second world war brought them back again into the Reich, a policy of Hitler's government, then in grave need of workers in the war industries. Guides to the whereabouts of these settlements were prepared for Wehrmacht use as it pressed eastward; one of these guides was *Die deutschen Siedlungen in der Sowjetunion* (the German settlements in the Soviet Union) which present-day genealogical researchers of Russian *Volksdeutsche* (ethnic German) and nonconformist groups (Mennonites, Russian Baptists, etc.) will find highly instructive. Similar guides for other German-speaking enclaves in eastern and southeastern Europe must also have been prepared for official use, but these seem no longer to be extant.

Beginning in 1952 many of these uprooted people were resettled in Australia, Canada, the United States, and Venezuela. Thus, it is that the records of Volksdeutsche migrations became, first of all, a matter of political clearance for emigration and, secondly, as time goes on, a genealogical record of first importance. These records, prepared by the German government, were captured by the American forces at the end of the second world war. They are housed in the Berlin Document Center; a description of them will be found in the present writers' *American Genealogical Resources in German Archives (AGRIGA)*. Many of the records have also been microfilmed in National Archives Microcopy Series T580, described hereinafter.

[Meynen, Emil, ed.] *Die deutsche Siedlungen in der Sowjetunion* [German settlements in the Soviet Union] 2 vols. Berlin: Sammlung Georg Leibbrandt, 1941.

GERMAN GENEALOGICAL PERIODICALS

INDEXED IN *DER SCHLÜSSEL*--Continued

	Period Indexed	In Der Schlüssel volume
Jahrbuch der Heimatgemeinschaft des Kreises Eckernförde [yearbook of the Local History Society of Eckernförde Administrative District]	1936–59	4
Familiengeschichtliche Mitteilungen aus Nordschleswig [genealogical reports from North Schleswig]	1942–44	4
Mitteilungen der Gesellschaft für Schleswig-Holsteinische Familienforschung und Wappenkunde [reports of the Society for Genealogy and Heraldry in Schleswig-Holstein]	1949–59	5

Western Germany and Holland

	Period Indexed	In Der Schlüssel volume
Beiträge zur westfälischen Familienforschung [contributions to Westphalian family research]	1938–60	5
Mitteilungen der Niederländischen Ahnengemeinschaft [reports of the Netherlands Genealogical Society]	1938–60	5
Pfälzische Familien- und Wappenkunde [Palatine genealogy and heraldry]	1952–60	5
Publications of the Westdeutschen Gesellschaft für Familienkunde e.V. [West German Society for Genealogy, Inc.]:		
a. *Mitteilungen* [reports]	1913–44	2
b. *Die Laterne* [the lantern]	1948–58	5
c. *Scholle und Schacht* [group and region]	1958	5

This publication was apparently intended for use only by officials in German-occupied Russia during the second world war; a copy of it is available in the Library of Congress, however. The first volume is a systematic listing of every village and administrative region in which German speakers lived and statistics on their numbers. The second volume consists of maps locating these settlements precisely.

Of significance to American genealogists is the fact that many of the German-Russians emigrated from Germany to the United States. This movement began with the Mennonite colonies in the period after 1873. Since 1948 other groups of German-speaking Russians, mainly Lutherans and Baptists but including some Roman Catholics, immigrated as *Volksdeutsche* to the United States under the Displaced Persons Act of 1948.

Before the second world war there were many unassimilated German settlements in the USSR. One writer has estimated that Germans tilled land in Russia amounting to about 25% of the area of the German Reich (*Altreich*). These settlements were located throughout the Soviet Union and were said to have been about 2,000 in number. Many German-speaking Russians came to Germany during the 1941-45 period and a great many more were among the refugees who fled before the Russian troops moving westward. After the re-establishment of Soviet control over areas of western Russia formerly occupied by the Germans, the remaining German speakers were deported to Siberia on the grounds that they had been disloyal to the Soviet Union; most of the old settlements have been entirely destroyed.

U.S. General Services Administration. National Archives. Microcopy Series T580: "Records of the *Einwandererzentrale* [central office for immigration into Germany] in the Berlin Document Center." Microfilm rolls 700-743.

Gives the names of settlers from France and the Slavic countries of eastern and southeastern Europe immigrating into Germany during the Third Reich period; includes *Lagerlisten* (resettlement barracks lists) and correspondence with individual settlers.

RECORDS OF THE
ENEMIES OF THE STATE

Among the saddest, yet most fascinating, of records are those of the political police having to do with enemies of the state. Those records which have come to light in Germany on the revolutionaries known as the Forty-Eighters are listed in AGRIGA, and biographies of some of them who fled to the United States

are to be found in Adolf Eduard Zucker's *The Forty-Eighters: Political Refugees of the German Revolution of 1848*. These émigrés were to have a profound impact on German-American cultural and political life.

At the end of the second world war the ten-volume blacklist of persons in Germany and Austria considered by the Reichsführer SS to have been enemies of the German state came to light; it is published in National Archives Microcopy Series T175. Correspondingly, in Microcopy Series T457, the German government's documentation concerning Jews is also available.

The policy of the Third Reich toward its nationals living abroad was such that most governments began to fear the so-called "fifth column." German nationals and naturalized German-Americans became the subjects of surveillance by the American government. Names and addresses of all known Nazi party members became a matter of public record in 1946 with the publication of a Senate subcommittee reprint of a document of the U.S. War Department. At about the same time, a list of emigrants from southwestern Germany living in the United States (many of whom were not Nazis, of course), prepared by the German Auslands-Institut, came to light. It is reproduced in National Archives Microcopy Series T81. All such records are grist for the mill of genealogical research.

Zucker, Adolf Eduard. *The Forty-Eighters: Political Refugees of the German Revolution of 1848*. New York: Russel & Russell, 1967.

The Forty-Eighters were a group of about 4,000 German political activists, usually in their twenties at the time they came to the attention of the German authorities, who fought to establish a liberal and unified Germany. Having lost the struggle during the revolution of 1848, many of them came to the United States as refugees from the reaction which then took place in Germany. Among this group of immigrants were many persons later to achieve distinction in America.

The revolution of 1848, it should be noted, was not strictly a German event. It first began in France, quickly spreading to Austria, Belgium, and Italy. The first effect was the overthrow of Count Metternich, the ultra-conservative foreign minister of the Austro-Hungarian Empire. In Germany there were revolts in Baden and Berlin. By the end of the year these revolts had been put down, after much bloodshed, and the proponents of liberty, democracy, and national unity had been put to flight by reactionary monarchists. Popular radicals, with more or less of a populistic or socialistic outlook, were bitterly hated by the traditionalists. Since the United States had no immigration barriers at that time and was thought to be the most promising area of the New World, most of the radicals came to this country in the period immediately after 1848. They were to distinguish themselves as writers, politicians, abolitionists, and artists.

U.S. General Services Administration. National Archives. Microcopy Series T175: "Records of the Reichsführer SS und Chef der deutschen Polizei" [Reichs Leader of the SS and chief of the German police]." Microfilm roll 451.

On this microfilm roll there is a ten-volume blacklist of persons in Germany and Austria who were considered enemies of the German state during the period of the Third Reich (1933-1945). The list is entitled "Erfassung führender Männer der Systemzeit" (summary of leading men of the System [Weimar] period); it will be found at the beginning of the microfilm roll. Included in the blacklist were personages classified as follows:

Marxist-Communists

Liberal-Pacifists

Confessional Parties (religious leaders)

Right-wing Opponents and Reactionaries

Austrian Elitists

Scientists

Artists

Writers and Journalists

These volumes, intended only for police use and classified geheim (secret), contain detailed summaries of the activities of each individual. Some of these persons found their ways to the United States as political refugees.

U.S. General Services Administration. National Archives. Microcopy Series T457: "Documentation Concerning Jews in the Berlin Documents Center." 14 microfilm rolls.

Gift of the Library of the Jewish Theological Center, New York, N. Y., under whose direction the information was apparently assembled from Nazi source materials. There is no guide to this collection.

U.S. War Department. Nazi Party Membership Records Submitted to the Subcommittee on War Mobilization of the Committee on Military Affairs, U.S. Senate [79th Cong., 2d. sess., Senate, Subcommittee print]. Washington: Government Printing Office, 1946.

During the second world war the United States government compiled lengthy lists of

Nazi party members in the United States and in countries other than Germany. Lists pertaining to the United States are to be found in the following:

Part I (March 1946), pp. 2-15.
Part II, pp. 2-18. Supplemental list.
Part III, pp. 2-9. Additional supplemental list.
Part IV, pp. 2-16.

These lists give names, birthplaces and dates, when entered the party, and a then-current address (1940-43?). Most Americans of German descent listed in the above-cited document were recent immigrants to the United States; some of them were repatriated to Germany during, or shortly after, the war. Their children, many born in the United States, have remained here, with a few exceptions.

U.S. General Services Administration. National Archives. Microcopy Series T81: "Records of the Deutsches Ausland-Institut. Part I: Records on resettlement. Part II: The general records."

This is a huge collection of records of unfathomed value to genealogical researchers. Most of the material is administrative correspondence, however, and would require a great deal of effort to make it accessible to the investigator. One item, noted at random, will be of great interest:

Microfilm roll 575, beginning at frame 5,355,401: List of names and addresses of German immigrants in the United States and where they came from in southwestern Germany. Alphabetized A-Z; many Gemeinde (communities); an extremely valuable record.

SEARCHING FOR THE

FLOTSAM AND JETSAM

There are indications, here and there, that in the eighteenth, perhaps even in the seventeenth, century there was a good deal of illegal emigration from Europe to the New World. Among the papers of the German Prince Salm-Salm is a statement, dated 1772, that hundreds of deserters of all nationality take refuge in Holland and from there go to America. Elsewhere, these writers have seen a list of "German" prisoners at Kinsale, England, captured on a vessel bound for Port-au-Prince in 1779 and giving their countries and parishes of origin. All of these prisoners were young men, many still in their teens. A number were from French towns, but the majority were registered as from "Hungary," by which we assume the Habsburg lands both within and without the Holy Roman Empire German Nation were meant, since the surnames of these captives and their places of origin were Belgian, German, and Luxemburger, never Hungarian. Elsewhere in this Encyclopedia we deal with the problem of desertions from the German mercenary forces brought over to fight for the British during the American Revolution, discovering these desertions to comprise a substantial, yet almost unknown, wave of immigration. Other German units served under the British in colonial North America at an earlier period, but we know almost nothing of them.

There has never been a systematic attempt to uncover the details of this clandestine immigration, and these writers feel that, because of the difficulty in finding traces of it, a considerable body of immigrants to the New World has escaped attention. Since, by the very nature of this immigration, there are few formal records upon which to rely, investigators will be forced to proceed indirectly, patiently retrieving the random name wherever it appears. We suggest that, being on the edge of the law and the prey of naval recruiters in any port of call, these fugitives would have struck out for the unsettled interior of America at first opportunity. Here, for example, they would have taken on any protective coloration possible; in one case, for example, the fugitive lived among the Indians, raised a family, and died at his clearing on the banks of the Mississippi.

We believe that some of these fugitives can be identified through a careful reading of travel descriptions of the period, for it frequently occurred that the traveler mentioned meeting such persons during his travels. We likewise assert that the accounts of captives of the Indians, of which there are a great number in such collections as the Ayer Collection at the Newberry Library, Chicago, would yield significant references to such fugitive immigrants. With regard to very early German descriptions of North America and possible mention of fugitive immigrants encountered during the travelers' wanderings, there is the excellent, but entirely unknown, bibliography by Philip Motley Palmer entitled "German Works on America 1492-1800" in *University of California Publications in Modern Philology*. In the detailed description of this work and its value to the genealogical researcher, we have listed a number of the rarest works and their locations, which the determined genealogical researcher may wish to consult.

Chicago. Newberry Library. Edward E. Ayer Collection. *Catalog of the Edward E. Ayer Collection of Americana and American Indians*. 8 vols. Boston: G. K. Hall, 1961.

This collection of some 90,000 items is particularly strong in early discoveries and explorations of America, the American Indian, missionary activities, western exploration and travel, cartography, and Latin American history.

Palmer, Philip Motley. "German Works on America 1492-1800." *University of California Publications in Modern Philology* 36 (1952): 271-412.

This monograph is the most complete bibliography of early works on America published in Germany. Of the 967 titles listed herein, 314 are not found in the older standard work by Joseph Sabin, *Dictionary of Books Relating to America . . .* (New York: Sabin, 1868-92; Biographical Soc. of America, 1928-36). Indeed, some 77 titles have not yet been found in any library; they have been included on the basis of references to them found elsewhere. The John Carter Brown Library, Providence, Rhode Island, has 477 of the titles--the largest number in any of the world's great libraries--the New York Public Library has 393, the British Museum 375, the Library of Congress 267, and the Preussische Nationalbibliothek in Berlin 262. The Bayerische Staatsbibliothek in Munich and Harvard College Library, Cambridge, Massachusetts, have far fewer entries.

The significance of this bibliography to the genealogical researcher cannot be precisely assessed. What is needed is a thorough search of all the travel descriptions and reports of missionaries to America for the occasional references to individual German immigrants. One title listed herein, the Simmendinger list of immigrants to New York, 1709, is of obvious value. Hereinafter follows a listing of titles which seem most likely to contain information of genealogical interest. Translations from other languages into German, of which there were many published in the 300 years before 1800, have not been included, for the most part. The location of known copies of these works is coded as follows:

B   Preussische Nationalbibliothek, Berlin

BA   Boston Athenaeum, Boston, Massachusetts

Basel   University Library, Basel, Switzerland

BM   British Museum, London, England

BPL   Boston Public Library, Boston, Massachusetts

De Renne   Wymberley Jones De Renne Library, Savannah, Georgia

H   Harvard College Library, Cambridge, Massachusetts

HEH   Henry E. Huntington Library, San Marino, California

JCB   John Carter Brown Library, Providence, Rhode Island

LC   Library of Congress, Washington, D. C.

Lehigh   Lehigh University Library, Bethlehem, Pennsylvania

M   Bayerische Staatsbibliothek, Munich, Germany

NYH   New York Historical Society, New York, N. Y.

NYP   New York Public Library, New York, N. Y.

PLC   Philadelphia Library Company, Philadelphia, Pennsylvania

Strass-   University Library, Strassburg, France
burg

UIl   University of Illinois Library, Urbana, Illinois

UMi   University of Michigan Library, Ann Arbor, Michigan

Zürich   Zentralbibliothek, Zürich, Switzerland

Titles are listed hereinafter under the name of the author, when known, or under the first substantive word of the title, when anonymously written. Only short titles are given; the lengthier ones should be referred to in Palmer.

Early German Works on America
of Potential Interest to Researchers

Abbildung Nordamerikanische Länder . . . [description of North American countries . . .] Erfurt, 1757 (another edition, Erfurt, 1787) Sabin 55453. Found in JCB, LC, NYP.

Contains police and regimental regulations operative during the French and Indian wars, etc. Might contain leads on early German mercenary troop units in British service at the time.

Abdruck einiger wahrhafften Berichte aus Germantown in Pensylvanien vom 17. Nov. 1738 [copies of some true reports from Germantown, Pennsylvania, of 17 November 1738] Berlenburg, 1738. Sabin 27153. Not found.

These would be accounts from early settlers at Germantown.

Adelung, Johann Christoph. *Versuch einer Neuen Geschichte des Jesuitenordens* . . . [draft of a new history of the Jesuit order] Berlin and Halle, 1769-70; 3 volumes in 2. Found in BM, NYP.

There are numerous references to America in this work.

Allerneuester Kriegsstaat . . . [latest conditions of warfare . . .] Leipzig, 1731; 14 volumes. Sabin 911. Not found.

Might contain information on early German mercenary units in British service in America much before the American Revolution.

Apollonius, Levinus. *Dritte Theil der Newen Welt* . . . [third part, the New World . . .] Basel, 1583. Found in BM, LC, M, NYP.

Although this work deals mainly with Peru, there is an appendix containing a plea to French King Charles XI regarding French widows, orphans, relatives, and residents in Florida, dating from 1565.

Ausführliche Historie derer Emigranten Oder Vertriebenen Lutheraner Aus den Ertz-Bissthum Saltzberg . . . [complete history of the Lutheran emigrants driven out of the Archbishopric of Salzburg . . .] Leipzig, 1732. Found in BM, NYP, de Renne.

In part, dealing with the Salzburger settlers in Georgia.

Auswahl kleiner Reisebeschreibungen . . . [selected small travel descriptions . . .] Leipzig, 1784-95; 22 volumes. Found in M.

Munich has only 14 volumes thereof, 1784-92.

Baegert, Jakob. *Brief eines Elsassers aus Californien in Nord Amerika an seinen Bruder in Schlettstadt (1752)* . . . [letter from an Alsatian in California to his brother in Schlettstadt, dated 1752 . . .] Strassburg, 1777. Found at Strassburg; typewritten copy and translation at the University of California.

Baegert was evidently a Catholic missionary.

Boehme, Anton Wilhelm. *Das Verlangte, nicht erlangte Canaan* . . . [the wished-for, unattained Canaan . . .] Frankfurt and Leipzig, 1711. Found in B, BM, HEH, LC, M, NYP.

Contains an account of the Kocherthal party of immigrants in New York.

Bolzius, Johann Martin. *Danksagungsbrief* . . . [letter of thanks . . .] Augsburg, 1749. Found in JCB.

Letter written from Ebenezer, Georgia, by the minister there.

Byrd, William. *Neu-Gefundenes Eden* . . . [new-found Eden . . .] Switzerland? 1737. Found in BM, JCB.

Entry does not state this to be a translation from English, although the author appears to have been English. It is a travel description of North Carolina, Virginia, Maryland, and Pennsylvania and contains many letters.

Cranz, David. *Alte und Neue Brüder-Historie* . . . [old and new history of the Brotherhood . . .] Barby, 1771. Found in BM, BPL, NYP (also H and LC for second edition).

History of the Evangelical Lutheran Brüder-Unität, active in America. *See also* Hegner, Johann Konrad

Der nunmehr in der Neuen Welt . . . lebende Schweitzer [Swiss now living in the New World] Bern, 1734. Sabin 10975. Found in BM.

Letters from Swiss immigrants in Carolina.

Eden in Virginia . . . Switzerland? 1736. Sabin 21829. Found in LC.

Account of a purchase of a tract of land (33,400 *Jucharten*) in Virginia by the Helvetischen Societet.

Erläuterung für Herrn Caspar Schwenckfeld . . . durch Etliche der ehemaligen Emigranten aus Schlesien . . . Innwohner in Pensylvanien . . . [reports to Caspar Schwenckfeld . . . from a number of the former emigrants from Silesia [now] living in Pennsylvania . . .] Breslau and Leipzig, 1771. Found in NYP.

Gives reports from Schwenckfelders in Pennsylvania to the year 1740.

Falckner, Daniel. *Curieuse Nachricht von Pensylvania* . . . [curious news from Pennsylvania . . .] Frankfurt and Leipzig, 1702. Sabin 23739. Found in B, BM, JCB, NYP, PLC.

Answers 103 questions from friends regarding Pennsylvania in 1702.

Feldzug der vereinigten Franzosen und Nordamerikaner in Virginien im Jahre 1781 . . . [march through Virginia in 1781 by the united French and American troops . . .] Vienna, 1782? Found in NYP.

This may give information regarding German mercenaries in French service during the American Revolution, of which we know little. Note also the seven appendices.

Franckenstein, Jacob August. *. . . Unmassgebliche Gedancken über das Emigrations-Recht wegen der Religion . . .* [some unofficial thoughts on the right of emigration for reasons of religion . . .] Leipzig, 1734. Sabin 25487. Found in NYP.

Regarding the Salzburger emigration to Georgia.

Freylinghausen, D. Gotlieb Anastasius, and Schulze, D. Johann Ludwig. *Neuere Geschichte der Evangelischen Missions-Anstalten . . .* [new history of the Lutheran mission offices . . .] Halle, 1784-99. Found in NYH.

Periodical missionary accounts from America relating chiefly to the history of the Germans.

Gegenwartiger Zustand der Finantzen von Franckreich . . . Unternehmungen des Herrn Law . . . Beschreibung des mississipischen Handels . . . [present condition of French finances . . . the enterprises of Mr. Law . . . description of the commerce on the Mississippi . . .] Leipzig, 1720. Sabin 39308. Found in LC.

May give insight into German Coast colony in Louisiana.

Geisler, Adam Friedrich [junior]. *Geschichte und Zustand . . .* [history and condition . . .] Dessau and Leipzig, 1784. Found in NYP.

Full title says it gives a list of German officers who were mercenaries in the American Revolution.

Georgia, Oder: Kurtze Nachricht Von der Christlichen Vorhaben der . . . Commissarien [Georgia, or cursory account of the plans of the . . . commissioners] Frankfurt, 1733. Found in JCB, M.

Apparently has to do with the colonization of Georgia.

Goecking, Gerhard Gottlieb Guenther. *Vollkommene Emigrations-Geschichte von denen aus den Ertz-Bissthum Saltzburg vertriebenen und grossentheils nach Preussen gegangenen Lutheranern . . .* [complete history of the emigration of Lutherans driven out of the Archbishopric of Salzburg and who went, for the most part, to Prussia . . .] Frankfurt, 1734-37; 2 volumes. Sabin 27627. Found in BM, BPL, UI1.

History of Salzburg emigrants, some of whom eventually came to Georgia.

Hazart, Cornelius. *Kirchen-Geschichte . . .* [church history . . .] Vienna, 1678-1701; 3 volumes. Sabin 31114. Found in JCB.

Volume 2 concerns the Catholic Church missionary effort in America.

Heckewelder, John Gottlieb Ernestus. *. . . Reise von Bethlehem in Pensilvanien bis zum Wabashfluss . . .* [. . . trip from Bethlehem, Pennsylvania, to the Wabash River . . .] Halle, 1797. Sabin 31207. Found in JCB, LC.

Heckewelder was a well-known Moravian missionary to the Indians.

Hegner, Johann Konrad. *Fortsetzung von David Cranzens Brüder-Historie . . .* [continuation of David Cranz's history of the Brotherhood . . .] Barby, 1791-(1816); four parts in 3 volumes. Sabin 17412. Found in BM, BPL, H, NYP.

Activities of the Lutheran Brotherhood in America. *See also* Cranz, David.

Hulzius, Levinus. *Sammlung von . . . Schiffahrten . . .* [collection of ship voyages]. Various places of publication, 1598–1650. Some volumes to be found in BM, JCB, NYP.

There were 26 volumes, usually including accounts from 20 voyages in each. A few German immigrants and sailors may have been included in this collection, although it antedates most German migration to America. Consult Palmer for details on each volume.

Jever, Johann. *Verzeichniss Allerhand Pietistischer Intriguen . . .* [list of various Pietist intrigues . . .] Wiburg, 1729. Sabin 36097. No copies found.

Presumably contained information on the Pietists who emigrated from Germany to America.

Kleinknecht, Conrad Daniel. *. . . Nachricht von . . . Georgien* [news from . . . Georgia] Augsburg, 1749. Sabin 38041. Found in JCB.

_____. *Zuverlässige Nachricht . . . von den Englischen Colonisten Georgiens zu Eben-Ezer* [trustworthy news regarding the settlers at Ebenezer in the English colony of Georgia] Augsburg, 1749. Sabin 38041. Found in JCB.

Both the above titles concern the Salzburger settlers in Georgia.

Kocherthal, Josua von. *Aussführlich- und umständlicher Bericht von der berühmten Landschaft Carolina . . .* [thorough and complete report on the famous interior of Carolina . . .] Frankfurt, 1709. Found in BM, LC, M.

The Kocherthal party of immigrants eventually settled in and around Newburgh, New York.

Kurtze Relation aus denen . . . Briefen von dem . . . nach Georgien . . . gehenden zweyten Transport Saltzburgischer Emigranten [summary account abstracted from letters of Salzburger immgrants on the second transport to Georgia] Place of publication unknown, 1734. Found in De Renne.

Kurtze Remarques über . . . missisippischen Actien-Handel in Paris . . . des Herrn Laws . . . [summary remarks regarding the trade in Mississippi shares in Paris [promoted by] Mr. Law] Leipzig, 1720. Found in BM, NYP.

Might contain information on German Coast settlers in Louisiana.

Kurze, zuverlässige Nachricht von der . . . Kirche Unitas Fratrum [summary of trustworthy news regarding the Moravian Brethren Church] No place of publication, 1757. Sabin 97851. Found in BPL, JCB, NYP.

The Moravians had settlements in North Carolina and Pennsylvania during this period.

Löber, Emanuel Christian. *. . . Nachrichten von dem Englischen America besonders von Carolina und . . . Georgia* [news from English America, especially from Carolina and Georgia] Jena, 1750. Sabin 41771. Not found.

Löber was a royal counselor in Saxony and taught medicine.

Loskiel, Georg Heinrich. *Geschichte der Mission der Evangelischen Brüder unter den Indianern in Nordamerika* [history of the mission of the Lutheran Brotherhood to the Indians in North America] Leipzig, 1789. Sabin 42109. Found in B, BM, BPL, JCB, LC.

Melsheimer, Fr[iedrich] V[alentin]. *Tagebuch von der Reise der Braunschweigischen Auxiliär Truppen von Wolfenbüttel nach Quebec . . .* [diary of the voyage of the Brunswick mercenary troops sent from Wolfenbüttel to Quebec . . .] Minden, 1776; 6 parts. Found in H, LC.

Mittelberger, Gottlieb. *. . . Reise nach Pennsylvanien im Jahr 1750. Und Rückreise nach Teutschland im Jahr 1754 . . .* [voyage to Pennsylvania in 1750 and return trip to Germany in 1754 . . .] Stuttgart, 1756. Found in BM, H, JCB, LC, M; another edition found in B, BM, NYP.

Describes the poor living conditions of German immigrants and might give the names of some.

Moser, Johann Jacob. *Nord-America nach den Friedenschlüssen vom Jahr 1783* [North America after the 1783 treaty of peace] Leipzig, 1784–85; 3 volumes. Found in B, JCB, LC, M, NYP, PLC.

Nachricht von der Provinz Virginien . . . [news from Virginia Province . . .] Frankfurt, 1772.

Contains information on Virginia and Pennsylvania and the regulators of North Carolina.

Nachrichten und Erinnerungen an verschiedene deutsche Völker die von ihren Fürsten nach Amerika geschickt worden sind [news and memorials to a number of German groups sent by their princes to America] Place of publication unknown, 1778. Sabin 51693. Found in JCB.

Neue Nachricht . . . und sichere Briefe von der Landschaft Carolina und übrigen Englischen Pflanz-Städten in Amerika [new information and trustworthy letters from the interior of Carolina and other English plantations in America] Zurich, 1783. Sabin 10974. Found in LC.

Neue Sammlung von kleinen interessanten Reisebeschreibungen [new collection of short interesting travel descriptions] Münster, 1787–92. Found in M.

Neueste Nachricht von der Landschaft Georgia [latest information from the interior of Georgia] Göttingen, 1726. Found in M.

Ochs, Johann Rudolff. *Americanischer Wegweiser . . . der Englischen Provintzen in Nord America, sonderlich . . . Landschafft Carolina* [guide to America . . . the English provinces in North America, particularly the interior of Carolina] Bern, 1711. Sabin 56647. Found in JCB.

Pastorius, Franz Daniel. *Copia eines . . . Briefes* [copy of a . . . letter] Switzerland? 1684. Found at Zürich.

This is a letter from America to his parents, dated 7 March 1684.

_____. *Sichere Nachricht auss America, wegen der Landschafft Pennsylvania, von einem dorthin gereissten Teutschen . . .* [true account of America, especially the interior of Pennsylvania, written by a German who has traveled there . . .] Place of publication unknown, 1684. Found at Zürich.

_____. *Umständige . . . Beschreibung . . . Provintzen Pensylvaniae* [complete description of the province of Pennsylvania] Frankfurt and Leipzig, 1700. Sabin 59028. Found in B, BM, JCB, LC, M, NYP, PLC.

Also contains a report from his father, Melchior Adam Pastorius.

von Reck, Philipp Georg Friedrich. *Kurz gefasste Nachricht von dem Etablissement derer Salzburgischen Emigranten zu Ebenezer . . . Georgien . . .* [summary report regarding the establishment of the Salzburger emigrants at Ebenezer . . . Georgia . . .] Hamburg, 1777. Sabin 38363. Found in H, JCB.

Risler, Jeremias. *Leben August Gottlieb Spangenbergs, Bischofs der evangelischen Brüderkirche* [life of August Gottlieb Spangenberg, bishop of the Lutheran Brotherhood church] Barby and Leipzig, 1794. Sabin 71550. Found in BM, JCB, NYP.

Successor to Count Zinzendorf; Spangenberg was in Virginia and North Carolina.

Sammlung der . . . Reisebeschreibungen . . . [collection . . . of travel descriptions . . .] Berlin, 1774-1802; 35 volumes. Sabin 75902. Not found.

Volume 11 related to America.

Schlözer, August Ludwig. *Briefwechsel meist historischen und politischen Inhalts . . .* [correspondence, mainly of historical and political content . . .] Göttingen, 1777-1782; 10 volumes. Sabin 77658. Found in BM, UI1, UMi; third edition JCB, LC, NYP.

Often cited as containing material from the Revolutionary War period.

Schulze, Johann Ludwig. *Nachrichten von der vereinigten Deutschen Evangelisch-Lutherischen Gemeinen in Nord-Amerika, absonderlich Pensylvanien . . .* [news of the united German Evangelical Lutheran congregations in North America, particularly in Pennsylvania . . .] Halle, 1787; 2 volumes. Found in B, BM, H, JCB, NYP, PLC.

Reports from Lutheran missionaries in America.

Simmendinger, Ulrich. *Warhaffte und glaubwürdige Verzeichnuss . . .*] Reutlingen, 1717? Found in NYP.

This is the original list, often republished, of the first group of German settlers in New York province, 1709.

Spangenberg, August Gottlieb. *Kurzgefasste historische Nachricht . . . Brüder-Unität augsburgische Confession* [short historical report on the Brotherhood of the Augsburg Confession] Barby, 1793. Sabin 88930. Found in BA, BM.

_____. *Leben des Herrn Nicholaus Ludwig Grafen und Herrn von Zinzendorf und Pottendorf* [life of Nicholaus Ludwig Count and Lord von Zinzendorf and Pottendorf] Barby, 1772-1775; 8 volumes. Sabin 88931. Found in BM, LC, NYP.

_____. *Von der Arbeit der evangelischen Brüder unter den Heiden* [the work of the Lutheran Brotherhood among the heathens] Barby, 1782. Sabin 88934. Found in BM, Lehigh, LC.

Spöri, Felix Christian. *Americanische Reiss Beschreibung nach . . . Neu Engelland* [American travel description . . . to New England] in *Vier Loblicher Staat Zürich verbürgeter Reisebeschreibungen* [four travel descriptions by praiseworthy citizens of the city of Zurich]. This latter title is found in BM, BPL, H, JCB, LC, NYP. See under *Vier Loblicher . . .* hereinafter.

Sprengel, Matthias Christian. *Geschichte der Europäer in Nordamerika* [history of the Europeans in North America] Leipzig, 1782. Sabin 89757. Found in B, H, NYP.

Stoecklein, Joseph. *Allerhand . . . Brief, Schrifften und Reis-beschreibungen . . .* [a number of letters, writings, and travel descriptions . . .] Augsburg and Graz, 1726-(1761); 38 parts in 5 volumes. Sabin 91981. Found in JCB, LC, NYP.

Concerns Jesuit missionaries in America.

Stöver, Johann Caspar. *Kurtze Nachrichten von einer Evangelisch-Lutherischen Deutschen Gemeinde in . . . Virginien . . .* [summary of information from a German Evangelical Lutheran congregation . . . in Virginia . . .] Hannover,

1737. Sabin 91984. Not found.

Concerns a congregation on "the furthest border of Spottsylvania administrative district."

Stuck, Gottlieb Heinrich. *Verzeichnis von . . . Reisebeschreibungen* [list of . . . travel descriptions] Halle, 1784. Found in BM, LC, NYP.

Valuable index to the then known works relating to America.

_____. *Nachtrag zu . . . Verzeichnis von . . . Reisebeschreibungen* [addendum to . . . the list of . . . travel descriptions . . .] Halle, 1785. Found in NYP.

Tagebuch der Seereise von Stade nach Quebec . . . durch die zweyte Division . . . Braunschweigischer Hülfsvölker [diary of the ocean voyage from Stade to Quebec . . . of the second division of Brunswick auxiliary troops] Frankfurt and Leipzig, 1776. Found in H, JCB, LC, NYP.

Urlsperger, Samuel. *Americanisches Ackerwerk Gottes . . .* [God's work in America . . .] Augsburg, 1754-(1757); 5 volumes in 3. Sabin 98131. Found in B, H, JCB, LC, NYP.

Report on the Salzburger immigrants at Ebenezer, Georgia.

_____. *Der Ausführliches Nachrichten von . . . Saltzburgischer Emigranten . . .* [detailed accounts from Salzburger emigrants . . .] Halle, 1731. Found in PLC. Another edition, dated 1744, Sabin 98132, found in BM, H, LC, NYP.

_____. *Die Sammlung und Führung des IVten Transports Saltzburgischer Emigranten . . .* [collection and leadership of the fourth transport of Salzburger emigrants . . .] Halle, 1741. Found in B, JCB, NYP, De Renne.

Velthusen, Johann Caspar. *Nordcarolinische Kirchennachrichten . . .* [church news from North Carolina . . .] Leipzig, 1790. Found in B.

Vier Loblicher Staat Zürich verbürgeter Reissbeschreibungen . . . [four travel descriptions by praiseworthy citizens of the canton of Zürich . . .] Zürich, 1677-1678. Sabin 99534. Found in BM, BPL, H, JCB, LC, NYP.

Parts 1 and 3 deal with America.

Vollständige . . . Nachricht von der Herrenhuthischen Brüderschafft . . . [complete account of the Moravian Brethren . . .] Frankfurt and Leipzig, 1735. Sabin 100687. Found in NYP.

Warhaffte Nachricht von einer Hochteutschen Evangelischen Colonie zu Germantown in Nord-Virginien . . . [true account of a High German Lutheran colony in Germantown, North Virginia . . .] Place of publication unknown, 1720. Sabin 27160. Found in NYP.

Weber, Ludwig. *Der hinckende Bott von Carolina . . .* [the limping messenger from Carolina] Zurich, 1735. Not found.

Weber accompanied a group of 194 emigrants under the leadership of Minister Götschi of Zurich.

von Zinzendorf, Nicolaus Ludwig *count. Pennsylvanische Nachrichten . . .* [news from Pennsylvania] Büdingen, 1742? Sabin 106359. Found in LC, NYP.

Concerns the founding of Lutheran churches.

GERMAN ETHNIC
RELIGIOUS BODIES IN AMERICA

INTRODUCTION

GERMAN ETHNIC RELIGIOUS BODIES IN AMERICA

Amana Society

Apostolic Christian Church

Brethren (River)

    Brethren in Christ

    Yorker, or Old Order, Brethren

    United Zion's Children

Catholic Apostolic Churches

Churches of God in North America, General Eldership

Dunkers, or German Baptist Brethren

    German Baptist Brethren Church (Conservative)

    Old Order German Baptist Brethren

    The Brethren Church (Progressive Dunkers)

    German Seventh-day Baptists

    Establishment of Congregations

Evangelical Bodies

    Evangelical Association

    United Evangelical Church

German Evangelical Protestant Bodies

    German Evangelical Protestant Ministers' Association

    German Evangelical Protestant Ministers' Conference

German Evangelical Synod of North America

German Reformed Church

Lutheran Bodies

    General historical statement

    General Synod of the Evangelical Lutheran Church in the United States of America

    United Synod of the Evangelical Lutheran Church in the South

    General Council of the Evangelical Lutheran Church of North America

    Evangelical Lutheran Synodical Conference of America

    Evangelical Lutheran Joint Synod of Ohio and Other States

    Lutheran Synod of Buffalo

    German Evangelical Lutheran Synod of Texas

    Evangelical Lutheran Synod of Iowa and Other States

    Evangelical Lutheran Synod of Michigan and Other States

    Immanuel Synod of the Evangelical Lutheran Church of North America

    Evangelical Lutheran Jehovah Conference

Mennonite Bodies

    Mennonite Church

    Brüderhof Mennonite Church (Hutterian Brethren; Hutterites)

    Amish Mennonite Church

Old Amish Mennonite Church

Reformed Mennonite Church

General Conference of Mennonites of North America

Church of God in Christ (Mennonite)

Old (Wisler) Mennonite Church

Defenceless Mennonites

Mennonite Brethren in Christ

Bundes Konferenz der Mennoniten Brüder-gemeinde [United Conference of Mennonite Brethren

    Krimmer Brüdergemeinde

    Schellenberger Brüdergemeinde

Central Illinois Conference of Mennonites

Nebraska and Minnesota Conference of Mennonites

Miscellaneous German-Speaking Congregations

Moravian Church (Unitas Fratrum)

Roman Catholic Church

Schwenkfelders

Temple Society in the United States (Friends of the Temple)

United Brethren Bodies

    Church of the United Brethren in Christ

    Church of the United Brethren in Christ (Old Constitution)

LOCATIONS OF GERMAN-SPEAKING CONGREGATIONS IN THE UNITED STATES, 1906

INTRODUCTION

The ultimate goal of the genealogist is not merely to construct an accurate lineage chart over several centuries but to identify the major influences, both external and internal, which have shaped the lives of his ancestors. It may be that, just as there is a biological inheritance passed on from generation to generation, there is likewise a sociological inheritance. If so, a main carrier of social genetics is religion. If one knows the religious affiliation of an ancestor, it is usually possible to determine a great deal about his social outlook and politics, his choice of a mate and of friends, frequently the reasons for his selection of one place of settlement over another, occasionally even his partners in business transactions.

In general, we believe that American researchers give too little attention to religion in their investigations; it is rare that systematic search of church records is undertaken. Indeed, there is not even an adequate bibliography of published church records or a list of established congregations for the seventeenth through nineteenth centuries. There is, however, a most valuable summary of the various denominations and their migrations in America to be found in

Edwin Scott Gaustad. *Historical Atlas of Religion in America*. New York: Harper & Row, 1962.

Although this work includes only the major religious groups, it is an invaluable reference tool for the researcher.

Much more important to genealogists are the census reports of the United States government. Information presented in this Encyclopedia has been gleaned from

U.S., Department of Commerce and Labor, Bureau of the Census, Special Reports, *Religious Bodies: 1906*. 2 volumes. Washington, D.C.: Government Printing Office, 1910.

No competent researcher should overlook the extraordinary amount of data, particularly on the locations of congregations, to be found in these volumes.

GERMAN ETHNIC RELIGIOUS BODIES IN AMERICA

For research in German-American genealogy the 1906 religious census is particularly useful because it reflects the size and composition of German-speaking settlements in America on the eve of their disintegration at the time of the first world war. Hereinafter will be found summaries, as of 1906, of the religious sects and denominations in which German ethnic groups have been predominant. The information for smaller sects is better than that for larger ones; for example, the locations of German-speaking congregations of Dunkards is more easily ascertained than those of the much larger congregations of German-speaking Roman Catholics. An inquiry at the National Archives regarding the working papers of the census bureau, from which the names of Catholic churches with German-speaking congregations could be determined, disclosed that these original supporting documents have been destroyed, certainly a sad event for genealogists.

Researchers should pay particular attention to the various smaller subdivisions within some denominations, such as the Mennonites and the Lutherans. These are nearly always clues as to the European places of origin of members. For example, members of the Mennonite Church were almost exclusively the descendants of eighteenth-century immigrants from the Palatinate and Switzerland to Pennsylvania, whereas members of the Brüderhof Mennonite Church (the Hutterites) are nineteenth-century immigrants from Slovakia and Austria, via Russia, to the northern plains of the United States and Canada. In like manner, members of the General Synod of the Evangelical Lutheran Church of the United States of America were usually the descendants of eighteenth-century Palatine and Swabian immigrants settling in Pennsylvania, whereas members of the Lutheran Synod of Buffalo (New York) were mainly nineteenth-century immigrants from Prussia and Saxony. Thus it is that, in 1906 if not later, the various smaller subdivisions and groups within a denomination are, in fact, the reflections of unassimilated regional ethnic groups quite as much as they are representatives of varying religious doctrines, by which these groups are ordinarily described.

Amana Society

About the time that the Dunkers in Germany were developing under the influence of Pietism, there arose a community more thoroughly representative of the mysticism of the period, the members of which were convinced that the days of direct inspiration by God had not passed, but that persons then living were endowed with the same divine power. Gradually they gathered strength, and in 1714 a small group of them, under the leadership of Johann Rock and Eberhard Gruber, met in Himbach, Hessen, and gave expression to their belief by a somewhat loose organization. They increased in numbers and in influence but suffered severely at the hands of the government. On the death of Johann Rock in 1749 "the gift of inspiration ceased."

Rock's successors contined to work along the lines of the founders, but the congregations diminished in number until 1817, when a new impulse was given by Michael Kraussert and a peasant girl from the Alsace, Barbara Heinemann, both of whom were recognized by a number of the older members as inspired and endowed with the gift of prophecy. With them, later, was associated Christian Metz. These leaders traveled considerably and gradually strengthened the scattered congregations. By 1826 it became apparent that the *Inspirierte* (the Inspired Ones), of whom there were many in Württemberg in particular, would have to renounce their faith and return to the fold of the state church, or leave their homes and seek refuge where they could follow their religious customs unmolested. A large estate at

Marienborn, Hessen, was leased, to which other properties were added, and by 1835 the community was quite prosperous. Difficulties with the government arose again, however. The authorities would not accept affirmation as the equivalent of the oath, which the members of the society refused to take. Already a revelation had come to Metz that they should be led out to a land of peace, and in 1842 it was decided that he and some other members should come to America.

They arrived in New York on 26 October 1842 and, learning that the Seneca Indian reservation was available, secured the property. Little by little, the entire community, numbering about 800 persons, came over from Germany, and the society was organized in 1843 under the name of the Ebenezer Society, with houses arranged in four villages, Lower, Middle, Upper, and New Ebenezer. Each village had its store, meetinghouse or place of worship, and school, and its own local government consisting of a board of elders. As the numbers increased, the quarters became too small and another change was suggested, resulting in removal to Iowa County, Iowa, where the villages of Amana, East, Middle, High, West, and South Amana, and Homestead were established in 1855.

In 1859 the society was incorporated as a religious and benevolent society under the name of the "Amana Society," although the term "Community of the True Inspiration" was also used. The purpose of this association was declared to be an entirely religious one. In order to accomplish this in full for all members, the entire property remained as a common estate with all improvements and additions. Every member, at the time of joining the society, was required to give his or her personal and real property to the trustees for the common fund. For such payments, each member was entitled to a credit on the books of the society and to a receipt signed by the president and secretary and secured by a pledge of the common property of the society. All claims for wages, interest, and income share were renounced, and each member was entitled to support throughout life. All children and minors, after the death of parents and relatives, were under the special guardianship of the trustees, and credits not disposed of by will, or debts left by parents, were assumed by their children. Persons leaving the society, either by their own choice or by expulsion, received the amount paid by them into the common fund, without interest or allowance for services during the time of their membership.

In 1906 the denomination had seven congregations with 1,756 members. All the congregations were in the state of Iowa. German, as well as English, was used in their services.

Apostolic Christian Church

The Apostolic Christian Church traces its origin to a Swiss national, the Reverend S. H. Froehlich, who came to the United States about the middle of the nineteenth century and established a number of German-Swiss churches. The principal characteristic of the sect was the development of the doctrine of entire sanctification. The different congregations were only loosely associated.

In 1906 the denomination had 42 congregations, 38 of which used German in their worship services, totaling 4,558 communicants, located in the following states:

Connecticut	1	Ohio	8	Iowa	3
New York	1	Indiana	6	Kansas	4
New Jersey	1	Illinois	15	Oregon	1
West Virginia	1	Michigan	1		

All the congregations were in rural areas, excepting the congregations at Akron and Toledo, Ohio.

Brethren (River)

In the latter part of 1750 about thirty Mennonite families in Canton Basel, Switzerland, after a long period of persecution, imprisonment, and property losses, decided to emigrate westward. They went first to England and, in the fall of 1751, set sail for America. The voyage across the Atlantic was disastrous, one of the ships with all their goods being lost, and they landed poor and destitute. One group, including Johann and Jakob Engel (Engle) and others whose names are uncertain, settled near the Susquehanna River in the southwestern part of Lancaster County, Pennsylvania, in the spring of 1752.

In 1770 some members of the Lutheran, Mennonite, and Baptist churches, who were grieved at what they considered the formalism which then characterized the churches, organized a notable revival at which many conversions occurred. The revival was conducted mainly by several ministers, Otterbein, Boehm, Bochran, and the Engles, representing the different bodies. Subsequently, differences of views arose regarding the form of baptism, some holding that the applicant should make his choice of method, while others claimed that trine immersion was the only proper form. The result was that the ministers mutually agreed to work independently, in accordance with their various interpretations of the Scriptures.

The believers in trine immersion had no regular organization but were in the habit of designating the various communities as brotherhoods. Thus, there was the Brotherhood Down by the River, meaning in the southern part of Lancaster County; also there were brotherhoods in the northern part of Lancaster County as well as in Dauphin, Lebanon, Bucks, and Montgomery counties. The outlying brotherhoods looked to the brotherhood in the southern part of Lancaster County as the home of the organization, and it was probably due to this fact that the general term "River Brethren" was given to the entire body. Another explanation has been given by some, namely, that the group was in the habit of baptizing in the river. With the development of these brotherhoods it seemed advisable to select someone to perform the duties of the ministerial office, and the choice fell upon Jacob Engle, who thus became their first minister.

In the course of time dissensions arose concerning what would now be called minor points, which ultimately caused divisions. In 1843 the body known as "Yorkers," or, as some have termed them, "Old Order" Brethren withdrew, and in 1853 the body known first as "Brinsers," but later as "United Zion's Children," also withdrew. In 1906 the three individual church organizations had a total of 111 congregations and 4,569 communicants.

Brethren in Christ. At first, the organization of the River Brethren was simple, but as their numbers increased a more permanent form became necessary, and about 1820 the present ecclesiastical organization was adopted. During the Civil War some of the members, although proclaiming the doctrine of nonresistance, were drafted for military service, and it became evident that the denomination must secure legal recognition as a religious organization holding that doctrine. Steps to secure such recognition were taken at a private council held in Lancaster, Pennsylvania, as early as 1862, at which time those who remained after the separation of the other two branches, and who constituted the great majority of the Brethren, decided to adopt the name "Brethren in Christ" instead of "River Brethren," which was done the following year. In 1904 the organization was incorporated according to the laws of the state of Pennsylvania with headquarters at Harrisburg. The ecclesiastical organization of the denomination includes the local church, a system of district councils, and a general conference. The officers of the church are bishops, ministers, and deacons. The bishops preside at all council meetings, officiate at marriages and in the observance of the sacraments, and exercise all functions of the ministry. The ministers are teachers, but also do parish visiting and, by request of the bishop, administer the sacraments in his absence. The deacons have charge of the business affairs of the churches, serve at the communion table, look after the poor, and also do some visiting in the parish.

In 1906 the Brethren in Christ had 74 congregations throughout the United States distributed as follows:

New York	2	Indiana	3	Kansas	10
Pennsylvania	33	Illinois	3	Oklahoma	3
Maryland	1	Michigan	3	Arizona	1
Ohio	11	Iowa	3	California	1

All of the congregations were in rural areas, excepting those in Buffalo, New York, Chicago, Philadelphia, Des Moines, Iowa, Harrisburg, Pennsylvania, and Canton, Ohio. None of the urban congregations had as many as 100 members. About 53 of the congregations were using English exclusively by 1906, and the remaining 21 used both English and German in their services.

Yorker, or Old Order, Brethren. In 1843 a number of the River Brethren withdrew from the main body, claiming that the original doctrines of the founders were being departed from, particularly in regard to nonresistance and nonconformity to the world. Most of those who withdrew resided in York County, Pennsylvania, whence they received the name of "Yorkers" or "Yorker Brethren." They are also known as the "Old Order Brethren" and thus are sometimes confused with the Old Order German Baptist Brethren. They have no church edifices, and their services are frequently held in large barns.

In 1906 there were a total of nine congregations with 423 members. Three of the congregations used English only in their services and the remainder used English and German. The congregations were located in the following states: Pennsylvania 5, Ohio 2, Indiana and Iowa 1 each. One of the congregations in Ohio was in Canton, all others were in rural areas.

United Zion's Children. Questions of administration and ceremonial detail, particularly in connection with a church building, arose among the River Brethren in 1852. The next year about fifty persons in Dauphin County, Pennsylvania, withdrew and organized under the leadership of Matthias Brinser as their first bishop. They were thus generally called "Brinsers," but later adopted the name "United Zion's Children." They are found principally in Dauphin, Lancaster, and Lebanon counties, Pennsylvania. In 1906 they had 28 congregations and 749 members. All the congregations remained in Pennsylvania; all were in rural areas.

Catholic Apostolic Churches

There are two groups, the Catholic Apostolic Church and the New Apostolic Church, of roughly similar beliefs. The former group was mainly an English-speaking one and the latter German-speaking. Before the first world war the German group had ties with similar groups at Hamburg and at Steinhagen, near Bielefeld, Westphalia, Germany. The New Apostolic Church had 13 congregations with 2,020 members in the following states in 1906:

New York	3	Indiana	2	Wisconsin	1
New Jersey	2	Illinois	1	Nebraska	1
Ohio	1	Michigan	2		

Nearly all the membership lived in urban areas: Buffalo, Chicago, Cleveland, New York, Detroit, Milwaukee, Newark, Omaha, Grand Rapids, Passaic, and South Bend.

Churches of God in North America, General Eldership

The revival movement which spread through the United States during the early part of the nineteenth century was not felt as much in the Reformed as in the Methodist, Baptist, and Presbyterian churches. In one case, however, it made itself apparent and its fruits were seen in the denomination known as the "General Eldership of the Churches of God in North America," popularly known as "Winebrennerian," from the name of its founder.

John Winebrenner was born in the Glade Valley, Woodsborough District, Frederick County, Maryland, in 1797. His parents were of German descent. He was baptized and confirmed in the German Reformed Church, where he early showed an inclination for the ministry. After completing his education in a district school, in an academy at Frederick, and Dickinson College, Carlisle, Pennsylvania, he went to Philadelphia to study theology under Dr. Samuel Helfenstein. While there, Winebrenner had a religious experience, which he took for conversion, and from that moment the work of the ministry, which he had hitherto regarded with more or less indifference, became the "uppermost desire of his heart."

In 1820 Winebrenner was ordained at Hagerstown, Maryland. He then accepted a call to Harrisburg, Pennsylvania, with charge of three other churches in the neighborhood. He was earnest and energetic in his ministrations, preached experimental religion, sought to raise the standard of piety, and organized Sunday schools and other church agencies. So searching and impressive was his preaching that many of his hearers became seriously alarmed about their spiritual condition. Revivals of religion were new experiences in the churches of that region, so that his ministry early wakened strong opposition. Some of the members of his charge became much dissatisfied, and the matter was brought to the attention of the Synod of the Reformed Church which met at Harrisburg in 1822. The case was not finally disposed of until 1828, when the Reverend Winebrenner's connection with the German Reformed Church was finally severed.

After his separation from the Reformed Church, Winebrenner's labors extended to surrounding districts and towns and were attended by extensive revivals of religion. Gradually his views changed on a number of doctrinal points and on the ordinances of the sacraments. In 1829 he organized an independent church, calling it simply the "Church of God." Several congregations were formed around Harrisburg, each assuming the name of "Church of God at ---." These churches, in which all baptized members had equal rights, elected and licensed men to preach, but had no common bond, general organization, or directing authority. Finally, for the purpose of adopting a regular system of cooperation, a meeting was held at Harrisburg in 1830 which was attended by six of the licensed ministers. At this meeting an "Eldership" consisting of an equal number of teaching and ruling elders was organized, which, to distinguish it from the local church eldership, was called "The General Eldership of the Church of God." The work continued to grow and spread to adjoining counties in Pennsylvania, to the state of Maryland, and to Ohio, where Elderships were organized. In 1845 delegates from the Elderships met at Pittsburg, Pennsylvania, and organized the General Eldership of the Church of God in North America," which name was changed in 1896 to the "General Eldership of the Churches of God in North America." The Eldership in eastern Pennsylvania dropped the word "General" and became the "East Pennsylvania Eldership of the Churches of God."

In 1906, the denomination had 518 congregations, with 24,356 communicants, in the following states:

Pennsylvania	178	Michigan	12	Kansas	12
Maryland	25	Minnesota	1	Arkansas	23
West Virginia	26	Iowa	24	Oklahoma	20
Ohio	74	Missouri	37	Washington	3
Indiana	35	Nebraska	12		
Illinois	32			Oregon	4

Only six of the congregations still used German in their worship services in 1906, attesting to the wide degree of assimilation of the communicants.

Dunkers, or German Baptist Brethren

There are four related bodies sharing the same ethnic and historical background, commonly called Dunkers or Dunkards: the German Baptist Brethren Church (Conservative), Old Order German Baptist Brethren, the Brethren Church (Progressive Dunkers), and the German Seventh-day Baptists. In 1906 these four bodies were divided into 1,097 congregations

with 97,144 members. Their history will be related under the parent body, the German Baptist Brethren Church (Conservative), by far the largest organization.

German Baptist Brethren Church (Conservative). Among the various communities which arose toward the close of the seventeenth century for the purpose of emphasizing the inner life of the Christian, above creed and dogma, ritual and form, ceremony and church polity, one of the most influential, though not one of the best known, was the Pietist movement of Germany. The movement did not arise as Protestants against Catholics, but rather as Protestants against what they considered the barrenness of Protestantism itself. With no purpose of organizing a sect, the created no violent upheaval, but started a wave of spiritual action within the state churches already organized. Among their leaders were Philip Jacob Spener and August Herman Francke, who together organized and supervised the mission, industrial, and orphan school at Halle. They gave a great impetus to the study of the Bible, struck a plane of moderation in theology, revived an interest in church history, and left a lasting testimony in at least one organization, the Dunkers or German Baptist Brethren.

Among the students at the Halle school was Ernst Christoph Hochmann, who, after the vicissitudes of an ascetic life, expulsion, arrest, and confinement in Detmold castle, fled to Schwarzenau, where he came into association with Alexander Mack, with whom he went on various preaching tours. In 1708, at Schwarzenau, eight of these Pietists went from the house of Alexander Mack to the Eder River. One of them, chosen by lot, led Alexander Mack into the water and immersed him three times in the name of the Father, the Son, and the Holy Ghost. Then Alexander Mack baptized the other seven, and these eight, probably the first to receive trine immersion in the history of the Protestant Church, organized a new congregation which became the basis of the *Täufer*, Tunkers or Dunkers, *Dompelaars*, or German Baptist Brethren as they have been variously called, as a separate church.

The members of the new organization waived the question of apostolic succession, subscribed to no written creed, differed from other Pietists in that they were not averse to church organization, did not abandon the ordinances which Christianity, as a whole, held to be necessary for salvation, and in general gave evidence that they were men of steadfastness. Gradually they worked out their doctrine, polity, and practice, following in many respects the same general line as the Quakers, Mennonites, and other so-called "plain people," though they have no association with them, and are to be held as entirely distinct.

The church in Schwarzenau grew, and other congregations were organized in the Palatinate, at Marienborn, Crefeld, and Epstein in Switzerland, and in West Friesland; all suffered at the hands of the state churches of Germany, Holland, and Switzerland the hardships which have been the usual lot of independents and separatists. It was from Crefeld that the first communicants, under the leadership of Peter Becker, sailed for America, settling in Germantown, Pennsylvania, in 1719. The next year, Alexander Mack, with the remaining members of the Schwarzenau community, fled to Westervain in West Friesland, and in 1729, 59 families, or 126 persons, crossed the Atlantic, landing at Philadelphia on 15 September. The fate of the communicants who did not come to America is not known; in all probability the greater number migrated, and thus the nucleus of the church was removed from European to American soil.

In 1728 Johann Konrad Beissel and his followers withdrew from the sect and organized the famous monastic community at Ephrata, Pennsylvania. No further divisions occurred until 1881, when a comparatively small company withdrew in protest against certain modifications which they felt to be inconsistent with their early history. The next year another division took place, based chiefly upon objections to the form of government which had developed within the larger body.

In 1906 the German Baptist Brethren (Conservative) had 822 congregations in 35 states and a membership of 76,547. Only 27 of these congregations, encompassing 5,300 members, still used German in their worship services. The distribution of their congregations throughout the United States was as follows:

New York	1	North Dakota	17
New Jersey	2	South Dakota	1
Pennsylvania	106	Nebraska	24
Maryland	23	Kansas	62
District of Columbia	1	Kentucky	1
Virginia	59	Tennessee	16
West Virginia	43	Alabama	1
North Carolina	14	Louisiana	3
South Carolina	1	Arkansas	9
Ohio	90	Oklahoma	24
Indiana	103	Texas	5
Illinois	49	Montana	1
Michigan	18	Idaho	7
Wisconsin	8	Colorado	6
Minnesota	7	Arizona	1
Iowa	43	Washington	9
Missouri	41	Oregon	9

There were also 17 congregations in California. Urban congregations were located in the following cities:

Chicago	Washington	Fort Wayne
Philadelphia	Dayton, Ohio	Johnstown, Pennsylvania
New York	Des Moines	
Pittsburg	Duluth	Lancaster, Pennsylvania
Denver	Hartford	Lincoln
Indianapolis	Kansas City, Kansas	Rockford
Los Angeles		South Bend
Minneapolis	Portland, Oregon	Spokane
St. Joseph, Missouri	Atlantic City	York, Pennsylvania
Cedar Rapids	Canton, Ohio	

Old Order German Baptist Brethren. Up to the latter part of the nineteenth century the history of the Dunkers was one of internal peace. Whatever disparity of individual opinion there was did not pass the bounds of mutual forbearance. As social customs developed along more modern lines during the latter part of that century, certain influences were manifested among the communities which tended to lessen the emphasis upon many of the special customs of earlier times. Accordingly, some of the members, fearful that the traditions of the founders of the denomination should be forgotten, and "the Scriptures suffer violence," withdrew in 1881 and formed the organization known as the "Old Order German Baptist Brethren."

In 1906 the Old Order Dunkers had 68 congregations, totaling 3,388 members; only one of the congregations was in an urban area (Dayton, Ohio). All the congregations used English in their services. Distribution throughout the United States was as follows:

Pennsylvania	3	Indiana	13	North Dakota	1
Maryland	2	Illinois	4	Nebraska	1
Virginia	6	Michigan	3	Kansas	3
West Virginia	3	Wisconsin	1	Oklahoma	1
North Carolina	1	Iowa	1		
Ohio	20	Missouri	2		

There was an additional group in Colorado and two in California.

The Brethren Church (Progressive Dunkers). As the Dunker communities in America grew in strength, there was a gradual departure from the early form of polity and discipline which had been distinctively congregational. The district, state, and annual meetings became practically courts, much after the presbyterian system of polity. Against this, there was considerable protest by those who held that the final power should be vested in the local church. The result was that, in 1882, there was a division and those who preferred the simple congregational form of government withdrew and organized under the name of "The Brethren Church," though they were generally known as "Progressive Dunkers."

In 1906 the Progressive Dunkers had 202 congregations with 17,402 members in 19 states. All congregations used English in their services. Distribution of the congregations was as follows:

New Jersey	2	Indiana	29	Nebraska	4
Pennsylvania	49	Illinois	7	Kansas	16
Maryland	5	Michigan	5	Arkansas	1
District of Columbia	1	Wisconsin	3	Texas	1
		Iowa	13	Cali-	
Virginia	26	Missouri	2	fornia	1
West Virginia	1	South			
Ohio	29	Dakota	1		

They had urban congregations in Chicago, Philadelphia, Pittsburgh, Los Angeles, Washington, D.C., Des Moines, Allentown and Altoona, Pennsylvania, Canton, Ohio, Johnstown, Pennsylvania, and South Bend, Indiana.

German Seventh-day Baptists. Among the earlier members of the Dunker community in the United States was Johann Konrad Beissel, who, with a few others, landed at Boston in 1720, the year after Peter Becker settled in Germantown, Pennsylvania. Beissel had not been identified with the Schwarzenau community in Germany, although he had sojourned there for a short time, but had acquired strong mystical tendencies as a result of his acquaintance with the writings of Gottfried Arnold and the teachings of Jakob Boehme and other Inspirationists, and his association with the Rosicrucians at Heidelberg. After his arrival in America, Beissel spent a short time in Germantown and then removed with three companions to Conestoga, Pennsylvania, at that time almost a wilderness, where they lived as hermits. In 1724 they were visited by Peter Becker of the Dunkers; Beissel and several others were baptized into that church, and a congregation was organized of which Beissel was chosen pastor. It was not long, however, before his ascetic and mystical tendencies, together with outside influences to which he was subjected, led him to embrace and teach doctrines, such as celibacy and the observance of the seventh day as the Sabbath, which were widely at variance with the tenets of the Dunkers, and finally, in 1728, he and his followers formally withdrew from the Dunker church.

In 1732 Beissel left his congregation and removed to Ephrata, Pennsylvania, a few

miles distant, there again to live as a hermit. Here he was joined from time to time by others of both sexes who shared his mystic and ascetic ideas and whom he organized into the "Ephrata Society." Celibacy was enjoined upon the members, and separate houses were built for the two sexes, each of which was organized in monastic fashion, the "Brothers' house" having its prior and the "Sisters' house" its prioress. The society grew rapidly and its activities were entered into with enthusiasm. Industries were organized on the communistic plan, which flourished for a time; but under the influence of Beissel, who thought them out of harmony with the spiritual purposes for which the community was organized, they were soon greatly curtailed and were kept subordinate to the religious idea. Ephrata had, however, one of the first schools (1735) in that part of the country, and its printing establishment (1750) was one of the earliest and best.

With the advancing tide of civilization and the disappearance of the wilderness the most characteristic features of the community lost their prominence. The celibate membership diminished. In 1764 there were 21 males and 25 females, while in 1769 there were but 14 celibate males in the brotherhood, and this is the last record of the exact number of celibates. By 1830 the community was so scattered that it was agreed that members might cast their votes in business meetings by proxy. The only trace of the communistic feature remaining in 1906 was the ownership of the property by the society, under control of a board of trustees. All five of the remaining congregations, with a total membership of 167, were in Pennsylvania.

Establishment of Congregations. The 1906 census contains information regarding establishment dates of congregations which may be indirectly helpful to researchers:

	1700 1799	1800 1849	1850 1879	1880 1906
German Baptist Brethren Church (Conservative)	11	87	262	403
Old Order German Baptist Brethren	*	*	*	*
Brethren Church (Progressive Dunkers)	-	-	5	193
German Seventh-day Baptists	3	1	1	-

*Included with the German Baptist Brethren Church (Conservative).

Extensive information on the genealogies of Dunkard families is to be found in the following archival collections:

Brethren Historical Library and Archives, Church of the Brethren General Offices, 1451 Dundee Avenue, Elgin, Illinois 60120

Evangelical Bodies

In 1906 there were two Evangelical organizations, as follows: the Evangelical Association and the United Evangelical Church. The communicants of both these denominations were ethnic Germans, usually of Lutheran or Reformed backgrounds.

Evangelical Association. The great religious awakening which took place in the United States at the close of the eighteenth century was at first largely confined to the English-speaking communities. It was inevitable, however, that others should feel the effect of the new spirit, and a number of leaders arose, through whose influence varying types of religious life developed, eventuating in different church organizations. In eastern Pennsylvania, there were a large number of German-speaking people, the descendants of those who in the preceding century had fled from the Palatinate. Among them was Jakob Albright (Albrecht), who was born in Pottstown, Pennsylvania, in 1759, and died in 1808. Baptized in infancy and confirmed in the Lutheran communion, Albright was later converted under the influence of a Reformed minister; but, coming into connection with the Methodists, he declared his adherence to them and was licensed to exhort. More and more, his interests were directed toward his own people. The leaders of the Methodist Church did not wish to engage in distinctively German work, as they believed that the language would soon become extinct in the United States, and therefore Albright, who had begun to preach in 1796, felt called upon to devote himself particularly to work among these people in their own language. Under his direction 20 converts from among them united in 1800 to pray with and for each other. It had not been his purpose to found a new church, but the language conditions and the opposition manifested by some Methodists to the modes of worship used by his converts made a separate ecclesiastical organization necessary. There was not schism; it was simply the development of a movement for the religious and spiritual awakening of the German populace in Pennsylvania.

It was not until 1803 that an ecclesiastical organization was effected at a general assembly held in eastern Pennsylvania, when Jakob Albright was set apart as a minister of the gospel and ordained as an elder. The act of consecration was performed by the laying on of hands and solemn prayer by two of his associates. The claim that this act was an ordination was opposed by the ecclesiastics of other denominations, but the Association held to its position and asserted that Albright's credentials were from a higher authority than that of the ecclesiastical succession.

Albright's training in the Methodist Episcopal Church influenced him in organizing the new movement, and many characteristic Methodist features, as the circuit system and the itinerancy of ministers, were adopted. The first field of operations included the counties of Bucks, Berks, and Northampton, and extended into portions of Northumberland and Center counties, Pennsylvania. The first annual conference was held in Lebanon County, Pennsylvania, in 1807. Albright was elected bishop, and articles of faith and the book of discipline were adopted, but a full form of church government was not devised for some years. The first general conference convened in Buffalo Valley, Center County, Pennsylvania, in 1816, at which the denomination adopted the title "Evangelical Association."

Although in the beginning, the activities of the church were confined to the German language, the scope was soon widened by taking up work in the English language also. The denomination spread into other Middle Atlantic states, throughout the northern and western states from New England to the Pacific coast and north into Canada. As early as 1815 a church publishing house had been founded, and what is said to have been the oldest German religious newspaper in the United States, *Der Christliche Botschafter*, was founded in 1836. A division in 1891, resulting in the organization of the United Evangelical Church, took from the denomination a large number of ministers and members.

In 1906 the Evangelical Association had 1,700 congregations, totaling 104,808 communicants, in the following states:

Maine	2	Indiana	112	Nebraska	66
Vermont	2	Illinois	127	Kansas	88
Massachusetts	10	Michigan	139	Kentucky	2
Rhode Island	2	Wisconsin	223	Oklahoma	18
Connecticut	1	Minnesota	126	Texas	14
New York	65	Iowa	110	Colorado	9
New Jersey	9	Missouri	22	Washington	22
Pennsylvania	234	North Dakota	53	Oregon	37
Maryland	8	South Dakota	51	California	15
West Virginia	7				
Ohio	186				

Of these 1,700 congregations, 917 were still using the German language in their worship services in 1906.

United Evangelical Church. As a separate ecclesiastical body, the United Evangelical Church dates from the year 1894. Previously, its members had constituted a part of the Evangelical Association. The division which resulted in the formation of the new church was due to differences of opinion as to what were considered fundamental principles of church polity, and official acts affecting the claims of a large minority of the ministers and members of the association. Seven annual conferences, with from 60,000 to 70,000 members, who were designated the "minority," entered a protest against what they regarded as "abuse of the powers conferred by the discipline and usurpation of powers in violation of the discipline." This protest availed nothing, and in due time a separate organization was effected, with articles of faith and a discipline in strict accord with the doctrine, spirit, and purpose of the original church. In 1894 the former members of the East Pennsylvania Conference met in convention and organized as the "East Pennsylvania Conference of the United Evangelical Church," and called a general conference to meet in Naperville, Illinois, in November of that year. Other conferences joined the call, and on the designated day the conference met, and on the following day declared itself to be the first General Conference of the United Evangelical Church.

In 1906 the denomination had 978 congregations, with 69,882 communicants, located in the following states:

New York	6	Wisconsin	4	Kansas	14
Pennsylvania	579	Minnesota	13	Oklahoma	7
Maryland	15	Iowa	84		
West Virginia	4	North Dakota	3	Washington	1
Ohio	45			Oregon	43
Indiana	2	South Dakota	8	California	1
Illinois	86	Nebraska	62		
Michigan	1				

Of the 978 congregations, 158 still used the German language in their worship services in 1906.

German Evangelical Protestant Bodies

In the 1890 census there was reported a German Evangelical Protestant Church. By 1906 the denomination was reported in two organizations, as follows: the German Evangelical Protestant Ministers' Association, and the German Evangelical Protestant Ministers' Conference.

German Evangelical Protestant Ministers' Association. A number of independent German congregations of liberal faith, located mainly in Pennsylvania, Ohio, and Illinois, united in 1885 in an association called the German Evangelical Ministers' Association (*Predigerverein*). The immediate object was to bring the ministers together in a social way, that they might be able to encourage and assist one another in the

discharge of their pastoral duties. They had not been members of any synods, but were independent of all organizations, as were the churches they served.

One of the most serious problems which the association had to meet in later years was the general demand for the use of the English language in church services. As it became increasingly difficult to satisfy this demand, several of the larger congregations were compelled to fill their pulpits with preachers belonging to what were known as the "Orthodox synods."

In 1906 the sect had 44 congregations, all of which used German in their worship services, and a total of 23,518 communicants. The congregations were located in the following states:

Pennsylvania	9	Ohio	17	Michigan	1
Maryland	2	Indiana	7	Iowa	2
West Virginia	1	Illinois	3	Kentucky	3

Ten of the 44 congregations were in cities and towns, as follows: Baltimore, Cincinnati, Cleveland, Pittsburgh, Allegheny (Pennsylvania), Columbus, Newport (Kentucky), Terre Haute (Indiana), McKeesport and Wheeling (Pennsylvania).

German Evangelical Protestant Ministers' Conference. This organization was formed in Cincinnati in 1895 by members of the German Evangelical Ministers' Association who were prompted to withdraw from that organization on account of differences arising in regard to polity.

In 1906 the Conference had 22 congregations, 18 of which used German in their worship services, with 11,186 communicants. The congregations were located in the following states:

Pennsylvania	2	Missouri	2
Ohio	9	Kentucky	3
Indiana	3	California	1
Illinois	2		

Six of the 22 congregations were located in urban areas, as follows: Cincinnati, Pittsburgh, St. Louis, San Francisco, Allegheny (Pennsylvania), and Dallas.

German Evangelical Synod
of North America

The German Evangelical Synod of North America traces its origin to six ministers of the State Church of Prussia (representing the union of the Lutheran and Reformed churches) who met and organized a synod at Gravois Settlement, Missouri, in 1840. Four of these were missionaries--two sent by the Rhenish Missionary Society and two by the Missionary Society of Basel, Switzerland. The two remaining ministers were independent--one coming from Bremen and the other from Strassburg. During subsequent years several similar organizations were effected, including the United Evangelical Synod of North America, the German Evangelical Society of Ohio, the United Evangelical Society of the East, and others. In 1872 these organizations, holding the same doctrines and governed by the same ecclesiastical principles, united in the organization known in 1906 as the "German Evangelical Synod of North America."

The denomination had 1,205 congregations, totaling 293,139 communicants in 1906; 952 of the congregations still used German exclusively in their services and 236 used German and English. Distribution of the congregations was as follows:

New York	64	Michigan	68	Alabama	2
New Jersey	7	Wisconsin	99	Louis-iana	4
Pennsylvania	18	Minnesota	69		
Maryland	17	Iowa	81	Arkansas	3
District of Columbia	1	Missouri	162	Okla-homa	17
Virginia	1	North Dakota	8	Texas	50
West Virginia	2	South Dakota	6	Wyoming	1
Georgia	1			Colorado	6
Ohio	110	Nebraska	28	Utah	2
Indiana	91	Kansas	35	Cali-fornia	14
Illinois	219	Kentucky	19		

German Reformed Church

The Reformed Church in the United States--for many years known as the "German Reformed Church"--traces its origin chiefly to the German, Swiss, and French people who settled in America early in the eighteenth century. Among its founders it includes Ulrich Zwingli and Jean Calvin, of Switzerland, while the fact that so many of its early members came from the Palatinate gives it close relation to Philip Melanchthon. The Heidelberg Catechism compiled by Zacharias Ursinus, a pupil of Melanchthon, and Caspar Olevianus, a pupil of Calvin, in 1563 during the reign of Friedrich III, the Palatine Elector, is still the Reformed Church's standard in teaching the Scriptures.

Emigration from the Palatinate during the seventeenth century was small and there was no continuity between the early, isolated pioneers and the churches in the succeeding century. Pastorius with a little company of mystics came to Pennsylvania in 1683 at the invitation of William Penn and founded Germantown; but it was not until 1709 that Reformed immigrants became at all numerous. About that

time more than 30,000 emigrants from the Palatinate had made their ways to England, encamped near London, clamoring for transportation to America. Some thousands of them were placed on unoccupied lands in Ireland and elsewhere, while large numbers were brought to America, where they established settlements in the South, in New York, and especially in Pennsylvania. These pioneers made provision for churches and parochial schools, although they were not well supplied with either preachers or qualified teachers. In some cases they had been accompanied by their pastors, and in this way Johann Friedrich Hager accompanied one of the parties, arriving in New York in 1709. Among others who proved energetic and useful workers were Johann Philipp Boehm, Georg Michael Weiss, and Johann B. Rieger. The general condition of the churches was poor; the number of divisions was very great and there were large companies of mystics. No regular method of securing ordination in this country existed, although Boehm was ordained by the Dutch Reformed ministers of New York, with the assent of the Classis of Amsterdam. Meanwhile, the ecclesiastical authorities of the Palatinate, appreciating their own inability to do much for the American churches, made application to the Classis of Amsterdam, and that classis commissioned Michael Schlatter as a missionary evangelist. He arrived in America in August 1746 and soon after had a conference with the pastors who were already in the churches. As a consequence, a coetus, or synod, was organized the next year. Some opposition arose in connection with the Dutch church, which, in its turn, was somewhat discouraged by the reports from America and also be the death in 1749 of Boehm, whose influence had been great.

In 1751 Schlatter made a visit to Europe, and so interested the people of Holland in the churches of Pennsylvania that he returned the next year with six ministers and a sum estimated at $60,000. This general assistance, however, was conditioned upon subordination to the Classis of Amsterdam, causing a great deal of friction which manifested itself in the development of two distinct parties in the coetus itself, differing in their views of polity, and resembling in a general way the "Old Side" and the "New Side" in the Presbyterian Church; the former emphasizing doctrinal regularity, the latter being more in accord with the evangelistic and pietistic developments of the time. Among the most prominent leaders in the latter group was Philipp Wilhelm Otterbein, later identified with the organization of the United Brethren in Christ. A number of independent ministers declined to identify themselves with the coetus, among whom one of the most prominent was John J. Zubly, pastor of a church in Charleston, South Carolina, and for a time a member of the Continental Congress.

The latter part of the eighteenth century was not a period of great growth, although the general status of the individual churches was good. With the general development of the feeling of independence and the association with other denominations--particularly the Lutherans under the leadership of Muhlenberg-- the German Reformed congregations became dissatisfied with the conditions of their connection with the Classis of Amsterdam. That connection had proved as heavy a burden for them as for the Dutch churches of New York and New Jersey, and it was finally decided to act independently of the classis.

The first synod of the German Reformed Church met at Lancaster, Pennsylvania, on 27 April 1793 and reported 178 congregations and 15,000 communicants. Of the congregations, at least 55 had no ministers. The churches were scattered through New York, northern New Jersey, Pennsylvania, Maryland, and Virginia, with several congregations west of the Alleghenies. The most important congregations were Philadelphia, Lancaster, and Germantown in Pennsylvania, and Frederick in Maryland. Many churches in sections of Pennsylvania, about which no certain information was available, were reported vacant. It was difficult for them to secure any ministers, either from their own synod or from the Dutch Reformed Church, especially ministers who could use the German language.

With the development of the Protestant Episcopal Church, some congregations joined that body and others joined in the organization of the United Brethren. Various movements sprang up for union with other bodies, such as the Dutch Reformed Church and especially the Lutheran, at the time of the organization of the first Lutheran ministerium. This latter union was especially encouraged by the union in 1817 of the Lutheran and Reformed churches of Prussia. It did not, however, materialize in this country, and after a few years was no longer spoken of.

Then followed the revival period, in which two opposing influences, liberal and conservative, became apparent. The conservative party was anxious to preserve the faith, and the liberal party laid greater stress on fellowship. Another complication arose from the fact that the younger element in the congregations preferred the English language in church services, while the older element preferred the German. As the difficulty of securing trained leaders became more urgent, a theological seminary was founded. During the discussions that followed, a number of churches withdrew and formed, in 1822, the "Synod of the Free German Reformed Congregations of Pennsylvania," later known as the "German Reformed Synod of Pennsylvania and Adjacent States." These churches returned in 1837, and eventually the discussion resulted in the establishment of a theological seminary at Mercersburg, Pennsylvania.

Meanwhile, the church had been forming congregations to the westward, but the difficulties of communication made the relations uncertain and the western classis soon developed into the Western Synod, which, while holding generally fraternal relations with the Eastern Synod, was not identified with it. As graduates of Mercersburg found their way into the distant regions, the two synods came into more intimate relations, and in 1844 a convention was called in which the Dutch Reformed Church and the two German Reformed synods were represented. Although the convention was purely advisory, it prepared the way for later union. The western congregations meanwhile had met the same difficulty as those in the East in securing ministers, and had established their own educational institutions, one of which, Heidelberg College, at Tiffin, Ohio, was founded in 1850.

In 1906 the denomination had 1,736 churches with 292,654 communicants. Only 57 of the 1,736 churches were in communities with more than 25,000 population. Distribution of the congregations was as follows:

Massachusetts	2	Indiana	58	Kentucky	12
Connecticut	3	Illinois	31	Tennessee	3
New York	18	Michigan	18	Arkansas	1
New Jersey	6	Wisconsin	64	Oklahoma	1
Pennsylvania	891	Minnesota	7	Colorado	1
Maryland	78	Iowa	44	Oregon	7
District of Columbia	2	Missouri	10	California	1
Virginia	25	North Dakota	21		
West Virginia	9	South Dakota	18		
North Carolina	55	Nebraska	18		
Ohio	310	Kansas	12		

The 1906 census contains information regarding establishment dates of congregations which may be indirectly helpful to researchers:

1683-1800	176	1860-1869	194	1890-1899	184
1800-1849	364	1870-1879	151	1900-1906	134
1850-1859	182	1880-1889	188		

In 1906 there were still 674 congregations, totaling 143,023 communicants, still using German in their services. In addition, the Dutch Reformed Churched (called in 1906 the Reformed Church in America) had 68 congregations, with 8,161 communicants, using German in their services.

Lutheran Bodies

In 1906 there were 24 Lutheran bodies within the United States, and their ethnic composition was complex. The eleven bodies having

German-speaking components were as follows:

	Total Congregations in Body	Congregations Using German
General Synod of the Evangelical Lutheran Church in the United States of America	1,734	261
United Synod of the Evangelical Lutheran Church in the South	449	5
General Council of the Evangelical Lutheran Church of North America	2,146	598
Evangelical Lutheran Synodical Conference of America	3,301	3,121
Evangelical Lutheran Joint Synod of Ohio and Other States	772	606
Lutheran Synod of Buffalo (New York)	33	33
German Evangelical Lutheran Synod of Texas	25	25
Evangelical Lutheran Synod of Iowa and Other States	828	819
Evangelical Lutheran Synod of Michigan and Other States	55	55
Immanuel Synod of the Evangelical Lutheran Church of North America	11	10
Evangelical Lutheran Jehovah Conference	9	9

General Historical Statement. The earliest Lutherans to settle in North America came from Holland to Manhattan Island in 1623 with the first Dutch colonists. For some years they had great difficulty in establishing worship of their own, the Dutch authorities, both ecclesiastical and civil, having received instructions "to encourage no other doctrine in the New Netherlands than the true Reformed." A Lutheran pastor, the Reverend Johann Ernst Goetwater, was sent to this country in 1657 by the Lutheran consistory of Amsterdam to minister to two Lutheran congregations in New York and Albany, but he was not allowed to enter upon his ministrations, and after a few months was sent back to Holland by representatives of the Reformed faith. When the English took possession of New York in 1674, the Lutherans were allowed full liberty of worship.

The first independent colony of Lutherans was established on the Delaware River by Swedes who were sent over in 1638 by the prime minister of King Gustavus Adolphus. Reorus Torkillus, the first Lutheran minister to settle in the territory of the United States, arrived in 1639. He held Lutheran services in Fort Christina, the first Lutheran church, a blockhouse, was built soon afterwards.

In 1643 the Reverend Johann Campanius, another Swedish Lutheran minister, arrived and in 1646 built a Lutheran church at Tinicum, Pennsylvania, nine miles southwest of Philadelphia. He also translated Luther's Catechism into the local Indian language. In 1669 a block church was erected by the Swedes at Wicaco, now a part of Philadelphia, and about 1694 the first English Lutheran services were held in Germantown and in Philadelphia by Heinrich Bernhard Koster. The block church at Wicaco was superseded in 1700 by the Gloria Dei Church, which is still standing, as is also Trinity Church in Wilmington, Delaware, the cornerstone of which was laid in 1698. The first German Lutheran church in Pennsylvania, that at Falckner's Swamp, Montgomery County, is thought to date from 1703, and the Reverend Daniel Falckner to have been its first pastor.

In 1710 a large number of exiles from the Palatinate settled in New York and Pennsylvania, and in 1734 a colony of Salzburgers founded the Lutheran Church in Georgia. In 1728 the Reverend Johann Kaspar Stoever traveled from Germantown and the banks of the Delaware River to the Susquehanna River at York, and finally into Maryland, organizing German Lutheran congregations in the interior of Pennsylvania. It was left to the Reverend Heinrich Melchior Muhlenberg, who arrived in Philadelphia in 1742, to bring these primitive congregations into some order, to infuse into them a sound piety and a true church life, to provide them with good pastors, and to introduce schools for the education of the children. The sphere of Muhlenberg's activities included the states of New York, New Jersey, Pennsylvania, and Maryland.

By the middle of the eighteenth century Pennsylvania contained about 30,000 Lutherans, of whom four-fifths were Germans and one-fifth Swedes. In 1748 Muhlenberg, with six other ministers and with lay delegates from the congregations, organized a Synod, or Ministerium, of Pennsylvania, the first Lutheran synod in this country. In 1786 the second synod, the Ministerium of New York, was formed, and in 1803 the Synod of North Carolina; but it was not until 1818, with the organization of the Synod of Ohio, that the growth of the denomination became rapid. During the nineteenth century the Lutheran communion in the United States grew with extraordinary rapidity, due primarily to immigration from Lutheran countries, a large portion of American Lutherans being either German immigrants or the offspring of German immigrants. There are also large bodies of Swedish, Norwegian, and Danish Lutherans, and a number from Finland and other European countries.

General Synod of the Evangelical Lutheran Church in the United States of America. Although Lutheran communities were to be found in the United States in the early part of the seventeenth century, it was not for another century that they were generally organized into churches or gathered into ecclesiastical bodies. The first synod was the Ministerium of Pennsylvania; the second, the Ministerium of New York, and the third, the Synod of North Carolina, each absolutely independent of the others, and jealous of its independence. The celebration in 1817 of the tercentennial of the Reformation served to bring the various communities together. With the organization of the Synod of Ohio in 1818 and the Synod of Maryland and Virginia early in 1820, a demand arose for a general body to unify these different elements. A call was issued for a convention at Hagerstown, Maryland, in the latter part of 1820. Representatives were present from all the Ministeriums, excepting Ohio. A form of constitution was agreed upon for an organization to be called the "General Synod," and was referred to the participating synods for ratification. Committees were appointed to consider the establishment of a theological seminary and a missionary institution, and also to provide means for the care of poor ministers and ministers' widows and orphans.

The organization was established with a hopeful outlook, but unexpected opposition soon developed among the congregations, many of which looked upon all organization as a form of ecclesiastical tyranny. The reason for the absence of representatives of the Synod of Ohio at the convention at Hagerstown was stated to be a fear that uniform hymn books and liturgies would be introduced, contrary to an article in the Augsburg Confession; that delegates to the General Synod would usurp the rights of other ministers and thus infringe upon the freedom and parity of the ministry; that incorporation would follow; and that in the General Synod the English language would soon prevail, whereas in other places German would remain the dominant language. The German element of Pennsylvania also made earnest protest against the new organization.

A year later, at the first meeting of the synod at Frederick, Maryland, only ten delegates were present, representing the Ministerium of Pennsylvania and the synods of North Carolina, and Maryland and Virginia. New York kept aloof entirely, and two years later the Ministerium of Pennsylvania withdrew, because its leaders were unable to overcome the opposition of the congregations in the rural districts, influenced probably by a protest in the Reformed Churches against a projected general synod in that denomination. Ohio had elected delegates to this convention, but learning of the withdrawal of the Ministerium of Pennsylvania, they did not attend. The result was that for a long time the General Synod remained practically confined to the three small synods of North Carolina, Maryland and Virginia, and Western Pennsylvania, which had been formed from the Ministerium of Pennsylvania after the latter's refusal to enter the General Synod.

Nevertheless, relations between the different bodies remained cordial; delegates were interchanged and many pastors and congregations which remained outside manifested their sympathy with the movements of the General Synod and contributed freely to them. This was in general the position of the Ministerium of New York, until in 1837 it joined the General Synod. In 1834 the single Ministerium of Pennsylvania, with 26,882 communicants, was larger than the whole General Synod, which had only 20,249. Other groups joined from time to time, and in 1839 the Ministerium of Pennsylvania entered its fellowship. When the Civil War broke out, the General Synod embraced 23 synods and more than two-thirds of the Lutheran communicants in the United States. The war, however, occasioned the loss of the five southern synods.

Meanwhile, the confessional question assumed greater and greater importance. In the General Synod the adoption of English as the language of worship proceeded with great rapidity, and the increasing fellowship with other denominations, which was one of its features, created a feeling on the part of many that it was not loyal to distinctive Lutheranism. The conservatism of many of its congregations was almost as strong as that of some of the older synods which stood aloof, yet on the other hand there was, in the General Synod, a very strong movement against what were considered rigid interpretations of Lutheran standards. In 1864 came the admission to the General Synod of the Franckean Synod, "which pressed 'new measures' to the extreme." The liberal tendency thus manifest in the organization of the General Synod was strongly opposed by the Ministerium of Pennsylvania, which refused to recognize the Franckean Synod. This refusal was interpreted as a virtual separation from the General Synod, and when the Pennsylvania delegates appeared in the convention of 1866 they were declined recognition until the situation should be clearly understood.

The matter thus came to a crisis and resulted in 1866 in a call by the Ministerium of Pennsylvania for a convention, at which the General Council was organized. The new organization gathered to itself those elements in the General Synod which were more conservative, not so much in their individual beliefs, as in their conception of the mutual relation of persons and churches holding different beliefs. While the withdrawal of these synods was a serious loss, the General Synod was left in greater harmony and freedom to develop along its special lines; thereafter, its growth was steady and substantial.

In 1906 the General Synod was comprised of 1,734 congregations, totaling 270,221 communicants in the following states:

Connecticut	2	Ohio	192	Kansas	55
New York	109	Indiana	89	Kentucky	17
New Jersey	27	Illinois	112	Tennessee	5
Pennsylvania	721	Michigan	13	Oklahoma	7
Delaware	1	Wisconsin	14	Wyoming	2
Maryland	115	Iowa	33	Colorado	7
District of Columbia	9	Missouri	20	New Mexico	2
		South Dakota	7	California	21
Virginia	4				
West Virginia	26	Nebraska	124		

Some 261 congregations, with 46,385 communicants, still used German in their worship services. Congregations were about evenly divided between urban and rural areas, with the urban congregations usually being the more liberal.

United Synod of the Evangelical Lutheran Church in the South. The Lutherans of the southern states shared in the general convictions of the southern people as to the permanency of the rupture of the federal union, and, believing the political separation from the northern bodies to be irrevocable, they considered it best to have a new general ecclesiastical organization. A few delegates in convention at Salisburg, North Carolina, arranged the preliminaries in 1862, and a year later delegations from the synods of North and South Carolina, Georgia, Virginia, and southwestern Virginia assembled at Concord, North Carolina, and formally organized the "General Synod of the Evangelical Lutheran Church of the Confederate States of America."

The doctrinal basis was declared to be the Old and New Testaments as the only infallible rule of faith and practice, and the ecumenical creeds and the Augsburg Confession the exponents of this faith. Already there had grown up a general desire for a more pronounced adherence to the Augsburg Confession, and a clause allowing liberty of construction upon certain articles, although accepted at the time, was later rejected. At the second annual meeting in 1864 a committee on domestic missions was appointed, but comparatively little else was done. The next year there was no meeting. In 1866 a new title became necessary to conform to the changed political situation, and the name "Evangelical Lutheran General Synod, South" was chosen. Questions of union with

other bodies arose, but it was finally decided that the wisest way to develop their own resources was not to renew organic relations with the General Synod. Negotiations were begun with the Tennessee Synod, and in 1868 a union was effected with the Holston Synod, and in 1872 with the Mississippi Synod. In 1886 the Tennessee Synod joined the body, which then became known as the "United Synod of the Evangelical Lutheran Church in the South."

In 1906 the United Synod had 449 congregations, totaling 47,747 communicants, located as follows:

Virginia	151	South Carolina	87	Tennessee	22
West Virginia	13	Georgia	22	Alabama	1
North Carolina	135	Florida	2	Mississippi	15
		Ohio	1		

General Council of the Evangelical Lutheran Church in North America. As the Swedish colony in Pennsylvania and Delaware owed its origin largely to the interest felt in the westward movement by King Gustavus Adolphus, so also it received from him much of the direction of its doctrinal development. The earliest governor of New Sweden was John Printz, who came over in 1643, with special instructions that divine service should be "zealously conducted according to the Unaltered Augsburg Confession . . . that the youth be properly instructed and trained in the fear of the Lord, and Christianity be spread among the Indians." Later religious leaders, such as Justus Falckner and John C. Stoever, emphasized the same position, and it was still further impressed upon the Pennsylvania churches by Henry Melchior Muhlenberg in 1742 and later. On this doctrinal basis the original Lutheran foundation in America was so well laid, especially by Muhlenberg, that European rationalism at the end of the eighteenth century had little effect on the Lutheran congregations.

The Ministerium of Pennsylvania, organized by Muhlenberg in 1748, the broad basis of which was indicated by the name it bore for many years--The Evangelical Lutheran Ministerium of North America--thus stood for a strong confessionalism, understanding by that term a recognition of the dominant authority of the confessions of the church, and particularly of the Augsburg Confession. Its churches were also chiefly German, and in view of the Unitarian influences which appeared to accompany the anglicizing tendencies manifest in the Ministerium of New York, it was natural that they should be anxious to retain their own language, particularly as it enabled their ministers to keep in touch with the literature of the Lutheran Church.

With the extension of settlement westward, progressive men in the eastern synods came to realize the advantage of a general body, and in 1820 a call was issued for a conference, which resulted in the organization of the General Synod. Although the leaders in this movement were chiefly members of the Pennsylvania Ministerium, the general tone of its churches was not sympathetic. This was due largely to their great conservatism; to their love of synodical liberty and dislike of centralization of power, a dislike strongly prevalent in the Lutheran churches in the twentieth century as well; to a spirit of inertia and an instinctive resistance to the English New England theology; and later to opposition to the revival movement which swept over the United States in the third and fourth decades of the nineteenth century. The Pennsylvania Ministerium entered into the General Synod reluctantly, for it seemed to them contrary to the whole spirit of the Lutheran Church.

After two years of trial, the Ministerium of Pennsylvania formally withdrew from the General Synod which, until the entrance of the New York Ministerium in 1873, included only four or five small synods. There was considerable friction within the General Synod, for congregations were rapidly passing from German to English; the new generation of pastors knew little of Lutheran theology except as they learned it from Calvinistic or American writers; the recurring waves of revival influence attracted them; and especially unfortunate from the standpoint of the earnest Lutheran was the lack of any decided form of church life. Preaching had become hortatory rather than doctrinal. The old ways of the fathers were looked upon with suspicion, and the very effort at compromise resulted in paralysis, as each party sought to avoid anything which might offend the other.

The reception into the General Synod of the Melanchthon and Franckean synods in 1859 and 1864, respectively, created much opposition, and when it appeared to the Ministerium of Pennsylvania that its continuance in the General Synod depended upon its acceptance, if not its endorsement, of the Franckean Synod, that Ministerium issued a call to all synods and congregations in the United States and Canada which adhered to the Augsburg Confession to attend a convention at Reading, Pennsylvania, in December 1866. At this convention the General Council was organized, and the "Principles of Faith and Church Polity," which thereafter formed the constitutional law of the council, were adopted. This constitution is composed of nine articles containing the fundamental principles of faith, and eleven articles on ecclesiastical power and church government, all based on the Lutheran confession.

The first convention was held at Fort Wayne, Indiana, in November 1867, and thirteen synods were represented. Two of the synods which participated, the Ohio and the (German)

Iowa, were not entirely satisfied on the so-called "four points," namely, the admission into Lutheran pulpits of ministers teaching non-Lutheran doctrine, the admission of non-Lutheran communicants to Lutheran altars, the attitude toward religious associations not divinely instituted (secret societies), and toward the question of the Second Advent. Wisconsin, Illinois, Minnesota, and Michigan—all German synods—withdrew one after another on similar grounds. Then the Synod of Missouri, which had sent delegates to the preliminary convention, followed the example of the General Council, organized the Synodical Conference in 1872, uniting those synods which had opposed the position taken by the General Council. That position, as finally expressed, was that "Lutheran pulpits are for Lutheran ministers only; Lutheran altars are for Lutheran communicants only; and exceptions to the rule belong to the sphere of privilege, not of right." With regard to secret societies, the General Council took a strong stand in opposition to them, but did not excommunicate members of such organizations.

The result was that the General Council occupied what might be regarded as an intermediate position between the General Synod and the Synodical Conference. On the one hand, the General Synod was considered to have laid more stress on a common fellowship with other churches and less stress on what it regarded as nonessentials in doctrinal principle; it interchanged delegates with evangelical denominations; and it enacted no restrictive law against a general fellowship of ministers in the pulpit and of Christians at the altar. On the other hand, the Synodical Conference laid no stress on the historical continuity of the Lutheran Church in America; cut itself off completely from the common Christianity of America; gave certain doctrines, such as predestination, a new emphasis in the history of Lutheranism; and carried doctrinal principle to governmental conclusions, prompting discipline on all points of faith. The Synodical Conference was more German, and the General Synod was more English, than the General Council. Two-thirds of all the Lutherans of the United States in 1906 belonged to these three general bodies.

In 1906 the General Council Lutherans had 2,146 congregations, totaling 462,177 communicants, located in the following states:

Maine	3	Connecticut	48	District of Columbia	1
New Hampshire	2	New York	177	West Virginia	5
Vermont	3	New Jersey	63		
Massachusetts	34	Pennsylvania	755	Florida	3
		Delaware	2	Ohio	104
Rhode Island	9	Maryland	1	Indiana	47

Illinois	128	South Dakota	29	Idaho	9
Michigan	68	Nebraska	47	Wyoming	2
Wisconsin	71	Kansas	43	Colorado	14
Minnesota	290	Kentucky	1	Utah	8
Iowa	72	Alabama	4	Washington	21
Missouri	6	Texas	16	Oregon	17
North Dakota	23	Montana	6	California	14

Evangelical Lutheran Synodical Conference of America. In the early part of the nineteenth century an effort was made by King Friedrich Wilhelm III of Prussia to unite the Lutheran and Reformed churches. To him, it seemed an easy matter to combine "the two slightly divergent confessions," but with the study of the sources of confessional divergence which followed, and particularly in the attempt to furnish a uniform liturgy for both bodies, old convictions were intensified and lines of demarcation which had been gradually fading out of sight were revived. Many of the Lutherans refused absolutely to recognize the union, formed separate congregations, and carried on an active controversy against what they believed to be a gross form of ecclesiastical tyranny.

During the following twenty years the situation grew more strained, and as Lutheran immigration to the United States began, several of the dissident communities emigrated. The first company, under the leadership of the Reverend F. C. D. Wyneken, landed at Baltimore in 1838 and settled in Fort Wayne, Indiana. A second group, under the leadership of the Reverend Martin Stephan of Dresden landed at New Orleans in 1839 and soon after established itself in Missouri. A third group, under the leadership of the Reverend J. A. A. Grabau of Erfurt, settled at or near Buffalo, New York, in 1839.

One of the six clergymen who came over with the Missouri colony, the Reverend C. F. W. Walther, proved as effective a leader in the West as Muhlenberg had earlier proved in the East. Among the important questions that came up before the community were: Did the colonists constitute a Christian congregation with authority to call ministers; what was the relation of the clergy to the church, and did the ultimate authority rest with the ordained clergy or with the congregations; what was the relation of acceptance of the confessions to the personal piety and church standing of the individual. Walther held firmly to the rights of the congregations, both in the ordination of its clergy and in its authority over them. On account of the strong pietistic influences of his early life, he emphasized also the necessity of absolute accord to the confessions of the Lutheran Church. To meet the peculiar needs of the situation, one of Walther's first steps was the establishment of Concordia Seminary in a log house at Altenburg, Missouri, its teachers receiving as compensation only their board, and working with the people for the enlargement of the church. In 1844 he began to publish a religious periodical, the *Lutheraner*, which became the exponent of the stricter interpretation of Lutheran doctrine and ritual.

Meanwhile, the Fort Wayne community had grown, and Wyneken, on a trip to Europe for his health, had secured the cordial interest and support of Pastor Löhe of Neuendettelsau, Bavaria. On returning to America Wyneken became acquainted with the *Lutheraner*, and the Missouri and Indiana congregations entered into hearty mutual relations. Other congregations also manifested their sympathy, and in 1847 twelve congregations, 22 ministers, and two candidates for the ministry united in forming the "German Evangelical Lutheran Synod of Missouri, Ohio, and Other States." Under the constitution adopted, only those ministers whose congregations had entered into membership with the synod, and the lay delegates representing those congregations, were entitled to suffrage. All the symbolical books were regarded as the "pure and uncorrupted explanation and statement of the Divine Word." All mingling of churches and faiths was disapproved. Purely Lutheran books were to be used in churches and schools. A permanent, not a temporary or licensed, ministry was affirmed, and at the same time freedom of the individual church was recognized, the synod having no authority over it.

Soon, however, there grew up conflicts with other Lutheran bodies. The Buffalo Synod, which had been organized in 1845, had developed what seemed to the Missourians a very strong ecclesiasticism, emphasizing the power of the clergy as against that of the congregation. Other controversies arose with the churches in Iowa. Walther maintained that every question was a confessional matter, that there could be no questions on which absolute unanimity was not essential. The Iowans held that there were certain subjects that were "open questions," and with regard to which difference of opinion might be tolerated. Among these were the doctrine of the ministry, eschatological opinions concerning the millennium, the first resurrection, the conversion of Israel, and the antichrist. The discussion resulted in the formation of the independent Iowa Synod.

Under the leadership of Walther the Missouri doctrine gained acceptance, and as one synod after another was formed on the same general basis, it seemed advantageous to effect some sort of union. At the time of the organization of the General Council in 1866, several of these synods were invited to participate, but those who held the stricter doctrine could not accept the position taken by the new body. The next few years emphasized anew the advantages of union, and in 1872 in Milwaukee, Wisconsin, the Evangelical Lutheran Synodical Conference of America was formed. Representatives of the Synod of Ohio, the Synod of Wisconsin, the Synod of Minnesota, the Synod of Illinois, the Norwegian Synod, and the Synod of Missouri, Ohio, and Other States were present and effected the organization. The Synod of Illinois was later absorbed by the Missouri synod, the Synod of Ohio and the Norwegian Synod withdrew in 1881, because of doctrinal differences; but other synods were added, so that in 1906 the Synodical Conference comprised the Synod of Missouri, Ohio, and Other States—by far the largest and strongest of the Conference—the Synod of Wisconsin, the Synod of Minnesota, the English Lutheran Missouri Synod, the Synod of Michigan, and the Synod of Nebraska. Each one of these synods conducted its own synodical and church work independently of the others. Their basis of union was not so much a matter of a common ecclesiastical relationship as of a common church life, and particularly of doctrinal purity.

In 1906 the Synodical Conference had 3,301 congregations, comprising 648,529 communicants, located in 42 states, as follows:

New Hampshire	1	Indiana	123	Arkansas	22
		Illinois	340	Oklahoma	72
Massachusetts	20	Michigan	207	Texas	81
		Wisconsin	612	Montana	7
Rhode Island	2	Minnesota	370	Idaho	12
Connecticut	19	Iowa	163	Wyoming	4
		Missouri	175	Colorado	26
New York	128	North Dakota	98	Utah	2
New Jersey	16			Nevada	2
Pennsylvania	56	South Dakota	125	Washington	18
Maryland	21	Nebraska	207	Oregon	15
District of Columbia	2	Kansas	118	California	46
		Kentucky	6		
Virginia	12	Tennessee	6		
West Virginia	4	Alabama	15		
North Carolina	32	Mississippi	8		
Florida	7	Louisiana	23		
Ohio	78				

Evangelical Lutheran Joint Synod of Ohio and Other States. At a meeting of the Ministerium of Pennsylvania in 1804, a plan was presented which provided for traveling missionaries to meet the needs of the rapidly growing western communities. Three such missionaries were appointed, who covered a great extent of territory and laid the foundations of synods in Ohio, Tennessee, Virginia, and North Carolina. As a result of the work in Ohio, eight pastors, all members of the Ministerium of Pennsylvania, who were engaged in missionary work in western Pennsylvania and eastern Ohio, met together with three lay delegates in Washington County, Pennsylvania, in October 1812 and organized a special conference of the general body with which they were connected. They applied for and received an honorable dismissal from the Ministerium of Pennsylvania, and having thus become independent, they reorganized at a convention held in September 1818 at Somerset, Ohio, under the name of the "General Conference of Evangelical Lutheran Ministers of Ohio and Adjacent States." In 1825 a more strictly ecclesiastical title was adopted, the "Evangelical Lutheran Synod of Ohio and Adjacent States."

The new synod was invited to participate in the formation of the General Synod, but representatives from the Ohio synod, though expected, failed to attend. Subsequently, delegates did attend, but the Ohio synod, declining to become identified with the General Synod, remained independent. In the year 1831, on grounds wholly of a practical nature, it was divided into two districts, Eastern and Western, to which a third, the First English, was added in 1836.

The general body was incorporated by a special act of the Ohio legislature in 1847, and continued to extend its borders until, by 1906, it included ten districts in the United States and a district in Canada, centered at Winnipeg. In the doctrinal discussions of its early years several small synods were formed from it, some of which entered the General Synod. In 1872 the Joint Synod of Ohio participated in the formation of the Synodical Conference, without losing its independent character, however, inasmuch as that Conference was a union of synods for the preservation and propagation of doctrine and faith rather than for cooperation in the work and government of the church. When the Missouri synod and some other members of the Synodical Conference adopted the Calvinistic doctrine of predestination in 1881, the Joint Synod of Ohio severed its relations with them, and thereafter had no formal connection with other Lutheran organizations. In 1906 it was reorganized under the name "Evangelical Lutheran Joint Synod of Ohio and Other States" and at that time became a representative body. From its early history, the Joint Synod had been a German-English organization. While in some districts English was the predominant language, and in others German, both were more or less used in all congregations, and at the conventions they were by statute placed on an equal footing.

In 1906 the Joint Synod of Ohio was comprised of 772 congregations, with 123,408 communicants, located in 31 states, as follows:

New York	2	Michigan	30	Louisiana		1
Pennsylvania	41	Wisconsin	92	Oklahoma		2
Delaware	1	Minnesota	67	Texas	14
Maryland	22	Iowa	22	Idaho	4
District of Columbia	2	Missouri	2	Colorado	6
Virginia	5	North Dakota	40	New Mexico		1
West Virginia	14	South Dakota	13	Washington		41
North Carolina	12	Nebraska	10	Oregon	10
Ohio	227	Kansas	16		
Indiana	46	Kentucky	4		
Illinois	22	Tennessee	1		
		Alabama	1		

Lutheran Synod of Buffalo. Among the Lutherans who withdrew from the State Church of Prussia after the attempt to unite the Lutheran and Reformed bodies, was a company called "Old Lutherans," or "Separatists," under the leadership of the Reverend Johann A. A. Grabau, pastor of St. Andrew's Church at Erfurt, Germany. He had been deposed from office and imprisoned for a year on account of his decided opposition to the union, and this, together with the general conditions of the time, led to the application to King Friedrich Wilhelm III for permission to emigrate to America. This was granted, and they arrived in New York in 1839, the majority settling in the city of Buffalo, New York, and its neighborhood. As the number of churches increased, Grabau, with three other pastors, organized, in 1845, the Buffalo Synod, or "Synod of the Lutheran Church Emigrated from Prussia."

For a time the synod was in conflict with other Lutheran synods, particularly the Synod of Missouri, Ohio, and Other States, on the subjects of doctrine, the church, the ministry, and ordination. As a consequence of this discussion, a number of ministers and congregations of the Buffalo Synod withdrew in 1866. Some of them joined the Missouri synod; others remained separate for a time, then gradually entered other synods. Those who remained faithful to the principles adopted by the Synod of Buffalo at its organization henceforth continued their denominational work under great difficulties.

In 1906, the Buffalo Synod was comprised of 33 congregations, with 5,270 communicants, in the following states: New York, 16; Illinois, 2; Michigan, 5; Wisconsin, 7; and Minnesota, 3.

German Evangelical Lutheran Synod of Texas. With the increase of Lutheran immigration to America there was a corresponding development of activity on the part of the different synods in reaching the newcomers. The Pittsburg synod, organized in 1845, was especially prominent in this respect, and one of its members, the Reverend Passavant, with his periodical, the *Missionary*, was a leader in the movement. In 1851 the Reverend C. Braun and eight other ministers who had come from the school at St. Chrischona, near Basel, Switzerland, went to Texas, where they soon afterwards organized the Synod of Texas. In 1854 the new synod, at the request of Dr. Passavant, joined the General Synod, but, not being altogether satisfied with its relations, transferred its membership to the General Council soon after the organization of that body.

Though most of the ministers of the Texas Synod came from the St. Chrischona school, ministers from other Lutheran synods were received. Largely under the influence of ministers who had not graduated from St. Chrischona an unsuccessful attempt was made between 1870 and 1874 to found a theological seminary. Then the question arose as to whether it was possible to satisfy the needs of the English-speaking churches by ministers from St. Chrischona, and the discussion grew quite earnest. The majority, withdrawing in 1895 from the General Council, became a part of the Synod of Iowa. A small remnant reorganized as an independent synod under the name "German Evangelical Lutheran Synod of Texas."

The Synod of Texas held that its prime duty was to take care of the German immigrants, and that for this a perfect knowledge of German was necessary. The English-speaking communicants could easily take care of themselves. Accordingly, ministers ought to be able to preach in both German and English, and as a consequence, it was claimed that its custom of sending young men to St. Chrischona for training met the immediate needs in the best manner. It recognized that, in time, the church would become entirely English-speaking, but believed that the development of an American Lutheran church would be hindered, rather than helped, by any effort to hasten the progress. In 1906 the Texas Synod had 25 congregations, with 2,440 communicants, all in the state of Texas.

Evangelical Lutheran Synod of Iowa and Other States. The situation of the Lutheran churches in America appealed strongly to many of the pastors in Europe. Among them, none was more interested than the Reverend Wilhelm Löhe, pastor at Neuendettelsau, Bavaria, who had come into relations with the Reverend F. C. D. Wyneken, leader of the Lutheran community at Fort Wayne, Indiana. Löhe entered into Wyneken's plans for the development of the churches, founded a society to carry on missionary work, and began to educate men for the ministry, with a special view to service in America. Coming to realize the impracticability of providing the entire supply of ministers from Europe, Löhe was instrumental in founding a theological seminary at Fort Wayne, and when the scarcity of parochial school teachers menaced the schooling of Lutheran children, he took steps to establish a teachers' seminary. A conference at Neuendettelsau, with Walther, the leader of the Missouri synod, led to Löhe's endorsement of the organization of that body, and to such cooperation in educational matters that quite a number of the graduates of his school entered that synod.

Among those who came to America under Löhe's auspices was the Reverend G. Grossmann, who established the first Lutheran normal school in North America at Saginaw, Michigan, in 1852. When he began his work he was questioned regarding his views as to the doctrines which had been under special discussion between the Missouri synod and Löhe, and it soon appeared that there was wide divergence between his views and those approved by the synod. Grossmann was supported by another Neuendettelsau pastor, the Reverend J. Deindorfer, and both were disciplined by the local pastor. It became evident that further cooperation was impracticable, and in order to avoid hostilities in the same territory, Grossmann, Deindorfer, a few students, and a small number of the colonists left Saginaw in 1853 and migrated to Iowa. Grossmann established his seminary in Dubuque, while Deindorfer and the colonists settled at St. Sebald, about 60 miles west of Dubuque. The next year they were joined by two men from Neuendettelsau, and these four organized in August 1854 the Evangelical Lutheran Synod of Iowa and Other States.

For some years the synod met with difficulties. The two congregations found it impossible to support the seminary, and in 1857 it was removed from Dubuque to St. Sebald, where a part of its support could be raised on a farm. Largely under the influence of two brothers, Sigmund and Gottfried Frischel, teachers in the seminary, the synod grew, and after ten years it had 39 ministers: 16 in Iowa, 6 in Wisconsin, 4 in Illinois, 2 in Missouri, 4 in Ohio, 5 in Michigan, and 1 each in Kentucky and Dakota Territory. In 1906 the Iowa Synod had 828 congregations, with 110,254 communicants, located in the following states:

Ohio	36	North Dakota	68	Oklahoma	8
Illinois	88			Texas	83
Michigan	38	South Dakota	55	Colorado	6
Wisconsin	98	Nebraska	60	Washington	6
Minnesota	57	Kansas	32		
Iowa	171	Arkansas	4	Oregon	1
Missouri	17				

Evangelical Lutheran Synod of Michigan and Other States. In 1833 a mission was begun by the Reverend F. Schmid among North American Indians in the neighborhood of Ann Arbor, Michigan. He gathered around him a number of pastors, many of them from the missionary seminary at Basel, Switzerland, and together they labored among the German immigrants. In 1860, eight ministers and three congregations united in organizing the Evangelical Lutheran Synod of Michigan and Other States, and from that time their numbers increased, though they were seriously hampered by the scarcity of faithful pastors. In 1867 the synod assisted in the organization of the General Council, but withdrew from that body in 1888 on account of dissatisfaction with its position on pulpit and altar fellowship, on secret societies, and on "open questions."

In order to meet the demand for ministers, a school was opened in 1885 at Manchester, Michigan, but two years later it was removed to Saginaw. It was known as the Lutheran Seminary of the Michigan Synod, and from it a large number of workers went forth.

In 1892 the synod joined the Wisconsin and Minnesota synods in forming the General Synod of Wisconsin, Minnesota, and Michigan, often called the Synod of the Northwest, and in 1893 it became a member of the Synodical Conference. These connections were severed again in 1896, owing to differences in regard to the future of the seminary and the management of the synod. A number of ministers and congregations at that time severed their connection with the Michigan synod and organized under the name of the District Synod of Michigan, but remained in connection with the Synodical Conference. In 1906 a reconciliation was effected between the two Michigan synods, resulting in the union of 55 congregations, with 9,697 communicants. Fifty of the congregations were in Michigan and five in Ohio.

Immanuel Synod of the Evangelical Lutheran Church of North America. A number of Lutheran ministers and churches, desiring to secure greater freedom of church life than was possible in some of the synods, met at Wall Rose, Pennsylvania, in 1885 and organized the Immanuel Synod of the Evangelical Lutheran Church in North America. While agreeing in doctrine with the whole Evangelical Lutheran Church, this synod differed from others in its attitude toward other religious bodies. It acknowledged other denominations as sister churches, and while it appreciated agreement with its own doctrines, it was not indifferent to doctrines from which it differed. In regard to the secret societies question, the synod was more liberal than some other Lutheran synods, welcoming all who were willing to join the church and cooperate with it, whether or not members of a secret society. In polity it was in general accord with other Lutheran synods.

In 1906 the Immanuel Synod had 11 congregations, with 3,275 communicants, in the following states: 5 in Pennsylvania; 2 in New York; 1 each in Massachusetts, New Jersey, Ohio, and Iowa.

Evangelical Lutheran Jehovah Conference. As the Lutheran immigration to the United States increased, the Lutheran churches in Europe became interested in the supply of ministers, and a number of organizations were formed there to assist in the training of ministers in the Lutheran faith. Among these was the Lower Hessian Mission Association, founded by the Reverend I. W. G. Vilmar, metropolitan and pastor of the church at Melsungen, Hessen-Kassel, Germany. In December 1870 a theological seminary was established at that place, which was for many years connected with the Lutheran Synod of Iowa. In 1880 the board of the seminary withdrew from connection with that synod, preferring to train ministers independently for missionary work in the United States. In November 1886 the Reverend W. Hartwig, an elder in the so-called "Resistant" Church of Hessen-Kassel, came to America and began mission work at Greenfield, Michigan, under the auspices of the Lower Hessian Mission Association. Other missionaries followed, and, as the work extended and it became necessary to form an association, the ministers identified with the movement organized the Evangelical Lutheran Jehovah Conference. This was not a synod in the usual sense of the term, but simply an association of ministers for mutual assistance in their church duties.

In 1906 the Jehovah Conference had nine congregations, totaling 735 communicants; eight of the congregations were in Michigan and one in Maryland.

Mennonite Bodies

The origin of the denominations classed under the heading of Mennonite bodies is traced by them to an early period in the history of the Christian Church. As various changes in doctrine and church organization came about, in both the East and the West, a number of communities, unwilling to accept them and preferring the simplicity of the Apostolic Church, remained more or less distinct through the middle ages. These communities received various names in different localities and in different centuries, but from the time of the first general council at Nicea in the early part of the fourth century to the Conference of Dort, Holland, in 1632, they represented a general protest against ecclesiastical rule and a rigid liturgy, and an appeal for the simpler organization, worship, and faith of the apostolic age.

At the time of the Reformation, the members of these scattered communities who laid particular stress upon the doctrine of believers' baptism, as opposed to infant baptism, found a leader in the person of Menno Simon, a former Roman Catholic priest who was born in Witmarsum, Holland, about 1496. He is regarded by the Mennonites, however, not so much as the founder of the church as a prominent factor in its organization. The name "Mennonite" dates from 1550, but would scarcely be recognized in Holland, where the usual name is *Doopgezinde* or *Dooper*, the Dutch equivalent of the English "Baptist." Similarly in parts of Germany, Switzerland, and Austria, the German form *Taufgesinnte* or *Täufer* was used to indicate Baptists, although this name was not applied to all Mennonites. It was to some of the Flemish Mennonites, who, upon the invitation of King Henry VIII, settled in England and became the pioneers of the great weaving industry of that country, that the Baptists of England were largely indebted for their organization as a religious body.

The hardships which these people suffered on account of the almost universal religious intolerance in Europe, both before and after the Reformation, caused them to look toward the New World, and early in the seventeenth century the first representatives crossed the Atlantic. For a time their hopes were not realized. The new colonies were not liberal in the modern sense of the term and had small patience with those who did not agree with them in matters of faith and practice.

When William Penn acquired Pennsylvania from the English crown, he offered homes to the Mennonites, where they might enjoy the free exercise of their religious beliefs. They were, for the most part, too poor to emigrate, but the Society of Friends (the Quakers) in England came to their relief. Forwarding agencies were established in several Dutch cities, to which funds gathered in England were sent; and thus means were provided by which large numbers from Holland, Switzerland, and Germany were enabled to come to America. Individual families settled in New York and New Jersey as early as 1640, but the first Mennonite colony was formed at Germantown, Pennsylvania, in 1683. As their numbers increased during the first third of the eighteenth century, the Mennonites spread northward from Germantown into Lancaster, Bucks, Berks, Montgomery, and other counties in Pennsylvania and from these original settlements they have since spread to western Pennsylvania, Ohio, Canada, Indiana, Illinois, and farther westward.

In the meanwhile, the Mennonites who had not immigrated to North America were finding it necessary for reasons of their pacifism to move eastward out of the Rhine Valley to

Prussia and from there into southern Russia, where they established a number of colonies early in the eighteenth century. In 1873-1874, because of newly-decreed universal military conscription in Russia, a second wave of migration to America came about. These German-speaking so-called "Russian Mennonites" settled in the Dakotas, Canada, and Kansas.

In 1906 there were fourteen Mennonite bodies in America as follows:

	Total Number Churches	Total Communicants
Mennonite Church	220	18,674
Brüderhof Mennonite Church	8	275
Amish Mennonite Church	57	7,640
Old Amish Mennonite Church	46	5,043
Reformed Mennonite Church	34	2,079
General Conference of Mennonites of North America	90	11,661
Church of God in Christ (Mennonite)	18	562
Old (Wisler) Mennonite Church	9	655
Defenceless Mennonites	14	967
Mennonite Brethren in Christ	68	2,801
Bundes Konferenz der Mennoniten Brüdergemeinde [United Conference of Mennonite Brethren]: Krimmer Brüdergemeinde	6	708
Schellenberger Brüdergemeinde	13	1,825
Central Illinois Conference of Mennonites	13	1,363
Nebraska and Minnesota Conference of Mennonites	8	545
Totals	604	54,798

The religious beliefs and origins of each of the above groups will be discussed separately hereinafter.

The Mennonite Church. The Mennonite Church, by far the largest of the different Mennonite bodies in 1906, represented the general trend of them all and was most closely identified with the history already given. In the controversy which resulted in the separation of the Amish Mennonite Church, it stood for the more liberal interpretation of the Confession of Faith, and included what may be called the conservatively progressive element of the

Mennonite communities. It was the most important factor in the westward extension of Mennonites from Pennsylvania. In 1906 there were 220 congregations with 18,674 members, located in the following states:

Pennsylvania	90	Michigan	6	Kansas	9
Maryland	16	Minnesota	1	Tennessee	1
Virginia	26	Iowa	1	Oklahoma	3
West Virginia	11	Missouri	7	Texas	1
Ohio	20	North Dakota	1	Idaho	1
Indiana	14	South Dakota	1	Colorado	3
Illinois	8	Nebraska	1	Oregon	2

All congregations were located in rural areas, excepting three (Canton, Ohio, Fort Wayne, Indiana, and Johnstown, Pennsylvania). In 1906 74 congregations still used German in their worship services.

Brüderhof Mennonite Church (Hutterian Brethren; Hutterites). Jakob Huter, an Anabaptist minister of the sixteenth century, advocated the communistic conception of the ownership of property, and his followers, with other Anabaptists of widely varying creeds and practices, were bitterly persecuted. He, himself, after being driven from place to place, was finally apprehended and burned at the stake at Inssbruck, Austria, in 1536, during what was probably the fiercest persecution suffered by any of the Anabaptist bodies in the sixteenth century. Despite the persecution, however, the community, which came to be known as the *Hutterische Brüder* and the Hutterite Society, flourished, and at the beginning of the Thirty Years' War had 24 branches in Moravia. Although the Emperor Joseph II had granted the members a certain measure of religious liberty, they were at length driven from Austria and found a home successively in Hungary, Roumania, and Russia. In Russia many of them gave up the communistic idea and united with other Mennonite congregations. When their religious liberty was circumscribed by the imperial ukases of 1863 to 1865, they, with many other Russian Mennonites, came to the United States, settling in Bonhomme County, South Dakota, in 1874, where they have prospered, and whence they spread into adjoining counties. During the first world war they met discrimination, because they still considered themselves German and use the German language exclusively in their religious services and in their homes. As a consequence, many of the Hutterites emigrated to Canada, settling in the plains provinces.

In doctrine the church is practically in accord with other Mennonite bodies, except in so far as it adheres to the communistic form of ownership. The general polity also is in accord with that of the other bodies.

In 1906 there were eight Hutterite communes in South Dakota with 275 members. In the half-century which has followed, their numbers have increased markedly, both in the United States and Canada.

Amish Mennonite Church. This branch of the Mennonite bodies became a separate organization in the closing years of the seventeenth century. Jakob Ammon, or Amen, from whose name the term "Amish" was derived, was a native of Amenthal, Switzerland; but, probably to escape persecution, he settled in the Alsace in 1659. There was a tendency on the part of many of the Mennonites of the time, during the interval of rest from persecution, to become lax in their religious life and discipline. Ammon was the acknowledged leader of those who held to the strict letter of Menno Simon's teachings and the literal interpretation of several points of doctrine presented in the Confession of Faith, adopted at the general conference held at Dort, Holland, in 1632. Maintaining that, because they were not literally and rigorously carried out, some of the articles of the confession were a dead letter with many of the congregations, he traveled extensively, laboring to restore the communities to the spiritual life and condition manifested during Simon's ministry among them. The special point of divergence between his followers and the other Mennonites was in regard to the exercise of the ban, or excommunication of disobedient members. The Amish party interpreted the scriptural injunctions calling for the ban to apply to daily life and the daily table; while the others understood them to mean simply the exclusion of expelled members from the communion table.

In 1690 two bishops, Ammon and Blank, acted as a committee to invetigate conditions in Switzerland and southern Germany. As those accused of laxity in the particulars mentioned did not appear when called upon to answer the charges preferred against them, the Amish leaders expelled them. They, in turn, disowned the Amish party, and the separation was completed in 1698. Some time after this, Ammon and his followers made overtures for a reconciliation and union of the two factions, but these were rejected, and it remained for the closing years of the nineteenth century, almost exactly two centuries later, to see the steps taken that virtually reunited the two bodies, or the main part of each, for in the meantime there had been other divisions between the extreme elements of both.

At about the time of the separation, the migration of Mennonites from Europe to the crown lands acquired by William Penn in America began to assume large proportions, and included many of the Amish Mennonites, who settled in what now comprises Lancaster, Mifflin, Somerset, Lawrence, and Union counties in Pennsylvania. William Penn himself traveled extensively among the Mennonites in Europe, preaching in their meetings, and rendering them aid in various ways. From Pennsylvania the Amish Mennonites moved with the westward tide of migration into Ohio, Indiana, Illinois, Nebraska, and other states. There was also a large exodus from Pennsylvania and from Europe directly to Canada, principally to the section westward of the large tract acquired by the early Mennonite settlers in Waterloo County, Ontario.

By 1906 there were 57 congregations, with 7,640 communicants, in the United States, as follows:

Pennsylvania	5	Illinois	7	Nebraska	5
Maryland	1	Michigan	2	Kansas	3
Virginia	1	Iowa	6	Arkansas	1
Ohio	11	Missouri	3	Oklahoma	1
Indiana	8	North Dakota	1	Oregon	2

All the congregations were located in rural areas; 48 of the 57 congregations still used German in their services in 1906.

Old Amish Mennonite Church. As the movement along more progressive lines in the Amish Mennonite Church developed, resulting in a virtual reunion of the conservatively progressive element in that body with a kindred element in the Mennonite Church, it encountered not a little opposition from the more strictly conservative members. The result was a gradual separation, and the organization of the Old Amish Mennonite Church about 1865.

The members were very strict in the exercise of the ban, or shunning of expelled members. They have had few Sunday schools, no evening or protracted meetings, church conferences, missions, or benevolent institutions. They worship for the most part in private houses, and use the German language exclusively in their services. They did not associate in religious work with other bodies, and were distinctive and severely plain in their dress, using hooks and eyes instead of buttons. They were, however, by no means a unit in all these things, and the line of distinction between them and the Amish Mennonites was in many cases not very clearly drawn.

In 1906 there were 46 congregations, with 5,043 communicants, located in the following states:

New York	1	Maryland	3	Indiana	6
Pennsylvania	10	Ohio	9	Illinois	4

Michigan	2	Missouri	2	Montana	1
Iowa	2	Kansas	5	Oregon	1

All of the congregations were located in rural areas.

Reformed Mennonite Church. A movement among the Mennonites in Pennsylvania along practically the same lines as that which, under the leadership of Jakob Ammon, had resulted in the division in Europe in 1698 was inaugurated by Francis Herr and his son John Herr and resulted in 1812 in the organization of the Reformed Mennonite Church, with John Herr as pastor and bishop. He condemned the church as "a corrupt and dead body," and labored for the restoration of purity in teaching and the maintenance of discipline.

The Reformed Mennonites accepted the eighteen articles of the Dort Confession of Faith and retained the general features of church organization of the Mennonite Church. They were very strict in their discipline, especially with other religious bodies, and held that the doctrine of nonresistance was one of the cardinal principles of the gospels.

In 1906 the Reformed Mennonites had 34 congregations, totaling 2,079 members, located in the following states:

New York	3	Ohio	7	Illinois	1
Pennsylvania	16	Indiana	2	Michigan	3
Maryland	2				

All the congregations were in rural areas; all used German in their worship services.

General Conference of Mennonites of North America. In March 1859 two small Mennonite congregations in Lee County, Iowa, composed of immigrants from southern Germany, held a conference to discuss the possible union of all the Mennonite bodies in America. Until that time, while in a general way the different organizations had held to the same doctrines, they had not cooperated actively, or at least had taken no concerted part in any particular work. The resolutions adopted at this meeting drew the attention of all the Mennonite bodies. Among those especially interested was John Oberholzer of Bucks County, Pennsylvania, who had taken advanced ground in the matter of aggressive work, and, together with 16 other ministers, having been charged with insubordination to the then established form of church government in his conference and having been disowned by that conference, had organized a separate conference in eastern Pennsylvania in October 1847. The publication by Oberholzer of the *Religiöser Botschafter* (religious messenger), founded in 1852 and later styled the *Christliches*

Volksblatt (Christian newspaper), gave wide publicity and strong support to the new union movement, which promised to advance along broader and more liberal lines than his conference had permitted. The Iowa congregations extended a general invitation to all Mennonite congregations and conferences, and in May 1860 at West Point, Iowa, the first effort was made to hold a general conference of Mennonites in America. While this conference was not completely representative, questions of education, missions, and unity were discussed, and the organization of the General Conference of Mennonites in America was brought about. On the basis of uniting in the support of mission work, other congregations were soon added, and the membership and influence of the body grew rapidly. Many of the congregations whose members had come from Russia and Germany since 1850 and who had become acquainted with the movement before leaving Europe joined the new organization. Among the Amish Mennonites who came from Europe and settled in Ohio about 1840 were some who favored greater leniency in discipline, and who separated from the Amish body on that account. They were known as the Apostolic Mennonite Church, but after the organization of the General Conference of Mennonites, they affiliated with that body, and in 1906 their sole remaining church was included in the latter's statistics.

In 1906 the General Conference of Mennonites of North America had 90 congregations, totaling 11,661 members, located in the following states:

New York	2	Iowa	4	Montana	1
Pennsylvania	14	Missouri	1	Arizona	1
Ohio	9	South Dakota	5	Washington	1
Indiana	2	Nebraska	5	Oregon	2
Illinois	1	Kansas	21	California	2
Minnesota	1	Oklahoma	18		

Seventy-seven congregations still used German in their services; all the congregations were in rural areas, excepting one in New York City and another in Allentown, Pennsylvania.

Church of God in Christ (Mennonite). Largely owing to the difficulty of communication between different sections of the country, the same general reform movement which resulted in the development of the Amish Mennonite Church in Europe and the Reformed Mennonite Church in Pennsylvania, occasioned in 1859 the organization in Ohio of the Church of God in Christ as a separate body. The leader in this movement was John Holdeman, who was born in Ohio in 1832 and united with the Mennonite Church at the age of 21 years. At the age of 25 years, believing that he was called of God to preach, but not being recognized by the church as a properly ordained preacher, he began to hold independent services and soon gathered a company of followers. Asserting that the Mennonite Church had shifted from the old foundation, he directed his efforts chiefly toward the reestablishment and maintenance of the order and discipline of the church as he understood it had been in Menno Simon's time. This included particularly the strict exercise of the ban, or the shunning of expelled members, and the refusal of fellowship with those of other denominations. Holdeman traveled extensively in an effort to bring others to his views, and in 1859 the full organization of the body was completed. As the Russian Mennonites began to come into the country in 1873, several hundreds of them joined the movement.

As the years passed by, and even before the death of Holdeman in 1900, the views on discipline were considerably relaxed, largely through the influence of the Russian Mennonite membership, increasing leniency appeared in the attitude of the denomination toward other religious bodies, especially toward the parent body. In addition to the strict interpretation of the letter of the Confession of Faith, some characteristic doctrines are taught, notable among them being the refusal to take interest on money loaned, which is called usury and considered wrong.

In 1906 the Holdeman Mennonites had eighteen congregations, totaling 562 communicants, located as follows:

Virginia	2	Illinois	1	Nebraska	2
Ohio	2	Michigan	3	Kansas	5
Indiana	1	Missouri	2		

All the congregations were located in rural areas; all of them used German in their worship services in 1906.

Old (Wisler) Mennonite Church. The development of the progressive movement in the Mennonite Church about the middle of the nineteenth century was accompanied by considerable opposition, manifesting itself especially in regard to the introduction of the English language into the church services, the practice of holding evening meetings, revival meetings, Sunday schools, and certain other "innovations" which were regarded as unorthodox. Other minor matters, magnified into important issues, were added to these differences of opinion, and under the lead of Jacob Wisler, the first Mennonite bishop in Indiana, a separation took place in 1870. He was disowned by the Mennonite Church and, although various efforts at reconciliation were subsequently made, he and a small following in Indiana and Ohio formed a separate conference, claiming to be the real Mennonite Church. In 1886 the corresponding conservative element of the Mennonite Church in Canada formed a separate

body along practically the same lines; other organizations were formed in Pennsylvania in 1893 and in Virginia in 1901.

In 1906 the Wisler Mennonites had nine congregations, totaling 655 members, in the following states: 6 in Ohio; 2 in Indiana; and 1 in Michigan. All congregations were located in rural areas; all used German in their worship services.

Defenceless Mennonites. About 1860 certain members of the Amish Mennonite Church under the lead of Henry Egli, separated from that body on the ground that the church did not emphasize sufficiently the need for a definite experience of conversion. In general doctrine and polity they were not distinguishable from the Amish Mennonites and the Mennonite Church. In 1906 the Defenceless Mennonites had 14 congregations, with 967 communicants, located in the following states:

Ohio	3	Missouri	2	Kansas	1
Indiana	4	Nebraska	1	Oklahoma	1
Illinois	2				

All congregations were located in rural areas; all of them used German in their worship services.

Mennonite Brethren in Christ. In 1853 several ministers and members of the Mennonite Church in Pennsylvania united in protracted evangelistic work. Their efforts were successful, and in 1858 they organized a conference in Lehigh County, Pennsylvania, under the name "Evangelical Mennonites."

Eleven years later a Mennonite minister in Canada professed conversion, although he had been in the ministry for some time, and by introducing protracted prayer and fellowship meetings into his work, incurred the censure of the bishops who at that time regarded such things as questionable innovations. The movement spread, however, and soon found many adherents in the United States and Canada. Being disowned by the parent body, these met in 1874 in Berlin, Ontario, and formed an organization known as the "Reformed Mennonites," which is not to be mistaken for the body now known as the Reformed Mennonite Church. The next year they were joined by a small body which had been organized into a separate religious society under the name of the "New Mennonites," the two bodies adopting the name "United Mennonites."

As the purpose of all three organizations was similar, and as there were no vital differences in method of work or form of doctrine, steps were soon taken for further consolidation, and in November 1879 at a special meeting held at Blair, Ontario, the Evangelical

Mennonites of Pennsylvania and the United Mennonites of Ontario, Canada, became one body and adopted the name "Evangelical United Mennonites."

The body continued to grow in numbers and began the publication of a church periodical and other religious literature. Three years later, in 1882, the Evangelical United Mennonites became acquainted with a small body called the "Brethren in Christ," which had, on account of doctrinal differences, separated from the River Brethren Church in 1838. The two bodies united in 1883, and the present name "Mennonite Brethren in Christ," was adopted.

In 1906 there were 68 congregations, with 2,801 members, located in the following states:

Pennsylvania	21	Indiana	9	Washing-
Ohio	12	Michigan	25	ton	1

Eleven of the congregations still used German in their worship services.

Bundes Konferenz der Mennoniten Brüdergemeinde [United Conference of Mennonite Brethren]. There were two groups within the Conference: the Krimmer Brüdergemeinde (Crimean Brethren) and the Schellenberger Brüdergemeinde (Schellenberger Brethren).

In the early part of the nineteenth century a number of Mennonite ministers and members in the Crimea and along the Molotchna River in Russia, believing that the church was drifting from the true foundation and becoming lax in religious life, effort, and discipline, separated from the greater body of the Mennonites in Russia. Both bodies joined in the immigration from Russia in 1873 to 1876 and settled chiefly in Kansas, Nebraska, and Minnesota, but afterwards spread into other states and Canada. The communities differed in some details, but preserved their identities, the community from the Crimea being known as the Krimmer Brethren, the other as the Schellenberger Brethren. In many matters, however, they affiliated in much the same way as the Mennonite and Amish Mennonite churches, and have been classed together as a Bundes (union) conference. In matters of doctrine the two bodies are in general harmony with other Mennonites, except that they baptize by immersion. Here, again, there is a distinction; the Crimean Brethren baptized backwards, the Schellenberger Brethren baptized forwards.

In 1906 the Crimean Brethren had six congregations, three of which were in Kansas and one each in Nebraska, Oklahoma, and South Dakota, totaling 708 communicants. The Schellenberger Brethren had thirteen congregations, all of which were in Kansas, totaling 1,825 communicants. Both groups used only German in their worship services.

Central Illinois Conference of Mennonites. At the time of the organization of the western district conference of the Amish Mennonite Church a number of congregations in Illinois, to whom the requirements of membership seemed to rigid, did not unit with the conference, but remained independent of all affiliations. In 1899 these congregations organized a conference, which has since met annually. While the Illinois congregations never formally separated from the Amish Mennonite Church and held the same confession, they were less strict in discipline and rules of order than the parent church.

In 1906 the Central Illinois Conference of Mennonites had 13 congregations, totaling 1,363 members. Eleven of the congregations were in Illinois and one each in Indiana and Nebraska. Only seven of the congregations still used German in their worship services in 1906; all congregations were in rural areas, excepting one in Chicago.

Nebraska and Minnesota Conference of Mennonites. This body includes a part of the Mennonites who came from Russia in 1873-1874. They hold the same doctrine and have the same polity as the Mennonite Church and the Amish Mennonite Church, and affiliate with those two bodies in the Mennonite General Conference. In 1906 they had eight congregations—3 in Minnesota, 3 in Nebraska, and one each in Kansas and Texas, totaling 545 communicants. All these congregations were in rural areas, and all used the German language in their worship services.

Miscellaneous German-
Speaking Congregations

Several of the major, and some of the minor, protestant bodies in the United States have had congregations which used the German language in their worship services, reflecting the special ethnic composition of individual congregations, rather than the intellectual origins of the sects themselves. Since the 1906 federal religious census does not give the location of these congregations, it is only possible to list them according to denomination, as follows:

	German Speaking Congregations	Total Congregations in Sect
Advent Christian Church	2	550
Seventh-Day Adventists	85	1,889
Baptist bodies:		
Northern Baptist Conference	191	8,272
Southern Baptist Conference	22	21,104

	German-Speaking Congregations	Total Congregations in Sect
Christian Catholic Church in Zion	4	17
General Convention of the New Jerusalem in the USA (Swedenborgian)	11	119
Congregationalists	158	5,713
Disciples of Christ	2	8,293
Church of Christ	1	2,649
Hephzibah Faith Missionary Association	2	10
Missionary Church Association	19	32
Church of Jesus Christ of Latter-day Saints	7	683
Reorganized Church of Jesus Christ of Latter-Day Saints	1	501
Methodist bodies:		
Methodist Protestant Church	1	2,843
Methodist Episcopal Church, South	35	17,831
Methodist Episcopal Church	864	29,943
Free Methodist Church of North America	3	1,553
Nonsectarian Churches of Bible Faith	13	204
Presbyterian Church in the USA	144	7,935
Presbyterian Church in the United States	2	3,104
Protestant Episcopal Church	15	6,835
Christian Reformed Church	15	174
Salvation Army	11	694
Spiritualists	19	455

It will be seen from the above listing that certain of the Protestant denominations commonly identified with English ethnic groups in America were willing to accommodate German-speaking communicants, and that other denominations were more reluctant to do so.

Moravian Church (Unitas Fratrum)

From the time of the first propagation of the gospel among them by Cyril and Methodius, the Bohemians and Moravians have stood for freedom in religion and in national life, and under the leadership of John Huss and Jerome of Prague they offered a firm resistance to the rule of both the Austrian Empire and the Roman Catholic Church. For several years after the martyrdom of Huss in 1415, and of Jerome in 1416, their followers had no special organization, but in 1457, near Kunwald in Bohemia, an association was formed to foster pure scriptural teaching and apostolic discipline.

In spite of continued persecution the union grew steadily, so that at the opening of the sixteenth century, before the German and Swiss reformations, it had about 11,000 adult male members in Bohemia and 100,000 in Moravia. Most cordial relations were maintained with Martin Luther and Jean Calvin, though no formal union with the German and Swiss churches was ever reached, and the Moravian confession of faith, published in 1535, had Luther's approval. In its organization the church was episcopal, having a supreme judge to preside in the assembly and a synod to decide matters of faith and discipline. Priest, living at first in celibacy, were ordained after the apostolic example, and pursued trades for their support. The administration of the congregations was in the hands of elected elders who had supervision over the church members, the women being under the control of matrons.

The union proved to be strongest in the fields of education and literature. In nearly every large town the Moravian Brethren had schools and a printing house. Their greatest achievement, however, was the translation of the Bible into both the Bohemian and Moravian languages (completed in 1593).

Meanwhile, the opposition of the Roman Catholic Church had increased, and the Thirty Years' War devastated the country. At its close in 1648, the evangelical churches of Bohemia and Moravia had been practically destroyed. Of the 200,000 members in those countries, large numbers had been put to the sword and others had fled into Hungary, Saxony, Holland, and Poland, in which countries, as well as in Bohemia and Moravia, they continued in scattered communities. The last bishop of the United Church, the famous John Amos Comenius, died at Amsterdam in 1670.

In 1722 a small company from Moravia, followed later by others who cherished the traditions of their ancestral church, were permitted to settle on an estate of Nicholas Louis Count von Zinzendorf, in Saxony, where the village of Herrnhut was established. Colonists from Germany also joined, and an association was formed in which the religious plans of Zinzendorf and those of the Moravians were combined. The Protestant confession of the realm was accepted, and a distinct order and discipline, perpetuating elements of the old Moravian Church, was established under royal concessions. In 1735 the historical Moravian episcopate was transferred to the association by two surviving bishops of the old line who were filling state church positions, and the Unitas Fratrum, or Church of the Brethren, known at the present time in America as the Moravian Church, was established.

The chief purpose of the church was to carry on evangelistic work in Christian and heathen lands. In accordance with this purpose, the first Moravian missionary came to Pennsylvania in 1734, and in the same year an attempt was made at colonization and missionary work in Georgia. David Nitschmann, the first Moravian bishop in America, who in 1732 had helped to found the first Moravian mission among the heathen in the West Indies, came to Georgia in 1735. Political disturbances ruined the work in Georgia, and in 1740 the colony moved to Pennsylvania. In 1741 Bishop Nitschmann and his associates founded the town of Bethlehem, and a little later the neighboring belonging to the evangelist, George Whitefield, was purchased. This second settlement was named Nazareth. A cooperative union to develop the settlements and support missionary work was formed by the colonists and was maintained until 1762. All members labored for a common cause and received sustenance from a common stock, but there was no surrender of private property or of personal liberty, nor any individual claim on the common estate. Missionary work was begun among the Indians and also among the white settlers.

In 1749 an act of the British Parliament recognized the Moravian Church as "an ancient Protestant Episcopal Church." This gave it standing and privileges in all British colonies; but its policy of doing undenominational leavening work, with the hope of furthering evangelical alliance, caused it to remain a comparatively small body. In subsequent years it was mainly active in cooperating with the European branches of the church in the conduct of missions among the heathens.

Bethlehem, Nazareth, and Lititz, in Pennsylvania, and Salem in North Carolina, were organized in colonial times as exclusive Moravian villages, after the model of the Moravian communities in Germany, England, and Holland. During the years between 1844 and 1856 this exclusive system was abolished, and the organization of the church was remodeled to meet modern conditions. At the same time home missionary work was revived, and since then the membership of the church in the United States has grown rapidly.

In 1906 the Moravian Church had 117 congregations, totaling 17,155 members, in sixteen states. Only 41 of the congregations still used German in their worship services. Distribution of the congregations was as follows:

New York	9	Ohio	6	Missouri	5
New Jersey	4	Indiana	3	North Dakota	6
Pennsylvania	19	Illinois	2		
		Michigan	1	California	3
Maryland	2	Wisconsin	20		
Virginia	2	Minnesota	11		
North Carolina	22	Iowa	2		

The only urban congregations were in the following cities: New York, Philadelphia, Indianapolis, Elizabeth (New Jersey), Utica (New York), Easton, Lancaster, and York (all in Pennsylvania).

Roman Catholic Church

One of the most important lacunae in the federal religious census of 1906 was the failure to identify, or to locate, the Catholic congregations using the German language in sermons. Of the 12,482 congregations of Roman Catholics in the United States, 1,881 used only German and English in sermons; in an additional 170 congregations German was used as well as other European languages. Most of the latter congregations were probably in urban areas. Thus, one may infer that 15% of all the Catholic congregations in America were purely German in ethnic composition, and an additional 1% were partially so.

In terms of communicants, 1,519,978 persons were members of Catholic churches in which German was the only foreign language used in sermons. This represented 13% of the total number of 12,079,142 Catholic communicants in the United States in 1906.

Schwenkfelders

One of the most enthusiastic advocates of the Reformation was Kaspar von Schwenkfeld of Ossig, Saxony (born 1489, died 1561), a councillor at the court of the Duke of Liegnitz. Mainly through his efforts the Reformation gained a stronghold in Silesia. He was independent in his thinking, however, and held mystical and pacifistic beliefs unacceptable to other reformers of the era. Strongly opposed to the formation of a hierarchical church, Schwenkfeld did no more than organize congregations. He and his followers were compelled to flee from place to place to escape persecution until he died at Ulm. After his death the congregations were bound together only by occasional meetings and conferences held in Silesia, Switzerland, and Italy.

In September 1734 about 200 members of the Schwenkfelder congregations landed at Philadelphia. Unable to secure land as they desired for a colony of their own, they bought homes in

Montgomery, Bucks, Berks, and Lehigh counties, Pennsylvania, where most of their descendants were still living in 1906, when they reported eight congregations and 725 members. Six of the eight congregations still used German in their worship services.

Temple Society in the United States

(Friends of the Temple)

The Temple Society, also known as the "Friends of the Temple," was founded in Württemberg, Germany, in 1853, by the Reverend Christoph Hoffmann. Adherents of the society emigrated to America a few years later and within ten years an organization was effected.

The Temple Society has no ecclesiastical forms of doctrines which were binding on its members. It held that the sum and substance of the New Testament is in the teachings of the Kingdom of God, the essence of which is contained in the words of Jesus, "Thou shalt love the Lord thy God, . . . and thy neighbor as thyself," and emphasizes the spiritual development of the kingdom. Accepting in full the prophecies of the Old Testament in regard to the future of the Holy Land, one great aim of the organization was the establishment of Christian colonies in Palestine which achieved a measure of success. The Society in Jerusalem was regarded as the chief organization, and its president exercised general supervision over the branches in Germany and America. In 1906 there were three local congregations in the United States, two being in New York state (Buffalo and Schenectady) and one in Kansas. All three groups used German in their worship services in 1906.

United Brethren Bodies

At the time of the 1906 religious census the United Brethren in Christ were divided into two bodies: the Church of the United Brethren in Christ, and the Church of the United Brethren in Christ (Old Constitution). The first of the two bodies mentioned was the parent organization.

Church of the United Brethren in Christ. Among the serious conditions facing the German Reformed churches in America in the early part of the eighteenth century were the lack of organization and the dearth of ministers. There were as yet no training schools in this country, and the congregations were compelled to look to the Old World for their ministerial supplies. The result was that they were not always provided for, and it was difficult to secure adequate ministers. General conditions within the congregations were deplorable. Appeals were made to the churches of the Palatinate, but they were unable to meet the need, so the colonists turned

to the Classis of Amsterdam, which had already given assistance to the Dutch Reformed churches in New York.

In 1746 the Reverend Michael Schlatter, a Swiss by birth, was sent as a missionary to the German Reformed churches in Pennsylvania, although under the general direction of the synod of Holland. In 1751 he returned to Europe to present an appeal for further aid and additional missionaries. Six young men responded to his presentation of the need in the new colonies. Among them was Philip Wilhelm Otterbein, born in the Duchy of Nassau, Germany, in 1726, who had already had some experience in pastoral work. The company arrived in New York in July 1752, and Otterbein soon found a field of labor with the congregation at Lancaster, Pennsylvania, at that time the second in importance among the German Reformed churches of the colonies.

A peculiar personal experience, in which Otterbein found himself unable to respond to an earnest appeal from one seeking spiritual counsel, led him to a prolonged struggle for a fuller witness to the regenerating power of the gospel in his personal life. The result was a spiritual transformation and an insistence upon the need for a deeper inward spirituality on the part of his people. About the same time he came into personal relations with Martin Boehm, a member of the Mennonite community, who had passed through a similar religious experience, and together they conducted evangelistic work among the scattered settlers in Pennsylvania. This was deemed irregular by Otterbein's fellow ministers, and offended the synod to such a degree and aroused such opposition to him that, in 1774, Otterbein accepted a call to the Baltimore, Maryland, congregation on an independent basis. For the next fifteen years Otterbein continued his evangelistic labors among the German-speaking communities, going into the surrounding country and holding two-day "great meetings," in which he became more closely associated with ministers of kindred spirit in other denominations. Under their preaching, converts rapidly multiplied, but church organizations were not yet formed, many of the converts uniting with English-speaking churches.

In 1789 a meeting of these revivalist preachers was held in Baltimore, and a confession of faith and rules of discipline were adopted, based upon the rules adopted four years before for the government of Otterbein's independent church in Baltimore. During the next decade similar councils were called at irregular intervals, culminating in a conference held in Frederick County, Maryland, in 1800, in the formation of a distinct ecclesiastical body under the name of "United Brethren in Christ." Thirteen preachers were in attendance, and Otterbein and Boehm were elected bishops, in which office they remained until the death of Boehm in 1812 and of Otterbein in

1813. This new organization was in no sense a schism from any other body, but a natural development on the part of the German-speaking congregations of that section which were desirous of a fuller evangelistic life.

Bishop Asbury, of the Methodist Church, and Bishop Otterbein, of the United Brethren, came into close relations and were warm friends, but as the Methodist Church was at that time unwilling to accede to the wishes of the German-speaking communities, and encourage German-speaking churches, the two bodies remained distant, and no specific effort to unite the forces was ever made.

The fact that those persons who joined the new organization represented different forms of church life necessitated mutual conference and some concessions. Of the fourteen ministers at the conference of 1789, nine were of German Reformed antecedents and five were Mennonites. The church members, however, were more widely distributed. The Reformed churches practiced infant baptism, but not footwashing; the Mennonites practiced footwashing and regarded believers' baptism by immersion as the only correct form. The result was that each generously conceded to the other freedom to follow personal convictions as to the form of baptism, the age of the persons baptized, and the observance of footwashing.

During the first years of the nineteenth century the movement continued to grow and many preaching places were established in Ohio and Indiana, and some in Kentucky, but the center of greatest activity was the Miami valley in Ohio.

The first general conference was held in 1815, four district conferences being represented by fourteen delegates. This general conference arranged and adopted a book of discipline, accepting in general the system agreed upon in the first conference of 1789. The same general conference was also significant for its recognition of a change that had been gradually taking place in the use of the English language in the churches. Until this time, almost all the churches had used German in their services, but as they came into closer contact with other religious bodies, the use of English increased, and, although many continued their German preaching, English-speaking churches became numerous. This change was further recognized by the conference held in 1817, which ordered the confession of faith and the book of discipline to be printed in both German and English.

In 1906 the United Brethren in Christ had 3,732 congregations, with 274,649 communicants; only 67 congregations still used German in their worship services. Congregations were to be found in the following states:

State	No.	State	No.	State	No.
New York	34	Illinois	287	Alabama	1
Pennsylvania	586	Michigan	66	Louisana	11
Maryland	63	Wisconsin	45	Oklahoma	67
District of Columbia	1	Minnesota	32	Idaho	4
		Iowa	187	Colorado	12
Virginia	91	Missouri	87	Washington	12
West Virginia	321	South Dakota	6	Oregon	32
Georgia	6	Nebraska	126	California	18
Florida	2	Kansas	298		
Ohio	702	Kentucky	22		
Indiana	568	Tennessee	60		

Only 48 of the 3,732 congregations were in cities about 25,000 in population (as of the 1900 census).

Church of the United Brethren in Christ (Old Constitution). With the growth of the Church of the United Brethren in Christ, as in other denominations, two parties developed--one which held closely to the original constitution, and another which sought to change it to meet what they considered the necessity of changed conditions. At the general conference of 1841, when final steps were taken toward adopting the full constitution, four points were emphasized, which later became objects of special discussion: the slavery question, secret societies, changes in the confession of faith, and changes in the constitution. The slavery question disappeared after the Civil War, but the others came to the front, and the last two became specially prominent. In 1885 the general conference set aside the constitutional provisions for change by pronouncing them impracticable, and arranged for another constitution, under the name of amending the constitution. The minority recorded a protest, but the majority proceeded to appoint a commission which drafted an amended constitution and presented it for adoption by the society in such a manner as, in the opinion of the minority, insured endorsement by the indifferent and youthful members. Although less than one-half the whole society voted, the general conference of 1889 accepted the results and pronounced the revised constitution in force. The minority chose to remain upon the unamended constitution, holding that the constitution of 1841 was still in force, and that they were the true United Brethren Church, and, as such, entitled to the church property. In Michigan the supreme court pronounced in favor of the "Old Constitution" body; in Virginia each congregation had a "deciding election" to determine which organization should hold the property; and in other states the matter was settled in various ways. In some places the Old Constitution body retained the property, while in others, possession was secured only by repurchase.

In 1906 the Old Constitution body of the United Brethren in Christ had a total of 572 congregations and 21,401 communicants. Only six congregations still used German in their worship services. Congregations were located in the following states:

New York	3	Michigan	117	Oklahoma	6
Pennsylvania	37	Wisconsin	9	Idaho	7
		Iowa	9	Washington	19
Maryland	1	Missouri	10		
Virginia	6	South		Oregon	22
Ohio	162	Dakota	1	California	6
Indiana	98	Nebraska	4		
Illinois	26	Kansas	29		

Only two congregations were to be found in urban areas in 1906--in Reading, Pennsylvania, with 67 members, and Kansas City, Missouri, with 13 members; all other congregations were in rural areas.

LOCATIONS OF GERMAN-SPEAKING CONGREGATIONS IN THE UNITED STATES, 1906

The 1906 federal religious census gave considerable, though incomplete data on a number of the larger German-speaking denominations, enabling the genealogical researcher to establish the county in which congregations were located. Unfortunately, the census did not separately list German-speaking Catholic congregations, thus vitiating somewhat the usefulness of this data. One may assume, however, that wherever numerous Protestant German-speaking congregations were located, there likewise one could frequently find a German-speaking Roman Catholic one. In like manner, the smaller sects and splinter groups are also regrettably slighted, although even they are reported in Table 6 of the general tables to the 1906 census of religions, part 1, if located in a town with a population above 25,000, as of 1900. (The researcher should check Table 6 especially when searching for a very obscure sect, because so many of them were exclusively urban phenomena.)

The tabulation which follows does not include all the states of the Union, because some states did not have concentrated German-speaking settlements, excepting perhaps a few Catholic ones, which were not identified. In order to present a large array of data in limited space, the denominations have been coded as follows:

01 Churches of God in North America, General Eldership

02 Dunkers (German Baptist Brethren Church, Conservative)

03 Evangelical Association

04 United Evangelical Church

05 German Evangelical Synod of North America

06 General Synod of the Evangelical Lutheran Church in the United States

07 United Synod of the Evangelical Lutheran Church in the South

08 General Council of the Evangelical Lutheran Church of North America

09 Evangelical Lutheran Synodical Conference of America

10 Evangelical Lutheran Joint Synod of Ohio and Other States

11 Evangelical Lutheran Synod of Iowa and Other States

12 Evangelical Lutheran Synod of Michigan and Other States

13 Mennonite Church

14 General Conference of Mennonites in North America

15 Moravian Church (Unitas Fratrum)

16 Reformed Church in America (mainly of Dutch origin, but with some German communicants)

17 Reformed Church in the United States (mainly German communicants)

18 United Brethren in Christ

19 Miscellaneous (see footnote in tabulation)

x denotes existence of a congregation, or congregations, in the county

* Not all counties listed. ** No German ethnic congregations in county.

LOCATIONS OF GERMAN-SPEAKING CONGREGATIONS IN THE UNITED STATES, 1906

State & County	01	02	03	04	05	06	07	08	09	10	11	12	13	14	15	16	17	18	19
Arkansas*																			
Arkansas									x										
Clay									x										

LOCATION OF GERMAN-SPEAKING CONGREGATIONS
IN THE UNITED STATES, 1906--*Continued*

State & County	01	02	03	04	05	06	07	08	09	10	11	12	13	14	15	16	17	18	19
Arkansas--*Cont.*																			
Conway									x										
Faulkner									x										
Greene									x										
Jefferson									x										
Johnson									x										
Poinsett									x										
Polk									x										
Pope									x										
Prairie									x										
Pulaski									x										
St. Francis									x										
Saline									x										
Sebastian									x										
Sharp									x										
Washington									x										
California*																			
Alameda						x			x										
Contra Costa									x										
Fresno						x			x										
Glenn									x										
Humboldt									x										
Kern									x										
Los Angeles						x			x										
Monterey						x													
Napa									x										
Nevada									x										
Orange									x										
Riverside						x													
Sacramento						x													
San Bernardino						x			x										
San Diego						x			x										
San Francisco									x										
San Joaquin									x										
San Luis Obispo									x										
Santa Clara						x			x										
Solano									x										
Sonoma									x										
Stanislaus									x										
Tulare									x										
Ventura									x										
Connecticut																			
Fairfield								x	x										
Hartford								x	x										
Litchfield								x	x										
Middlesex								x	x										
New Haven								x	x										
New London								x											
Tolland								x	x										
Windham								x											
Delaware																			
Newcastle								x											

LOCATIONS OF GERMAN-SPEAKING CONGREGATIONS
IN THE UNITED STATES, 1906--*Continued*

State & County	01	02	03	04	05	06	07	08	09	10	11	12	13	14	15	16	17	18	19
Illinois																			
Adams					x	x			x		x							x	
Alexander						x													
Bond					x				x										
Boone			x		x			x	x										
Brown									x										
Bureau			x		x	x					x							x	
Calhoun						x			x										
Carroll			x			x			x										
Cass						x			x										
Champaign					x				x		x							x	
Christian					x				x									x	
Clark			x															x	
Clay					x													x	
Clinton					x				x		x								
Coles					x				x									x	
Cook			x		x	x		x	x		x							x	
Crawford																		x	
Cumberland																		x	
DeKalb			x		x			x	x		x							x	
Dewitt																		x	
Douglas			x						x									x	
Dupage			x		x				x									x	
Edgar			x															x	
Edwards			x															x	
Effingham			x						x		x							x	
Fayette			x		x	x		x	x		x							x	
Ford						x					x							x	
Franklin									x										
Fulton						x		x			x							x	
Gallatin**																			
Greene**																			
Grundy			x					x	x										
Hamilton																			
Hancock					x	x			x		x							x	
Hardin**																			
Henderson								x											
Henry			x		x			x	x		x							x	
Iroquois					x			x	x		x							x	
Jackson					x	x			x									x	
Jasper								x										x	
Jefferson																		x	
Jersey					x														
Jo Daviess						x			x		x								
Johnson																		x	
Kane			x		x			x	x										
Kankakee			x		x				x									x	
Kendall			x		x			x	x										
Knox								x	x									x	
Lake			x		x			x	x										
Lasalle			x		x			x	x		x							x	

LOCATIONS OF GERMAN-SPEAKING CONGREGATIONS
IN THE UNITED STATES, 1906--*Continued*

State & County	01	02	03	04	05	06	07	08	09	10	11	12	13	14	15	16	17	18	19
Illinois--*Cont.*																			
Lawrence																		x	
Lee			x			x					x							x	
Livingston			x						x		x							x	
Logan			x		x	x			x		x							x	
McDonough						x												x	
McHenry					x	x			x										
McLean					x			x	x		x							x	
Macon								x	x									x	
Macoupin					x	x			x		x								
Madison					x				x										
Marion					x				x									x	
Marshall								x	x		x								
Mason			x						x									x	
Massac					x						x								
Menard					x				x										
Mercer								x	x									x	
Monroe					x				x										
Montgomery					x	x			x		x								
Morgan						x			x										
Moultrie																		x	
Ogle			x		x	x		x	x		x							x	
Peoria			x			x		x	x		x							x	
Perry					x				x										
Piatt																		x	
Pike						x												x	
Pope											x							x	
Pulaski						x													
Putnam								x											
Randolph					x	x			x										
Richland			x					x										x	
Rock Island					x				x									x	
St. Clair					x				x										
Saline**																			
Sangamon						x			x									x	
Schuyler																		x	
Scott						x			x										
Shelby			x		x			x	x									x	
Stark											x								
Stephenson			x		x	x			x									x	
Tazewell			x		x	x			x										
Union						x					x								
Vermilion					x			x	x									x	
Wabash			x		x	x			x									x	
Warren								x										x	
Washington					x				x										
Wayne																		x	
White			x		x														
Whiteside			x			x		x	x		x							x	
Will			x			x	x	x	x									x	

LOCATIONS OF GERMAN-SPEAKING CONGREGATIONS

IN THE UNITED STATES, 1906--*Continued*

State & County	01	02	03	04	05	06	07	08	09	10	11	12	13	14	15	16	17	18	19
Illinois--*Cont.*																			
Williamson					x				x										
Winnebago						x		x	x										
Woodford			x		x				x		x								
Indiana																			
Adams		x	x			x			x								x	x	
Allen		x	x			x			x	x							x	x	
Bartholomew						x			x									x	
Benton																		x	
Blackford		x								x								x	
Boone																		x	
Brown																		x	
Carroll		x				x			x								x	x	
Cass		x	x			x			x									x	
Clark																		x	
Clay		x	x		x				x	x							x	x	
Clinton		x															x	x	
Crawford																		x	
Daviess																		x	
Dearborn					x				x	x									
Decatur																		x	
DeKalb		x	x			x			x								x	x	
Delaware		x			x	x												x	
Dubois					x				x	x									
Elkhart		x	x		x	x			x	x							x	x	
Fayette						x												x	
Floyd					x													x	
Fountain																		x	
Franklin										x								x	
Fulton		x	x						x									x	
Gibson			x		x													x	
Grant		x								x							x	x	
Greene																	x	x	
Hamilton		x	x			x			x									x	
Hancock		x			x				x									x	
Harrison						x			x								x	x	
Hendricks**																			
Henry		x																x	
Howard		x	x						x									x	
Huntington		x	x		x	x			x	x							x	x	
Jackson		x			x				x	x							x	x	
Jasper									x									x	
Jay		x	x			x				x							x	x	
Jefferson					x													x	
Jennings																		x	
Johnson																		x	
Knox					x				x									x	
Kosciusko		x	x			x												x	
Lagrange		x	x			x												x	
Lake			x		x				x										

LOCATIONS OF GERMAN-SPEAKING CONGREGATIONS
IN THE UNITED STATES, 1906--*Continued*

State & County	01	02	03	04	05	06	07	08	09	10	11	12	13	14	15	16	17	18	19
Indiana--*Cont.*																			
Laporte		x	x		x				x	x									
Lawrence																		x	
Madison		x				x			x									x	
Marion		x	x		x	x			x	x							x	x	
Marshall		x	x		x				x	x							x	x	
Martin										x								x	
Miami		x	x		x				x									x	
Monroe**																			
Montgomery		x																x	
Morgan**																			
Newton									x									x	
Noble		x	x			x			x	x								x	
Ohio										x							x		
Orange																		x	
Owen										x								x	
Parke																		x	
Perry					x				x									x	
Pike					x					x								x	
Porter																			
Posey					x														
Pulaski		x	x		x				x									x	
Putnam		x																x	
Randolph		x	x							x							x	x	
Ripley									x	x									
Rush																		x	
St. Joseph		x	x						x	x							x	x	
Scott																		x	
Shelby						x											x	x	
Spencer			x		x	x			x									x	
Starke			x		x				x									x	
Steuben		x	x														x	x	
Sullivan																		x	
Switzerland																	x	x	
Tippecanoe					x	x			x								x	x	
Tipton									x										
Union		x																x	
Vanderburg			x		x	x			x	x									
Vermilion									x									x	
Vigo			x						x								x	x	
Wabash		x	x		x	x			x	x								x	
Warren																		x	
Warrick			x						x	x								x	
Washington																		x	
Wayne		x	x			x				x								x	
Wells		x	x			x			x								x	x	
White		x	x						x										
Whitley		x	x			x			x	x								x	

LOCATIONS OF GERMAN-SPEAKING CONGREGATIONS

IN THE UNITED STATES, 1906--*Continued*

State & County	01	02	03	04	05	06	07	08	09	10	11	12	13	14	15	16	17	18	19
Iowa																			
Adair			x	x					x		x								
Adams			x															x	
Allamakee			x		x	x					x								
Appanoose								x										x	
Audubon					x				x									x	
Benton			x	x	x				x									x	
Blackhawk			x	x	x				x		x							x	
Boone								x	x									x	
Bremer			x		x				x		x							x	
Buchanan			x						x		x								
Buena Vista					x			x	x										
Butler			x	x	x				x		x					x		x	
Calhoun			x	x	x			x	x		x							x	
Carroll									x		x							x	
Cass			x	x	x			x	x									x	
Cedar						x			x									x	
Cerro Gordo			x								x							x	
Cherokee			x		x			x	x									x	
Chickasaw			x		x				x		x								
Clarke																		x	
Clay			x					x	x							x			
Clayton			x		x			x	x		x							x	
Clinton			x		x	x		x	x		x								
Crawford			x		x				x		x							x	
Dallas			x						x									x	
Davis**																			
Decatur																		x	
Delaware								x			x							x	
Des Moines					x	x		x			x								
Dickinson									x							x			
Dubuque			x			x			x		x								
Emmet									x										
Fayette			x	x					x		x							x	
Floyd			x	x							x								
Franklin			x	x	x				x		x					x		x	
Fremont					x	x													
Greene			x						x									x	
Grundy						x			x		x					x			
Guthrie									x									x	
Hamilton						x		x	x									x	
Hancock			x						x		x							x	
Hardin			x	x	x				x										
Harrison			x						x		x							x	
Henry								x											
Howard			x						x		x								
Humboldt			x						x		x								
Ida									x		x								
Iowa									x										
Jackson			x								x								
Jasper			x		x	x					x					x		x	

LOCATIONS OF GERMAN-SPEAKING CONGREGATIONS
IN THE UNITED STATES, 1906--*Continued*

State & County	01	02	03	04	05	06	07	08	09	10	11	12	13	14	15	16	17	18	19
Iowa--*Cont.*																			
Jefferson						x		x	x		x								
Johnson			x			x					x								
Jones			x			x			x		x								
Keokuk					x				x		x								
Kossuth			x		x			x	x							x		x	
Lee					x	x		x											
Linn			x	x		x		x	x									x	
Louisa				x														x	
Lucas				x				x										x	
Lyon			x	x	x				x		x					x			
Madison			x	x														x	
Mahaska											x					x			
Marion									x							x		x	
Marshall			x	x	x			x	x		x								
Mills											x							x	
Mitchell									x		x								
Monona									x										
Monroe								x										x	
Montgomery				x	x														
Muscatine			x		x	x			x		x					x		x	
O'Brien			x		x				x		x					x			
Osceola			x	x					x		x					x			
Page								x	x									x	
Palo Alto				x				x	x										
Plymouth			x	x	x				x		x					x		x	
Pocahontas			x					x			x								
Polk			x	x		x		x	x		x								
Pottawattamie			x	x	x	x		x	x		x							x	
Poweshiek											x								
Ringgold				x														x	
Sac				x				x	x		x								
Scott						x		x	x		x								
Shelby				x	x													x	
Sioux									x		x					x			
Story			x	x		x												x	
Tama			x		x						x							x	
Taylor			x															x	
Union			x	x	x			x										x	
Van Buren					x	x					x								
Wapello								x			x								
Warren											x							x	
Washington					x													x	
Wayne																		x	
Webster			x					x	x										
Winnebago			x													x		x	
Winneshiek			x								x							x	
Woodbury			x	x	x	x		x	x		x							x	
Worth				x	x						x					x			
Wright				x							x								

LOCATIONS OF GERMAN-SPEAKING CONGREGATIONS

IN THE UNITED STATES--*Continued*

State & County	01	02	03	04	05	06	07	08	09	10	11	12	13	14	15	16	17	18	19
Kansas																			
Allen			x					x	x									x	
Anderson		x				x												x	
Atchison			x		x	x			x										
Barber					x									x				x	
Barton		x	x		x	x			x									x	
Bourbon		x																x	
Brown		x	x		x				x									x	
Butler			x			x			x					x					
Chase									x										
Chautauqua																		x	
Cherokee																		x	
Cheyenne			x								x								
Clark**																			
Clay			x					x	x									x	
Cloud			x			x		x										x	
Coffey		x							x									x	
Comanche**																			
Cowley		x	x						x									x	
Crawford		x						x	x		x							x	
Decatur						x			x									x	
Dickinson		x	x			x		x	x		x							x	
Doniphan			x			x			x									x	
Douglas		x	x		x	x		x										x	
Edwards			x								x							x	
Elk		x																x	
Ellis						x					x								
Ellsworth					x	x			x									x	
Finney		x																	
Ford			x						x										
Franklin		x				x		x										x	
Geary					x				x									x	
Gove		x						x											
Graham																		x	
Grant**																			
Gray																		x	
Greeley**																			
Greenwood						x												x	
Hamilton**																			
Harper																		x	
Harvey		x	x		x				x		x								
Haskell		x																	
Hodgeman									x					x					
Jackson		x	x						x									x	
Jefferson		x	x			x			x									x	
Jewell		x	x			x												x	
Johnson		x																	
Kearny									x										
Kingman									x					x				x	
Kiowa																		x	
Labette		x	x						x									x	

LOCATIONS OF GERMAN-SPEAKING CONGREGATIONS
IN THE UNITED STATES--*Continued*

State & County	01	02	03	04	05	06	07	08	09	10	11	12	13	14	15	16	17	18	19
Kansas--*Cont.*																			
Lane									x									x	
Leavenworth			x		x				x									x	
Lincoln		x	x		x				x									x	
Linn																		x	
Logan								x											
Lyon		x	x		x				x									x	
McPherson		x	x		x			x	x					x				x	
Marion		x	x		x				x		x			x				x	
Marshall		x	x		x	x		x	x									x	
Meade									x		x								
Miami		x			x				x									x	
Mitchell						x			x		x							x	
Montgomery		x	x						x									x	
Morris		x	x					x	x									x	
Morton**																			
Nemaha		x	x		x				x									x	
Neosho		x									x							x	
Ness									x		x			x					
Norton		x	x															x	
Osage			x					x	x									x	
Osborne		x	x						x		x							x	
Ottawa						x												x	
Pawnee								x										x	
Phillips		x	x		x						x							x	
Pottawatomie			x					x	x									x	
Pratt									x										
Rawlins					x			x	x										
Reno		x	x		x	x		x	x					x				x	
Republic		x							x									x	
Rice		x	x						x									x	
Riley			x					x	x									x	
Rooks																		x	
Rush									x		x								
Russell			x			x			x		x							x	
Saline					x	x		x										x	
Scott		x							x										
Sedgwick		x	x		x				x									x	
Seward**																			
Shawnee		x	x		x				x									x	
Sheridan**																			
Sherman									x									x	
Smith									x		x							x	
Stafford		x			x													x	
Stanton**																			
Stevens**																			
Sumner		x				x			x									x	
Thomas																		x	
Trego								x			x								
Wabaunsee					x				x									x	
Wallace								x											

LOCATIONS OF GERMAN-SPEAKING CONGREGATIONS

IN THE UNITED STATES--*Continued*

State & County	01	02	03	04	05	06	07	08	09	10	11	12	13	14	15	16	17	18	19
Kansas--*Cont.*																			
Washington		x	x		x	x			x									x	
Wichita									x		x								
Wilson		x	x					x										x	
Woodson			x						x									x	
Wyandotte		x			x	x		x	x										
Kentucky*																			
Boone						x													
Bullitt						x													
Campbell					x	x													
Daviess					x														
Henderson					x														
Jefferson					x	x											x		
Kenton					x												x		
Laurel																	x		
Lincoln																	x		
McCracken					x														
Montgomery																	x		
Pendleton					x														
Simpson						x													
Louisiana*																			
Acadia									x										
Assumption									x										
Avoyelles									x										
Calcasieu									x										
East Feliciana									x										
Jefferson									x										
Orleans									x										
St. Tammany									x										
Tangipahoa									x										
Maryland																			
Allegany			x		x	x			x								x	x	
Anne Arundel					x					x									
Baltimore			x		x	x			x	x							x	x	
Baltimore City			x		x	x			x	x							x	x	
Calvert**																			
Caroline		x							x								x		
Carroll	x	x				x											x	x	
Cecil**																			
Charles**																			
Dorchester					x				x										
Frederick	x					x											x	x	
Garrett						x			x								x	x	
Harford			x							x									
Howard			x							x									
Kent**																			
Montgomery										x									
Prince Georges**																			
Queen Annes**																			
St. Marys**																			

LOCATIONS OF GERMAN-SPEAKING CONGREGATIONS
IN THE UNITED STATES--*Continued*

State & County	01	02	03	04	05	06	07	08	09	10	11	12	13	14	15	16	17	18	19
Maryland--*Cont.*																			
Somerset**																			
Talbot		x			x														
Washington	x					x											x	x	
Wicomico**																			
Worcester**																			
Massachusetts																			
Barnstable**																			
Berkshire								x											
Bristol								x											
Dukes**																			
Essex								x											
Franklin								x											
Hampden								x	x										
Hampshire									x										
Middlesex								x											
Nantucket**																			
Norfolk								x	x										
Plymouth								x	x										
Suffolk								x	x										
Worcester								x	x										
Michigan																			
Alcona									x										
Alger								x											
Allegan			x					x				x				x			
Alpena									x		x	x							
Antrim								x	x							x			
Arenac									x			x							
Baraga								x											
Barry			x							x									
Bay			x					x	x			x							
Benzie**																			
Berrien			x		x			x	x			x				x			
Branch			x						x										
Calhoun			x		x					x		x							
Cass			x		x			x											
Charlevoix			x		x			x											
Cheboygan								x	x		x								
Chippewa								x	x										
Clare									x			x							
Clinton			x						x			x							
Crawford								x											
Delta								x	x			x							
Dickinson								x				x							
Eaton**																			
Emmet			x		x				x										
Genesee			x																
Gladwin			x																
Gogebic								x	x										
Grand Traverse			x		x			x	x										

LOCATIONS OF GERMAN-SPEAKING CONGREGATIONS

IN THE UNITED STATES--*Continued*

State & County	01	02	03	04	05	06	07	08	09	10	11	12	13	14	15	16	17	18	19
Michigan--*Cont.*																			
Gratiot			x						x										
Hillsdale			x						x										
Houghton								x	x										
Huron									x			x							
Ingham					x														
Ionia									x			x							
Iosco								x	x										
Iron								x											
Isabella			x						x			x							
Jackson			x		x				x			x							
Kalamazoo			x									x				x			
Kalkaska**																			
Kent			x		x			x	x							x			
Keweenaw**																			
Lake**																			
Lapeer			x		x				x		x	x							
Leelanau			x						x										
Lenawee			x		x				x		x	x				x			
Livingston			x							x									
Luce								x											
Mackinac								x			x								
Macomb			x		x				x		x								
Manistee			x					x	x	x									
Marquette								x	x										
Mason			x					x	x			x							
Mecosta								x	x			x							
Menominee					x			x	x			x							
Midland			x						x			x							
Missaukee								x	x			x				x			
Monroe			x						x	x	x	x							
Montcalm			x		x				x										
Montmorency									x										
Muskegon					x			x	x							x			
Newaygo								x								x			
Oakland					x				x										
Oceana									x							x			
Ogemaw									x										
Ontonagon								x											
Osceola			x					x	x	x									
Oscoda**																			
Otsego**																			
Ottawa					x				x							x			
Presque Isle									x		x								
Roscommon**																			
Saginaw			x		x				x	x	x	x							
St. Clair			x		x				x	x	x	x							
St. Joseph			x						x			x				x			
Sanilac			x		x				x										
Schoolcraft								x	x										

LOCATIONS OF GERMAN-SPEAKING CONGREGATIONS

IN THE UNITED STATES, 1906--*Continued*

State & County	01	02	03	04	05	06	07	08	09	10	11	12	13	14	15	16	17	18	19
Michigan--*Cont.*																			
Shiawassee			x		x				x										
Tuscola			x						x			x				x			
Van Buren			x						x	x									
Washtenaw			x		x				x	x	x								
Wayne			x		x			x	x	x	x	x				x			
Wexford			x		x			x	x										
Minnesota																			
Aitkin								x	x										
Anoka								x	x										
Becker								x	x										
Beltrami									x										
Benton			x					x	x										
Bigstone								x	x										
Blue Earth								x	x	x									
Brown			x		x			x	x	x									
Carlton								x	x										
Carver			x		x			x	x										
Cass									x		x								
Chippewa								x	x	x	x								
Chisago					x			x	x										
Clay					x			x	x										
Clearwater								x											
Cook**																			
Cottonwood			x					x	x	x									
Crow Wing			x					x	x	x									
Dakota			x					x	x	x	x								
Dodge			x						x										
Douglas			x		x			x	x										
Faribault			x		x				x	x	x								
Fillmore			x						x		x								
Freeborn								x		x	x								
Goodhue			x		x			x	x	x									
Grant					x			x	x										
Hennepin			x		x			x	x	x	x								
Houston			x		x				x										
Hubbard					x				x										
Isanti			x					x	x										
Itasca								x	x										
Jackson			x		x			x	x	x	x								
Kanabec								x	x										
Kandiyohi								x	x		x								
Kittson			x					x			x								
Koochiching**																			
Lac qui Parle			x					x	x	x									
Lake								x											
Lesueur			x		x			x	x		x								
Lincoln			x					x	x										
Lyon			x					x	x										
McLeod			x		x				x	x									

LOCATIONS OF GERMAN-SPEAKING CONGREGATIONS

IN THE UNITED STATES, 1906--*Continued*

State & County	01	02	03	04	05	06	07	08	09	10	11	12	13	14	15	16	17	18	19
Minnesota--*Cont.*																			
Marshall								x	x										
Martin			x		x			x	x	x	x								
Meeker								x	x										
Millelacs								x	x	x									
Morrison			x		x			x	x		x								
Mower			x					x	x		x								
Murray								x	x		x								
Nicollet					x			x	x										
Nobles			x					x	x		x								
Norman								x			x								
Olmsted			x		x				x	x									
Otter Tail			x		x			x	x										
Pine					x			x	x		x								
Pipestone			x						x										
Polk								x	x	x									
Pope								x	x		x								
Ramsey			x		x			x	x		x								
Red Lake			x					x	x										
Redwood			x		x			x	x	x									
Renville			x		x			x	x	x									
Rice			x		x			x	x										
Rock			x						x										
Roseau								x											
St. Louis			x		x			x	x	x									
Scott								x	x	x									
Sherburne								x		x									
Sibley			x		x			x	x	x									
Stearns			x		x				x		x								
Steele									x		x								
Stevens								x	x	x									
Swift			x					x	x	x									
Todd			x		x			x	x										
Traverse					x			x	x										
Wabasha			x		x			x	x										
Wadena			x		x			x	x										
Waseca			x		x			x	x	x	x								
Washington					x			x	x	x	x								
Watonwan								x	x										
Wilkin			x		x				x										
Winona			x		x				x										
Wright			x		x			x	x	x									
Yellow Medicine								x	x	x									
Missouri*																			
Adair																		x	
Audrain			x						x										
Barry									x										
Barton																		x	
Bates									x									x	
Benton									x									x	

LOCATIONS OF GERMAN-SPEAKING CONGREGATIONS

IN THE UNITED STATES, 1906--*Continued*

State & County	01	02	03	04	05	06	07	08	09	10	11	12	13	14	15	16	17	18	19
Missouri--*Cont.*																			
Bollinger									x										
Boone					x														
Buchanan					x				x										
Butler									x										
Caldwell																		x	
Callaway					x													x	
Camden																		x	
Cape Girardeau					x				x										
Carroll					x				x										
Cass																		x	
Cedar									x										
Chariton									x									x	
Christian					x				x										
Clark					x														
Cole					x				x										
Cooper					x				x										
Crawford									x										
Dade									x										
Dallas																		x	
Daviess																		x	
Dent																		x	
Franklin					x				x										
Gasconade					x				x										
Gentry																		x	
Greene					x														
Grundy																		x	
Harrison																		x	
Henry									x									x	
Hickory																		x	
Holt									x									x	
Howard					x														
Iron									x										
Jackson					x				x										
Jasper									x									x	
Jefferson					x				x										
Knox																		x	
Lafayette					x				x										
Lawrence					x				x										
Lewis					x				x										
Lincoln					x														
Linn																		x	
Livingston																		x	
Macon									x									x	
Madison									x										
Maries					x				x										
Marion									x										
Mercer																		x	
Moniteau					x				x										
Montgomery					x				x										

LOCATIONS OF GERMAN-SPEAKING CONGREGATIONS

IN THE UNITED STATES, 1906--*Continued*

State & County	01	02	03	04	05	06	07	08	09	10	11	12	13	14	15	16	17	18	19
Missouri--*Cont.*																			
Morgan					x				x									x	
Newton					x														
Oregon									x										
Osage					x				x										
Perry									x										
Pettis					x				x										
Phelps									x										
Platte					x				x										
Polk									x										
Putnam																		x	
Randolph									x										
Ray					x														
St. Charles					x				x										
St. Clair					x				x									x	
St. Francois									x										
St. Louis					x				x										
St. Louis City									x										
Ste. Genevieve									x										
Saline					x				x										
Scotland																		x	
Scott									x										
Shelby									x										
Stoddard				x															
Stone																		x	
Sullivan																		x	
Vernon									x									x	
Warren					x														
Wayne									x										
Webster									x										
Nebraska																			
Adams			x	x		x			x									x	
Antelope					x				x									x	
Banner																		x	
Blaine						x													
Boone								x			x								
Boxbutte									x										
Boyd								x	x		x								
Brown									x									x	
Buffalo			x	x		x		x	x									x	
Burt						x		x	x										
Butler						x			x										
Cass			x	x	x	x			x										
Cedar						x		x	x		x						x	x	
Chase									x									x	
Cherry									x										
Cheyenne						x		x	x		x							x	
Clay			x	x	x	x		x									x		
Colfax						x			x										
Cuming			x		x	x			x										
Custer			x	x					x									x	

LOCATIONS OF GERMAN-SPEAKING CONGREGATIONS
IN THE UNITED STATES, 1906--*Continued*

State & County	01	02	03	04	05	06	07	08	09	10	11	12	13	14	15	16	17	18	19
Nebraska--*Cont.*																			
Dakota						x													
Dawes**																			
Dawson			x	x		x			x		x							x	
Deuel			x			x		x	x										
Dixon						x		x	x										
Dodge			x			x		x	x										
Douglas			x	x	x	x		x	x		x						x		
Dundy**																			
Fillmore				x		x		x	x		x							x	
Franklin				x		x			x		x							x	
Frontier				x					x		x								
Furnas				x		x			x									x	
Gage				x	x	x			x		x							x	
Garfield**																			
Gosper									x		x							x	
Grant**																			
Greeley			x			x		x	x										
Hall			x	x		x			x									x	
Hamilton				x	x	x		x	x									x	
Harlan			x	x		x		x	x		x							x	
Hayes									x									x	
Hitchcock			x						x									x	
Holt			x						x		x								
Hooker**																			
Howard									x									x	
Jefferson			x		x				x		x						x	x	
Johnson								x	x									x	
Kearney								x	x									x	
Keith						x			x										
Keyapaha									x										
Kimball								x											
Knox			x			x		x	x		x							x	
Lancaster			x	x	x	x		x	x		x						x	x	
Lincoln						x			x										
Logan**																			
Loup**																			
McPherson**																			
Madison			x			x		x	x									x	
Merrick			x			x			x										
Nance				x							x								
Nemaha				x		x			x		x							x	
Nuckolls			x			x			x		x							x	
Otoe					x	x					x							x	
Pawnee					x	x											x	x	
Perkins									x										
Phelps								x	x										
Pierce			x	x		x			x		x								
Platte			x		x	x		x	x								x	x	
Polk								x	x									x	
Redwillow				x					x									x	

LOCATIONS OF GERMAN-SPEAKING CONGREGATIONS

IN THE UNITED STATES, 1906--*Continued*

State & County	01	02	03	04	05	06	07	08	09	10	11	12	13	14	15	16	17	18	19
Nebraska--*Cont.*																			
Richardson			x	x	x	x			x								x	x	
Rock									x										
Saline			x		x	x			x									x	
Sarpy									x										
Saunders			x		x	x		x	x		x						x	x	
Scotts Bluff**																			
Seward			x	x	x				x		x							x	
Sheridan											x								
Sherman			x		x				x									x	
Sioux**																			
Stanton			x			x			x								x		
Thayer						x			x		x								
Thomas						x													
Thurston						x													
Valley			x						x									x	
Washington			x			x			x										
Wayne			x		x	x			x								x		
Webster			x			x			x		x							x	
Wheeler						x													
York				x		x		x	x								x	x	
Nevada																			
Douglas									x										
Washoe									x										
New Jersey																			
Atlantic								x											
Bergen								x								x			
Burlington								x											
Camden								x											
Cape May								x											
Cumberland								x											
Essex								x								x			
Gloucester								x											
Hudson								x								x			
Hunterdon																x			
Mercer								x											
Middlesex								x								x			
Monmouth								x								x			
Morris								x								x			
Ocean**																			
Passaic								x								x			
Salem**																			
Somerset								x								x			
Sussex																x			
Union								x								x			
Warren								x											
New York																			
Albany			x		x	x		x	x							x			
Allegany			x					x	x										

LOCATIONS OF GERMAN-SPEAKING CONGREGATIONS
IN THE UNITED STATES, 1906--*Continued*

State & County	01	02	03	04	05	06	07	08	09	10	11	12	13	14	15	16	17	18	19
New York--*Cont.*																			
Broome			x					x											
Cattaraugus			x					x	x										
Cayuga					x											x			
Chautauqua			x		x			x	x							x			
Chemung					x			x											
Chenango**																			
Clinton**																			
Columbia						x		x	x							x			
Cortland**																			
Delaware																x			
Dutchess						x		x								x			
Erie			x		x	x		x	x							x	x		
Essex**																			
Franklin**																			
Fulton			x		x				x							x			
Genesee			x	x					x										
Greene					x											x			
Hamilton**																			
Herkimer			x		x											x			
Jefferson					x			x								x			
Kings			x		x	x		x	x							x	x		
Lewis																x			
Livingston					x			x											
Madison			x																
Monroe			x		x			x	x							x	x		
Montgomery			x		x	x		x								x			
Nassau								x	x							x			
New York			x		x	x		x	x							x	x		
Niagara			x		x	x		x	x										
Oneida			x		x	x		x	x							x			
Onondaga			x		x	x		x								x			
Ontario			x					x	x										
Orange								x	x							x			
Orleans								x	x										
Oswego						x													
Otsego						x													
Putnam																x			
Queens			x					x	x							x	x		
Rensselaer			x		x	x		x								x			
Richmond									x							x			
Rockland						x		x	x							x			
St. Lawrence						x													
Saratoga									x							x			
Schenectady					x	x		x	x							x			
Schoharie						x										x			
Schuyler**																			
Seneca						x										x	x		
Steuben					x			x	x										
Suffolk								x	x							x			
Sullivan								x											

LOCATIONS OF GERMAN-SPEAKING CONGREGATIONS

IN THE UNITED STATES, 1906--*Continued*

State & County	01	02	03	04	05	06	07	08	09	10	11	12	13	14	15	16	17	18	19
New York--*Cont.*																			
Tioga																			
Tompkins**																x			
Ulster						x		x	x										
Warren**																x			
Washington																x			
Wayne		x						x								x			
Westchester					x			x	x							x			
Wyoming			x		x														
Yates								x											
North Carolina*																			
Alamance							x	x									x		
Alexander							x	x											
Buncombe								x											
Burke							x	x											
Cabarrus							x	x									x		
Caldwell							x										x		
Catawba							x	x									x		
Cleveland							x										x		
Davidson							x								x		x		
Davie							x								x				
Forsyth															x		x		
Franklin							x												
Gaston							x												
Guilford							x	x							x		x		
Jackson							x												
Lincoln																	x		
McDowell							x												
Mecklenburg							x	x											
Moore								x											
New Hanover							x												
Randolph							x												
Rowan							x	x									x		
Stanly							x										x		
Stokes							x												
Union							x	x											
Warren								x											
Watauga							x										x		
North Dakota																			
Barnes								x		x									
Benson**																			
Billings**																			
Bottineau								x											
Burleigh								x											
Cass								x		x									
Cavalier								x											
Dickey								x		x									
Dunn**								x		x									
Eddy								x											

LOCATIONS OF GERMAN-SPEAKING CONGREGATIONS
IN THE UNITED STATES, 1906--*Continued*

State & County	01	02	03	04	05	06	07	08	09	10	11	12	13	14	15	16	17	18	19
North Dakota--*Cont.*																			
Emmons									x		x								
Foster									x										
Grand Forks									x										
Griggs									x										
Hettinger**																			
Kidder											x								
Lamoure									x		x								
Logan											x								
McHenry									x		x								
McIntosh									x		x								
McKenzie**																			
McLean									x		x								
Mercer									x		x								
Morton									x		x								
Nelson									x										
Oliver									x		x								
Pembina									x										
Pierce**																			
Ramsey									x										
Ransom											x								
Richland									x										
Rolette									x										
Sargent									x										
Stark**																			
Steele									x										
Stutsman									x		x								
Towner									x		x								
Traill									x										
Walsh									x										
Ward									x		x								
Wells									x		x								
Williams									x		x								
Ohio																			
Adams		x																x	
Allen		x			x			x	x		x						x	x	
Ashland		x	x		x	x					x						x	x	
Ashtabula								x	x									x	
Athens																		x	
Auglaize			x		x	x		x	x		x						x	x	x
Belmont								x			x						x		x
Brown				x							x							x	
Butler				x	x				x		x						x	x	x
Carroll								x			x						x	x	
Champaign					x						x						x	x	
Clark		x		x	x		x				x						x	x	
Clermont		x		x					x									x	
Clinton																		x	
Columbiana		x	x		x		x		x								x	x	

[Ohio denomination 19 = German Evangelical Protestant Ministers' Association.]

LOCATIONS OF GERMAN-SPEAKING CONGREGATIONS

IN THE UNITED STATES, 1906--*Continued*

State & County	01	02	03	04	05	06	07	08	09	10	11	12	13	14	15	16	17	18	19
Ohio--*Cont.*																			
Coshocton			x		x			x		x							x	x	
Crawford			x			x				x							x	x	
Cuyahoga			x		x	x		x	x	x							x	x	x
Darke		x	x			x		x		x							x	x	
Defiance		x	x					x	x								x	x	
Delaware						x				x							x	x	
Erie			x		x					x							x		
Fairfield		x	x			x		x	x	x							x	x	
Fayette**																			
Franklin			x		x	x		x	x	x							x	x	x
Fulton		x	x						x								x	x	
Gallia																		x	
Geauga**																			
Greene		x				x											x		
Guernsey						x												x	
Hamilton					x	x			x	x							x	x	x
Hancock		x	x			x				x							x	x	
Hardin					x			x									x	x	
Harrison								x									x	x	
Henry		x	x			x		x	x	x							x	x	
Highland		x				x											x	x	
Hocking									x	x								x	
Holmes					x	x			x	x							x	x	
Huron			x		x					x							x	x	
Jackson					x												x	x	
Jefferson								x		x							x	x	x
Knox		x								x									
Lake									x										
Lawrence										x							x	x	
Licking			x		x	x				x							x	x	
Logan		x	x			x											x	x	
Lorain			x			x											x	x	
Lucas			x			x			x								x	x	
Madison								x										x	
Mahoning		x	x			x		x	x	x							x		
Marion			x		x					x							x	x	
Medina		x				x		x	x	x							x	x	
Meigs					x				x	x								x	
Mercer		x	x		x	x				x								x	
Miami		x			x	x		x		x							x	x	
Monroe					x													x	
Montgomery		x	x		x	x		x		x							x	x	
Morgan								x		x								x	
Morrow			x			x											x	x	
Muskingum		x			x	x		x	x	x								x	
Noble						x													
Ottawa			x		x				x	x								x	
Paulding		x	x					x		x							x	x	

[Ohio denomination 19 = German Evangelical Protestant Ministers' Association.]

LOCATIONS OF GERMAN-SPEAKING CONGREGATIONS

IN THE UNITED STATES, 1906--*Continued*

State & County	01	02	03	04	05	06	07	08	09	10	11	12	13	14	15	16	17	18	19
Ohio--*Cont.*																			
Perry		x						x		x							x	x	
Pickaway			x					x		x							x	x	
Pike					x												x	x	
Portage						x			x								x	x	
Preble		x	x			x		x		x							x	x	
Putnam		x	x			x				x								x	
Richland		x	x		x	x		x									x	x	
Ross		x			x	x											x	x	
Sandusky			x							x							x	x	
Scioto					x					x								x	
Seneca		x	x		x	x				x							x	x	
Shelby		x			x					x							x	x	
Stark		x	x		x	x		x		x							x	x	
Summit		x	x			x		x	x	x							x	x	
Trumbull						x				x							x	x	
Tuscarawas		x			x	x		x		x							x	x	
Union									x	x								x	
Van Wert		x	x		x	x		x	x									x	
Vinton																		x	
Warren										x							x	x	
Washington					x	x												x	
Wayne		x	x			x		x		x							x	x	
Williams		x	x			x											x	x	
Wood		x	x			x		x		x							x	x	
Wyandot		x	x			x				x							x	x	
Oklahoma*																			
Alfalfa									x										
Blaine									x					x				x	
Caddo									x					x				x	
Canadian									x									x	
Cleveland									x									x	
Coal									x										
Comanche									x										
Creek									x									x	
Custer														x				x	
Dewey														x					
Ellis									x									x	
Garfield									x										
Grady									x										
Grant														x				x	
Greer									x										
Harper									x										
Kay									x									x	
Kingfisher									x									x	
Kiowa									x										
Lincoln									x									x	
Logan									x									x	
Major									x					x					
Muskogee									x										

LOCATIONS OF GERMAN-SPEAKING CONGREGATIONS

IN THE UNITED STATES, 1906--*Continued*

State & County	01	02	03	04	05	06	07	08	09	10	11	12	13	14	15	16	17	18	19
Oklahoma--*Cont.*																			
Noble									x					x					
Oklahoma									x									x	
Osage									x										
Pawnee									x									x	
Payne																		x	
Pottawatomie									x									x	
Tillman									x										
Tulsa									x										
Wagoner									x										
Washita									x					x					
Woods									x					x				x	
Woodward									x									x	
Pennsylvania																			
Adams		x		x		x											x	x	
Allegheny		x	x	x		x		x	x								x	x	
Armstrong		x	x	x		x		x									x		
Beaver			x					x	x									x	
Bedford		x	x	x		x											x	x	
Berks		x	x	x		x		x					x				x	x	
Blair		x	x	x		x		x					x				x	x	
Bradford			x					x									x		
Bucks		x	x	x		x		x					x				x		
Butler			x	x		x		x	x								x	x	
Cambria		x	x	x		x		x					x				x	x	
Cameron**																			
Carbon			x	x				x									x		
Center			x	x		x											x	x	
Chester		x	x	x		x		x					x				x	x	
Clarion			x	x		x		x									x		
Clearfield		x	x	x		x		x	x				x				x	x	
Clinton		x	x	x		x		x									x		
Columbia			x			x		x									x	x	
Crawford			x					x									x	x	
Cumberland		x		x		x		x					x				x	x	
Dauphin		x	x	x		x		x	x				x				x	x	
Delaware						x		x	x										
Elk								x										x	
Erie			x					x	x									x	
Fayette		x	x	x		x		x	x				x				x	x	
Forest			x	x				x										x	
Franklin		x				x							x				x	x	
Fulton		x				x											x	x	
Greene						x			x										
Huntingdon		x				x											x	x	
Indiana		x	x	x		x		x									x	x	
Jefferson			x	x		x		x	x								x	x	
Juniata		x		x		x		x					x				x	x	
Lackawanna			x	x		x		x	x								x		

LOCATIONS OF GERMAN-SPEAKING CONGREGATIONS
IN THE UNITED STATES, 1906--Continued

State & County	01	02	03	04	05	06	07	08	09	10	11	12	13	14	15	16	17	18	19
Pennsylvania--Cont.																			
Lancaster		x	x	x		x		x	x				x				x	x	
Lawrence			x			x		x									x		
Lebanon		x	x	x		x		x					x				x	x	
Lehigh			x	x		x		x									x	x	
Luzerne			x	x		x		x	x								x		
Lycoming			x	x		x		x									x	x	
McKean			x					x	x									x	
Mercer			x					x									x	x	
Mifflin		x	x	x		x		x									x	x	
Monroe			x			x		x									x		
Montgomery		x	x	x		x		x					x				x	x	
Montour			x			x		x									x		
Northampton			x	x		x		x									x	x	
Northumberland			x	x		x		x									x	x	
Perry		x		x		x											x	x	
Philadelphia		x	x	x		x		x	x								x	x	
Pike			x																
Potter								x	x									x	
Schuylkill		x	x	x		x		x									x	x	
Snyder			x	x		x		x					x				x	x	
Somerset		x	x	x		x		x	x				x				x	x	
Sullivan			x					x									x		
Susquehanna			x																
Tioga			x	x		x		x	x										
Union		x		x		x											x		
Venango			x	x				x	x								x	x	
Warren			x	x				x									x	x	
Washington		x		x		x		x	x									x	
Wayne			x	x				x											
Westmoreland		x	x	x		x		x	x								x	x	
Wyoming								x											
York		x	x	x		x			x				x				x	x	
Rhode Island*																			
Kent								x											
Newport								x											
Providence								x											
South Carolina*																			
Aiken							x												
Bamberg							x												
Barnwell							x												
Charleston							x												
Edgefield							x												
Florence							x												
Greenwood							x												
Lexington							x												
Newberry							x												
Oconee							x												
Orangeburg							x												

LOCATIONS OF GERMAN-SPEAKING CONGREGATIONS

IN THE UNITED STATES, 1906--*Continued*

State & County	01	02	03	04	05	06	07	08	09	10	11	12	13	14	15	16	17	18	19
South Carolina--*Cont.*																			
Richland							x												
Saluda							x												
Spartanburg							x												
Sumter							x												
South Dakota*																			
Aurora									x		x								
Beadie									x		x								
Bonhomme									x		x								
Brookings									x										
Brown									x		x								
Brule									x		x								
Buffalo											x								
Campbell									x		x								
Charles Mix									x										
Clark									x										
Codington									x										
Davison									x		x								
Day									x										
Dewey									x										
Douglas									x		x								
Edmunds									x		x								
Fall River											x								
Faulk									x										
Grant									x		x								
Gregory									x		x								
Hamlin									x		x								
Hanson									x										
Hutchinson									x		x								
Jerauld									x										
Kingsbury											x								
Lake									x		x								
Lyman									x										
McCook									x										
McPherson									x		x								
Miner									x										
Minnehaha									x										
Moody									x										
Potter									x										
Roberts									x		x								
Spink									x		x								
Stanley									x										
Sully									x										
Turner									x										
Union									x										
Walworth									x		x								
Yankton									x		x								
Tennessee*																			
Anderson																	x		
Bedford																	x		

LOCATIONS OF GERMAN-SPEAKING CONGREGATIONS
IN THE UNITED STATES, 1906--Continued

State & County	01	02	03	04	05	06	07	08	09	10	11	12	13	14	15	16	17	18	19
Tennessee--Cont.																			
Carroll																		x	
Carter																		x	
Cocke							x											x	
Coffee																		x	
Davidson																		x	
Dickson																		x	
Greene							x											x	
Hamblen							x											x	
Hamilton																		x	
Jefferson																		x	
Knox							x											x	
Lawrence																		x	
Lincoln																		x	
Montgomery							x												
Sevier																		x	
Sullivan							x												
Union																		x	
Washington							x											x	
Texas*																			
Austin									x		x								
Bastrop											x								
Baylor									x										
Bell									x		x								
Bexar					x						x								
Blanco											x								
Bosque					x				x										
Brazos					x				x										
Burleson					x				x		x								
Caldwell											x								
Calhoun											x								
Clay									x										
Colorado					x						x								
Comal					x														
Coryell									x		x								
Cottle									x										
Dallas					x				x										
De Witt									x										x
Denton					x				x										
Donley									x										
Eastland									x										
El Paso									x										
Falls					x				x		x								
Fannin									x										
Fayette					x				x		x								x
Fort Bend					x				x										
Galveston											x								
Gillespie					x						x								

[Texas denomination 19 = German Evangelical Lutheran Synod of Texas.]

LOCATIONS OF GERMAN-SPEAKING CONGREGATIONS

IN THE UNITED STATES, 1906--*Continued*

State & County	01	02	03	04	05	06	07	08	09	10	11	12	13	14	15	16	17	18	19
Texas--*Cont.*																			
Goliad											x								x
Gonzales																			x
Grayson									x										
Grimes									x										
Guadalupe					x				x										
Hamilton									x		x								
Harris					x				x										
Haskell											x								
Hays					x														
Hill									x		x								
Howard									x										
Jefferson									x										
Kendall											x								
Kerr											x								
Lavaca									x		x								x
Lee									x		x								
Leon									x										
Llano											x								
McLennan					x						x								
Madison									x										
Mason											x								
Matagorda									x										
Medina											x								
Milam					x				x		x								x
Mills											x								x
Montague									x										
Orange									x										
Robertson					x														
Runnels					x						x								
Tarrant					x				x										
Taylor									x										
Tom Green					x														
Travis					x				x		x								
Uvalde											x								
Victoria																			x
Waller									x										
Washington					x				x		x								
Wharton									x		x								
Wichita									x										
Wilbarger									x										
Williamson					x				x		x								
Wise									x										
Young									x										

[Texas denomination 19 = German Evangelical Lutheran Synod of Texas.]

Virginia*

Albemarle																		x	
Alleghany			x																x

[Virginia denomination 19 = The Brethren Church (Progressive Dunkers).]

LOCATIONS OF GERMAN-SPEAKING CONGREGATIONS
IN THE UNITED STATES, 1906--Continued

State & County	01	02	03	04	05	06	07	08	09	10	11	12	13	14	15	16	17	18	19
Virginia--*Cont.*																			
Amherst																			x
Augusta		x					x										x	x	
Bedford		x																	x
Bland							x												
Botetourt		x					x												
Campbell		x																	
Carroll		x					x												
Craig							x												
Culpeper							x												
Fairfax		x																	
Fauquier		x																x	
Floyd		x					x												x
Franklin		x																	x
Frederick		x					x										x	x	
Giles							x												
Grayson		x																	
Greene		x																x	
Highland		x																x	
Loudoun																	x		
Lunenburg																			x
Madison		x					x												
Montgomery		x					x												
Orange		x																x	
Page		x					x												
Patrick		x																	
Pittsylvania		x																	x
Prince William		x					x											x	
Pulaski							x												
Rappahannock																			x
Roanoke		x					x												x
Rockbridge							x											x	x
Rockingham		x					x										x	x	x
Scott							x												
Shenandoah		x					x										x	x	x
Smyth							x												
Tazewell							x												
Warren																		x	x
Washington		x					x												
Wythe							x												
Bristol City							x												
Buena Vista City		x					x												x
Lunchburg City							x												
Newport News City							x												
Norfolk City							x												
Richmond City							x												
Roanoke City		x					x										x	x	x
Staunton City		x					x											x	
Winchester City							x										x	x	

[Virginia denomination 19 = The Brethren Church (Progressive Dunkers).]

LOCATIONS OF GERMAN-SPEAKING CONGREGATIONS

IN THE UNITED STATES, 1906--*Continued*

State & County	01	02	03	04	05	06	07	08	09	10	11	12	13	14	15	16	17	18	19
West Virginia																			
Barbour		x																x	
Berkeley		x				x												x	
Boone**																			
Braxton		x																x	
Brooke**																			
Cabell																		x	
Calhoun																		x	
Clay**																			
Doddridge		x																x	
Fayette**																			
Gilmer		x																x	
Grant		x								x								x	
Greenbrier		x																x	
Hampshire		x																x	
Hancock**																			
Hardy										x								x	
Harrison						x												x	
Jackson																		x	
Jefferson						x													
Kanawha		x								x									
Lewis																		x	
Lincoln**																			
Logan**																			
McDowell**																			
Marion						x												x	
Marshall								x											
Mason																		x	
Mercer		x																	
Mineral		x				x												x	
Mingo**																			
Monongalia		x						x											
Monroe		x																	
Morgan																		x	
Nicholas**																			
Ohio						x		x		x									
Pendleton		x								x								x	
Pleasants																		x	
Pocahontas		x																	
Preston		x				x												x	
Putnam																		x	
Raleigh		x																	
Randolph		x				x												x	
Ritchie																		x	
Roane																		x	
Summers**																			
Taylor		x				x												x	
Tucker						x												x	
Tyler																		x	
Upshur		x																x	
Wayne**																			

LOCATIONS OF GERMAN-SPEAKING CONGREGATIONS
IN THE UNITED STATES, 1906--*Continued*

State & County	01	02	03	04	05	06	07	08	09	10	11	12	13	14	15	16	17	18	19
West Virginia--*Cont.*																			
Webster**																		x	
Wetzel																	x		
Wirt																	x		
Wood								x									x		
Wyoming**																			
Wisconsin																			
Adams									x										
Ashland			x					x	x										
Barron			x					x	x	x	x								
Bayfield								x	x		x								
Brown			x						x	x					x		x		
Buffalo			x						x		x						x		
Burnett								x											
Calumet			x	x					x								x		
Chippewa			x						x		x								
Clark			x	x					x	x							x		
Columbia			x	x					x	x	x					x			
Crawford			x						x		x								
Dane								x	x	x	x				x		x		
Dodge			x						x	x	x					x	x		
Door			x						x	x					x				
Douglas			x					x	x		x								
Dunn			x						x		x								
Eau Claire			x	x				x	x		x								
Florence								x											
Fond du Lac			x	x					x		x						x	x	
Forest				x					x										
Grant			x	x				x	x	x	x								
Green			x	x					x	x							x		
Green Lake			x						x										
Iowa			x						x		x								
Iron									x										
Jackson								x	x								x		
Jefferson			x	x				x	x	x	x				x				
Juneau			x						x								x		
Kenosha			x					x	x	x									
Kewaunee			x						x										
La Crosse			x					x	x	x									
Lafayette			x	x													x		
Langlade			x	x					x	x									
Lincoln				x				x	x	x									
Manitowoc			x	x					x								x		
Marathon			x	x				x	x	x						x	x		
Marinette			x	x				x	x								x		
Marquette			x						x		x								
Milwaukee			x	x				x	x		x					x	x		
Monroe			x						x										
Oconto			x	x				x	x	x	x								
Oneida				x				x	x										

LOCATIONS OF GERMAN-SPEAKING CONGREGATIONS

IN THE UNITED STATES, 1906--*Continued*

State & County	01	02	03	04	05	06	07	08	09	10	11	12	13	14	15	16	17	18	19
Wisconsin--Cont.																			
Outagamie			x		x				x	x					x		x		
Ozaukee			x		x			x	x		x								
Pepin								x	x		x								
Pierce					x			x	x		x								
Polk								x	x										
Portage					x				x	x	x								
Price								x	x		x								
Racine			x					x	x	x									
Richland			x						x		x								
Rock			x					x	x	x	x								
Rusk								x			x								
St. Croix			x					x	x	x						x			
Sauk			x					x	x	x	x						x		
Sawyer									x										
Shawano			x		x				x	x									
Sheboygan			x		x				x		x					x	x		
Taylor					x			x	x										
Trempealeau			x						x										
Vernon									x										
Vilas								x	x										
Walsworth			x		x				x	x									
Washburn								x	x		x								
Washington			x		x				x								x		
Waukesha			x		x				x								x		
Waupaca			x					x	x	x									
Waushara			x						x		x								
Winnebago			x		x				x	x	x						x		
Wood			x		x			x	x	x	x			x					

LANGUAGE AND ONOMASTICS

GERMANIC TRIBES AND DIALECTS

CLASSES OF GERMAN SURNAMES

INTERNAL DIALECTAL CLUES IN GERMAN SURNAMES

PERSONAL, OR CHRISTIAN, NAMES

GERMAN SURNAMES IN AMERICA

When the mainly illiterate German immigrants to eighteenth-century Pennsylvania came to be registered by the government--on the occasion of entry into the Province, the rendering of oaths of allegiance, taxation, and military service--they encountered officials unfamiliar with their language. German surnames became distorted, first through the peasant dialects the immigrants spoke and second through the attempts of English-speaking officials to reproduce on paper what they heard. Since most of the officials in eastern and central Pennsylvania during this period were Scotch-Irish themselves, the German surnames took on orthographic traits of Scotland and Ulster; thus a German surname, perhaps Richartzbach, became Rickabaugh and so on. It is, therefore, axiomatic that the surnames of eighteenth-century German immigrants have become widely distorted in spelling; those of the nineteenth century and thereafter, on the other hand, are likely to preserve acceptable German orthography, reflecting both the improved literacy of the immigrants and the heightened sophistication of American officials. Researchers in German-American genealogy can use this observation to estimate very roughly the date of arrival of a German immigrant to America.

GERMANIC TRIBES AND DIALECTS

Germany is not a homogenous nation; it is in fact a collection of peoples of diverse cultures and languages. The historical leitmotiv of the country has been the struggle, never completed, to attain unity. Researchers need some knowledge of the cultural differences in order to understand the rich variety of German personal names, their dialectic origins, and the effect dialect has had on the German-American adaptations of these names.

To begin with, a German ancestor rarely referred to himself by the political unit from which he came, but to the ancient tribal group to which he belonged and to one of whose dialects he normally spoke. Thus, an emigrant from Baden or Württemberg is less likely to have referred to himself as a Badenser or Württemberger than as a Swabian, the Alemannic tribal group which has, since Roman times, lived in the territory now called Baden-Württemberg, and to *Schwäbisch*, one of about four major dialects of the Alemannen. In like manner, a person of the northern lowlands would more likely have identified himself as a Low German, a Westphalian, or a Rhinelander, than to have named the political entity in which he was born. Tribal areas are not contiguous with political boundaries and never have been; always there have been cultural enclaves and exclaves within, and without, the political units.

It is thought that the homeland of the Germanic peoples before the Roman occupation of western Europe was in southern Scandinavia, Denmark, and Schleswig-Holstein. Beginning in Roman times, Germanic tribes were pushing south and westward out of their northern homelands. Two major groups, the Alemannen and the Bajuwaren, settled in the rolling lands on the northern flanks of the Alps. The Alemannen, to the westward in modern-day Baden-Württemberg, Switzerland, and the Alsace (France), are exceedingly important to the German-American genealogical researcher interested in eighteenth-century immigration, because a large part of the immigration was from Alemannic territories. These immigrants spoke local dialects of a general Swabian variety of German. Directly to the east of the Alemannen were the Bajuwaren, the modern-day Bavarians and Austrians, whose immigration to the New

World was mainly a nineteenth-century phenomenon.

Directly north of the Alemannen and Bajuwaren was a far-flung tribe called the Franks or Franconians. Their tribal areas stretched from the Slavic lands in present-day Czechoslovakia westward along the Main, Mosel, and Rhine rivers into France (the Lorraine) and Luxemburg, and northwestward into Belgium and the Netherlands. The Franks were divided into several subgroups forming dialects and languages, even subcultures, all their own. Some of them, particularly the Palatines, were also important components in the eighteenth-century immigration to America.

North of the Franks were the Low Germans--a term referring not to any inferiority of culture or social condition, but to the fact that they lived in lands very little elevated above sea level. The territory of the Low Germans, a mixed group of Saxon and Frisian tribes, extended from the Zuider Zee on the west, northeastward to the lands of the Danes, and further eastward until it impinged upon lands of Slavic-speaking Wends (or Sorbs) and Poles. Low German immigration to the New World is a phenomenon almost entirely of the nineteenth century, despite the fact that, as a group, they are a venturesome, seafaring people, with easier access to America than Germans who came in the eighteenth century.

GERMANIC TRIBES, TERRITORIES, AND DIALECTS IN GERMANY

Tribal Groups	Modern National Territories	Present-day Dialects (in Germany only)
North Germanic	Norway Sweden Denmark Iceland (later) England (east coast)	
North Sea Germanic:		
Frisians	Germany Netherlands	Ostfriesisch Westfriesisch
Angles	England	
Saxons	Germany	Nordniedersächsisch, Mecklenburg-Pommerisch, Nordmärkisch, Mittelmärkisch, Westfälisch, Ostfälisch, Thuringisch-Obersächsisch
	Netherlands England	
Weser-Rhine Germanic:		
Franconians	Germany	Niederfränkisch, Ripuarisch, Mosel-Fränkisch, Rhein-Fränkisch, Rhein-Pfälzisch, Sudfränkisch, Ostfränkisch
	Netherlands Belgium France (Lorraine)	
Hessians	Germany	Hessisch
Elbe Germanic:		
Lombards	Italy (northern)	
Alemannen	Germany Switzerland Austria (Vorarlberg) France (Alsace)	Schwäbisch, Niederalemannisch
Bajuwaren	Germany (Bavaria) Austria	Nordbairisch, Mittelbairisch
East Germanic:		
Goths	)	
Vandals	) now submerged in France and Spain	
Burgundians	)	

Wedged between the Low Germans on the north and the Franks on the south was a large and vigorous tribe called the Saxons. Their territories on the east and southwest were threatened by Slavic groups--Bohemians, Moravians, Silesians (Poles)--and internally by large unassimilated Wendish (Sorbic) groups. Saxons, also did not immigrate to America until the nineteenth century, but then in a mighty flood.

In eastern Germany the linguistic and cultural characteristics become exceedingly complex. Centuries of German migrations and Slavic counter-migrations left ethnic pockets in great number and variety. The possibility of aggrandizement attracted hundreds of petty and great nobles from western Germany in the wake of the crusades. Religious persecution in Austria brought thousands of South Germans (Salzburgers) into the east during the sixteenth and seventeenth centuries. In like manner Jews and Huguenots from southwestern Germany and France settled in family groups, even in small villages otherwise inhabited by Slavs. Eastern Germany was, then, a colonial land of mainly unassimilated groups from the west superimposed upon an indigenous Slavic populace. As of 1945, when the great migration came about as a consequence of the fall of the Third Reich, all these groups were dissolved, swept aside in the westward march of the Slavic-speaking peoples inflamed by a new ideology, much as the Germans had been inflamed in their march eastward in the centuries before by a new religious impetus. Little remains today, excepting material monuments, of the diverse ethnic colonies; where individual ethnic inhabitants have survived, they are submerged, their distinctive cultures widely prohibited and decaying.

Cultural isolation, the rule in tribal regions, has fostered the existence of numerous dialects, all having their roots in a basic Aryan stock of words and concepts. The particularism of the tribal groups was a centrifugal force within the Holy Roman Empire German Nation; religion and higher education were centripetal forces. History and language are inextricable.

For genealogical researchers wishing to explore the development of the German language further than can be described here will find two recently published books of interest:

Chambers, W. Walker, and Wilkie, John R. *A Short History of the German Language*. London: Methuen & Co., 1970;

Waterman, John T. *A History of the German Language with Special Reference to the Cultural and Social Forces that Shaped the Standard Literary Language*. Seattle & London: University of Washington Press, 1966.

These books describe in some detail the development of the German language. Neither gives much attention to the dialects which most Germans still speak today, to one degree or another. What has happened in Germany is that, for general communication, the *Schriftsprache* (written language) or *Hochdeutsch* (High German) has been developed and, although used on all formal occasions--the stage, radio, television, publications, office, and school--it is likely to be replaced in the streets by older, more indigenous, dialects. And, even when speaking High German, the accents used in dialect come through clearly and strongly, attesting to the vigor and tenacity of ancient tribal folkways.

CLASSES OF GERMAN SURNAMES

The study of German surnames is of some usefulness to the genealogical researcher, because names often afford clues as to places of origin, at least in a regional sense. Unlike the names of England, those of Germany are of great variety, due mainly to the varying methods of fashioning them.

The patronymic, frequent in both countries, has greater variety in Germany than in England because of the numerous dialects of the German language. Where, in England, it would be hard to find many variations of patronymics such as Jacobs or Jacobson, in Germany there are many--Jacob, Jacober, Jacobi, Jacobs, Jacobsen, Jacobsohn, Jakobs, Jakobi, Jäck, Jack, Jäckle, Jäggli, Jacke, Jockl, Köbi, Köbes, Köpkes, Köppen, not to mention about ten other forms from eastern Germany reflecting the influence of Slavic and Lithuanian cultures.

Another considerable class of surnames in both Germany and England has to do with ancestral occupation. But here, again, dialectic variations have led to a multitude of surnames in Germany. The Smiths of England are met in Germany by Schmid, Schmitt, Schmitz, Schmidt, Schmedeke, Schmiedel, Schmiedecke, Smid, Smedes, Smets, Smieds, and even the name Eisenhauer (distorted to Eisenhower in America) is but another designation for the same profession. And, since most of the German Schmid-Schmidt-Schmitz immigrants to eighteenth-century America promptly had their names changed to Smith upon arrival, it can be asserted that more Americans of this surname are of German than of English origin. Another example of the variety of surnames arising from one profession, that of butcher, is again attributable to dialectic variation: A butcher in southern Germany is a Metzger or Mezeler; in other regions of Germany he is a Schlachter (then changed to Slaughter in America), Schlächter, Fleischer, Fleischner, Fleischhauer, Fleischhaker, even Knochenhauer. It would be a useful tool to have a list of the common terms for occupations in the various German dialects, if for no other reason than to suggest some of the surnames translatable into their English equivalents upon immigration to America.

Another category of German surname is that based upon a physical attribute or a humorous appellation. One would not easily find an English equivalent for Krumbein (crooked leg), but the Grumbines of Pennsylvania were originally Krumbeins in Germany; nor would one likely find an English name similar to Kukuk (coo-coo) or Blöd (silly) or Uebler (evildoer).

One category of German surnames—a very common one—has some equivalence in English practice. Particularly in southwestern Germany it was customary to take the name of one's village as surname. Among commoners this was usually done by adding an -er suffix to the place name; thus, Bamberg becomes Bamberger, Frankfurt becomes Frankfurter. A similar practice among nobles was to add a preposition (von or zu) to the place name; thus, von Eschenbach, von und zu Löwenstein.

Onomastics has been more thoroughly studied, it seems, in Germany than in English-speaking countries, probably because of the greater variety of personal names and because of the German academic interest in linguistics. Although there is no complete or definitive reference work on German surnames, there are a number of lists which may contain a surname of interest to the genealogical researcher. Here are some of the important ones:

Bach, Adolf. *Die deutschen Personennamen* [German personal names] 2 vols in 4 parts. Heidelberg: Carl Winter-Universitätsverlag, 1952.

A very thorough discussion of the literature, bringing the study of onomastics up-to-date.

Bahlow, Hans. *Deutsches Namenlexikon: Familien- und Vornamen nach Ursprung und Sinn erklärt* [German name lexicon: family and Christian names explained according to origin and meaning] Munich: Keysersche Verlagsbuchhandlung GmbH., 1967.

This handy book can also be obtained as a paperback in the Suhrkamp Taschenbuch edition.

Brechenmacher, Josef Karlmann. *Etymologisches Wörterbuch der deutschen Familiennamen* [Etymological dictionary of German surnames] 2d ed., 2 vols. Limburg/Lahn: C. A. Starke-Verlag, 1957.

A lengthy compilation of names collected from ancient tax, citizenship, and other lists before the "Ueberfremdung"

(literally, the over-alienation or introduction of undesirable foreign elements).

Gottschald, Max. *Deutsche Namenkunde: Unsere Familiennamen nach Entstehung und Bedeutung* [German onomastics: our surnames according to origin and meaning] 4th ed. Berlin: Walter de Gruyter & Co., 1971.

Has many of the same surnames as in the Heintze-Cascorbi below.

Heintze, Albert. . . . *Die deutschen Familiennamen; geschichtlich, geographisch, sprachlich* [. . . German surnames historically, geographically, linguistically (explained)] 7th ed. rev. & enl. by Paul Cascorbi. Halle & Berlin: Buchhandlung des Waisenhauses GmbH., 1933.

This authoritative work, from which many of the observations presented hereinafter have been gleaned, is often called "the Heintze-Cascorbi." It lists thousands of German surnames, giving origins and metamorphoses.

INTERNAL DIALECTAL CLUES
IN GERMAN SURNAMES

A distinctive feature of many German family names is the existence of internal clues as to their origins—the prefixes, suffixes, occasionally the internal vowel shifts and consonant combinations. Listed hereinafter are such clues. They should be used with caution, as they do not invariably apply, but in general they will help the researcher to make hypotheses as to the regions of origins of the families he seeks.

Surname Particle

-a   In East Friesland, and only there, some surnames end in the genitive plural; thus, Wiarda, Ebbinga, Reemtsma, Ukena, Beninga, Bojunga, Hajunga, Mennenga, Thedinga. Note, however, that -a and -ma suffixes are entirely missing from surnames of the Jeverland region of East Friesland.

Accent marks   *see under* Frenchified German surnames

-ack   A particle in Wendisch (Sorbic) surnames; thus, Noack.

-aff or -laff   A suffix appearing in Wendisch (Sorbic) surnames; thus, Mitzlaff. Also commonly encountered in Slavic names, as in Bogislaw, transcribed Boguslaff.

*Surname
Particle*

-ai-, -ay-	In Hessen-Darmstadt the internal particles -ai- and -ay- often replace the normal -ei-; thus, Mayer instead of Meyer, Hainz rather than Heinz. In Swabian and Bavarian areas -ai- also replaces -ei- with frequency, thus Aichele, Sailer, Stainer, Schnaithmann, Crailsheim, Waiblingen.
-aitis, -atis, -at, -eit	Lithuanian surname suffixes which are found in Germany among families formerly in the Memel, Tilsit, and Heidekrug administrative districts of East Prussia. In Germany, these suffixes usually are shortened to the -at or -eit form; thus, Petschulat, Josupeit.
American- ized German names	*see* German Surnames in America in this article
-atz	A suffix found in Wendisch (Slavic) surnames; thus, Glabbatz.
Auf dem	Prepositional particles found in Westphalian surnames; thus, auf dem Brauke.
-bach, -bacher	A frequent suffix (-bach) in south-western German place names (it means pond); thus Sulzbach, Auerbach, Amorbach. When used in personal names it ordinarily becomes -bacher; thus, Sulzbacher, Auerbacher.
-beck	A Westphalian particle and spelling variation of -bach; thus Möllenbeck.
-bek	Similar to -beck but found mainly in Schleswig-Holstein; thus, Reinbek.
-berg, -berger	A place name suffix (it means hill) in southern Germany, particularly. When used in personal names it becomes -berger; thus, Miltenberg makes Miltenberger. In southwestern Germany two-thirds of all surnames in some areas have -berger suffixes.
-borg	In the Oldenburger lowlands, the suffix -borg often replaces the more usual -burg.
-bostel	A Westphalian suffix in place names; thus, Fallingbostel, Rodenbostel. It may occasionally occur in personal names.

*Surname
Particle*

Brink-, -brink, -brinker	A Westphalian and Eastphalian particle (meaning grassy place or pasture); thus, Hasenbrink, Steinbrinker.
Brock-, -brock	A Westphalian and Eastphalian particle (meaning bridge); thus, Uhlenbrock, Brockmeyer.
-brugger	A Swabian suffix; thus Moosbrugger.
-burg, -burger	The -burg suffix (meaning fortress) occurs frequently in place names throughout Germany. When used in surnames, the -burger form is used; thus, Hamburg makes Hamburger, Coburg makes Coburger.
-diek	A Westphalian particle (meaning a pond); thus, Buddendiek, Griesediek.
-é	*see under* Frenchified German surnames
-ecke	*see* -icke
-eder, -öder	Bavarian personal name suffixes; thus, Hocheder, Ameisöder.
-egg, -egger	Swabian personal name suffixes; thus, Königsegg, Danegger.
-eit	*see* -aitis
-ek	A Wendisch surname particle; thus, Peschek. In Upper Silesia frequently found; thus Adamek.
-el	A diminutive personal name suffix often found in the southern part of Saxony; thus, Hähnel, Seidel, Siegel, Weigel, Barthel, Jäckel.
-en	*see* Patronymics
English surnames in Germany	Since the end of the seventeenth century there have been some Scottish surnames in East Prussia; thus, Douglas, Forster, Hobson, Kant, Motherby, Oldsloe, Pickering.
-er	A very frequent southern German surname ending to place names. It is also found accompanied by an umlaut; thus, Strassburger, Weinsberger, Dillinger, and Dörrenbecher, Oppenhäuser, Lichtenthäler.
-et, -eth	In Switzerland the German suffixes -hard and -hart are often abbreviated to -et; thus, Bernhard becomes Bernet, Ehrhart becomes Ehret.

*Surname
Particle*

Frenchi- | Examples of transliterations: Sol-
fied | ger=Saulier, Nagler=Naguillier,
German | Witzel=Ficelle, Kleemann=Clément,
Sur- | Vogler=Fouclair. The affectation
names | of Frenchified surnames was especi-
ally prevalent in Thuringia. Examples of added accent marks to
preserve original pronunciations:
Nestle=Nestlé, Kothe=Kothé,
Nägele=Nägelé. This became necessary in areas where local dialects
tended to omit the final endings.
In America same purpose was accom-
plished by adding -ey or -y; thus,
Kothé became Coty.

French | Families with French surnames were
Surnames | frequently encountered in the Eupen
in Ger- | and Malmedy districts, Luxemburg,
many | and in the Alsace and Lorraine;
thus, Dieudonné, Dollibois. Usually, these surnames have retained
their original French form, though
the German pronunciation of them
may leave something to be desired.
In the cities of Germany there
were also many Huguenot families
originally from France.

-gard | A German variation of the Slavic
-gorod (meaning fortress).

-gen | A Lower Rheinland diminutive suf-
fix, prevalent in Franconian dialects.

-halter | An exclusively Swabian suffix; thus,
Winterhalter.

-hammer | A Bavarian variation of the more
normal -heimer; thus, Niethammer,
Esterhammer (for Oesterheimer).

-hard, | A frequent High German suffix; *see
-hart | also* -et and -eth.

-haus | A Westphalian suffix (meaning house).

-heim, | A common place name suffix in south-
-heimer | western Germany, becoming -heimer in
personal names; thus, Flörsheim makes
Flörsheimer, Heppenheim makes Heppen-
heimer.

-hövel | A Westphalian suffix (meaning hill);
thus, Windhövel, van den Hövel.

-hofer, | A south German suffix; -hofer is
-höfer | more frequent than -höfer.

-hof, | A Westphalian particle (meaning a
-hoff | farmstead). In Münster and the
northern parts of Minden and

Arnsberg administration districts,
where farmsteads are solitary rather
than collected in villages, there
are many names, both geographic and
personal, containing this particle;
thus, Lohoff.

-holt | A Westphalian particle (meaning woods);
thus, Eichholt.

-horn | A Westphalian suffix in place names;
thus, Ehrhorn, Gifhorn.

-horst, | A Westphalian and Eastphalian suffix;
-hörster | thus, Behrhorst becomes Behrhörster
in the surname form.

-hues | A particle found in Münsterland (West-
phalia) substituting for the more
usual one -haus; thus Grothues.

Hungarian- | Occasionally German surnames have
ized Ger- | been "Hungarianized," usually by
man Sur- | simply twisting syllables; thus,
names | Bamberger=Vambéry, Hundsdörfer=
Hunfalvy, Benkert=Kertbeny. The
practice was common only in Austria.

-husen | A Low (northern) German place name
particle, the equivalent of -hausen
in High German; thus, Kellinghusen.

-i, | A diminutive particle typically Swiss;
-y | thus, Erni, Bläsi, Rudy.

-iak | In Silesia frequently encountered;
thus Stepaniak.

-ich, | A place name particle, particularly
-nich | north of the Mosel River in the
Lower Rhineland.

-ick | A Wendisch surname particle; thus,
Petrick, Nowick.

-icke, | A diminutive particle found especi-
-ecke | ally in Hessen and Thuringia; thus,
Heinicke, Meinecke, Fricke.

-iecki | A Slavic surname suffix; thus Lisi-
ecki (pronounced Lisiëzki).

-ien | Wendisch surname suffix.

-in | This is a feminine ending on any sur-
name. Particularly common in eighteenth-century German-American documents are names, such as Müllerin,
Schmidtin, Meyerin, etc., indicating
that a woman, usually married, was
referred to. Genealogists should
eliminate or ignore this ending,

*Surname
Particle*

equating such names with Müller, Schmidt, and Meyer in modern terms. The suffix also occurs in Wendisch place names and in surnames stemming from them.

-ing
In the Papenburg administrative district of northern Hannover the -ing suffix appears in about fifty percent of all surnames. It becomes less frequent the further southward one goes and disappears near the Saale River.

-ingen, -inger
A Swabian place name suffix typical of Württemberg and Baden. It becomes -inger when used in personal names; thus, Zähringen makes Zähringer.

-inski
Frequently encountered in Upper Silesia; thus, Lipinski.

Italianized German surnames
Occasionally German singers have "Italianized" their otherwise ordinary German surnames; thus, Stiegele became Stighelli, Crüwell became Cruvelli, Röder became Rodani. Such modifications are not to be confused with real Italian surnames which are to be found in Germany, usually among descendants of Italian trading families, such as von Brentano.

-itz
A Wendisch surname suffix; thus, Wiebelitz.

-ius
see Latinized German surnames

-je
An East Frisian diminutive suffix.

-kamp, -kämper
A Westphalian and Eastphalian suffix; thus, Bornkamp, Roggenkämper.

-ke
A Westphalian and Eastphalian diminutive suffix, particularly prevalent in the eastern-most areas near the lands of the Wends and Altmark; thus, Lemke, Wilke, Jahnke. *See also* -schke, -ske, -ski, -zke

-ken
A Lower Rhenish diminutive suffix.

-kk-
In East Friesland a double -kk- sometimes appears in a surname; thus, Dekker for Decker.

Kötter-, -kötter
A Westphalian particle (meaning a cottage dweller).

-kofer
A Bavarian personal name suffix; thus, Hüttenkofer.

*Surname
Particle*

-1
A diminutive particle to be found in many areas of Germany, even in the German Northeast, but typical of Bavaria and Austria. Its occurrence in northeastern Germany is due entirely to the forced emigration of protestant Salzburgers, however; thus, Märkl, Simmerl, Hocherl.

-laff
see -aff

Latinized German surnames
During the periods in which Latin was an important means of communication, a number of German surnames were Latinized; so, for example, Pastorius, of fame in early-day Pennsylvania, probably stems from the common German surname Schäfer, meaning shepherd.

-le
In Baden the diminutive form is typical; thus, Merkle, Bürkle, Enderle, Eberle. The suffix is also used in 75 percent of the Württemberg and Hohenzollern personal names, thus Bäuerle, Mayerle, Schwämmle.

-leb
In Hessen the Saxon and Thuringian suffix -leben is usually abbreviated; thus, Witzleben becomes Witzleb.

-leben
A suffix common in Saxony and Thuringia.

-lein
A diminutive suffix, especially in Thuringia; thus, Henlein, Gäbelein.

Leiter, Leitner, Leutner
Bavarian derivations from *Leite*, a cliff. Stands alone or as suffix.

-ler
A Bavarian suffix; thus, Hitler, Bichler.

-li
A diminutive particle typically Swiss; thus, Merkli.

-lin
A diminutive particle in the Upper Rhenish districts and westward to the Alsace, especially in the Palatinate; thus, Bürklin, Bundlin, Sütterlin, Oberlin, Köchlin.

Loh-, -loh
A Westphalian particle (meaning a thicket); thus, Lohoff.

-ma
Only found in East Friesland. *see also* -a

Maier-, -maier, -mayer
A frequent prefix and suffix in Bavaria and Württemberg and always spelled with 'a'; thus, Steinmaier, Katzenmaier, Stegmayer.

*Surname
Particle*

-mann   A German surname suffix so wide-spread as to give no clues to geographic origin.

Meyer-,
-meyer   This particle is very widely encountered in Westphalian and East-phalian surnames; thus, Brinkmeyer, Meyerhoff. It originally signified the administrator of a noble estate but came to mean a farmer of means. The particle Meyer- is usual in Eastphalia, and the particle -meyer in Westphalia.

Möller   This spelling of the surname Müller frequently occurs in Hessen.

-moos,
-mooser,
-moser   A Bavarian place name suffix which becomes -mooser or -moser in personal names; thus, Entmoos becomes Entmooser.

-ner   A Bavarian and Austrian personal name suffix; thus, Hubner, Löschner, Mautner.

-nich   *see* -ich

-nick   A suffix found in Wendisch (Slavic) surnames; thus, Bausnick.

-o,
-o-   An ancient Germanic particle which survives most frequently in Westphalia; thus, Teuto, Danco, Otto. In Low (northern) German -o- often replaces another vowel in High German; thus, Soltwedel instead of Salzwedel, Moller and Möller instead of Müller. *See also* Möller

-ou-   In East Prussia an -ou- often replaces an -au-; thus, Wildebouer instead of Wildebauer.

-ow   Frequently encountered place name suffix in Dannenberg district having a Wendisch (Slavic) origin; also found further eastward in areas contested with the Slavs; thus, Flotow, Grabow, Vangerow. Note, however, that the 'w' is silent.

-owski   A Polish surname suffix. *See also* Polishized German Surnames. Note, however, that there are many thousands of Germans with real Polish surnames, particularly in Upper Silesia, a mining area. Many Silesian miners then migrated to the Ruhr mining and smelting region of western Germany in the nineteenth and twentieth centuries.

*Surname
Particle*

P-,
-p   In Bavaria 'P' often replaces 'B' in customary in other areas; thus, Brücker becomes Prücker, Pannebecher becomes Pannepecher.

Patronymics   Particularly prevalent in the genitive form (with -s, -en, or -sen) in East Friesland and Jeverland; over half the surnames in Aurich and Emden regions and about one-third of those in the Leer region are so formed; thus, Reiners, Gerdes, Gerjets, Dirks, Focken, Rippen, Tjaden, Ufken, Bennens, Dudden, Habben, Hayen, Heeren, Jansen, Mommen, Onken, Popken, Folkers, Gerels, Harms, Sybolts. In Stadeland and Bütjadingen: Lübsen, Siebsen, Tanzen. In Osterstade and Wührden: Betken, Campsen, Hancken, Pecksen. In Land Würsten: Adickes, Camps, Frers, Johanns, Lubs, Pecks. In North Friesland: Andresen, Christiansen, Claussen, Janssen, Johansen, Lützen, Mommsen, Paulsen, Petersen, Thomsen, Todsen. Note that in Jeverland patronymics ending in -en and -sen account for eighty percent of all surnames, but that -a and -ma endings are entirely absent. In Schleswig -sen endings are found on ninety percent of all surnames, but in neighboring Eckernförde they disappear almost entirely.

Patronymics with -s endings are extremely important also in the Koblenz and Trier governmental regions; thus, Henrichs, Reichartz, Caspers, Eckes. They are also very common in Oldenburg; thus, Redlefs, Oltmanns, Rienitz (or Rienits).

Place
Names
as Sur-
names   In Hessen place names are used as surnames without any endings; thus, Henneberg, Sonnefeld.

Polishized
German
Surnames   Reflecting the propinquity of Germans and Poles in Prussia and Silesia, many German surnames have been spelled according to Polish orthography; thus, Schulz=Szulc, Schumann=Szuman, Schreiber=Szraiber. Another mode of "Polishizing" German surnames was to add the -owski suffix to the German root; thus, Feldmann=Feldmanowski, Krautshofer=Krauthofski.

Professional
Names   Although common, in one form or another, in all parts of Germany, Westphalians were apt to be more descriptive or specific; thus Bowenschulte, Brankschröder, Oberste-Kampmann.

*Surname
Particle*

-r   In southern German dialects the normal -er suffix is sometimes elided to -r, or dropped entirely; thus, Pfarrer becomes Pfarr, Bräuer becomes Bräu.

-rath   A place name particle, especially north of the Mosel River in the Lower Rhineland.

-reuth, -reuther, -reut   A Bavarian place name suffix becoming -reuther in personal names; thus, Bayreuth, Hütschenreuther.

-ried, -rieder   A Bavarian and Swabian place name suffix which becomes -rieder in surnames; thus, Bernried becomes Bernrieder.

-roth   A place name suffix, replacing -rath in the Cologne district of the Lower Rhineland and eastward to Thuringia.

-s   *see* Patronymics

-scheid   A place name suffix, especially north of the Mosel River in the Lower Rhineland.

-schke   Frequently occurs in eastern Pomerania where it substitutes for the Polish -ski ending; thus, Paaschke.

Schmid   This is the common form of the surname in Württemberg.

Schmidt   Frequently encountered in Hessen.

-sen   Mainly a patronymic suffix but is also a Westphalian particle in place names (an abbreviation of -heim); thus, Bellersen (Bellersheim), Wennigsen (Wennigsheim).

-ske, -zke   In eastern Pomerania often substitutes for the Polish -ski particle.

-ski -sky   A Polish surname suffix, often written in German -sky; thus, Kaminsky, Loschitzky. Frequently used with a patronymic to denote "son of;" thus, Adamski, Jakubski, Janski.

Sm-   In East Friesland Sch- becomes Sm-; thus, Smidt for Schmidt.

Ten-   A prepositional particle found in Westphalian surnames; thus, Tenberge.

Ter-   A prepositional particle found in Westphalian surnames; thus, Terbeck.

*Surname
Particle*

-tj-   In East Friesland a -tj- sometimes appears in a surname; thus, Tjark for Tiark, Warntjes for Warnties, Luitjens for Lütgens.

-tsch   A diminutive suffix similar to -z found mainly in Electoral Hessen; thus, Fritsch, Götsch replacing Fritze and Götze.

Tzsch-, -tzsch   *see* Zsch-

-üsch   A suffix found in Wendisch (Slavic) surnames; thus, Gramüsch.

-ui-   In East Friesland an -ui- particle often substitutes for the more normal -ü-; thus, Lütgen becomes Luitjens.

-uo-   In southern German -uo- occasionally replaces -u-; thus, Ruof, Schraishuon. Rare.

van   A prepositional prefix frequently found in Westphalian and Dutch surnames; thus, van den Berg (Westphalian) and van Hoogstraten (Dutch).

von   A prepositional prefix in nearly all noble surnames. However, it is not exclusively of noble usage. When found in lists of the nobility (or in muster rolls) it is nearly always abbreviated; thus, v. Kleist-Retzow. When written out in muster rolls it may refer to a commoner; thus, Von der Aa.

-wangen, -wanger, -wänger   An exclusively Swabian place name suffix which becomes -wanger or -wänger in surnames; thus, Ellwangen, the town, and Ellwanger the person, Naiswangen and Naiswanger.

-z, -ze   A diminutive form found in both High and Low German dialects; thus, Barz, Kunze. Sometimes the diminutive is doubled, as in Neitzke, Neitzel, Wetzel.

-zke   *see* -ske

Zsch-, -zsch, -tzsch   Found in Saxon personal names showing the Slavic influence; thus, Fritzsche, Klotzsche, Zschweigert, Zschinsky, Tschucke, Tzschackel.

PERSONAL, OR CHRISTIAN, NAMES

German personal names are of two main types, the ancient ones of the Germanic tribes and the biblical ones. Use of these names has varied considerably in place and time. The only general comment which can be made is that Lutherans and Catholics have diverged somewhat in namegiving, and this divergence can occasionally be useful to the genealogical researcher seeking to determine the religious affiliation of an ancestor. Hereinafter follows a summary of namegiving in several areas of German-speaking Europe over the centuries adapted from Karl Heinrichs' work entitled *Studien über die Namengebung in deutschen Seit dem Anfang des XVI. Jahrhunderts* [Studies regarding German namegiving since the sixteenth century] Strassburg: Karl J. Trübner, 1908:

Upper Alsace, Rufach. A Catholic district. The tax rolls of 1598 disclose no double names. By 1660 thirty percent of the male names were double, nearly always using Hans as the first of the pair; thus, in order of popularity:

Hans Jacob	Hans Martin	Hans Heinrich
Hans Diebolt	Hans Ulrich	Hans Baschen
Hans Jörg	Hans Wilhelm	Hans Paul
Hans Conrad	Hans Andreas	Johann Melchior

Other double names were Carly Ludwig, Görg Alexander, Philipps Heinrich, and Wende Christoph.

By the end of the nineteenth century the following were typical names in Rufach, sometimes elided in speaking:

Anna Maria (Annemarei, Annemei)

Maria Anna (Marianna)

Maria Rosa (Mariros)

Maria Therese

Maria Reginia

Franz Joseph (Franzsepp)

Franz Xaver

Johann Baptist (Schambetis, adapted from Jean-Baptiste)

Johann Peter (Schambiär, adapted from Jean-Pierre)

Germanic personal names, which had accounted for over two-thirds of all names in 1428, were no longer popular and by 1894 had fallen to only one-fourth.

Württemberg, Ulm. A mainly protestant area. Christenings recorded in the sixteenth century showed a marked preference for double names, usually the first being Hans (occasionally Johannes) plus an Old Testament name; for girls Maria and Anna were of about equal importance as forenames. The second or middle names for boys and girls were commonly:

Abraham	Jacob	Rebecca
Andreas	Jeremias	Samuel
Bartholomäus	Matthias	Sara
Gabriel	Michael	Zacharias
Gedeon	Petrus	

Among the non-biblical names Angelica, Apollonia, Barbara, Catharina, Christian, Georg, Magdalena, and Martin (only in protestant families, of course) were popular.

In the seventeenth century a number of additional Old Testament names became popular: Adam, Esther, Eva, Joseph, Josua, Moses, and Tobias. Additional Germanic names were also noted: Albrecht, Conrad, Gotthard, Leonhard.

Austria, Vienna. Almost entirely Catholic. In the late nineteenth century the frequency of forenames was as follows:

Carl	11.7%	Maria	16.7%
Joseph	9.6	Anna	10.0
Franz	9.3	Rosa(lie)	4.7
Johann	7.1	Leopoldine	4.6
Rudolf	5.3	Hermine	3.6
Leopold	4.4	Therese	3.6
Friedrich	3.1	Catharina	3.3
Otto	3.1	Johanna	3.0

Braunschweig (city). Strongly protestant. Double names became stylish only at the beginning of the seventeenth century. By the eighteenth century city-dwellers were again using single names, but use of double names continued in rural areas of the Duchy of Braunschweig until the middle of the nineteenth century. At the end of the nineteenth century city-dwellers were again giving double names to their children. In the local dialect, particularly in rural areas, double names tended to be elided; thus, Anna Dorothea became Anndortjen, Anna Sophie became Annefike, Catharine Sophie became Trinefike, and Johann Georg became Hannjörg.

Silesia, Görlitz. A mixed Catholic and protestant population. In the early eighteenth century both single and double names were to be found. Among boys with single names the following preferences were noted:

Johann	11.1%	Michael	4.0%
Christian	10.7	Andreas	4.0
Georg	10.0	Caspar	3.2
Gottfried	9.3	Elias	3.0
Christoph	7.0	Mathäus	3.0
Martin	4.3		

Old Testament names among protestants in order of preference were:

Elias	David	Michäus
Daniel	Jeremias	Nathaniel
Tobias	Hiob	Salomon

Only twenty percent of the boys were given double names; the first of the pair was usually Johann or Hans followed, in order of preference, by:

Georg	Friedrich	David
Christoph	Jacob	Gottfried
Heinrich	Caspar	Wilhelm
Christian	Daniel	

Other double names that appeared only occasionally were:

Carl Christoph	Florian Friedrich
Carl Gottfried	Friedrich Dietrich
Caspar Siegfried	Jeremias Victorinus
Christian Friedrich	Julius Ernst
Christian Gottlob	Otto Heinrich
Daniel Ludwig	Tobias Martin

In 1884 namegiving in Görlitz had changed markedly. The following preferences were noted:

Paul	14.5%	Wilhelm (Willi)	3.6%
Max	11.3	Otto	3.6
Richard	6.0	Arthur	3.3
Carl	5.6	Gustav	3.3
Alfred	4.0	Fritz	3.0
Bruno	4.0	Georg	3.0
		Hans	1.9

Occasionally, the names Hermann, Curt, Ernst, Oskar, Robert, Adolf, Emil, and Hugo occurred. In the Catholic primary school Franz and Joseph were popular names and Guido, Lorenz, Ottomar, Ignaz, and Hieronymus were used.

It is notable that the lowest social classes selected names from a smaller range of choices than did the higher classes.

Among feminine names in Görlitz the following were frequently found in the late nineteenth century:

Anna	12.0%	Bertha	4.3%
Martha	10.0	Margaretha	4.2
Emma	7.3	Helene	4.0
Maria	6.5	Hedwig	3.8
Clara	6.0	Ida	3.4
Elisabetha or Elise	5.5		

The names Gertrude, Selma, Agnes, Alma, Minna, Luise, Frida, Meta, Lina, Olga, Auguste, and Pauline also occurred.

Some general observations. Germans have tended to fashion derivative names (*Cosenamen*=cute names, or those of endearment) from some of the standard ones:

Standard Form	Derivatives
Johannes	Johann, Johanne (feminine), Hans
Nikolaus	Niklas, Claus (or Klaus)
Michael	Michel
Christoph	Stoffel
Andreas	Anders, Drews
Elisabeth	Elsbeth, Else, Elise
Margarethe	Grete, Gretel

They have also invented names reflecting religiosity, such as Gottlieb (God loving), Traugott (Trust God), Leberecht (Live Right), Himmelreich (Kingdom of Heaven).

GERMAN SURNAMES IN AMERICA

The surnames of eighteenth-century German immigrants to America underwent distinct, often drastic, changes in American official records. These changes can be summarized as follows:

¶ Wherever there was an obvious near-equivalent in English to the German surname, American officials were likely to use it, with or without permission of the bearer; thus, Schmid-Schmidt-Schmitz usually was recorded as Smith, Müller-Möller became Miller, Braun became Brown.

¶ Wherever there was a translatable equivalent for a German surname, some family members were likely sooner or later to adopt it, usually in the third generation and thereafter; thus, Zimmermann became Carpenter, Schneider became Taylor, Dürr became Dry, Gerber became Tanner, Bauer became Farmer.

¶ Wherever American pronunciation was confounded by German orthography, the German surname was likely to be changed in such manner as to preserve the original German pronunciation of it; thus, Ewald became Awalt, Dreier became Dryer, Meier-Maier became Myer, Koch became Cook, Bauer became Bower.

¶ Orthographic accommodations occurred in a large portion of the German surnames almost entirely with the intention of retaining the original pronunciation in dialect. As a consequence, genealogical researchers should consider all surnames which can be soundexed in the same class to be possible equivalents and their bearers to be related. *See* National Archives Soundex Rules *infra*

¶ Since many of the early-day officials in eastern Pennsylvania were Scotch-Irish, the orthographic changes in German surnames often betray Scotch-Irish spelling notions; thus, German surnames with the suffix -bach are frequently written -baugh; Strasbach becomes Strasbaugh, Richartzbach becomes Rickabaugh.

Very little can be said about orthographic shifts in German surnames for immigrants of the nineteenth century. In general, it appears that literacy was much higher than it had been among immigrants of the previous century and that the later immigrants tended to demand correct spelling of their surnames in American records. For that reason, genealogical researchers are less likely to encounter the anomalies common among surnames of eighteenth-century immigrants to America.

¶ When a German surname in America appears in the same form as it would in a modern-day telephone book of a German city, one can usually be certain it pertains to a family immigrating to America since the Civil War.

¶ Wherever a German surname in America still retains an umlauted vowel, such as

ä = ae, as in Hähnisch (in America, written Haehnisch)

ö = oe, as in Österreicher (in America, written Oesterreicher)

ü = ue, as in Dürr (in America, written Duerr),

it pertains almost certainly to an immigrant since the Civil War.

¶ As noted in a preceding section of this article, German immigration from Alemannic areas of Germany (Baden-Württemberg, Rheinland-Pfalz) antedates that of northern and eastern Germany and Bavaria by as much as a century. One can therefore state that, as a rule of thumb, Westphalian and Saxon surnames, of which there are very many in the United States, will be encountered only among nineteenth-century immigrants.

National Archives Soundex Rules[1]

The problem of indexing millions of names from a hundred countries, transliterated from several alphabets, syllabaries, even ideographies, would make accurate access to larger series of records in the National Archives--such as immigration records--an almost impossible task. As a consequence, during the 1930s, it was decided that records should be soundexed, not indexed. Rather than following the orthographic notions of either the immigrants or of officials of the U.S. Immigration and Naturalization Service, for example, it was decided that access should be through sound. To do this, similar sounds represented by a number of letters and combinations of letters in the various alphabets, were classed together. The result is that, when properly coded according to soundex rules, names which sound similar, though very different in orthography, are grouped together. For German-American genealogical researchers soundexing provides a powerful tool allowing them to consider together the most likely spelling variations of a surname and uncovering possible relationships between lineages apparently entirely unrelated. For example, the index to Strassburger's and Hinke's *Pennsylvania German Pioneers* shows the following entries for families of similar sounding surnames, some of which may be related, despite the spelling variations. Under soundex rules all these surname entries would have appeared together:

- Deile (Theyle)   - Teul

- Deill   - Theil (Teyle, Theyl)

- Diehl (Diel, Dihll,   - Thiel (Tiel, Dihl,
   Tiel, Till)   Tiell, Till)

- Diele   - Thiele (Teele)

- Doll (Dohl)   - Toll (Dill, Tholl)

- Dölle (Dolle)   - Tölly

General soundex rules. Surnames are coded according to the following code:

Code Class	Coded Letters
1	b, p, f, v
2	c, s, k, g, j, q, x, z
3	d, t
4	l
5	m, n
6	r
[7]	*see rule 1 below*

Rule 1: The letters a, e, i, o, u, y, w, and h are not coded.

Rule 2: The first letter of a surname is not coded.

Rule 3: Every soundex number must be a three-digit number. A name yielding no code numbers, as Lee, would thus be L000; one yielding one code number would have two zeros added, as Kuhne, coded as K500; and one yielding two code numbers would have one zero added, as Ebell, coded as E140. Not more than three digits are to be used, so Ebelson would be coded as E142, not E1425.

Rule 4: When two key letters or equivalents appear together, or one key letter immediately follows or precedes an equivalent, the two are coded as one letter, by a single number, as follows: Kelly, coded as K400; Buerck, coded as B620; Lloyd, coded as L300; and Schaefer, coded as S160.

Rule 5: Such prefixes as van, von, di, de, le, D', de la, or du are sometimes disregarded in alphabetizing and in coding.

Additional measures for German surnames. Despite the great power of the soundex system, further steps can be taken to enhance its usefulness in tracing German surnames. We suggest the following:

Step 1: After having coded the German surname under normal soundex rules above, compare it with all other initial letters of the same code class.

Example 1: Crumbine (C651), Grumbine (G651), and Krumbein (K651). Since C, G, and K are of the same code class 2 in the soundex rules, one is led to the assumption that the three surnames are variations. Because Krumbein is the original German surname (it means crooked leg), it is clear that Crumbine and Grumbine are American variations unlikely to appear in German emigration and vital records.

Example 2: Awalt (A430) and Ewald (E430). Since A and E are of the same code class 7 (vowels), the two surnames are equivalents. German speakers will quickly point out that the immigrant probably sought to preserve the German pronunciation of Ewald by changing it to Awalt.

Example 3: Folz (F420) and Volz (V420). F and V being of the same code class 1, the two surnames are equivalents; Folz is American, Volz is German.

Step 2: In general, it can be said that, wherever possible, German immigrants sought to preserve the pronunciation of their surnames, not the original German spellings. A few letters of the alphabet are pronounced differently in German and English, thus causing orthographic change when

they are written by English speakers. These possibilities are not fully encompassed by the present soundex rules.

The German W is pronounced like the English V. The German surname West might become Vest in English. German surnames beginning with W should be listed in code class 1, rather than with the vowels (code class 7) as shown in basic soundex rules, in order to disclose possible surname variations.

The German J is pronounced like the English Y. The German surname Jaeger is often written as Yeager in America, thus preserving the original German pronunciation. In soundex lists of surnames, one should include German surnames beginning with J in code class 7 with the vowels.

It is said that some German surnames beginning with G have been softened to Y in early Pennsylvania.[2] Goder is said to have become Yoder; Goetter became Yetter. This was caused by German dialect shifts. We suggest that such shifts be dealt with, if at all, only when soundexing the first generations of Pennsylvania Germans; probably it is not necessary for name lists of immigrants after the American Revolution.

Step 3: Finally, and quite apart from soundex considerations, researchers will want to consider the possibility of complete name translation. This occurs, in particular, when the German surname denotes a trade, quality, color, or day of the week. Here are some examples:

In Germany	*In America*
Zimmermann	Carpenter
Jaeger	Hunter
Schaefer	Shepherd
Vogel	Bird
Koenig	King
Gerber	Tanner
Weiss	White
Schreiner	Joiner
Schneider	Taylor
Suess	Sweet
Fuchs	Fox
Freitag	Friday
Schwartz	Black
Dürr	Dry
Roth	Redd
Grünbaum	Greentree

There is, of course, no certain way to determine when a direct translation has taken place. There are, however, some clues:

¶ When a German given name accompanies an English-sounding surname, one may suspect such translation. For example, Johannes Farmer was probably Johannes Bauer or Meier; Franz Josef Carpenter might have been Franz Josef Zimmermann.

¶ When an English surname oddly appears in a group of German surnames, here also a translation may be suspected. The rule is hardly invariable, of course; Horace Greely Hjalmar Schacht, Hitler's economics minister, is an exception and, no doubt, there are others.

¶ Finally, when a translatable English surname cannot be traced in America before the first world war, one should look for its German equivalent. Anti-German feeling was then high and some German-Americans found it advantageous to change their names.

---

1. Major portions of this essay have been adapted from our article, of the same title, in the *National Genealogical Society Quarterly* 62 (1974): 13-16, with permission.

2. Researchers wishing to study the surnames of Pennsylvania Germans in detail should refer to the *Annual Report of the American Historical Association for the Year 1931* (Washington: Government Printing Office) 1 (1932): 312-318.

ORGANIZATION OF THE HOLY ROMAN EMPIRE GERMAN NATION

INTRODUCTION

THE EARLY SETTLEMENT OF GERMANY

THE SOCIOLOGICAL STRUCTURE OF THE *ALTREICH*

THE ORGANIZATION OF THE GERMAN REICH FROM
    1495 TO 1806

A. The Imperial Government

    The kaiser

    The imperial administration (*Hof- und Reichsregierung*)

    The Reichstag

    Territorial organization (the *Reichs-kreise*)

    Defense of the realm

    Imperial finances

    The imperial church

    Imperial cities (*Reichsstädte*)

    Imperial knights (*Reichsritterschaft*)

B. The Territorial States

C. Organization of the Social Classes

    Nobility

    Burghers

    Peasants

    Jews

ALPHABETICAL LISTING OF THE PRINCIPAL SOVER-
    EIGN TERRITORIES OF IMPERIAL GERMANY

INTRODUCTION

The Holy Roman Empire German Nation was a congeries of small principalities, free towns and cities, and feudal estates. Under elected emperors, the Germans never attained a state of political cohesion which the French and British had long since taken for granted. Few of the sovereign territories of German-speaking Europe could even boast of a king—a title rarely used in Germany until quite late in its history—most were ruled by *Fürsten* (ruling princes), *Markgrafen* (marquises), *Grafen* (counts), and petty *Freiherren* (free lords or barons). Essentially, then, the re-curring theme of eighteenth-century German history is the struggle to reach political unity through dynastic hegemony. When the Holy Roman Empire fell in 1806 there began a massive re-organization and consolidation of territories which has not been entirely resolved, even today.

For the genealogical researcher inter-ested in documenting lineages with archival materials over and beyond the data to be found in church registers, knowledge of local, parti-cularly administrative, history becomes cru-cial. One cannot look to the public records of a central government; instead, one must seek out the records of the dynasties and petty magnates who were the effective lords over es-tates upon which the great mass of the populace was bound as serfs until near the end of the eighteenth century. In these estate records, the researcher can find manumission records (for ex-serfs permitted to emigrate to America), hereditary leasehold documents (for peasants tilling a portion of the lord's estate), lists of serfs (the equivalent of censuses), contri-bution records (a primitive form of taxation), and the like. In order to enter the appropri-ate corpus of archival materials, it becomes necessary first for the researcher to identify the dynasty or petty lord to whom an ancestor may have been subservient. This, then, is the purpose of this article.

THE EARLY SETTLEMENT OF GERMANY

German-speaking tribes and clans began moving south and westward, it is thought, from a Baltic homeland during the time of the Roman Empire. The four main groupings of peoples comprising the Germans today were the Franks, the Alemannen, the Saxons, and the Bajuwaren (the Bavarians). The Franks overran a portion of Germany along the lower Rhine; some groups of Franks were stopped by the Roman outposts along the river, but eventually the Franks settled in much of Belgium and France, as well as in their lower Rhenish lands. To the south of them--and not always as friends--were the Alemannen or Swabians. Their lands lay south of the Main River to the Alps and included most of Switzerland and the Alsace. Pushing out of the east behind these two tribal groups were the Saxons to the north and the Bajuwaren to the south. The Saxons settled along the Elbe and Weser rivers. The Bavarians settled along the upper Danube to a north-south line which passed near the present city of Augsburg, then a Roman settlement.

Modern genealogists will find these ancient tribal locations of some significance, for, even in the twentieth century, the cultural and linguistic differences among the principal ethnic divisions of Germany are pronounced. An immigrant to America is more likely to have reported that he was a Bavarian, or a Pfälzer (Palatine), or a Swabian, for example, than he was to have given a more precise term for his place of origin. Then, too, the four great ethnic subdivisions correspond roughly to the dialectic variations of the German language; most eighteenth-century German emigrants spoke dialect, rather than the Hochdeutsch (high German) of the educated classes.

THE SOCIOLOGICAL STRUCTURE OF THE *ALTREICH*

Germans were divided into *Stände* (social classes or estates) verging upon a caste system. Remnants of the system are still quite evident to the observer, although the vicissitudes of the two world wars and a monstrous inflation in the 1920s have brough down the mighty and elevated the crafty in a manner which before 1918 would hardly have been thought possible.

At the top of the sociological pyramid was an elected emperor (the Kaiser), ordinarily a Habsburg dynast, chosen by a small group of electors. The powers of the kaisers were important theoretically, but, in fact, the emperor's ability to rule--to control his tenants-in-chief and important magnates--was often limited by geography, ethnic differences, and the forecefulness, or lack of it, of his own personality. Ordinary mortals felt very little direct effect of imperial law; mainly they were the subjects of intermediate lords whose will was much more immediate, even in matters of life and death.

Directly below the kaiser was a group of noblemen called the *Reichsadel* (nobles of the realm). Ordinarily, they were tenants-in-chief with hereditary rights to land held

directly of the imperial crown. Nine or ten of these great nobles were also electors of the kaisers. It is this group of nobles which most completely asserted what would be thought of today as the rights of sovereignty over territories and the populaces living in them. It is confusing that there was no one title designating a territorial magnate exercising sovereignty. Not all sovereigns held the title of prince (*Fürst*), or duke (*Herzog*), or marquis (*Markgraf*). Numerous counts (*Grafen*), for example, were tenants-in-chief holding directly of the imperial crown and, thus, sovereigns in their own right; other counts held no such direct tenancies and were not *Reichsadel*. For modern genealogical researchers, the nobles of the realm almost always are significant, for, when one knows the precise locality from whence an ancestor came, one can usually determine the imperial administrative jurisdiction, if any, to which the ancestor was subject and the corresponding archival corpus in which to search.

Below the *Reichsadel* was a numerous minor nobility, some with the title of count, but mainly *Freiherren* (free lords or barons) who were tenants of the kaiser's various tenants-in-chief. Some of the *Reichsadel* had the right to ennoble their own subtenants. This is clearly reflected, for example, in the granting of heraldic devices and titles of nobility by such tenants-in-chief of the kaiser as the electoral princes of Hessen or the princes of Fürstenberg or Schwarzburg (see the article on heraldry herein). For the genealogist this distinction between the higher and lower nobility--though easy enough to determine by consulting an *adelige Taschenbuch* (small directory of the nobility)--can bring a perplexing problem: Some minor nobles exercised powers over their subjects almost indistinguishable from those of the territorial magnates. Thus, it may be difficult to know whether the emigration permits of a former serf might be found among the house papers of a minor baron upon whose lands the emigrant had formerly been bound, or whether such papers would more likely be found in the archives of the ruling prince to whom the baron himself was subject.

Both classes of noblemen might be either clerical or secular. Until 1806 the Roman Catholic Church and its Lutheran and Reformed successors owned much land, and the bishops and abbots exercised secular powers therein. Several of the *Fürstbischöfe* (prince bishops) were also electors of the kaiser. In addition, there were two orders of religious knights, the Deutschorden (Teutonic order of knights) and the Johanniterorden (commonly called the Knights of Malta) which held vast lands and ruled their subjects quite as absolutely as any secular magnate.

Below, or perhaps parallel to, the nobles of Germany were the citizens of free towns and cities. There were about 85 such towns which, over the centuries, had bought from the kaiser the privileges of self-government. In theory, these towns and their citizens were direct dependencies and subjects of the kaiser, but, in fact, imperial influence was usually most indirect. The actual rulers of the free cities were patrician elites, often called *Ratsherren* (councillors) who presided over an organized system of guilds and the citizenry. This has considerable significance to the genealogical researcher, for citizenship in a free city was highly prized and correspondingly difficult to obtain. Because of this, the records of free cities are likely to be especially valuable to the researcher; these records often contain detailed information over several generations on their citizens and their qualifications for citizenship. Sometimes this information will antedate the entries to be found in church registers.

At the bottom of the social structure was a large body of persons who were serfs, or practically so. In northwestern Germany many of the more prosperous peasants had won a considerable degree of freedom over the centuries, and their noble landlords were correspondingly lacking in sovereign powers and frequently impoverished. In the German East, however, serfs were almost completely bound to the soil upon which they were born, and their duties and obligations vis-à-vis their noble landlords were more onerous. In only two regions were there some free peasants--in the marshes of East Friesland, a region so difficult to traverse as to make the passage of military forces a practical impossibility, and in the remoter valleys of the Swiss Alps.

THE ORGANIZATION OF THE
GERMAN REICH FROM 1495 TO 1806

It is not the writers' purpose to explore in depth the constitutional history of the German Reich, but it does seem useful to set forth in aphoristic form such of the major features as might have significance to modern genealogical investigators. Administrative organization, rights and privileges, and jurisdiction determine the kinds of records which were kept and provide clues to their whereabouts.

A. The Imperial Government

1. The kaiser (emperor)

¶ The kaiser, nearly always a Habsburg, was chosen by eight to ten electors at a convocation normally held at Frankfurt/Main. Early coronations were at the cathedral in Aachen, but later they, too, were held at Frankfurt.

¶ Imperial sovereignty was restricted by the *Reichsstände* (the imperial estates). The election of the kaiser was itself an opportunity for further restricting imperial power, because the kaiser-elect was required to sign a *Wahlkapitulation* (election agreement) confirming, and occasionally expanding, the powers of the *Reichsstände*.

¶ The kaiser had oversight of foreign relations, but he could not enter into treaties, ally the Reich with another power, or declare war without the approval of the *Reichsstände*.

¶ The kaiser convened the Reichstag and presented the major proposals to be considered.

¶ The kaiser ratified laws passed by the Reichstag; only thereafter were such laws in force.

¶ The kaiser was the instance of ultimate appeal and administered the imperial court system (the *Reichskammergericht*), but the *Reichsstände* had a say in the selection of judges.

¶ The kaiser had the right to grant lands and territories (*Reichslehen*) and to require his tenants-in-chief to renew their feudal vows of fealty to him. Whenever important tenancies-in-chief became vacant (usually through the extinction of a vassal dynasty), the kaiser had the right to grant the vacated territories to another tenant only with the approval of the electoral princes.

¶ The kaiser had the right, subject to no other magnates or bodies, to ennoble commoners and to promote nobles to higher rank, to grant academic degrees and titles, to found universities and to specify their privileges, to appoint notaries, to declare the majority of minor children (usually in the event of succession to a tenancy), and to legitimate illegitimate persons. (The kaiser's declarations of legal competence and of legitimacy were usually undertaken only with the concurrence of the territorial overlords, however.)

¶ The Empire had no designated capital. The Reichstag met at Regensburg, but the first meeting of a Reichstag after the election of a new kaiser was held at Nürnberg, where the imperial crown and other regalia of office were kept. The Reichskammergericht (the court of highest instance) met at Speyer and later at Wetzlar. The kaisers usually resided at Prague or, in later centuries, at Vienna.

2. The imperial administration (*Hof- und Reichsregierung*)

¶ There were three classes of ministerial offices at the imperial court: (i) *Erzämtern* (arch- or superior offices), (ii) *Reichserbämtern* (imperial hereditary offices), and (iii) *kaiserliche Haus- und Hofämtern* (imperial house and court offices).

(1) The *Erzämtern* were controlled by the electoral princes. These offices were, for the most part, empty ceremonial titles and rarely exercised by the electoral princes themselves; instead, these positions devolved on lower nobles and made hereditary in certain families (*Reichserbämtern*).

(ii) Among the *Reichserbämtern* were the following: *Reichserbmarschall* (imperial hereditary marshal) which belonged to the counts v. Pappenheim and controlled the personnel in the imperial service; *Reichserbtruchsessen* (imperial hereditary seneschal) which had charge of the imperial palaces and was hereditary in the family von Waldburg (counts and imperial princes); the *Reichsbannerherramt* (office of imperial nobles), a position hereditary in the dukes of Württemberg; the *Reichs-Obrist-Jägermeister* (master of the imperial hunt), a position hereditary in the marquises of Meissen and later in the electoral prince of Saxony; the *Reichs-General-Postmeister* (imperial postmaster general), belonging to the princes von Thurn und Taxis. Especially important hereditary officials were the *Hofpfalzgrafen* (counts palatine) whose prerogatives included the appointment of notaries, the legitimation of bastards, the oversight of adoptions, the granting of academic titles and degrees and of coats of arms, and the crowning of poets laureate. There were several of these positions for the larger regions of the Empire; the territorial princes were much opposed to the *Hofpfalzgrafen* as interlopers in the affairs of their territories.

(iii) The *Haus- und Hofämtern* were offices filled by imperial appointment; as such, not all officials were nobles. Their offices were in Vienna. Among this group were the secretaries, the tax officials, clerks, and office personnel. The *Reichsvizekanzler* (imperial vice-chancellor), the effective head of the administrative offices of the kaiser, was usually in a powerful political position.

¶ The *Reichshofrat* (imperial council), led by a president who had to be a tenant-in-chief of the kaiser, was a body of 18 to 30 personages composed of nobles and academicians. When a kaiser died, his council was disbanded. The major duties of the council had to do with the administration of justice and, in certain questions of state, with the presentation of alternative courses of action upon which the kaiser was to base his decisions. The *Reichshofrat* had its offices in Vienna.

¶ The *Geheimer Rat* (privy council) was the most prestigious group at the imperial court. Its principal function had to do with foreign affairs and with financial matters. There were usually only about four to six officials in this group.

3. The Reichstag

¶ The Reichstag was the legislative body of the Empire. There were three colleges in the Reichstag: (i) the *Kurfürstenkollegium* (college of electoral princes); (ii) the *Fürstenrat* (college of princes, prelates, counts, and lords); and (iii) *Kollegium der Reichsstädte* (college of imperial free cities).

¶ The kaiser or his representative, an imperial prince, attended the Reichstag in person. Members of the Reichstag could send delegates, if they did not themselves attend.

¶ Although the right to a seat and a vote in the Reichstag was originally a personal right, it came later to require the ownership of a territory held directly of the kaiser (a tenancy-in-chief). Thus, membership in the Reichstag became the equivalent of territorial representation. Quite late in the history of the Reichstag, a number of *Personalisten* (personal representatives) were admitted; these magnates had no lands held directly of the kaiser but they were invariably great landowners of political importance.

¶ Membership in the Reichstag could be cancelled, (i) if the territory was permanently lost to a foreign power; (ii) if the imperial nobleman was expelled from the Reichstag; (iii) by mediatisation, wherein a prince, formerly a tenant-in-chief of the kaiser, lost this imperial status when the territory he controlled came under the jurisdiction of another tenant-in-chief.

¶ Some nobles had only *Kuriatstimmen* (a vote exercised conjointly with others). Thus, there were *Kreisen* (circles) of counts and lords which voted as a unit, but not individually (the Fränkische, Schwäbische, Westfälische, and Wetterauische Grafenkollegien).

¶ There were secular and ecclesiastical members in the Reichstag. In matters having to do with religion, the membership of the Reichstag--both ecclesiastical and secular--was divided into a Catholic corpus and a Protestant one.

¶ A prince might exercise more than one vote in the Reichstag, if he held more than one territory directly of the kaiser.

4. Territorial organization (the *Reichskreise*)

¶ Various regions, or Kreise, of the Reich had the power to assemble in their own Kreistage (local legislative bodies), usually for the purpose of imposing law and order within their borders or jointly to provide troops for a foreign war. These Kreistage also had broad powers in the matters of taxation, regulation of commerce, roadbuilding, and welfare.

5. Defense of the realm

¶ In the event of warfare outside the borders of the Reich, the members of the *Reichsstände* were required to provide cavalry and infantry soldiers in accordance with a fixed levy. In later centuries, some or all of this obligation might be met by the payment of money. As a consequence of the varying quality of training and equipment provided these units, it was extremely difficult for the Reich to put an effective army into the field.

¶ The imperial army was led in the field by the kaiser himself or by a lieutenant general field marshall appointed jointly by the kaiser and the Reichstag. An army of the Reich was required to have as many Catholic generals as it had Protestant ones, in accordance with the Treaty of Westphalia.

¶ Early attempts to halt the vicious practice of recruiting troops for service in foreign armies and, instead, to

strengthen the imperial armies, came to nothing because the Protestant members of the *Reichsstände* feared the Catholic kaiser's increase in power more than they objected to hiring out their peasants to foreign princes. (It is therefore not surprising that all of the princes who provided mercenaries to the British for service in the American Revolution were Protestant ones.)

6. Imperial finances

¶ The kaiser's income from taxation was severely restricted. Wherever possible, his rights of taxation were disputed by the territorial magnates; even in those cases where an imperial tax was undisputed, many territorial lords were in arrears or refused to forward collections to the imperial treasury.

¶ During the period of Turkish expansion in central Europe, the kaiser imposed a *Turkensteuer* (Turk tax) to provide for the common defense. Many of these tax lists are extant and provide genealogical researchers with useful data.

¶ One of the ancient levies which has implications for genealogists was the *Wildfangregal* (the right to the proceeds of catching wild animals). Despite its title, the right also covered illegitimate persons and foreigners. The electoral prince of the Palatinate, for example, reserved to himself the right to declare any bastard or free foreigner in his lands to be his personal property along with all their chattels. Thus, illegitimate children automatically became serfs of the prince. The *Wildfangregal* was in use in the eighteenth century in the Palatinate as a matter of public law.

7. The imperial church

¶ Relations with Catholic and Protestant churches were defined in the Augsburg Agreement (1555) and the Peace of Westphalia (1648) for the purpose of accommodating the contending forces having their origins in the Reformation.

¶ Each member of the *Reichsstände* (the imperial territorial magnates and the free cities) had the right to adhere to the Catholic, Lutheran, or Reformed confession and to require all their subjects to conform thereto. Those persons unable to do so were given the freedom to remove themselves from the territory.

¶ Certain of the free cities were allowed

to have both Catholic and Protestant parishes within their walls (Augsburg, Biberach, Dinkelsbühl, Kaufbeuren, and Ravensburg) and to permit an equal number of Catholics and Protestants to participate in the government of these cities (the so-called parity provision).

¶ According to the Peace of Westphalia, no other sects were to be permitted within the borders of the Empire, with the exception that the Greek Catholics in the Ruthenian possessions of Austria were not to be affected. This arrangement fell hard upon the Jews, the Anabaptists (Amish, Hutterites, Mennonites), and the groups having their origins in the teachings of Jan Hus (the Moravian Brethren) and George Fox (the Quakers), and other small groups.

¶ On 17 June 1662 Count Friedrich III zu Wied granted the newly-established town of Neuwied the privilege of permitting various small sectarian groups to practice their religions therein. Even though the privilege ran directly counter to the Peace of Westphalia, it was not contested by the kaiser or other magnates and became part of the imperial common law. Similar toleration of the minor sects was also practiced in some of the territories of the princes von Isenburg (Ysenburg).

¶ Through the centuries, powerful magnates had occasionally secularized territories controlled by church authorities. On 25 February 1803, all church lands in the Empire were secularized, excepting those of the Deutschorden (Teutonic knights), the Johanniterorden (Maltese order), the newly-founded archbishopric of Aschaffenburg-Regensburg, and those of the archbishopric of Mainz east of the Rhine River. This meant that the properties of most of the bishoprics and all of the abbeys and prelates were expropriated. The lands were distributed among the territorial magnates and constituted probably the largest internal transfer of land ownership heretofore seen in the Empire's history.

8. The imperial cities (*Reichsstädte*)

¶ The imperial cities were direct dependencies of the kaiser. Most of the imperial cities had territories, towns, and villages outside their walls over which they exercised sovereignty.

¶ Certain of the weaker imperial cities became clients of stronger *Reichsstädte*; for example, Dinkelsbühl, Schweinfurt, Weissenburg am Nordgau, and Windsheim were clients of Nürnberg; Heilbronn, Kaufbeuren, Schwäbisch-Hall, Schwäbisch-Wörth (now Donauwörth), and Wimpfen were clients of Augsburg.

¶ Imperial cities were governed by councils composed of the representatives of patrician families. In some cities the guilds had important influence in the governance of the cities.

¶ The residents of the *Reichsstädte* were divided into two classes: citizens with full rights, and tolerated persons. The legal rights of the residents depended upon grants of citizenship (an extremely valuable source of information for genealogists, because ancestry was an important consideration in the granting of citizenship). Jews were tolerated in some imperial cities but not in others; they were never citizens. Inhabitants of territories owned by imperial cities were treated as subjects or serfs; very rarely did they have any influence in the government.

9. The imperial knights (*Reichsritterschaft*)

¶ In southern and western Germany many noble families were able to avoid mediatization under the territorial magnates and remained direct vassals of the kaiser. These imperial vassals formed three *Ritterkreise*, the Franconian, Rhenish, and Swabian circles of knights. Members of these *Kreise* (circles) were not accepted in the *Reichsstandschaft*.

¶ The *Reichsrittern* exercised full powers of government within the lands they held directly of the kaiser, and these vassals usually acted in concert with other members of their circle. The three circles were divided into cantons as follows:

Franconian Circle	Swabian Circle
Altmühl	Allgäu-Bodensee
Gebirg*	Donau
Odenwald	Hegau
Rhon-Werra*	Kocher
Steigerwald	Kraichgau
	Neckar, Schwarz-
Rhenish Circle	wald, Ortenau
Mittelrheinstrom*	
Niederrheinstrom	
Oberrheinstrom	

*Further divided into *Quartiere* or *Bezirke* (districts).

B. The Territorial States

Territorial states were geographic and political entites controlled by magnates (*Fürsten*, *Markgrafen*, and *Grafen*, if secular; or *Fürstbischöfe*, *Bischöfe*, and *Prelaten*, if ecclesiastic) who were direct tenants-in-chief of the kaiser. The struggle between the kaisers and the territorial magnates is the leitmotiv of German history. For the genealogical researcher, the records of the territorial states are likely to be more useful than the imperial records, because the governments of the territorial states more directly impinged upon the lives of their subjects than did that of the kaiser.

¶ The territorial dynasties usually had special rules regarding the inheritance of the territory. Instead of splitting up the territory among all male heirs, it was customary that all the estate devolved upon the first-born male heir (primogeniture). These rules of inheritance and the indivisibility of territory were set forth in *Hausgesetze* (house or dynastic laws).

¶ The territorial magnates had the right to convene a Landtag (territorial parliament) within their territories. In a few states, these parliaments could convene without the permission or convocation of the magnate, but this was hardly usual.

¶ Membership in a Landtag was limited to the landed nobility, for the most part. Generally speaking, the territorial magnate could not levy a tax or raise an army without their approbation.

¶ After the Reformation, church prelates were no longer active in the territorial parliaments. In Protestant states representatives from the universities were seated in the territorial parliaments; in Catholic states this was not usual until near the end of the eighteenth century.

¶ In some territorial parliaments all towns and cities had representation; in other parliaments only the major cities were seated. In eastern Germany the cities were rarely admitted to the Landtage.

¶ Since one of the most important prerogatives of the territorial magnate had to do with taxation, it is at the territorial level that genealogical researchers are most likely to find early tax lists, a particularly common one being the *Turkensteuer*, a tax levied at the time of the Turkish invasion of central Europe. Tax lists became more comprehensive and reliable in the seventeenth century; records of land taxes usually date from about the middle of the eighteenth century.

¶ In earlier centuries soldiers were mainly hirelings, rarely from the territory for which they were engaged to fight or to defend. By the seventeenth century it was generally held that soldiers drafted locally and fighting under the officers who were local *Landadel* (nobles) proved more dependable. This brought about a system not unlike a local militia, but it weakened the power of the territorial magnate vis-à-vis his local nobles. By the eighteenth century strong magnates had begun to consolidate such militia groups into larger military units, but it seems clear that many military records (muster rolls, pension lists) are likely to be found in the archives of individual *Landadel*, as well as among the papers of state left by territorial magnates.

¶ The beginnings of communal records vary from region to region. In Kurtrier (Electoral Trier) the beginnings of local self-government can be detected by 1742; in Kurmainz (Electoral Mainz) by 1770. During the French occupation of the Rhine region, the movement gained impetus. Shortly thereafter (1808), local self-government was introduced in Prussian territories.

C. The Organization
of the Social Classes

Until the fall of the Holy Roman Empire German Nation in 1806, there were three major classes of society in Germany--the nobility, the burghers, and the peasants. In addition, there were the Jews, perhaps more assimilated to the burghers than to other classes, but nonetheless subject to special restrictions. During the nineteenth and twentieth centuries, although much of the legal foundation upon which the three social classes had been based was no longer applicable, the habits of centuries were not immediately to be eradicated; indeed, even today in Germany, remnants of the old class structure are still visible. Genealogical researchers will need to know the main characteristics of each social class, for these characteristics give insight into the conditions under which Germans lived before their emigration and the motivations for their journeys to the New World.

1. The nobility

¶ In law, there were only two classes of nobles: the *Reichsunmittelbare* (direct vassals of the kaiser, or tenants-in-chief) and the *Reichsmittelbare* (the indirect vassals of the kaiser, or those whose fealty was owed to a prince who was himself an imperial tenant-in-chief).

¶ Noblemen were distinguishable by their names, usually preceded by the *von* or *zu* preposition (although not all surnames with *von* are noble, for example, von der Aue); by their right to armorial bearings (although many burghers and some peasants had coats of arms); by their membership in noble organizations; and by their eligibility for nomination to court and honorary positions.

¶ The right of ennoblement belonged exclusively to the kaiser, but he could, and did, delegate this right to certain other princes. As a consequence, a great many of the noble families of Germany owe their titles not to imperial favor but to that of other territorial magnates, such as Prussia, Hessen, the Palatine counts, and the princes von Fürstenberg. In later centuries, Bavaria and Prussia prohibited their subjects from accepting titles of nobility from other princes, including the kaiser.

¶ In later centuries, the kaiser could promote a noble to princely rank only with the approval of the electoral princes.

¶ Some noblemen had no titles other than the distinguishing preposition *von* before their surnames. In ascending order of rank, others might be named *Edler*, *Ritter*, *Edler Herr*, *Freiherr*, *Graf*, and *Fürst*. The first three of these titles were more usual in Bavaria than elsewhere.

¶ The higher nobility observed the principle of *Ebenbürtigkeit* which required that marriages be between nobles of equal rank. Among the lower nobility *Ebenbürtigkeit* was not required, but it was widely practiced.

¶ The lower nobility were of two groups--those who were tenants-in-chief of the kaiser (*Reichsritter*), and those who were vassals of a territorial magnate, himself a tenant-in-chief of the kaiser. The *Reichsrittern* disappeared entirely in 1806 when they were all mediatized.

¶ The lower nobility inherited title from noble fathers. In Prussia, by a decree of 1794, marriages between noblemen and commoner women were declared null and void on the grounds that, in a military state, the proper sense of patriotism and duty toward the state was a characteristic exclusively to be found in the noble caste; the children of an ignoble mother could not be expected to have such characteristics. In other areas of Germany the children of a father of the lower nobility received his title

regardless of their mother's class origins. The children of noble mothers and commoner fathers, on the other hand, did not receive their mother's title and, therefore, were commoners.

¶ A nobleman could lose his right to title by engaging in an occupation not allowed to him. Any commercial activity or the practice of a trade or profession brought with it immediate loss of nobility. Adoption of a noble child by a commoner was also a grounds for the child's loss of nobility. The simple failure to use one's title did not result in loss of nobility, however.

2. The burghers

¶ Burghers were town and city dwellers pursuing commerce, trade, and handicrafts. They were not allowed to own lands reserved to noblemen.

¶ Within the bourgeoisie there came to be numerous subclasses. The highest were the patrician elites who governed the towns (if an imperial free city) and who were rentiers. Often these patrician families married only among themselves and otherwise maintained customs very similar to the nobility with whom they claimed parity. The entrepreneurs and the traders with ventures abroad often comprised a second social class. Often they were joined by the university-educated professionals, the lawyers, clerics, and doctors. A third group was the master craftsmen organized in guilds. Under these layers were a multitudinous class of journeymen craftsmen, small tradesmen, and workmen, some with citizenship, others without.

3. The peasants

¶ By definition, the peasants included all persons engaged in agriculture. There were two classes, the freemen and the serfs. Freemen continued to exist only in a few remote areas, such as the outer marsh reaches along the North Sea and in the valleys of the Alps.

¶ Serfs were subject to varying degrees of servility to their noble lords. In the west of Germany serfs often had only to pay rent for the lands they tilled; in the east of Germany there was a more abject servility--serfs were required to render personal services to their lords, and their ownership of chattel property was limited. Succinctly put, the landlord of eastern Germany became a governing prince in his own villages.

¶ As a general rule, the kaiser and the territorial magnates tended to take the side of the serfs in disputes with the serfs' lords. Usually this was for the purpose of keeping the power of the lords in check, but occasionally it arose from humanitarian considerations.

¶ The freeing of the serfs began in the late eighteenth century and was completed in Germany by the middle of the nineteenth century:

- In Prussia the emanicipation process began in 1777 and was completed by 1807.

- In Austria, Maria Theresia began the distribution of land to peasants in 1771-1775; in Bohemia, Moravia, and Silesia serfdom was abolished in 1781.

- In Baden serfdom was abolished in 1783.

- In German lands under French occupation (the *Rheinbundstaaten*) serfdom was abolished in 1808; in the Kingdom of Westphalia in 1807; in the Grandduchy of Berg in 1808; in the Grandduchy of Frankfurt in 1810.

4. The Jews

¶ Jews entered Germany with the Romans and have lived there continuously down to modern times.

¶ Jews were not considered to be members of the community, because they were not Christians. They were permitted to live in specified places and in specified numbers only.

¶ In matters of internal governance and the distribution of the tax burden imposed upon them, Jews were subject to their own laws and leaders, rather than to those of the communities in which they lived. The relationships between Jews and gentiles were subject to special laws not otherwise applicable.

¶ In 1812 the Jews then living legally in Prussia were granted citizenship for the first time. Emancipation of the Jews in Bavaria came only in the latter half of the nineteenth century.

ALPHABETICAL LISTING OF THE PRINCIPAL
SOVEREIGN TERRITORIES OF IMPERIAL GERMANY

Most of the inhabitants of the Holy Roman Empire German Nation belonged to the land upon which they lived. Often a village was jointly owned by a number of noblemen, and the inhabitants of the village were subjects of the individual noble owners, depending upon the houses in which the inhabitants lived and the fields they tilled. As a consequence, precise knowledge of the political jurisdiction to which ancestors were subject becomes important to genealogical researchers, because of the need to locate ancestral records. No historian has yet satisfactorily delineated--or completely listed--all the territorial entities which had a measure of autonomy in imperial Germany. So serious is the problem that it is impossible to present a map completely depicting the complex jurisdiction and sovereignty as it was on the local level. Researchers must examine land records in the archives of Germany and study the numerous journals of local history for clues to these jurisdictions.

Hereinafter are listed the *Reichsunmittelbare* (tenancies-in-chief) ecclesiastic and secular principalities, *Reichsstädte* (imperial free cities), and other political entities having a large degree of autonomy within the Empire. Below the imperial tenants-in-chief or territorial magnates were a numerous class of feudal lords whose exercise of sovereignty over their subjects was scarcely less complete than that of the magnates. Some of these lords were imperial knights, others were direct vassals of the territorial magnates. There are no complete lists of feudal *Herrschaften*, the territories and estates of these minor feudal lords; perhaps the best inventory of all the noble families which exercised a degree of sovereignty are those listed in the volumes of the *Siebmacher'schen Wappenbücher* (see the article on Heraldry herein).

The entities listed hereinafter are those of the *Reichsmatrikel* (imperial inscription) of 1521 with changes made in later centuries down to the fall of the Empire in 1806. The participation of each of the territories in the Peace of Westphalia (1648) is given, thus affording the genealogist a clue to the religion which an ancestor professed. It will be noted that the preponderant religious affiliation of modern-day residents is frequently different from that of 1648. A few terms have not been translated from German to English because of their special application in German constitutional history:

Amt local office

Ballei regional administrative office of the Deutschorden (Teutonic knights); an office immediately above the *Landkomtur*

Bezirk district

Grafenkolleg a collegium of counts; a regional deliberative body

Grafschaft the territory governed by a count (not the equivalent of county in English)

Herrschaft the territory of a nobleman, usually of the lower nobility

Kanton canton, a geographic and political term mainly used in southern Germany and Switzerland

Kreis circle, or regional grouping; in modern terms, a group of communities

Kur a prefix to a territorial designation (as in Kurmainz) signifying that the ruling prince was also an elector of the emperor

Landkomtur district office of the Deutschorden (Teutonic knights); an office immediately below the *Ballei*

Landkreis rural circle or grouping of communities

Landvogtei regional administrative district under the supervision of a *Vogt*, or vice-regent

Personalist a personal member of the Reichstag. Until the eighteenth century membership in the Reichstag was limited to nobles holding tenancies-in-chief of the emperor; thereafter, a few important landholding nobles were given seats in the Reichstag, even though they held no such direct tenancies of the kaiser

Regierungsbezirk governmental district

Reich empire, or imperial

Reichsadel imperial nobles

Reichsstadt imperial city, sometimes called a free city; a town granted a charter of self-governance by the kaiser. Such cities were ruled by a local patrician elite and were independent of the territorial magnates whose lands may have surrounded them

Reichsstand, Reichsstände, Reichsstandschaft the class, or classes, of imperial ecclesiastic and secular nobles having seats in the Reichstag

Reichstag the imperial parliament

Verwaltungsbezirk administrative district

SUMMARY OF THE

TENANTS-IN-CHIEF AND OTHER

DIRECT DEPENDENTS OF THE KAISER

	As of 1521	As of 1755		As of 1792
Kurfürsten (electoral princes)	7	9	*Kurfürstenkolleg* (college of electoral princes)	8
Fürsten (ruling princes):			*Reichsfürstenrat* (council of princes):	
Archbishops and bishops	51	43	Archbishops, dukes, Deutschmeister	5
Deutschorden Balleien	4	2	Bishops	27
Prelates nullius: abbots and cathedral chapters	65	24	Abbots	3
Prelates nullius: abbesses	14	13	Swabian prelates nullius	23*
			Rhenish prelates nullius	19*
Secular princes (German)	21	34	Princes and marquises	59
Secular princes (foreign)	3	1	Wetterauische counts	25*
Counts and lords	145	92	Schwäbische counts	24*
			Fränkische counts	17*
			Westfälische counts	21*
Reichsstädte (imperial cities)	85	51	*Collegium of cities:*	
			Rhenish bench	14
			Swabian bench	37

*Had only one vote which was exercised conjointly.

Alphabetical Listing of Tenancies-in-Chief

and Other Dependencies of the Kaiser

AACHEN (also called Aix-la-Chapelle), now in Nordrhein-Westfalen; former Reichsstadt. Member of Catholic corpus at Peace of Westphalia; the Landkreis is now 88% Catholic.

AALEN, now in Baden-Württemberg; former Reichsstadt. Represented by Ulm in Protestant corpus at Peace of Westphalia; town is now 56% Catholic; Landkreis is 70% Catholic. Town once had a small area of sovereignty surrounding it, but this fell to Württemberg. Many of the nearby villagers were subjects of the Grafen von Oettingen.

AARBURG, now in Bezirk Zofingen, Kanton Aargau, Switzerland; former Grafschaft; then became part of Kanton Bern (now Aargau). Population is about two-thirds Reformed.

AICHHEIM. See Iller-Aichheim

ALSCHHAUSEN, now in France; former Grafschaft and Landkomtur of the Deutschorden (Teutonic knights), Ballei Elsass und Burgund (Alsace and Burgundy). Member of the Swabian Grafenkolleg.

ALTENKIRCHEN. See Ansbach; Westfälische Grafenkolleg (Sayn-Altenkirchen)

ANHALT, now in the German Democratic Republic; former principality. Subordinate and associated territories were Zerbst, Herrschaft Jever (in Oldenburg); see also Barby und Mühlingen; the Prince zu Anhalt-Bernburg-Schaumburg represented Grafschaft Holzappel in the Westfälische Grafenkolleg. Anhalt was a member of the Protestant corpus at the Treaty of Westphalia and represented the Protestant interests of the Palatine Grafschaften Lautern and Simmern therein; the Anhalt dynasty was Protestant. The Anhalt-Köthen (Dessau) branch of the dynasty was regnant until 1918. It is hypothesized that the small contingent of mercenaries sent to America during the Revolution was from Herrschaft Jever.

ANHOLT, now in Kreis Borken, Nordrhein-Westfalen; former Herrschaft and Grafschaft. Member of the Westfälische Grafenkolleg and represented by the princes zu Salm-Salm. Population is now 85% Catholic; the Salm-Salm dynasty is Catholic. In 1810 Anholt fell to the French and in 1815 to Prussia.

ANSBACH, now in Regierungsbezirk Mittelfranken, Bayern (Bavaria); former marquisate and principality. Associated estates were Uffenheim, Crailsheim, Feuchtwangen, Gunzenhausen, Schwabach, Abenberg-Cadolzburg, Neustadt-Windsheim, Erlangen, and an area around Hof. Represented by Brandenburg-Kulmbach in the Protestant corpus at the Peace of Westphalia; town population is now 67% Protestant; Landkreis is 80% Protestant. Represented by the princes zu Sayn-Altenkirchen in the Westfälische Grafenkolleg. Once ruled by the counts von Oettingen, thereafter by Hohenzollern dynasty (as Marquises of Brandenburg); in 1791 territory became Prussian; in 1806 territory became Bavarian. The principality is often called Ansbach-Bayreuth. There was a settlement of Huguenots at Erlangen. Ansbach and Bayreuth sent contingents of troops to serve under the British during the American Revolution and many remained in America, as listed in the following publication: Clifford Neal Smith, *Mercenaries from Ansbach and Bayreuth, Germany, Who Remained in America after the Revolution*. German-American Genealogical Research Monograph No. 2 (DeKalb, Ill.: Westland Publications, 1974).

AREMBERG (or Arenberg), Dukes of; also called House of Ligne. Owned much property in Belgium and France; Duchy of Arenberg-Meppen (Hannover); Grafschaft Recklinghausen. Dynasty is Catholic.

ASPREMONT (also Aspermont), Grafen von; associated with the Leiningen dynasty. See Reckum (or Reckheim)

AUERSBERG, Dukes and princes of. Held much property in Austria; the Tengen estate (*Vorderösterreich*) was held as a tenancy-in-chief of the kaiser. House of Auersberg is Catholic; family originated in the Krain.

AUGSBURG, now in Regierungsbezirk Schwaben, Bayern (Bavaria); former Reichsstadt and bishopric. The bishopric of Augsburg was represented by Osnabrück in the Catholic corpus at the Peace of Westphalia; the Reichsstadt was a member of the Catholic corpus in its own right; Protestant citizens of the Reichsstadt were represented by Esslingen in the Protestant corpus at the Peace of Westphalia. Stadtkreis (city) is now 74% Catholic; Landkreis is 82% Catholic. Since 1548 all religious properties have been jointly administered by Catholics and Lutherans.

AULENDORF, now in Kreis Ravensburg, Baden-Württemberg. Town is now 84% Catholic. *See also* Königsegg-Aulendorf

BADEN (various principalities), now in Baden-Württemberg. Baden-Baden represented Grafschaft Eberstein in the Schwäbische Grafenkolleg. Marquisate of Baden-Baden was a member of the Catholic corpus at the Peace of Westphalia; marquisates of Baden-Durlach and Baden-Hochberg were members of the Protestant corpus at the Peace of Westphalia. The dynasty of Zähringen (Baden) is Catholic.

During the eighteenth century the territories were divided between Baden-Durlach (Lutheran) and Baden-Baden (Catholic). Baden-Durlach also held Amt Rhodt (Kreis Landau) until the time of the French Revolution. Baden-Baden owned Herrschaft Beinheim in Lower Alsace, Amt Gräfenstein (around the town of Rodalben, Kreis Pirmasens), Herrschaft Hesperingen and Herrschaft Rodemachern in Luxemburg, and a portion of Grafschaft Sponheim in the Hunsrück. After 1803 the Grandduchy of Baden was organized, expanding the territory to include the Breisgau (formerly Austrian territory), and the city of Constance. Serfdom was abolished in Baden in 1783.

BAINDT, now in Kreis Ravensburg, Baden-Württemberg; former abbey for women religious. Village is now 85% Catholic. Abbey was secularized in 1803.

BAMBERG, now in Regierungsbezirk Oberfranken, Bayern (Bavaria); former bishopric, now archbishopric. Bishopric was a member of the Catholic corpus at the Peace of Westphalia; city is now 77% Catholic; Landkreis is 95% Catholic. The bishopric also owned Villach in Carinthia until 1759, when it was sold to Austria.

BARBY UND MUEHLINGEN, in Kreis Schönebeck, Bezirk Magdeburg, German Democratic Republic; former Grafschaften. Represented by Kursachsen (Electoral Saxony) until 1659; Sachsen-Weissenfels, Anhalt-Zerbst, and Magdeburg controlled the territory. Population is mostly Protestant.

BASEL, now in Switzerland; former Reichsstadt and bishopric. Herrschaft Schliengen was associated. When most of the inhabitants of the bishopric became Protestant in the time of the Reformation, the Catholic bishop removed to Freiburg in Breisgau; population is now about two-thirds Protestant. The Reichsstadt became a member of the Swiss Confederation in 1501 and took no further part in the German Reichstag after 1531.

BAYERN (Bavaria), now a West German state; former kingdom and electoral principality; branches of the Wittelsbach dynasty also ruled the Pfalz (Palatinate) and so the history of Bavaria and the Palatinate is closely related. Kurbayern (Electoral Bavaria) represented the Grafschaft Helfenstein in the Schwäbische Grafenkolleg. Both Kurbayern (Electoral Bavaria) and the Duchy of Bavaria were members of the Catholic corpus at the Peace of Westphalia; the Wittelsbach dynasty is Catholic. Bavaria was one of the larger principalities of the German Reich. The Wittelsbach dynasty began as tribal leaders of the Bajuwaren; the family was divided into several lines, mainly

Oberbayern (with the Rheinpfalz and the electoral right) and Niederbayern which later became extinct. A later division weakened the dynasty and much territory was lost to competitors.

BAYREUTH, now in Regierungsbezirk Oberfranken, Bayern (Bavaria); former marquisate. City is now 70% Protestant; Landkreis is 74% Protestant. See also Ansbach; Brandenburg (Franconian Line)

BECKENRIED, now in Switzerland; former prelate nullius. Estate merged into Swiss Confederation.

BEILSTEIN. See Winneburg und Beilstein

BENTHEIM, Fürsten and Grafen von; also called the House of Güterswyk. Owned Tecklenburg-Rheda. Family is Reformed. See also Steinfurt

BERCHTESGADEN, now in Bayern (Bavaria); former prince-bishop and prelate nullius. Represented by Kurköln (Electoral Cologne) in Catholic corpus at the Peace of Westphalia; Landkreis is now 82% Catholic. Close historic association with Salzburg.

BERG, now in Nordrhein-Westfalen; former duchy east of the Rhine between the Ruhr and Sieg rivers, capital Düsseldorf. Early became a possession of the Pfalz-Neuburg branch of the Wittelsbach dynasty (Bavaria) and thereafter passed to Kurpfalz (Electoral Palatinate). In 1815 became Prussian territory.

BERGEN, former Grafschaft. Became Dutch territory in 1581 but regained membership in German Grafenkolleg in 1654; seat was cancelled in 1712 and has been a part of The Netherlands, Province Zutphen, thereafter.

BERGEN UND WALEN (Bergen op Zoom), former Grafschaft. Became Dutch in 1567 or 1648; previously had been a tenancy-in-chief of the German kaiser.

BERLEBURG. See Wetterauische Grafenkolleg (Sayn-Wittgenstein-Berleburg)

BERNBURG. See Anhalt

BESANCON, now in Département Doubs, France; former Reichsstadt and archbishopric. Both Reichsstadt and bishopric were members of the Catholic corpus at the Peace of Westphalia. Area taken over by Burgundy and in 1674-1679 became French with the Franche-Comté.

BEUCHLINGEN, former Grafschaft. Reichstag vote cancelled in 1560.

BIBERACH, now in Baden-Württemberg, former

Reichsstadt. Member of the Catholic corpus at the Peace of Westphalia; the town elite was Catholic, the populace Protestant. In 1649 religious strife was ended by a treaty giving equal rights to both parties; Stadt-kreis (town) is now 58% Protestant; Land-kreis is 80% Catholic. The town was destroyed during the Thirty Years War.

BIRSTEIN. *See* Wetterauische Grafenkolleg (Isenburg-Birstein)

BITSCH, now in Lorraine, France; former Graf-schaft. Reichstag vote was cancelled in 1570 and the territory merged with Lothringen (Lorraine).

BLANKENBERG, now Lorraine, France; former Graf-schaft. Merged with Lothringen (Lorraine) in 1542.

BLANKENBURG; former prelate nullius. The identity of this former clerical honor is uncertain; the estate is thought to have been in Lorraine or Oldenburg.

BLANKENHEIM und GEROLDSTEIN, now in Kreis Schleiden, Nordrhein-Westfalen; former Graf-schaft. Associated estates were Gerolstein, Kronenburg, Dollendorf (all Eifel Herrschaft-en). Member of the Westfälische Grafenkolleg. Area is now 80% Catholic. Represented by Grafen von Manderscheid-Blankenheim and, since 1780, by the Grafen von Sternberg.

BÖHMEN (Bohemia), now province in Czechoslo-vakia; former kingdom and electoral princi-pality. Bohemia was an original member of the electoral college, but lost the position in the seventeenth century; readmitted to electoral college in 1708. A number of Prot-estant sects originated in Bohemia; in the early seventeenth century Protestant nobles and burghers had to emigrate as a result of a decree of the ruling Habsburg dynasty favoring Catholicism; all serfs were forced to become Catholics; three-fourths of the noble estates, excluding those of the king, changed hands during the period 1620-1627. About 36,000 families were forced to emi-grate, including nearly one-fourth of all nobles and burghers.

BONNDORF, now in Kreis Hochschwarzwald, Baden-Württemberg; former Herrschaft. Member of the Schwäbische Grafenkolleg; represented by the Abbot of St. Blasien since 1613; in 1803 administration taken over by the Johanniter-orden (Knights of Malta); in 1805 the admin-istration passed to Württemberg, and in 1806 estate was absorbed by Baden.

BOPFINGEN, now in Kreis Aalen, Baden-Württem-berg; former Reichsstadt. Represented by Ulm in the Protestant corpus at the Peace of Westphalia; town is now 51% Catholic.

In 1802 town was taken over by Bavaria and in 1810 transferred to Württemberg.

BRAKEL, now in Kreis Höxter, Nordrhein-West-falen; former Reichsstadt. Hinnenburg estate was associated. Administration was taken over by Bishop of Paderborn; town is now 80% Catholic.

BRANDENBURG, now in German Democratic Republic; former electoral principality and bishopric. Associated estates were Uckermark, Prignitz, Herrschaft Cottbus, Herrschaft Peitz, Crossen, Züllichau, Beeskow, Storkow, Kleve, Mark, Ravensberg, Ravenstein, Duchy of Prussia. Electoral Brandenburg was a member of the Protestant corpus at the Peace of Westphalia. Bishopric was absorbed (*landsässig*) by Brandenburg but again exercised vote after 1544. Brandenburg came into the possession of the Hohenzollern dynasty in 1411. *See also* Prussia

BRANDENBURG (Franconian Line), now territories in Bavaria; former marquisates of Ansbach, Bayreuth, Kulmbach. Marquisates of Branden-burg-Ansbach and Brandenburg-Kulmbach were both in the Protestant Corpus at the Peace of Westphalia. Raised to the Kurfürstenrat (Council of Electoral Princes) in 1692. Territories associated with the Hohenzollern dynasty since the thirteenth century.

BRANDENSTEIN-ROENIS, former Grafschaft. As-similated in the fifteenth century by the Saxon dynasties.

BRAUNFELS. *See* Wetterauische Grafenkolleg (Solms-Braunfels)

BRAUNSCHWEIG-LÜNEBURG, now in Niedersachsen; former duchy. Member of the Protestant cor-pus at the Peace of Westphalia, with branches Braunschweig-Lüneburg-Kalenberg and Braun-schweig-Lüneburg-Grubenhagen; ruling house of Welf (Braunschweig-Lüneburg) is Protestant. There were two main lines to this house and duchy--Braunschweig and Lüneburg--adminis-tered separately. Several cadet lines of the Welf dynasty ruled from time to time. Between 1807 and 1813 the duchy was occupied by the French who made it part of the King-dom of Westphalia; thereafter, it returned to its former position but was, quite il-legally, ruled by Hohenzollern and Mecklen-burg regents until 1913. Braunschweig fur-nished a large contingent of troops serving with the British in the American Revolution; many soldiers of this contingent remained in America after 1783, and are listed in Clif-ford Neal Smith, *Brunswick Deserter-Immi-grants of the American Revolution*. German-American Genealogical Research Monograph No. 1 (DeKalb, Ill.: Westland Publications, 1973).

BRAUNSCHWEIG (often called Kurbraunschweig).

See also Hannover; Lauenburg

BREMEN, now free state in German Federal Republic; former Reichsstadt and archbishopric. Both archbishopric and Reichsstadt were members of the Protestant corpus at the Peace of Westphalia; city is now 84% Protestant; much influenced by Reformation movement in Holland; Bremen has a modified Calvinistic creed. The vote in the archbishopal bench was secularized in 1648 when taken over by Sweden; then taken over by Hannover in 1719. Reichsstadt and archbishopric disagreed as to extent of Reichsstadt privileges, but city has been active in the Reichstag since 1640.

BRIXEN (or Bressanone), now in Province Bozen, Italy; formerly ruled by bishop. Represented by Trient in the Catholic corpus at the Peace of Westphalia. Area much associated historically with the Austrian Tirol and the Vorarlberg. Many of the inhabitants of this region are German speaking.

BRONKHORST, former Herrschaft. Vote in Reichstag cancelled in 1719. The lords of Bronkhorst (princes zu Salm-Salm) also owned Anholt.

BRUNNEN (Landstrass in Krain); former prelate nullius. Doubtful membership in the Reichsstand.

BUCHAU AM FEDERSEE, now in Kreis Saulgau, Baden-Württemberg; former abbey for women religious and Reichsstadt. The abbey was a member of the Schwäbische Grafenkolleg. Reichsstadt was a member of the Catholic corpus at the Peace of Westphalia; village is now 80% Catholic. Both Reichsstadt and abbey were listed in the Reichsmatrikel of 1521 and reaffirmed after 1792. In 1802 the town and abbey came to the Thurn und Taxis family; in 1806 administration passed to Württemberg. Status as Reichsstadt was never denied but apparently privileges were forgotten over the years; town had no lands and was very poor. The abbey was headed by a *gefürstete Abtissin* (princess-abbess).

BUCHHORN (now called Friedrichshafen), Baden-Württemberg; former Reichsstadt. Associated estates were Herrschaft Baumgarten-Eriskirch, Kloster Hofen. Member of the Catholic corpus at the Peace of Westphalia; town is now 65% Catholic. Administration passed to Württemberg in 1810. Name changed from Buchhorn to Friedrichshafen in 1811.

BÜCKEBURG, now in Kreis Schaumburg-Lippe, Niedersachsen; former Grafschaft. Town is mainly Protestant; former ruling house of Lippe is Reformed. The town was the residence town of the princes of Schaumburg-Lippe.

BÜDINGEN. *See* Wetterauische Grafenkolleg (Isenburg-Büdingen-Meerholz-Wächtersbach)

BURGUND (Burgundy), now in France; former duchy. Associated lands included Brabant, Namur, Limburg, Hennegau, Holland, Seeland, Luxemburg. The *Hoch-Freigrafschaft* Burgund (Exalted and Free Graviate of Burgundy) was a member of the Catholic corpus at the Peace of Westphalia. The region was the scene of bitter contention between the Habsburg dynasty and France.

BURSCHEID, now in Rhein-Wupper-Kreis, Nordrhein-Westfalen; former prelate nullius. Town is now 66% Protestant. Membership in the Reichsstand is doubtful, as it is not listed in any Matrikel and belonged to no Reichskreis.

CASTELL, now in Kreis Gerolzhofen, Regierungsbezirk Unterfranken, Bayern (Bavaria); former Grafschaft. Member of Fränkische Grafenkolleg. Castell family of counts was divided into two lines: Castell-Castell (Protestant) and Castell-Rüdenhausen (Protestant and Catholic). Grafschaft Castell was itself held in tenancy from Württemberg, and the family was Reichsadel only as Personalisten. The family controlled three territories (*Flecken*) and 28 villages; they were mediatized in 1806 and became Bavarian princes in 1901.

CHALON, now Chalon-sur-Saône, France; former Grafschaft. Became a direct possession of Burgundy in 1237.

CHIEMSEE, now in Bavaria; former bishopric. Absorbed (*landsässig*) by Archbishopric of Salzburg; Chiemgau secularized in 1803.

CHUR, now in Kanton Graubünden, Switzerland; former bishopric. Represented by Osnabrück in the Catholic corpus at the Peace of Westphalia; population is now 55% Protestant. Territory joined the Swiss Confederation in 1648, but the Catholic bishop remained a member of the Reichsstand without any lands directly held of the kaiser.

COLLOREDO, princes of. Associated estate was the Freiherrschaft of Waldsee (Wallsee). Member of the Schwäbische Grafenkolleg. Family of Colloredo-Mannsfeld is Catholic. The family became Reichsadel after 1792 as Personalisten and held no estates directly of the kaiser.

COLMAR, Département Haut-Rhin, France; former Reichsstadt. Member of the Protestant corpus at the Peace of Westphalia. Formerly belonged to the Landvogtei Hagenau, but became French after 1648.

COMBURG, former prelate nullius. Estate seized

by Württemberg whose action was approved by the Reichskammergericht (imperial court) in 1587.

CORVEY, now Höxter, Nordrhein-Westfalen; former prince-bishop, prelate nullius, and duchy. Ruled by the Hereditary Prince of Orange-Nassau when secularized in 1803. In 1807 the territory (Höxter and 16 villages) became part of the Kingdom of Westphalia, and in 1815 devolved to Prussia. The domain estates were formed in 1820-1822 into a mediatized Principality of Corvey. In 1834 the territory was transferred from the family of Hessen-Rotenburg to the Princes of Hohenlohe-Schillingsfürst (after 1840 styled Dukes of Ratibor, Princes of Corvey).

DÄNEMARK (Denmark), kingdom. The Oldenburg dynasty was a tenant-in-chief of the kaiser through tenancies of Holstein and Oldenburg. The house of Oldenburg is Lutheran.

DANZIG, now in Poland; former Reichsstadt. The city was Lutheran from 1557 to 1945 but is now predominantly Catholic. Obtained independence in 1454 when the citizens threw off the rule of the Teutonic knights; city then came under Poland, but the Polish king had few rights within the city.

DEGENBERG, now in lower Bavaria; former Grafschaft. The main town of Degendorf is 84% Catholic; the Landkreis is 93% Catholic. Vote in the Reichstag was cancelled when the territory became Bavarian.

DEUTSCHORDEN. See Hoch- und Deutschmeister

DIEPHOLZ, now Landkreis Diepholz, Niedersachsen; former Grafschaft. Member of the Westfälische Grafenkolleg and represented by Braunschweig, Kurbraunschweig (or Hannover), or the King of England since 1858.

DIESSEN, now Kreis Landsberg am Lech, Oberbayern (Upper Bavaria); former Grafschaft. Population is now 85% Catholic. Vote in Reichstag is said to have been cancelled by 1326 when it became Bavarian.

DIETRICHSTEIN, now Austria; former Grafschaft and principality. Associated estates were Tarasp (in Kanton Graubünden, Switzerland, but Austrian territory before 1803), Herrschaft Proskau und Czrhelitz, Leslie, Reichsherrschaft Neu-Ravensburg (in Swabia, later sold to Württemberg), Nikolsburg, Hollenburg, Finkenstein, Thalberg, Mensdorf-Pouilly. All lands were held under tenancy from Austria, excepting Tarasp which was a tenancy-in-chief of the kaiser. The family v. Dietrichstein is Catholic.

DINKELSBÜHL, now in Mittelfranken, Bayern (Bavaria); former Reichsstadt. Member of the

Catholic corpus at the Peace of Westphalia; in 1534 most of the population became Protestant but after 1648 both Protestants and Catholics were tolerated; the town is now 56% Protestant; the Landkreis is 71% Protestant.

DISSENTIS, former prelate nullius. Territory joined the Swiss Confederation.

DONAUWÖRTH. See Schwäbisch-Wörth

DORTMUND, now in Regierungsbezirk Arnsberg, Nordrhein-Westfalen; former Reichsstadt. Member of the Protestant corpus at the Peace of Westphalia. Withstood numerous incursions, mainly from the Grafen von der Mark; in 1803 the city passed to the house of Orange, then to the Duchy of Berg; in 1809 it became the capital of the French Ruhrdépartement; after 1815 it was in Prussian territory.

DÜREN, now in Nordrhein-Westfalen; former Reichsstadt. Town is now 76% Catholic; Landkreis is 85% Catholic. The town was mortgaged to Jülich in 1242, but the loan was never repaid; however, the town retained its status as Reichsstadt at least until 1548.

DUISBURG, now in Regierungsbezirk Düsseldorf, Nordrhein-Westfalen; former Reichsstadt. City is now 47% Catholic. Historically, the city has been associated with Jülich-Kleve.

DURLACH. See Baden

DYCK, now Gemeinde Bedburdyck, Kreis Grevenbroich, Nordrhein-Westfalen; former Grafschaft. Population is mainly Catholic. Ruled by the counts zu Salm-Reifferscheid-Krautheim et Dyck, a Catholic house.

EBERSTEIN, in Murgtal, Baden (near Baden-Baden); former Grafschaft. Member of the Schwäbische Grafenkolleg. Represented by Baden-Baden since 1660.

ECHTERNACH, in Luxemburg; former prelate nullius. Taken over by Burgundy (Austria).

EGGENBERG, in Austria?; former principality. Reichstag vote cancelled in 1717.

EGLINGEN, now in Kreis Heidenheim, Baden-Württemberg; former Herrschaft. Represented by the counts v. Grafeneck until 1728, thereafter by the princes v. Thurn und Taxis. In 1806 the territory was absorbed by Württemberg and in 1810 by Bavaria. The Thurn und Taxis dynasty is Catholic.

EGLOF(S), in Oberschwaben (Upper Swabia); former Herrschaft and Grafschaft. Member of the Schwäbische Grafenkolleg. Represented by counts v. Abensberg und Traun after 1668; in 1804 taken over by princes v. Windisch-

Grätz, and in 1806 absorbed by Württemberg. The peasants maintained their liberties and rights of self-administration until the nineteenth century; these rights apparently stem from special privileges granted to them during the early middle ages when the Franks were encroaching upon Swabian territory.

EGMONT und ISELSTEIN, now in The Netherlands; former Grafschaft. Territory became Dutch in 1648; Reichstag vote cancelled in 1548 or 1707. *See also* Iselstein

EHRENFELS, near Rüdesheim, Rheingaukreis, Hessen; former Grafschaft. Town of Rüdesheim is now 74% Catholic. Grafschaft became a member of Grafenkolleg in 1766, but vote was not exercised. Associated with the Kurpfalz (Electoral Palatinate).

EICHSTÄDT, now in Mittelfranken, Bayern (Bavaria); former bishopric. Associated estates were Beilngries, Herrieden, Ornbau, Pleinfeld, and the Hirschberger Erbe. Represented by Osnabrück in the Catholic corpus at the Peace of Westphalia; town is presently 88% Catholic; Landkreis is 96% Catholic. Secularized in 1803-1806 and became Bavarian territory; from 1817-1855 parts of the territory were included in the Duchy of Leuchtenberg; after 1817-1821 the bishopric was merged with that of Bamberg.

EINSIEDELN, in Kanton Schwyz, Switzerland; former prelate nullius. Territories became part of the Swiss Confederation and Reichstag vote was cancelled.

ELBING, in East Prussia, now Polish; former Reichsstadt. Until 1945 most of the populace was Protestant; after 1945 mainly inhabited by Polish Catholics. Elbing fell to Prussia in 1772. The city archives were not destroyed in 1945.

ELCHINGEN, now in Kreis Neu-Ulm, Regierungsbezirk Oberschwaben, Bayern (Bavaria); former prelate nullius. The Benedictine abbey at Elchingen was secularized in 1802.

ELLWANGEN, now in Kreis Aalen, Baden-Württemberg; former prince-bishop and prelate nullius. Represented by Augsburg in the Catholic corpus at the Peace of Westphalia; town is now 73% Catholic. Ellwangen was the most important territory in Württemberg under clerical control--about 400 square kilometers--divided into six district offices. In 1802 the Duchy of Ellwangen devolved on Württemberg as a consequence of secularization.

ELSASS UND BURGUND (Alsace and Burgundy), now in France; former Ballei (regional administration) of the Deutschorden (Teutonic order). *See* Hoch- und Deutschmeister

EMDEN. *See* Ostfriesland

ENGLAND, King of. *See* Diepholz; Hannover; Hoya; Spiegelberg

EPPSTEIN, now in Main-Taunus-Kreis, Hessen; former Grafschaft. Town is now 50% Protestant. The territory, mainly in the eastern Taunus hills, was comprised of lands of the Reich and of the Archbishopric of Mainz; when the Eppstein family died out in 1535, lands were divided among Hessen, Trier, and Stolberg. *See also* Königstein

ERBACH, in Odenwald, Hessen; former Grafschaft. Member of the Fränkische Grafenkolleg. Town is now 77% Protestant; Landkreis is 79% Protestant; the counts of Erbach-Erbach are Lutheran. The counts of Erbach were mediatized in 1806 and sovereignty passed to Hessen-Darmstadt.

ESSEN, now in Nordrhein-Westfalen; former abbey for women religious. Associated estates were Werden and Steele. Presently Essen is 50.3% Catholic. After 1609 Essen became a protectorate of the marquises of Brandenburg; in 1802-1803 the territory was secularized and fell to Prussia; from 1806-1813 it was part of the Grandduchy of Berg, but then came again into administrative control of Prussia.

ESSLINGEN AM NECKAR, now in Baden-Württemberg; former Reichsstadt. Member of the Protestant corpus at the Peace of Westphalia; town is now 52% Protestant. In the fourteenth century Esslingen tried to obtain more territory, but met with resistance from Württemberg; consequently, its sovereignty extended only over twelve small villages west of the Neckar River and a small bridgehead east of the river, plus the villages of Deizisau, Möhringen, and Vaihingen. In 1802 Esslingen was merged with Württemberg.

an der ETSCH (also called Adige), now Italy; former Ballei (regional administration of the Deutschorden (Teutonic knights). Absorbed by Austria. *See also* Hoch- und Deutschmeister

FALKENSTEIN, probably Kreis Rottweil, Baden-Württemberg; former Grafschaft. Absorbed (*landsässig*) by Austria in the fifteenth century. There were several estates of this name, as follows: in Kreis Roding, Bavaria, which belonged to the Bavarian duke and purchased in 1829 by Prince v. Thurn und Taxis; another in Obertaunuskreis, Hessen, belonging to the family of Nassau-Weilburg; another in Kreis Heidenheim, Württemberg; another in Kreis Hettstedt, Bezirk Halle, German Democratic Republic, belonging to the bishopric of Halberstadt.

FINSTINGEN (Fénétrange), now in Département

Moselle, Lorraine, France; former Herrschaft. Vote in the Reichstag was cancelled in 1458. This estate was later much fragmented but then was reassembled in 1751 under the house of Lothringen (Lorraine). House of Habsburg-Lothringen is Catholic.

FRANKFURT/MAIN, now in Hessen; former Reichs-stadt. Member of the Protestant corpus at the Peace of Westphalia; city is now 56% Protestant; the cathedral remained Catholic, even after most of the town's populace became Protestant; a great many Dutch and Walloon refugees of the Reformed Church were given refuge in Frankfurt. Because the cathedral remained Catholic, it continued to be the site of the election and crowning of the German kaiser. From 1806-1813 the city was the capital of the Rheinbund, and in 1810 capital of a Grandduchy of Frankfurt, which included Hanau, Fulda, Wetzlar, and Aschaffenburg. Annexed by Prussia in 1866.

FRÄNKISCHE GRAFENKOLLEG (Franconian Collegium of Counts). The Collegium was a member of the Protestant corpus at the Peace of Westphalia (although not all the participating nobles were Protestant). The participating nobles of the Collegium were:

- Princes and counts v. Hohenlohe

- Counts v. Castell

- Princes and counts v. Löwenstein representing Grafschaft Wertheim

- Gräflich Limpurgischen Allodialerben (heirs of the Limpurg estate with the rank of counts)

- Counts v. Nostitz representing Grafschaft Rieneck

- Princes v. Schwarzenberg representing Herrschaft Seinsheim and the gefürstete Grafschaft Schwarzenberg

- Gräfliche Wolfsteinische Allodialerben (heirs of the Wolfstein estate with the rank of counts), namely Prince v. Hohenlohe-Kirchberg and Count v. Giech

- Counts v. Schönborn representing Herrschaft Reichsberg and Herrschaft Wiesentheid

- Counts v. Windisch-Grätz, Personalists

- Counts Ursin von Rosenberg, Personalists

- Counts v. Wurmbrand, Personalists

- Counts v. Giech, Personalists

- Counts v. Grävenitz, Personalists

- Counts v. Pückler, Personalists

FREISING, now Oberbayern (Upper Bavaria); bishopric. Associated estates were Grafschaft Ismaning and Werdenfels and widely scattered lands--Innichen in Tirol, Bischoflack in Krain (Skofja Loka), Oberwölz in Styria. Represented by Salzburg in Catholic corpus at the Peace of Westphalia; town is now 86% Catholic; Landkreis is 92% Catholic. Territory was secularized in 1802-1803, part being absorbed by Bavaria, the remainder by Austria.

FRIEDBERG, now in Hessen (Wetterau); former Reichsstadt and Grafschaft. Member of the Protestant corpus at the Peace of Westphalia; town is now mainly Protestant; Landkreis is 64% Protestant. The Reichsstadt paid imperial taxes but was not a member of the Reichs-stände. Until 1729 Friedberg was the headquarters of the Rheinische Ritterkreises. In 1806 land was merged with Hessen-Darmstadt as a result of mediatization.

FRIEDRICHSHAFEN. *See* Buchhorn

FRIESLAND, now a province of The Netherlands (capital Leeuwarden), also a Landkreis in Niedersachsen, Verwaltungsbezirk Oldenburg (capital Jever); former Grafschaften. The Dutch province of this name became a Habsburg possession in 1524 and in 1579-1648 a part of The Netherlands. There was an early division into West and East Friesland; West Friesland is the Dutch province; East Friesland is now in Germany. *See also* Ostfriesland

FÜRSTENBERG, now in Kreis Donaueschingen, Baden-Württemberg; former Grafschaft and principality. Associated estates were Feldberg, Kniebis, Möhringen/Donau, Schöneberg, Grafschaft Heiligenberg, Herrschaft Messkirch, Landgrafschaft Stühlingen, Herrschaft Hewen (other properties in Bohemia and Austria). Another branch of the family had estates in Silesia. The Fürstenberg dynasty is Catholic. In 1806 Fürstenberg fell to Baden through mediatization.

FUGGER, Counts von. Associated estates were Grafschaft Kirchberg, Herrschaften Weissenhorn, Schmeihen, Pfaffenhofen, Marstetten, Fussendorf, Disachhausen, Wullenstetten, Babenhausen. The Fugger family is Catholic and supported a Jesuit college at Augsburg, "an act which has never been forgotten by protestant historians." This is one of the few families which freely admits its original bourgeois beginnings from "an honorable weaver and owner of a *Tagwerkes* [measure of land] . . . in Graben am Lechfeld." Through marriage the ancestor became a citizen of Augsburg in 1370. His savings allowed the sons to begin an international trade, mainly to the Levant and later to the West Indies.

FULDA, now Landkreis Fulda, Hessen; former principality under a prince-abbot. The Abbey of Fulda was represented by Bamberg in the Catholic corpus at the Peace of Westphalia; city is now 77% Catholic; Landkreis is 81%

Catholic. The prince-abbot controlled a small territory in the Rhön Mountains and from Brückenau to Hammelburg in Franconia. There was much fighting in this area at the time of the Reformation, but Fulda remained on the Catholic side. The territory was secularized in 1802 and fell to Hessen-Kassel in 1815.

GANDERSHEIM, now in Verwaltungsbezirk Braunschweig, Niedersachsen; former prelate nullius. In 1589 the territory became the property of a Protestant abbess; the town is now mainly Protestant. The abbey was dissolved in 1810. Territory was not held directly of the kaiser and membership in the Reichsstand is unclear. Until 1709 Braunschweig-Wolfenbüttel had sovereignty over the estates and continued to assert sovereignty thereafter.

GEDERN. *See* Wetterauische Grafenkolleg (Stolberg-Gedern-Ortenberg)

GELDERN, now in Nordrhein-Westfalen (also Gelderland in The Netherlands); former duchy. Associated estates included Erkelenz, Roermond, Grafschaft Zutphen, Goch, Arnheim, Venlo. The German areas remained Catholic at the time of the Reformation; the city of Geldern is now 75% Catholic; Landkreis is 84% Catholic. In 1543 the duchy became party of Burgundy; later the northern portion became Dutch and the southern part remained under Spanish control; in 1713 the southern portion became Prussian and Erkelenz fell to Kurpfalz (Electoral Palatinate).

GELNHAUSEN, now in Hessen; former Reichsstadt and Ritterschaft. The Reichsstadt paid imperial taxes but was not a member of the Reichsstände. The Reichsstadt was mortgaged in 1349; through sale and inheritance the mortgage came to Kurpfalz (Electoral Palatinate) and Hanau; later came to Hessen-Kassel. In 1549 a case was brought before the Reichskammergericht, which was resolved in 1745 by the town's becoming fully obligated to the mortgage holders. In 1746 the Kurpfalz' share in the mortgage was sold to Hessen-Kassel. In 1803 Gelnhausen was merged with Hessen.

GEMEN, now in Kreis Borken, Nordrhein-Westfalen; former Herrschaft. *See* Schaumburg und Gemen

GENF (Geneva), now in Switzerland; former bishopric. When Geneva became Protestant, the Catholic bishop removed to Annecy in France. Territories joined the Swiss Confederation.

GENGENBACH, now in Kreis Offenburg, Baden-Württemberg; former Reichsstadt and prelate nullius. The Reichsstadt was a member of the Catholic corpus at the Peace of Westphalia; the town is now 76% Catholic. Status as a Reichsstadt was questionable, and the matter was dropped by 1755; both Reichsstadt and Reichsabtei (imperial abbey) were mediatized in 1803 and merged with Baden.

GERA, now in Thuringia, German Democratic Republic; former Herrschaft. Vote in the Reichstag was cancelled in 1550. From 1562 Gera has been the seat of the junior line of the house of Reuss; the Reuss dynasty is Lutheran.

GERNRODE, now in Kreis Quedlinburg, Bezirk Halle, German Democratic Republic; former abbey for women religious. Abbey became Protestant about 1525; Reichstag vote was controlled by Anhalt after 1614.

GEROLDSTEIN (or Gerolstein), now in Kreis Daun, Rheinland-Pfalz; former Grafschaft. Estate was originally a tenancy of Jülich; fell to Blankenstein in 1469 and was ruled by a branch of the counts v. Manderscheid family. *See also* Blankenstein und Geroldstein; Manderscheid

GIECH, Counts von. Associated estate was Herrschaft Thurnau. Giech represented the Gräfliche Wolfsteinische Allodialerben (heirs of Wolfstein estate with the rank of counts) in the Fränkische Grafenkolleg, and was also a Personalist of the Collegium. This Franconian noble family is Protestant and Lutheran. Sovereignty over Herrschaft Thurnau was lost to Prussia in 1796. After 1806 territories of the family were merged with Bavaria.

GIENGEN AN DER BRENZ, now in Kreis Heidenheim, Baden-Württemberg; former Reichsstadt. Represented by Ulm in the Protestant corpus at the Peace of Westphalia; town is now 45% Protestant and 45% Catholic. Merged with Württemberg in 1803.

GIMBORN-NEUSTADT, now in Oberbergischen Kreis, Nordrhein-Westfalen; former Grafschaft. Territory comprised of about 50 small villages; represented by the princes v. Schwarzenberg and, after 1760, by the counts v. Wallmoden. Amt Neustadt was formerly a part of Grafschaft Mark. The Schwarzenberg family is Catholic, but Gimborn is now 65% Protestant.

GLEICHEN, now in Thuringia, German Democratic Republic; former Grafschaft. Apparently sold to the Archbishopric of Mainz when the Gleichen ruling family died out; Reichstag vote was cancelled in 1569 or 1631.

GÖRZ, now the Italian province of Gorizia; former gefürstete Grafschaft. Reichstag vote was cancelled in 1501; property fell to the house of Habsburg (Austria); under Napoleon's control 1809-1815, and from 1815-1918 an Austrian crown land; became Italian territory after 1919 with portion to Yugoslavia.

GÖTTINGEN, now in Niedersachsen; former Reichsstadt (false). City is now 81% Protestant. Göttingen was not a Reichsstadt, although so stated erroneously in old lists; however, the town did have a considerable amount of freedom, partially because it was the site of a university.

GOSLAR, now in Niedersachsen; former Reichsstadt. Represented by Lübeck in the Protestant corpus at the Peace of Westphalia; city is now 67% Protestant. In 1802 Goslar fell to Prussia; in 1815 to Hannover; in 1866 again to Prussia; and in 1941 to Braunschweig.

GOTTORP. See Dänemark; Holstein; Oldenburg

GRÄVENITZ, Counts von. Personalists in the Fränkische Grafenkolleg. Closely allied to the dukes of Württemberg as the consequence of a morganatic marriage in 1707.

GRONSFELD, former Grafschaft. Member of the Westfälische Grafenkolleg. Represented by the counts v. Törring-Jettenbach since 1719; the v. Törring family is Catholic.

GRUMBACH. See Wetterauische Grafenkolleg (Wild- und Rheingraf zu Grumbach)

GUNDELFINGEN, now in Kreis Münsingen, Baden-Württemberg; former Herrschaft. Reichstag vote cancelled in the fifteenth century.

GUNTERSBLUM, now in Kreis Mainz, Rheinland-Pfalz; former Grafschaft. Since 1660 the seat of the Guntersblum branch of the Leiningen dynasty. In Guntersblum there was also an office of the Teutonic knights (Deutschorden). The family of Leiningen-Billigheim (Guntersblum) is Catholic. See also Hoch- und Deutschmeister; Wetterauische Grafenkolleg (Leiningen-Guntersblum)

GURK, now in Bezirk St. Veit/Glan, Carinthia, Austria; former bishopric. Absorbed (landsässig) by Austria.

GUTENZELL, now in Kreis Biberach, Baden-Württemberg; former abbey for women religious. Territories included 11 villages. Administered by the Abbot of Salem until 1753; secularized in 1803 and assigned to the counts v. Törring.

HAAG IM OBERBAYERN, now in Kreis Wasserburg am Inn, Oberbayern (Upper Bavaria); former free Herrschaft. Town is now 91% Catholic. Reichstag vote was cancelled in 1567, when the Herrschaft was absorbed by Bavaria.

HACHENBURG, now in Oberwesterwaldkreis, Rheinland-Pfalz. See Westfälische Grafenkolleg (Sayn-Hachenburg)

HAGENAU, now in Département Bas-Rhine, France; former Reichsstadt and Landvogtei. Associated political entities of the Landvogtei were Kaiserberg, Colmar, Schlettstadt, Weissenburg/Elsass, Oberehnheim (Obernai), Rosheim, Landau, Türkheim, Münster in St. Gregoriental. Territory became French in 1648.

HALBERSTADT, now in Bezirk Magdeburg, German Democratic Republic; former bishopric. Represented by Deutschorden (Teutonic knights) in the Catholic corpus at the Peace of Westphalia. Secularized in 1648 with Reichstag vote exercised by Brandenburg.

HALLERMUND (or Hallermünde), former Grafschaft. Represented by the counts v. Platen since 1706; the family v. Platen-Hallermund is Lutheran and Catholic.

HAMBURG, now a state; former Reichsstadt. Associated areas were Cuxhaven, Geesthacht, and a few smaller villages. Member of the Protestant corpus at the Peace of Westphalia. The Reichskammergericht decreed Hamburg's free status in 1618, but the city was unable to take a seat or vote in the Reichstag until 1770. Excepting for the period of French occupation (1806-1814), Hamburg has successfully maintained its freedom under a local aristocracy.

HANAU-LICHTENBERG, now in Hessen; former Grafschaft. Associated estates were Babenhausen, Bornheim. City of Hanau is 64% Protestant; Landkreis is 73% Protestant; the house of Brabant (Hessen) is Lutheran. Lichtenberg was the senior line of the Brabant dynasty; by treaty of inheritance, the properties fell to Hessen-Kassel in 1736. Reichstag vote cancelled in 1736.

HANAU-MÜNZENBERG, now in Hessen; former Grafschaft. Associated with Hanau-Lichtenberg and merged with Hessen-Kassel in 1736.

HANNOVER (also called Kur-Braunschweig), now in Niedersachsen; former electoral principality. The Duchy of Braunschweig-Wolfenbüttel was a member of the Protestant corpus at the Peace of Westphalia; city of Hannover is presently 75% Protestant; there is a large Evangelisch-Lutherische Landeskirche (1,392 congregations) and a smaller Evangelische Reformierte Kirche (129 congregations).

Kurhannover achieved electoral status in 1692-1708 and is more correctly called Kur-Braunschweig, which is the legal title (Kurhannover is a popular appellation). From 1714 to 1837 Hannover and England were under the same sovereign in personal union. (This may have implications for genealogical researchers, because the Hannoverian subjects of the king of England would not have been required to swear oaths of allegiance upon landing in the American colonies, as were the other German immigrants before the Revolution.) Bremen and

Verden fell to Hannover in 1720.

The principality was occupied by Prussia in 1801 and 1805, by Napoleon in 1803 and 1806. From 1807 to 1813 the southern part of Hannover was part of the Kingdom of Westphalia; from 1810 to 1813 the northern part was occupied by France. In 1813 Hannover was liberated and became a kingdom enlarged by merger with Osnabrück, Emsland, Ostfriesland, Hildesheim, Goslar, and Untereichfeld. In 1866 Hannover became a Prussian province. In 1922 Grafschaft Pyrmont and Schaumburg were added, and Kreis Ilfeld transferred to Saxony.

HARDECK, former Grafschaft. Absorbed by Austria.

HARRACH, Counts von. Family also owned Herrschaft Ruhrau in Lower Austria. Member of the Schwäbische Grafenkolleg. The family v. Harrach has Catholic and Protestant branches.

HARTENBURG. See Wetterauische Grafenkolleg (Leiningen-Hartenburg)

HAVELBERG, now in Bezirk Magdeburg, German Democratic Republic; former bishopric. The diocese became Protestant in 1561 and most of the populace is now Protestant. The bishopric had large estates which were absorbed by Brandenburg in 1571.

HEBEN (or Hohenhewen), near Engen in Hegau (northwest of Lake Constance), Baden-Württemberg. Reichstag vote was cancelled in 1570. Territory held by Austria until 1805, when it fell to Württemberg; in 1810 it was transferred to Baden.

HEGAU. See Heben (or Hohenhewen); St. Georgenschild im Hegau

HEGGBACH, now within the town of Maselheim, Kreis Biberach, Baden-Württemberg; former abbey for women religious. Estate contained five villages. Administered by the Abbot of Salem until secularized in 1803; thereafter administered by the counts v. Waldbott-Bassenheim until 1873.

HEIDECK, now in Kreis Hilpoltstein, Mittelfranken, Bayern (Bavaria); former Herrschaft. Territory has been Bavarian since 1471; administered by the Pfalz-Neuburg branch of the Wittelsbach dynasty after 1505.

HEIDESHEIM. See Wetterauische Grafenkolleg (Leiningen-Heidesheim)

HEILBRONN, now in Baden-Württemberg; former Reichsstadt. Represented by Esslingen in the Protestant corpus at the Peace of Westphalia; Landkreis is now 57% Protestant.

HEILIGENBERG, now in Kreis Überlingen, Baden-Württemberg; former Grafschaft. Member of the Schwäbische Grafenkolleg and represented by the princes zu Fürstenberg since 1534. In 1806 the territory was merged with Baden. The Fürstenberg family is Catholic. See also Werdenberg (und Heiligenberg)

HELFENSTEIN, near Geislingen an der Steige, Baden-Württemberg; former Grafschaft. Member of the Schwäbische Grafenkolleg with Reichstag vote controlled by Bavaria. Lands were divided among Reichsstadt Ulm, Württemberg, and Bavaria; in 1810 nearly all its former territory was within Württemberg.

HENNEBERG, near Meiningen, Bezirk Suhl, German Democratic Republic; former gefürstete Grafschaft. Herrschaft Schmalkalden (to Hessen-Kassel) was formerly associated with Henneberg. Represented by Sachsen-Altenburg (in the name of the entire house of Saxony) in the Protestant corpus at the Peace of Westphalia. From 1680 to 1920 most of the former territory was in the Duchy of Sachsen-Meiningen. The Kursächsische (Electoral Saxon) portion became Prussian in 1851 and the Hessian portion merged with Prussia in 1866.

HERFORD, now in Nordrhein-Westfalen; former Reichsstadt and abbey for women religious. City is now 82% Protestant; Landkreis is 90% Protestant. The Reichsstadt was taken over by the abbey and transferred to Jülich in 1547; status as Reichsstadt reaffirmed in 1631; invaded by Brandenburg shortly thereafter and retained despite later court decisions.

HERRENALB, now in Kreis Calw, Baden-Württemberg; former prelate nullius. The area is now 90% Protestant. The territory, which once comprised 40 villages, was secularized by Württemberg in 1535.

HERSFELD, now in Hessen; former principality and prelate nullius. The abbey of Hersfeld was represented by the Deutschorden (Teutonic knights) in the Catholic corpus at the Peace of Westphalia; the city is now 76% Protestant; the Landkreis is 83% Protestant. Secularized in 1606-1648 under the principality of Hessen-Kassel.

HESSEN (Hesse), now a state; former principality, electoral principality, landgraviate, and Grafschaft. Both Hessen-Kassel and Hessen-Darmstadt were members of the Protestant corpus at the Peace of Westphalia. Hessen-Kassel, the senior line, became Reformed in 1604; Hessen-Darmstadt, the junior line, remained Lutheran.

HESSEN-DARMSTADT, now part of Hessen; former principality. Member of the Protestant corpus at the Peace of Westphalia; reigning house was Lutheran. Grafschaft Hanau-

Lichtenberg was lost in 1736. Between 1790 and 1830 Hessen-Darmstadt gained Kurmainz and Kurpfalz territories east of the Rhine, the Kurkölnische Duchy of Westphalia (Brilon and Arnsberg), and Reichsstadt Friedberg. In 1806 Darmstadt gained Grafschaft Erbach and certain baronial (Reichsritterschaftliche) territories. In 1815 Westphalia was exchanged with Prussia for the principality of Isenberg-Birstein (Offenbach), Worms, Alzey, and Bingen. In 1816 the fortress of Mainz also passed to Darmstadt. Hessen-Homburg, Kreis Biedenkopf, and Kreis Vöhl were lost to Prussia; in 1866 and 1867 Darmstadt was more or less a Prussian protectorate.

HESSEN-KASSEL, now in the state of Hessen; former electoral principality. Represented Schaumburg in the Westfälische Grafenkolleg. Member of the Protestant corpus at the Peace of Westphalia; reigning house is Reformed since 1604. There have been two subsidiary branches of this family: Hessen-Rotenburg-Rheinfels (1627-1834) and Hessen-Philippsthal (since 1685). Acquired Herrschaft Schmalkalden in 1583 and Grafschaft Hanau-Münzenberg in 1736. In 1807 Hessen-Kassel merged with the kingdom of Westphalia; in 1813-1815 the Kurfürstentum (electoral principality) of Hessen was re-established and acquired the Niedergrafschaft (Lower Grafschaft) of Katzenelnbogen. In 1866 Hessen-Kassel was annexed by Prussia.

HESSEN-NASSAU, now in the state of Hessen; former Prussian province. Territory was a Prussian province from 1868 to 1944; included territories taken from Hessen-Kassel and Hessen-Darmstadt in 1866, Duchy of Nassau, Hessen-Homburg, the former Bavarian Bezirke Gersfeld and Orb, districts of Biedenkopf and Vöhl (formerly in Hessen-Darmstadt), and the city of Frankfurt/Main. In 1929 Waldeck was added; in 1932 Kreis Wetzlar was added, and Kreis Rinteln (Grafschaft Schaumburg) was merged with Hannover. (The political entity called Hessen-Nassau, a modern creation, has otherwise no history of its own and was not one of the former imperial designations.)

HILDESHEIM, now in Niedersachsen; former bishopric. Represented by Kurköln in the Catholic corpus at the Peace of Westphalia; now the majority of the city populace, as well as that of Amt Peine, is Protestant; other areas of the former bishopric remain Catholic. By 1519-1523 most of the lands of the diocese had been seized by Braunschweig-Lüneburg and the remainder of the lands were secularized in 1802. Territory was under Prussian administration from 1802 to 1807, then part of the kingdom of Westphalia from 1807 to 1813, thereafter merged with Hannover.

HOCHBERG. *See* Baden-Hochberg

HOCH- UND DEUTSCHMEISTER (the Teutonic order of knights), formerly a prelate nullius with lands scattered throughout Germany, Burgundy, and Italy. Represented in the Catholic corpus at the Peace of Westphalia. The Order (known by several names) was founded in Palestine during the Crusades as a religious order of warriors fightin for the cause of Christianity. Later, the Order returned to Europe, where it was especially notable for conquering the western Slavic lands, particularly East Prussia and the Baltic region.

By 1530 the Order had established its central administration at Mergentheim (now Bad Mergentheim, Baden-Württemberg) and had divided its possessions into twelve regions (*Balleien*) as follows:

- Thuringia
- Austria
- Hessen (Marburg)
- Franconia (Mergentheim)
- Koblenz
- Alsace-Burgundy-Swabia (with estates also in Switzerland)
- Utrecht (which became free after 1637)
- Bolzano (called An der Etsch)
- Altenbiesen (near Maastricht with lands now mainly in Belgium)
- Lorraine
- Saxony
- Westphalia

Each of the Balleien had a number of district offices (*Komtureien*); Utrecht, for example, had twelve district offices. Under the district offices there were often a number of local offices (*Ämtern*); Komtur Nürnberg, for example, had four Ämtern with 96 villages.

In 1809 Napoleon suppressed the Order in Germany and the estates were taken over by a number of secular lords. The Order was re-established in 1834 by Austria, again suppressed under Hitler, and revived in 1945 solely as a charitable organization.

A leading work on the various administrative offices of the Order is that of Walter Ziesemer, *Das grosse Ämterbuch des Deutschen Orden* [The great office book of the Teutonic Order] (Danzig: A. W. Kafemann, 1921). The principal archives of the Order are to be found in Vienna I, Singerstrasse 7. Contents are described, in part, in Klemens Wieser, *Die Bedeutung des Zentralarchivs des Deutschen Ordens für die Geschichte Schlesien und Mähren: Quellen und Darstellungen zur schlesischen Geschichte* [The importance of the Central Archives of the Teutonic Order for the history of Silesia and Moravia: Sources and accounts on Silesian history] Band 13 (Wurzburg: Holzner Verlag, 1967). See, in particular, the following entries therein:

- "Untertanen-verzeichnisse zu allen Orten des Meistertum Mergentheim 1527-1723" [Lists of subjects in all the places of the Mergentheim Chapter, 1527-1723], catalog number Mei 42/4, at page 39.

- "Zum Meistertum gehörige Städte, Schlösser, Ämter, Flecken, Dorfschaften, Weiler, und Gehöfte (alphabetisch . . . um 1700)" [Towns, castles, offices, districts, villages, marketplaces, and farms (alphabetically arranged . . . dated about 1700)], catalog number Mei 490/3, at page 48.

HOHENEMS, now in Bezirk Feldkirch, Vorarlberg, Austria; former Grafschaft. Member of the Schwäbische Grafenkolleg. Represented by Austria since 1759. Since 1617 the town has had a Jewish ghetto and synagogue.

HOHENFELS UND REIPOLTSKIRCHEN, now Kalkofen, Kreis Sigmaringen, Baden-Württemberg; former Herrschaft. Vote cancelled in 1602; Herrschaft belonged to Deutschorden (Teutonic knights).

HOHENGEROLDSECK (UND KRONBERG), now Schönburg, Kreis Lahr, Baden-Württemberg; former Herrschaft. Associated estates were Lahr and Mahlberg. Member of the Schwäbische Grafenkolleg. Represented by the counts von der Leyen since 1692. In 1819 the Herrschaft was sold to Baden. Half the estate was owned by the counts v. Veldenz and inherited by the counts v. Mörs-Saarwerden. The original owners (von der Leyen) were Catholics.

HOHENHEWEN (or Hohen-Höwen). See Heben

HOHENKÖNIGSBERG. See Tierstein und Hohenkönigsberg

HOHENLOHE, princes and counts of. Represented the Wolfstein heirs in the Franconian Grafenkolleg. There are two main lines of this dynasty: Hohenlohe-Neuenstein which is Protestant, and Hohenlohe-Waldenburg which is Catholic. There are a number of Hohenlohe branch lines--Langenburg, Öhringen, Ingelfingen, Bartenstein, Jagstberg, Waldenburg-Schillingsfürst, and Schillingsfürst (the Dukes of Ratibor und Corvey). Most of the lands of this dynasty were in Württemberg with a smaller portion in Bavaria. One branch was prominent in Silesia (Ratibor).

HOHENSOLMS, Kreis Wetzlar. See Wetterauische Grafenkolleg (Solms-Hohensolms)

HOHENSTEIN, now in Kreis Hersbruck, Mittelfranken, Bayern (Bavaria); former Grafschaft. Reichstag vote was cancelled in 1593; Grafschaft was under the administration of Nürnberg. (There was a second Grafschaft Hohenstein, now in Landkreis Nordhausen, Bezirk Erfurt, German Democratic Republic, which belonged to the Deutschorden (Teutonic knights).

HOHEN-WALDECK UND MAXLRAIN, former Grafschaft. Represented by the Electoral Prince of Bavaria, who voted only in the Kreistagen (local assemblies) but not in the Grafenkolleg.

HOHENZOLLERN, now in Baden-Württemberg; former double principality. Erroneously admitted to the Schwäbische Grafenkolleg. The populace of both Hohenzollern-Hechingen and Hohenzollern-Sigmaringen is mainly Catholic. Since 1695 both were Prussian (Hohenzollern) territories, because of an agreement between Kurbrandenburg and the Markgrafen von Ansbach und Bayreuth regarding rights of inheritance and succession. The Hechingen branch of the family is Protestant and formerly kings in Prussia; the Sigmaringen branch of the family is Catholic.

HOLSTEIN, now part of the state of Schleswig-Holstein; former duchy. Subordinate estates were Stormarn and Dithmarschen. The dukes of Holstein-Gottorp-Oldenburg were members of the Westfälische Grafenkolleg. The Duchy of Holstein was represented in the Protestant corpus at the Peace of Westphalia, and the populace is mainly Protestant today; the house of Holstein (Oldenburg) is Lutheran. From 1867 to 1945 Holstein was a Prussian province.

HOLZAPPEL, now in Unterlahnkreis, Rheinland-Pfalz; former Grafschaft. Member of the Westfälische Grafenkolleg. Represented by the princes v. Anhalt-Bernburg-Hoym who also owned Nassau-Hadamar. The house of Anhalt is Protestant.

HOORN, now in The Netherlands; former Grafschaft. When the count proposed to tolerate Protestants during the Reformation, he was beheaded by the Spanish Duke of Alba and his property seized. The Reichstag vote was then cancelled in 1586, and the territory fell to Liège.

HOYA, now in Niedersachsen; former Grafschaft. Represented by the king of England (as Braunschweig-Lüneburg and Kur-Braunschweig) in the Westfälische Grafenkolleg. Populace is mainly Protestant today.

HONOLZHAUSEN (or HYNOLTSHUSEN), may have been Honnecourt near Cambrai, France; former prelate nullius. Very doubtful membership in the Reichsstandschaft; not certainly identified.

ILLER-AICHHEIM, former Grafschaft. Represented by the counts v. Rechberg and later by the counts v. Limburg-Stirum. At an early date the Reichstag vote was cancelled, and the estate was listed among the Reichsritterschaft.

The family of Rechberg und Röthenlowen is Catholic.

IRRSEE, now in Upper Austria near the Salzburg border; former prelate nullius.

ISELSTEIN, former Grafschaft. Suppressed by Burgundy, then taken over by The Netherlands. *See also* Egmont

ISENBURG (or YSENBURG), princes and counts of. Associated estates were Birstein, Büdingen, Meerholz, Wächtersbach, Marienborn, Bönnstadt (*see also* Nieder-Isenburg). Members of the Wetterauische Grafenkolleg. Through the Edict of Tolerance, Isenburg-Büdingen became a haven for religious persecutees-- *Sektierer* (Sectarians), *Inspirierter* (the Inspired), *Herrnhuter* (Moravian Brethren). The Birstein branch of the dynasty is Catholic; all other lines are Reformed. The two principal lines of the dynasty were Isenburg-Büdingen and Isenburg-Birstein. From 1806 to 1815 the territories were a *Reichsbundstaat* (imperial federated state); the reigning family was mediatized after 1815, and the territories were incorporated into Hessen.

ISNY, now in Kreis Wangen, Baden-Württemberg; former Reichsstadt and prelate nullius. Represented by Esslingen in the Protestant corpus at the Peace of Westphalia; populace is now 67% Catholic. In 1803 the territory fell to the counts v. Quadt-Wykradt and in 1806 was incorporated into Württemberg.

JOHANNITERMEISTER (master of the Maltese knights), former prelate nullius. The Order was represented by the Deutschorden (Teutonic knights) in the Catholic corpus at the Peace of Westphalia; it seems likely that most of the subjects of the Order in Germany were Protestants, however, because of the Order's domination by Brandenburg. The Ballei Brandenburg (regional organization) was dissolved in 1811 and secularized by Prussia. Today, the organization is simply a charitable one with membership limited to nobles.

JÜLICH UND BERG, now in Nordrhein-Westfalen; former duchy. Associated estates were Monschau, Randerath, Euskirchen, Grafschaft Heinsberg, and Kleve. The city of Jülich is now 75% Catholic; Landkreis is 85% Catholic. The Reichstag vote was not exercised, because of a controversy among Kursachsen (Saxony), Kurbrandenburg, and Pfalz-Neuburg as to ownership through inheritance. From 1777 Jülich was in personal union with Bavaria; occupied by France 1794-1814; thereafter administered by Prussia.

JUSTINGEN. *See* Stöffeln und Justingen

KAISERSBERG, now in France; former Reichsstadt. Pertained to the Landvogtei Hagenau and became French in 1648.

KAISERSHEIM, former prelate nullius.

KAMMERICH, now Cambrai, France; former Reichsstadt and bishopric. Fell to France in 1678.

KAMMIN, former bishopric. Secularized in 1648 and Reichstag vote exercised by Brandenburg.

KAUFBEUREN, now in Bavaria; former Reichsstadt. Member of the Catholic corpus at the Peace of Westphalia; city populace is now 72% Catholic; Landkreis is 92% Catholic.

KAUFMANNS-SAARBRÜCKEN (also called Saarburg), now in France. Taken over by the bishopric of Metz, transferred to Lorraine, and thence to France.

KAUFUNGEN, now in Hessen; former abbey for women religious. Absorbed by Hessen-Kassel.

KAUNITZ, princes von. Associated estates were Esens, Stedesdorff, Wittmund, Austerlitz, Questenberg. This Catholic family was mainly in Bohemia and Moravia; also in Ostfriesland. *See also* Rietberg

KEMPTEN, now in the Allgäu, Bavaria; former Reichsstadt and prince-bishopric. The bishopric was a member of the Catholic corpus at the Peace of Westphalia, and the Reichsstadt was a member of the Protestant corpus; there had been much strife between the burghers and the bishop, so the burghers became Protestant in 1525; the town is now 76% Catholic; the Landkreis is 85% Catholic. Until 1803 the prince-bishop of Kempten owned the second largest clerical territory in Swabia (after Augsburg). The territories of the bishopric and of the Reichsstadt fell to Bavaria in 1803 and were united in 1811-1818.

KERPEN-LOMMERSUM, now in Kreis Bergheim (Erft) and Kreis Euskirchen, Nordrhein-Westfalen; former Grafschaft. Represented by the counts v. Schaesberg from 1712 to 1794. Because these two estates had belonged to the Spanish Netherlands (Belgium) before 1712, they are still called "Little Spain."

KHEVENHÜLLER, princes and counts of. Associated estates were Metsch, Aichelberg, Hohenosterwitz, Annabühl, Landskron, Werberg, Grafschaft Hardegg, Fronsberg, Prutzendorf, Starrein, Peygarten, Ladendorf, Kammerburg, Frankenburg. Member of the Schwäbische Grafenkolleg; personal members of the imperial nobility after 1792, although they controlled no tenancies-in-chief. Originally the family came from Carinthia but were also prominent in Mittelfranken. There were two principal lines: Khevenhüller-Frankenburg (which died out in 1884) and Khevenhüller-Metsch. The family is Catholic.

KIRCHBERG, former Grafschaft (Burggraf). Member of the Westfälische Grafenkolleg. Estate owned since 1530 by the Fugger family which is Catholic.

KITZINGEN, now in Unterfranken, Bayern (Bavaria); former prelate nullius. The town is 51% Protestant; the Landkreis is 53% Catholic. Town originally belonged to the archbishopric of Würzburg, but fell to Bavaria in 1802-1814.

KLETTGAU, on lower Wutach River, near Schaffhausen, in Baden-Württemberg and Switzerland; former Landgrafschaft. Member of the Schwäbische Grafenkolleg. Represented by the princes v. Schwarzenberg (a Catholic family) until 1805 when the territory was merged with Baden.

KOBLENZ, now in Rheinland-Pfalz; former Ballei (administrative region) of the Deutschorden (Teutonic knights). The city is mainly Catholic. Occupied by the French in 1794 and in 1798 became the capital of their Rhein-Mosel-Département. In 1816 the city fell to Prussia.

KÖLN (or Cologne), now in Nordrhein-Westfalen; former Reichsstadt and electoral prince-archbishopric. Associated estates and territories included a small strip along the west bank of the Rhine from Andernach to Rheinberg, Deutz, and Linz-Altenwied on the east bank, Vest Recklinghausen, the Duchy of Westfalen, Grafschaft Arnsberg, Hülchrath. The bishoprics of Münster, Paderborn, and Trier were suffragans to Köln. Both the electoral prince-archbishopric (Kurköln) and the Reichsstadt were members of the Catholic corpus at the Peace of Westphalia; the city is now 64% Catholic. The archbishops are usually also cardinals and therefore very influential in German church history and politics. The city itself was free, and the archbishop resided at Bonn. From 1583 to 1761 the archdiocese was controlled by Bavarian princes (Wittelsbach). In 1794 the French occupied the Kurköln west-bank territories and in 1803 the east-bank territories. Both territories fell to Prussia in 1815. A church reorganization in 1821 caused the transfer of northern and northeastern territories to the bishoprics of Münster and Paderborn. Eupen and Malmedy (now in Belgium) were transferred to Liège diocese after the first world war.

KÖNIGSBRONN, now in Kreis Heidenheim, Baden-Württemberg; former Grafschaft. Grafschaft Rothenfels (Allgäu) was an associated estate. The family v. Königsegg-Aulendorf is Catholic. Rothenfels was sold to Austria in 1804; Aulendorf came under Württemberg sovereignty in 1806.

KÖNIGSTEIN UND EPPSTEIN, now in Obertaunuskreis, Hessen; former Herrschaft. The Reichstag seat was cancelled in 1535, when the tenancy was assumed by the v. Stollberg family. The Stollbergs introduced protestantism, but the archbishop of Mainz overpowered them, and the territory was re-Catholicized; it is now 52% Catholic. The territories were captured by the French in 1793; the fortress was blown up.

KONSTANZ (or Constance), now in Baden-Württemberg; former Reichsstadt and bishopric. Reichenau and Propstei Öhningen were associated territories. The bishopric was a member of the Catholic corpus at the Peace of Westphalia; the Reichsstadt was a member of the Protestant corpus; the city populace is now 61% Catholic; the Landkreis is 81% Catholic. The city was Protestant at the time of the Reformation, and the bishop lived at Meersburg; under Austria, however, the populace was re-Catholicized. The Reichsstadt became Austrian in 1548 and remained so until 1805, when it fell to Baden.

KORNELIMÜNSTER, now in Kreis Aachen, Nordrhein-Westfalen; former prelate nullius. Town is now 92% Catholic.

KREUZLINGEN, now in Canton Thurgau, Switzerland; former prelate nullius.

KRIECHINGEN (or Créhange), now in Département Moselle, France; former Grafschaft. Member of the Wetterauische Grafenkolleg. Reichstag vote was cancelled in 1697 but revived in 1765 with representation by Wied-Runkel. The Grafschaft was dissolved during the French Revolution. *See also* Wied-Runkel

KRONBERG, now in Obertaunuskreis, Hessen. *See* Hohengeroldseck (und Kronberg)

KUFSTEIN, now in the Tirol, Austria; former Grafschaft. Member of the Schwäbische Grafenkolleg. Area is mainly Catholic, and the ruling family v. Kufstein is Catholic. Family members were Personalisten only after 1792.

LAHR, now in Baden-Württemberg; former Herrschaft. The town is now 56% Protestant; Landkreis is 56% Catholic. The territory fell to Nassau-Saarbrücken in 1629 and in 1803 to Baden. *See also* Saarwerden und Lahr

LANDAU/PFALZ, now in Rheinland-Pfalz; former Reichsstadt. Town became Lutheran at the time of the Reformation, but is now 50% Catholic. Town formerly pertained to the Landvogtei Hagenau; became French in 1648 and ownership was confirmed in 1714; it remained French until 1815, when it passed to Bavaria.

LANDSBERG. *See* Schenken v. Landsberg

LAUBACH, now in Kreis Giessen, Hessen; former Grafschaft. Town is now 76% Protestant. *See also* Wetterauische Grafenkolleg (Solms-Laubach)

LAUENBURG, now in Schleswig-Holstein; former duchy. The Sachsenwald was an associated estate. The Duchy of Sachsen-Lauenburg was a member of the Protestant corpus at the Treaty of Westphalia. Ownership passed to Braunschweig-Lüneburg in 1689; transferred to Prussia in 1815 and a year later to Denmark. In 1864 the duchy was again Prussian, and in 1876 was made a Kreis in Provinz Schleswig-Holstein.

LAUSANNE, now in Canton Vaud, Switzerland; former bishopric. The canton is now 60% Reformed.

LAUTERN. See Anhalt; Pfalz

LAVANT, now in Carinthia, Austria; former bishopric. Absorbed by Austria.

LEBUS, now in Kreis Seelow, Bezirk Frankfurt/Oder, German Democratic Republic; former bishopric. Absorbed by Brandenburg in 1598.

LEININGEN, princes and counts of. Associated estates were Dagsburg (Dachsburg), Hartenburg, Amorbach, Miltenberg, Mosbach, Ilbenstadt, Reinek, Aspermont. The main branches of the Leiningen dynasty are Protestant. The family has its origins in the Rheinpfalz. In 1779 a new Duchy of Leiningen was established but was dismembered in 1806 with parts going to Baden, Bavaria, and Hessen.

LEININGEN-WESTERBURG, counts of. Associated estates were Hartenburg, Heidesheim, Guntersblum, Westerburg, Ilbenstadt. Members of the Wetterauische Grafenkolleg. The family of Leiningen-Westerburg is Protestant. This is the main branch of the Leiningen dynasty; mediatized in 1806.

LEISSNIGK, former Grafschaft. Reichstag vote was cancelled in 1538; apparently the territories were in Saxony.

LEMGO, now in Nordrhein-Westfalen; former Reichsstadt. The town is 95% Protestant; Landkreis is 86% Protestant; the surrounding region was Reformed (Calvinist), but Lemgo itself remained Lutheran. Taken over by Lippe.

LEUCHTENBERG, now in the Oberpfalz, Bayern (Bavaria); former Landgrafschaft. Represented by Kurköln (Electoral Cologne) and then by Bavaria in the Catholic corpus at the Peace of Westphalia; the house of Leuchtenberg (Beauharnais) is Orthodox (most of their former eastern estates being in Russia). In 1648-1717 the Landgrafschaft became Bavarian territory.

LEUTKIRCH, now in Kreis Wangen, Baden-Württemberg; former Reichsstadt. Represented by Esslingen in the Protestant corpus at the

Peace of Westphalia; town is now 73% Catholic. Fell to Württemberg in 1810.

LICH, now in Kreis Giessen, Hessen; former Grafschaft. The town is now 72% Protestant. See also Wetterauische Grafenkolleg (Solms-Lich)

LICHTENBERG, now in Kreis Dieburg, Hessen. See Hanau-Lichtenberg

LIECHTENSTEIN (sometimes called Vaduz), the only remaining German-speaking principality. Diplomatic representation for the principality is administered by Switzerland. The Catholic princes of Liechtenstein were originally Austrian; branches of the family lived in Moravia, Silesia, and Austria.

LIMBURG-STIRUM. See Schaumburg und Gemen; Iller-Aichheim

LIMPURG, now in Baden-Württemberg; former Grafschaft. Member of the Fränkische Grafenkolleg. Since 1690 and 1713 represented by various allodial heirs.

LINDAU, now in Schwaben, Bayern (Bavaria); former Reichsstadt and abbey for women religious. The Reichsstadt was a member of the Protestant corpus at the Peace of Westphalia; the city is now 58% Catholic; Landkreis is 80% Catholic. In 1755 it was discovered that the Reichsmatrikel (imperial certification) for the abbey had been falsified and that it was not a member of the Prelatenkolleg. In 1802 the estates fell to the princes v. Bretzenheim, then to Austria; in 1805 the lands were transferred to Bavaria.

LIPPE, princes and counts of. The principality of Lippe is now the Regierungsbezirk Detmold, Nordrhein-Westfalen. Associated estates were the Herrschaft Rheda and the Grafschaften Schwalenburg and Sternberg. Members of the Westfälische Grafenkolleg. The house of Lippe is Reformed. There were several branches of this family. In 1806, when most other princely houses of Germany were mediatized, the reigning duchess of Lippe refused the change in status, and Lippe remained a separate state until forceably absorbed during the National Socialist era (1933-1945).

LIPPE-BÜCKEBURG. See Schaumburg und Gemen

LOBKOWITZ, princes of. Associated estates were the Duchy of Sagan (in Silesia), Raudnitz, Neustadt/Waldnaab, and the gefürstete Grafschaft Sternstein, plus numerous estates in Bohemia and Styria. The Herrschaft Neustadt/Waldnaab became the gefürstete Grafschaft Sternstein in 1641; in 1807 it fell to Bavaria. The Lobkowitz family is Catholic.

LÖWENSTEIN, now in Kreis Heilbronn, Baden-Württemberg; former Grafschaft. Associated estates were Grafschaft Wertheim (in Kreis Tauberbischofsheim), and Rochefort (Province Namur), Königstein im Taunus, Herrschaft Brenberg. Represented Virneburg in the West-fälische Grafenkolleg; represented Wertheim in the Fränkische Grafenkolleg. One branch of this family, Löwenstein-Wertheim-Freuden-berg was Protestant and held Virneburg and, later, Amt Freudenberg (in Kreis Tauberbisch-ofsheim); the junior line, Löwenstein-Wert-heim-Rosenberg was Catholic and held Graf-schaft Püttlingen and Rochefort, Amt Rothen-fels, and the abbey of Bronnbach. Both lines were mediatized in 1806. Many of these es-tates were absorbed by Württemberg.

LOMMERSUM, now in Kreis Euskirchen, Nordrhein-Westfalen; former Grafschaft. See Kerpen-Lommersum

LOSENSTEIN, former Grafschaft. Absorbed by Austria, and Reichstag vote cancelled in 1629.

LOTHRINGEN (or Lorraine), now in France; for-mer principality. France seized Lorraine in 1735, and the Lorraine dynasty was given a Reichstag vote representing Nomeny as indem-nification for the loss of their territories. After 1766 Lorraine was a French province un-til 1871, when large parts again were seized by Germany. From 1919 to 1940 all areas of Lorraine were again French; from 1940 to 1945 again held by Germany; after 1945 the French again took over these territories.

LÜBECK, now in Schleswig-Holstein; former Reichsstadt and bishopric. Both the Reichs-stadt and the bishopric were members of the Protestant corpus at the Peace of Westphalia; the populace is now 87% Protestant. The Reichstag vote was exercised by the Evangel-ical Lutheran bishops from the dynasty of Holstein-Gottorp. From 1810 to 1813 the city was occupied by the French; thereafter, it was a free state in the German Federation. In 1937 the city became part of Schleswig-Holstein, and its various exclaves were ab-sorbed by Prussia and Mecklenburg.

LUEDERS, former prince-bishopric. Represented by the Deutschorden (Teutonic knights) in the Catholic corpus at the Peace of West-phalia. Associated with the abbey of Murbach in the Upper Alsace.

LÜNEBURG, now in Niedersachsen. City is mainly Protestant; Landkreis is 90% Protestant. See also Braunschweig-Lüneburg

LÜTTICH (or Liège), now in Belgium; former (and present) bishopric. Represented by Kurköln (Electoral Cologne) in the Catholic corpus at the Peace of Westphalia.

LUPFEN, former Grafschaft or Herrschaft. Vote cancelled in 1582.

MAAS (or Meuse), now in France; former duchy. Probably also called the Duchy of Bar, which passed to Lorraine in 1431.

MAGDEBURG, now in the German Democratic Repub-lic; former principality and archbishopric. Member of the Protestant corpus at the Peace of Westphalia. The Reichstag vote was secu-larized and exercised by Brandenburg. From 1679 to 1740 many French and Palatine refu-gees fled to Magdeburg which was a center of Lutheranism.

MAINZ (or Mayence), now in Rheinland-Pfalz; former ecclesiastical electoral principality. Associated estates, titles, and territories were Erthal, Schönborn, Bassenheim, Ostein, Stadion, Dalberg, Aschaffenburg, parts of the Taubertal and Spessart regions, Kinzigtal; also held lands in Thuringia, Eichsfeld, and Hessen, Erfurt, Amöneburg. Kurmainz (Elec-toral Mainz) was a leader in the Catholic cor-pus at the Peace of Westphalia; the city is now mainly Catholic, but is the seat of an Evengelical Propstei; only areas around Mainz, Bingen, Dieburg, Seligenstadt, Bensheim-Hep-penheim have remained solidly Catholic. After 1648 the archbishopric had ten suffragan bish-ops and originally encompassed even more (Chur, Konstanz, Augsburg, Strassburg, Speyer, Worms, Würzburg, Eichstätt, Paderborn, Verden, Hildesheim, Halberstadt, Prague, Olomouc (Olmütz), and Fulda). After 1802 the arch-bishopric was confined to an area west of the Rhine River. During the French occupation period (1798-1816) Mainz was the capital of the Département of Mont-Tonnère. After 1816 the city fell to Hessen-Darmstadt.

MANDERSCHEID, now in Kreis Bernkastel-Wittlich, Rheinland-Pfalz; former Herrschaft and Graf-schaft. The Reformation was introduced into the territory but failed. Mediatized by the Habsburgs in 1546; it was occupied for a time by the French and then fell to Prussia in 1814.

MANSFELD, now in Kreis Hettstedt, Bezirk Halle, German Democratic Republic; former Grafschaft. The territory is mainly Protestant today; one line of the ruling family, Mansfeld-Bornstädter, was Catholic, however. The estates were ab-sorbed by, or mortgaged to, Saxony and Prus-sia. The name Mansfeld and certain allodial possessions were inherited by the Colloredo dynasty.

MARCHTAL, former prelate nullius.

MATSCH, former Grafschaft. Absorbed in the Tirol; Reichstag seat was cancelled in 1505.

MAULBRONN, now in Kreis Vaihingen, Baden-Würt-temberg; former prelate nullius. The abbey became Protestant in 1557, and the town is now 68% Protestant. The abbey once owned over 100 villages; secularized by Württemberg in 1504.

MAXLRAIN. *See* Hohen-Waldeck und Maxlrain

MECKLENBURG, now in the German Democratic Republic; former principality and duchy. The duchies of Mecklenburg-Schwerin and Mecklenburg-Güstrow were both members of the Protestant corpus at the Peace of Westphalia. The burghers of Mecklenburg were not submissive to the reigning dukes, and there was always much strife between them.

MEERHOLZ, now in Kreis Gelnhausen, Hessen. *See* Wetterauische Grafenkolleg (Isenburg-Büdingen-Meerholz-Wächtersbach)

MEERSBURG, in the Alsace, France; former Grafschaft. Became Austrian in the sixteenth century. (There is also a town of this name on Lake Constance.)

MEISSEN, now in Bezirk Dresden, German Democratic Republic; former marquisate and bishopric. The ecclesiastical lands became Protestant in 1587. Absorbed by Kursachsen (Electoral Saxony).

MEMMINGEN, now in Swabia, Bayern (Bavaria); former Reichsstadt. Member of the Protestant corpus at the Peace of Westphalia; city is now 62% Catholic; Landkreis is 78% Catholic. Reichsstadt formerly controlled 12 villages; territory fell to Bavaria in 1803.

MERSEBURG, now in Bezirk Halle, German Democratic Republic; former bishopric. Territories became Protestant in 1543-1561; secularized by Kursachsen (Electoral Saxony).

METTERNICH, counts of. This Catholic family originated in the lower Rhine region and Luxemburg. *See* Winneburg und Beilstein

METZ, now in Département Moselle, France; former Reichsstadt and bishopric. Became French in 1552, but was German again from 1871 to 1918 and 1940 to 1944.

MINDEN, now in Nordrhein-Westfalen; former bishopric. Associated territory was Grafschaft Ravensberg. Represented by Osnabrück in the Catholic corpus at the Peace of Westphalia; city is now 80% Protestant; Landkreis is 88% Protestant. Secularized and Reichstag vote exercised by Brandenburg in 1648. Merged with Grafschaft Ravensberg for administrative purposes in 1719. In 1808 Minden became part of the Kingdom of Westphalia. In 1811-1813 the portion of its territory west of the Weser River and the city of Minden fell to the French. After 1815 it was all again under Prussian control.

MOERS, now in Nordrhein-Westfalen; former Grafschaft. The Grafschaft became Protestant at the time of the Reformation, replacing the then ruling family with the house of Orange; city is now 56% Protestant; Landkreis is 50% Protestant. Territory fell to Brandenburg in 1702.

MÖMPELGARD (or Montbéliard), now in Département Doubs, France; former Grafschaft and principality. Territory had belonged to the house of Württemberg from 1397; occupied by France in 1676-1679 and again in 1793; annexed to France in 1801.

MONTFORT (or Menthor), now in Vorarlberg, Austria; former Grafschaft. Member of the Schwäbische Grafenkolleg. The family of Montfort-Tettnang (extinguished in 1787) also owned Rotenfels/Allgäu; thereafter territories represented by Austria.

MÜHLHAUSEN/THÜRINGEN, now Bezirk Erfurt, Thuringia, German Democratic Republic; former Reichsstadt. Member of the Protestant corpus at the Peace of Westphalia; now mainly Protestant populace. Although a free city itself, Mühlhausen was the administrative center for a number of imperial estates.

MÜHLINGEN. *See* Barby und Muehlingen

MÜLHAUSEN/ELSASS (or Mulhouse), in the Alsace, France; former Reichsstadt. Became a member of the Swiss Confederation in 1515; became French in 1797.

MÜNCHENROTH, former prelate nullius.

MÜNSTER/WESTFALEN, now in Nordrhein-Westfalen; former (and present) bishopric. Associated territories were Herrschaft Stromberg, Emsland, Vechta, Horstmar, Lohn, Cloppenburg, Ahaus, Ottenstein. Represented by Kurköln (Electoral Cologne) in the Catholic corpus at the Peace of Westphalia; city is now 66% Catholic; Landkreis is 83% Catholic; city was the site of the "Thousand-year Kingdom" of the Wiedertäufer (Baptists or Mennonites) in 1534-1535. Münster always had a close connection with Cologne and the latter's archbishops (usually Bavarian Wittelsbach family members). The territories were secularized in 1802-1803 and divided among the following: Prussia, Oldenburg, Arenberg, Looz-Corswarem, Salm-Grumbach, Salm-Salm, and Croy. There was an ecclesiastical reorganization in 1821 which divided the old areas into Bezirk Münster (with some lands from Düsseldorf) and Bezirk Oldenburg.

MÜNSTER IM ST. GREGORIENTAL, now in France; former prelate nullius. The town of Münster/Alsace joined the Protestants in 1536; pertained to the Landvogtei Hagenau; became French in 1648.

MÜNZENBERG, now in Kreis Friedberg, Hessen; former Herrschaft. Town is now 88% Protestant. Once belonged to the Stollberg family and to Kurmainz (Electoral Mainz).

MURBACH, near Gebweiler, Upper Alsace, France; former prince-bishopric. Represented by the Deutschorden (Teutonic knights) in the Catholic corpus at the Peace of Westphalia. De facto French territory since 1648 but legally still a member of the Reichsstand. Associated with Lüders. In 1764 the territory was secularized.

MYLLENDONK, former Grafschaft. Controlled by the counts v. Ostein.

NASSAU, now in Hessen; former duchy and Grafschaft. Associated territories were Usingen, Weilburg, Saarbrücken. Members of the Wetterauische Grafenkolleg. Territories became Calvinist (Reformed) during the Reformation. The reigning house is usually referred to as the house of Orange, the royal family of The Netherlands. Their possessions in Germany were divided among five lines of the dynasty but were again merged in 1743. Fulda, Corvey, and Weingarten were associated for a time. One branch of the family also owned Grafschaft Saarbrücken (to 1723), Ottweiler (to 1728), Idstein (to 1721), Usingen (to 1816), and Weilburg (to 1912). Diez, Dillenburg, and Hadamar were exchanged with Prussia in 1815. In 1866 Nassau became Prussian territory.

NAUMBURG/SAALE, now in Bezirk Halle, German Democratic Republic; former bishopric. Became Protestant during the Reformation. Absorbed by Kursachsen (Electoral Saxony).

NEIPPERG, counts von. Members of the Schwäbische Grafenkolleg. The family is Catholic and achieved the Reichsstand as Personalisten only after 1792. The family was originally Franconian; one branch thereof settled in Italy during Napoleonic times and styled itself the princes von Montenuovo.

NERESHEIM, now in Kreis Aalen, Baden-Württemberg; former prelate nullius. The town is now 80% Catholic. Originally belonged to the v. Oettingen family, but, as a result of a legal controversy, the abbey became *Reichsunmittelbar* (direct tenancy of the kaiser) from 1763 to 1803. Thereafter, it was secularized and administered by the counts v. Thurn und Taxis. In 1806 it was placed under Bavarian sovereignty and transferred to Württemberg in 1810.

NEUBURG, now in Bavaria; former principality and Pfalzgrafschaft. The Pfalzgrafschaft was a member of the Catholic corpus at the Peace of Westphalia; the ruling family, a branch of the Bavarian Wittelsbach dynasty, is Catholic. In 1742 Pfalz-Neuburg was inherited by Pfalz-Sulzbach. In 1777 Neuburg was in personal union with Bavaria; after 1799 it was called Province Neuburg and joined with Bavaria in 1808.

NEUENAHR, now in Kreis Ahrweiler, Rheinland-Pfalz; former Grafschaft. Area is now mainly Catholic. Reichstag vote was cancelled in 1600.

NIEDER-ISENBURG, former Grafschaft. Reichstag vote was cancelled in 1664. *See also* Isenburg

NIEDERMÜNSTER, former abbey for women religious.

NIEDERWESEL (or Wesel), now in Kreis Rees, Nordrhein-Westfalen; former Reichsstadt. Populace is now about equally divided between Catholics and Protestants. City was taken over by Jülich and came to Brandenburg in 1666. Occupied by the French during the Napoleonic period, and fell to Prussia thereafter.

NÖRDLINGEN, now in Bavaria; former Reichsstadt. Represented by Esslingen in the Protestant corpus at the Peace of Westphalia; now about equally Catholic and Protestant in both city and Landkreis. Absorbed by Bavaria in 1803.

NOMENY, now in Lorraine, France; former marquisate and principality. Member of the Catholic corpus at the Peace of Westphalia. Reichstag vote was introduced in 1736 for the house of Lorraine as indemnity for the loss of their former Lorraine territories which had fallen to France.

NORDHAUSEN, now in Bezirk Erfurt, German Democratic Republic; former Reichsstadt. Represented by Lübeck in the Protestant corpus at the Peace of Westphalia. Became Prussian territory in 1802.

NOSTITZ, counts v. A Saxon noble family from the Oberlausitz; branches thereof were located in Bohemia, Poland, and Silesia. *See also* Rieneck

NÜRNBERG, now in Bavaria; former Reichsstadt. Member of the Protestant corpus at the Peace of Westphalia; the city is now 58% Protestant; Landkreis is 66% Protestant. Formerly owned large estates and numerous market towns. In 1806 Nürnberg was absorbed by Bavaria.

OBEREHNHEIM (or Obernai), Département Bas-Rhin, France; former Reichsstadt. Pertained to the Landvogtei Hagenau; became French in 1648.

OBERMÜNSTER, former abbey for women religious.

OBERSTEIN, now in Kreis Birkenfeld, Rheinland-Pfalz; former Grafschaft. Town is now 80% Protestant. Reichstag vote was cancelled in 1682.

OCHSENHAUSEN, now in Kreis Biberach, Baden-Württemberg; former prelate nullius. Historically connected with the Abbey St. Blasien. When secularized in 1803, its territory was comprised of 35 villages in four Ämter (offices).

ODELHEIM, former prelate nullius. Otherwise unidentified, possibly in the Kraichgau, now in Baden-Württemberg.

ÖSTERREICH (or Austria), former marquisate, duchy, grandduchy, and empire. The Grandduchy of Austria was a member of the Catholic corpus at the Peace of Westphalia; most Austrian lands are staunchly Catholic today; the ruling house of Habsburg was, and remains, a loyal supporter of the Roman Catholic Church. The Habsburgers had extensive lands throughout Europe, only one concentration being in central Europe (Austria, Bohemia, Moravia, Silesia). In Germany, the Habsburgers held lands in what is now Baden-Württemberg; in addition, one branch of the house ruled in Lothringen (Lorraine) until it was taken over be the French. A member of the Habsburg family was usually elected kaiser of the Holy Roman Empire German Nation and was, therefore, the highest authority in all of Germany.

ÖSTERREICH, former Ballei (regional administration) of the Deutschorden (Teutonic knights). Member of the Schwäbische Grafenkolleg. Converted to Landstand, the equivalent of absorption, by Austria.

OETTINGEN, princes and counts von. Associated territories were Wallerstein and Spielberg. Members of the Schwäbische Grafenkolleg. One of the oldest dynasties in Germany. In 1806 the family was mediatized and its territories were merged with Bavaria and Württemberg. The family is Catholic.

OFFENBURG, now in Baden-Württemberg; former Reichsstadt. Member of the Catholic corpus at the Peace of Westphalia; city is now 63% Catholic; Landkreis is 80% Catholic. Since the sixteenth century Offenburg was the seat of the imperial Landvögte of Ortenau, a title held by the Markgrafen v. Baden from 1701. In 1803 the city was taken over by Baden; in 1848-1849 it was a focal point of the Revolution.

OLDENBURG, now in Niedersachsen; former grandduchy. Associated territories were Herrschaft Varel, duchy of Birkenfeld (in 1814); Herrschaft Jever (in 1818), and Herrschaft Knyphausen (in 1825). The Duke of Holstein-Gottorp-Oldenburg was a member of the Westfälische Grafenkolleg. The city of Oldenburg is now 70% Protestant; the Landkreis is 85% Protestant; the Oldenburg dynasty is Lutheran. The kings of Denmark are members of the Oldenburg dynasty. Some Oldenburger lands (the Ämter Friesoythe, Vechta, and Cloppenburg)

fell to the bishopric of Münster in 1803 in return for Amt Wildeshausen (formerly Hannoverian territory).

ORTENBERG, now in Kreis Offenburg, Baden-Württemberg. See Wetterauische Grafenkolleg (Stolberg-Gedern-Ortenberg)

ORTENBURG, now in Kreis Vilshofen, Niederbayern (Bavaria); former Grafschaft. Member of the Wetterauische Grafenkolleg. Ownership of the Grafschaft was long disputed by the Wittelsbach dynasty. In 1805 Bavaria finally got Ortenburg in exchange for Amt Tambach and Amt Sessbach.

OSNABRÜCK, now in Niedersachsen; former bishopric. Associated territory was the exclave Reckenberg (in Kreis Wiedenbrück). Member of the Catholic corpus at the Peace of Westphalia. As a consequence of this treaty, all parishes of the bishopric were divided equally between Catholic and Protestant congregations. In the cathedral, a Catholic prince-bishop and a Saxon (Welf) prince ruled alternately. The city populace is now 58% Protestant; the Landkreis is 58% Catholic. Territories mainly lost to the bishopric of Münster.

OSTFRIESLAND (East Friesland; also called Emden), now the Regierungsbezirk Aurich, Niedersachsen, and the coastal area between Oldenburg and the Dutch border; former principality and Grafschaft. There was much controversy between the ruling princes who were Lutheran and the city of Emden whose populace was Calvinist (as in The Netherlands). The territory became Prussian, then Dutch, and in 1810 French. After the Congress of Vienna, it was given to Hannover; in 1866 it came once again to Prussia.

PADERBORN, now in Nordrhein-Westfalen; former bishopric. Represented by Kurköln in the Catholic corpus at the Peace of Westphalia; the city is now 70% Catholic; the Landkries is 82% Catholic. At the time of the Reformation some territories were given up to Ravensberg, Lippe, and Waldeck; in 1732 some parishes were transferred to Kurkoln; in 1792 other parishes assigned to the new bishopric of Corvey. During the seventeenth and eighteenth centuries the house of Lippe supplied several of the bishops; thereafter, they were supplied by the house of Fürstenberg.

PASSAU, now in Niederbayern (Bavaria); former bishopric. Represented by the Deutschorden (Teutonic knights) in the Catholic corpus at the Peace of Westphalia; city is now 87% Catholic; Landkreis is 93% Catholic. Some territories were lost to the bishopric of Linz (1783) and to St. Pölten (1783); in 1803 the remaining territories became Bavarian.

PETERSHAUSEN ZU KONSTANZ (now in the city of

Constance, Baden-Württemberg); former prelate nullius. Associated territory was the Herrschaft Hilzingen und Herdwangen.

PFALZ (or The Palatinate), now divided among Hessen, Rheinland-Pfalz, and Baden-Württemberg; former electoral principality and numerous Grafschaften. Divisions were Pfalz-Simmern and Pfalz-Zweibrücken. The Oberpfalz (Upper Palatinate), Pfalz-Neuburg, and Pfalz-Sulzbach, so named because of dynastic relationships, were in what is now Bavaria and not contiguous with Simmern and Zweibrücken.

The religious history of the various divisions of the Pfalz was as follows: At the Peace of Westphalia all divisions were represented in the Protestant corpus: Pfalz-Simmern and Pfalz-Zweibrücken were represented by Anhalt, Pfalz-Veldenz and Pfalz-Lauterecken by Württemberg; the Kurpfalz (Electoral Palatinate) was itself a member of the Protestant corpus. In Pfalz-Simmern Calvinism (the Reformed Church) became established, but a succeeding prince declared the territory to be Lutheran; when a new dynastic line ascended the throne, Catholicism was declared; the controversy was such that in 1707 all church edifices were distributed among the three sects; today, Protestants are slightly in the ascendancy (52%).

Before Napoleon reorganized the Palatinate in 1803, the area was divided into 44 different sovereignties whose rulers often transferred their religious loyalties from one confession to another, with the consequence, that the religious and political history of the region is extraordinarily complicated. Pfalz-Zweibrücken set up Pfalz-Birkenfeld in 1569 for the younger line of the ruling family; in 1671 this territory became Pfalz-Bischweiler and Grafschaft Rappoltstein. Pfalz-Lautern, comprised of the Oberämtern Lautern, Neustadt, and Amt Sobernheim, was independent from 1576 to 1583 and the populace was Calvinist. Pfalz-Simmern, independent from 1459 to 1598 and 1611 to 1674, was comprised of Simmern and a part of Grafschaft Sponheim. Pfalz-Veldenz, indepedent from 1543 to 1694, was comprised of the Amtern Veldenz and Lauterecken with Remigiusberg cloister, Grafschaf Lützelstein, and the half-Herrschaft Guttenberg; this principality rejoined the Kurpfalz again in 1733. Pfalz-Zweibrücken, a duchy from 1410 to 1801, originally included Simmern, Zweibrücken, Veldenz, and part of Grafschaft Sponheim.

PFULLENDORF, now in Kreis Überlingen, Baden-Württemberg; former Reichsstadt. Member of the Catholic corpus at the Peace of Westphalia; now 75% Catholic. Territories fell to Baden in 1803.

PLAUEN, now in Bezirk Chemnitz, German Democratic Republic. *See* Reuss und Plauen

PLESSE, now in Leinstal bei Eddigehausen, Kreis Göttingen, Niedersachsen; former Herrschaft. Reichstag vote was cancelled in 1571, when the ruling house died out; thereafter it was Hessian territory until 1816 when it came to Hannover.

POLHEIM, former Grafschaft. Absorbed by Austria.

POMMERN (or Pomerania), now in the German Democratic Republic and Poland; former duchy. Vorpommern was Swedish territory; Hinterpommern belonged to Brandenburg. The duchies of Pommern-Stettin and Pommern-Wolgast were represented by Kurbrandenburg (Electoral Brandenburg) in the Protestant corpus at the Peace of Westphalia. Part of Pomerania was conquered by Prussia in 1648, further areas in 1720. Settled by refugees and Palatines. In 1815 the Swedish territory in Pomerania was taken over by Prussia.

PREUSSEN (or Prussia), now mainly in the German Democratic Republic, Poland, and the Soviet Union; former principality and kingdom. Prussia was a term denoting wider possessions of Brandenburg; the term also means the territories brought together in the Baltic Sea are by the Deutschorden (Teutonic knights) and secularized in 1525 under the rule of Brandenburg. Prussia was represented in the Westfälische Grafenkolleg. Under the Great Elector (*Grosse Kurfürst*) Friedrich Wilhelm, Brandenburg was Calvinistic (the Reformed Church); other areas were mainly Lutheran. The great coat-of-arms of the Kingdom of Prussia of 1853 was divided into 48 fields representing the following possessions:

1.	Silesia	15.	Duchy of the Wenden
2.	Grandduchy of Niederrhein	16.	Mecklenburg
3.	Grandduchy of Posen	17.	Duchy of Crossen
4.	Duchy of Saxony	18.	Thuringia
5.	Duchy of Engern	19.	Oberlausitz
6.	Duchy of Westphalia	20.	Niederlausitz
7.	Duchy of Geldern	21.	Oranien und Neuenburg
8.	Duchy of Magdeburg	22.	Rügen
9.	Duchy of Cleve	23.	Pyrmont
10.	Duchy of Jülich	24.	Paderborn
11.	Duchy of Berg	25.	Münster
12.	Duchy of Stettin	26.	Minden
13.	Duchy of Pommern	27.	Camin (Kamin)
14.	Duchy of Cassubia	28.	*Fürstl.* Wenden
		29.	*Fürstl.* Schwerin
		30.	Ratzeburg

31. Moers	40. Grafschaft Tecklenburg
32. Eichsfeld	41. Grafschaft Lingen
33. Erfurt	42. Grafschaft Schwerin
34. Nassau	43. Sayn
35. Grafschaft Henneberg	44. Rostock
36. Ruppin	45. Stargard
37. Grafschaft Mark	46. Grafschaft Arensberg
38. Ravensberg	47. Grafschaft Barby
39. Hohenstein	48. --

The period 1640-1714 may be considered the period during which Brandenburg was transferred into Prussia through acquisition and consolidation of territories and the reorganization of governmental administration. From 1713 to 1792 was the flowering of the Kingdom of Prussia. From 1792 to 1815 Prussia suffered reverses, rivalry with Austria and defeat from Napoleon. After 1815 there were numerous social and economic reforms, a revolution in 1848, the 1871 war with France, and the great consolidation of territory brought about by the Congress of Vienna and through Bismarck's efforts. The end of world war one brought about the fall of the monarchy and the beginnings of popular government.

PRÜM, now in Kreis Bitburg-Prüm, Rheinland-Pfalz; former prince-bishop and prelate nullius. Represented by Trier in the Catholic corpus at the Peace of Westphalia; mainly Catholic today. The archbishop of Trier took over the administration of Prüm in 1576 and controlled the territory as an Oberamt. The present Kreis contains some communities formerly in Kreise Wittlich and Trier.

PÜCKLER, counts von. Associated estates were Muskau and Limpurg. Personalisten in the Fränkische Grafenkolleg. This is a Silesian family with a Franconian branch since the eighteenth century; the Pückler-Limpurg branch is Lutheran.

PYRMONT, now in Kreis Hameln-Pyrmont, Niedersachsen; former Grafschaft. Member of the Westfälische Grafenkolleg; represented by the princes v. Waldeck since 1625. The area is mainly Protestant today, and the family v. Waldeck-Pyrmont is Protestant.

QUEDLINBURG, now in Bezirk Halle, German Democratic Republic; former abbey for women religious. The territory became Protestant in 1540. In 1698 administration passed by agreement from Kursachsen (Electoral Saxony) to Brandenburg and in 1813 the territory was completely absorbed by Prussia.

RAPPOLTSTEIN (or Haut-Ribeaupierre), near

Rappoltsweiler in the Vosges mountains, France; former Herrschaft. Reichstag vote was cancelled in 1673 because it had been superseded by Austria. When the original ruling family died out, the Herrschaft was taken over by Pfalz-Birkenfeld and transferred to Pfalz-Saarbrücken in 1734. In 1789-1801 it was merged with the Alsace. Since the fourteenth century the lords of Rappoltstein have been the lords of all the pipers and musicians in the Alsace and were accorded the honor of being "Piper King."

RATZEBURG, now in Kreis Herzogtum Lauenburg, Schleswig-Holstein; former bishopric. Secularized under Mecklenburg-Schwerin in 1648; passed to Mecklenburg-Strelitz in 1701 and so remained until 1934. In 1869 the Duchy was allowed its own Landtag but, because of opposition from the peasants, it did not convene until 1906, after having made several revisions of its constitution.

RAVENSBURG, now in Baden-Württemberg; former Reichsstadt. Member of the Catholic corpus at the Peace of Westphalia. Since the time of the Reformation, all governmental offices have been divided equally between Protestants and Catholics. The city is now 71% Catholic and the Landkreis 69% Catholic. In 1802 the city fell to Bavaria and after 1810 to Württemberg.

RECKLINGHAUSEN (or Rechenhausen), now in Nordrhein-Westfalen; former prelate nullius. City is now 58% Catholic; Landkreis is 57% Catholic. The abbey of Essen (for women religious) exercised sovereignty, but the territory was mortgaged to the Herren v. Gemen and their descendants the counts v. Schaumburg. In 1794 it became a possession of Kurköln (Electoral Cologne) and in 1802 of the dukes v. Arenberg. In 1811 the territory passed to Grafschaft Berg and in 1815 to Prussia.

RECKUM (or Reckheim), now Rekheim bei Tongern, Belgium; former Grafschaft. Member of the Westfälische Grafenkolleg. Represented by the counts v. Aspremont since 1623.

REGENSBURG (or Ratisbon), now in Regierungsbezirk Oberpfalz, Bayern (Bavaria); former Reichsstadt and bishopric. Associated estate was the Herrschaft Donaustauf. The Reichsstadt was represented by Hessen-Darmstadt in the Protestant corpus at the Peace of Westphalia; the bishopric was represented by Osnabrück in the Catholic corpus; the city is now 83% Catholic; Landkreis is 93% Catholic. The bishopric was secularized in 1803, and its territories passed to the princes v. Thurn und Taxis.

REGENSTEIN, near Blankenburg, Bezirk Magdeburg, German Democratic Republic; former Grafschaft.

Represented by Brandenburg since 1670. Until 1945 the territory was a Prussian exclave within Kreis Blankenburg, which belonged to Braunschweig.

REICHENAU, an island in Lake Constance, Baden-Württemberg; former prelate nullius. Now 74% Catholic. Territory was merged with the bishopric of Konstanz and lost its Reichstag vote in 1548. In 1757 it again became free of the bishopric and in 1803 was secularized.

REICHENSTEIN, now in Nordrhein-Westfalen; former Grafschaft. Represented by the v. Nesselrode family since 1698.

REICHSBERG UND WIESENTHEID, former Grafschaft. Represented by the counts v. Schönborn in the Fränkische Grafenkolleg. The v. Schönborn family is Catholic.

REIFFERSCHEID, now a community in Kreis Ahrweiler, Rheinland-Pfalz; former Grafschaft. From 1794 to 1814 the area was occupied by the French. The ruling Salm-Reifferscheid family is Catholic.

REIPOLTSKIRCHEN, now in Kreis Kusel, Rheinland-Pfalz; former Herrschaft. The Herrschaft was a tenancy-in-chief of the kaiser until 1792-1801. See Hohenfels und Reipoltskirchen

REUSS UND PLAUEN, now in Thuringia, German Democratic Republic; former Grafschaft. Associated estates were Burg, Dölau, Saalburg, Schleiz, Köstritz, Lobenstein, Ebersdorf. Member of the Wetterauische Grafenkolleg. The rulers were the princes v. Reuss, a Lutheran house. There were two principalities and branches of the family: Reuss Senior Line (Reuss-Greiz) and Reuss Junior Line (Reuss-Gera). Some properties were held jointly by as many as 12 subbranches of the dynasty. This family has a marked preference for the name Heinrich; the Erbprinz (Hereditary Prince) Heinrich XLV died in 1945.

REUTLINGEN, now in Baden-Württemberg; former Reichsstadt. Represented by Esslingen in the Protestant corpus at the Peace of Westphalia; city is now 71% Protestant; Landkreis is 67% Protestant. Territory fell to Württemberg in 1803.

RHEINECK, probably near Brohl, Kreis Ahrweiler, Rheinland-Pfalz; former Grafschaft. Represented by the v. Sinzendorf family since 1654.

RHEINGRAFEN, the "counts of the Rhine." Members of the Wetterauische Grafenkolleg. The Rheingrafen had fortresses and estates in the Nahe River region. They inherited the estates of the Wildgrafen (Dhaun, Kyrburg bei Kirn), and then styled themselves the Wild- und Rheingrafen thereafter. Connected with the Salm-Kyrburg branch of the Salm

dynasty; the Salm-Kyrburg family is Catholic. See also Wild- und Rheingrafen

RIDDAGSHAUSEN, now a part of the city of Braunschweig, Niedersachsen; former prelate nullius. Became Protestant in 1568 and since that time has been in the Braunschweig-Wolfenbüttel Landstand only.

RIENECK, now in Kreis Gemünden, Unterfranken, Bayern (Bavaria), former Grafschaft. Member of the Fränkische Grafenkolleg. Represented by the v. Nostitz family since 1674. The family was mediatized in 1814, and the territory was merged with Bavaria.

RIETBERG, now in Kreis Wiedenbrück, Nordrhein-Westfalen; former Grafschaft. Member of the Westfälische Grafenkolleg. Town is now 87% Catholic. Represented by the v. Kaunitz family since 1692. In 1807 the territory was merged in the Kingdom of Westphalia and after 1815 became Prussian territory.

ROCKENHAUSEN, may have been near Kaiserslautern or by Schaffhausen; former prelate nullius. Not positively identifiable.

RÖDELHEIM, former Grafschaft. The ruling family v. Solms-Rödelheim-Assenheim is Lutheran. See Wetterauische Grafenkolleg (Solms-Rödelheim)

RÖNIS. See Brandenstein-Rönis

ROGENDORF, former Grafschaft. Became Austrian territory after 1600.

ROGGENBURG, now Messhofen, Kreis Neu-Ulm, Schwaben, Bayern (Bavaria); former prelate nullius. The territory had four Ämtern; came to Bavaria in 1803.

ROSENBERG, counts von. The Orsini (Ursin) von Rosenberg family is thought to have a faulty lineage and not, in fact, to be related to the Orsini family of Italy. The Rosenberg family is Catholic and originated in Carinthia, Austria. See also Ursin v. Rosenberg

ROSHEIM, now in Département Bas-Rhin, France; former Reichsstadt. Pertained to the Landvogtei Hagenau; became French territory in 1648.

ROTH, either Münchenroth or Roth im Bayern; former prelate nullius. Not positively identifiable.

ROTHENBURG OB DER TAUBER, now in Mittelfranken, Bayern (Bavaria); former Reichsstadt. Member of the Protestant corpus at the Peace of Westphalia; the town is now 72% Protestant; the Landkreis is 86% Protestant.

ROTTMÜNSTER, former abbey for women religious. Location unknown.

ROTTWEIL, now in Baden-Wurttemberg; former Reichsstadt. Member of the Catholic corpus at the Peace of Westphalia; city is now 69% Catholic; Landkreis is 63% Catholic.

RUNKEL, now in Oberlahnkreis, Hessen; former principality. Associated estates were the Herrschaften Westerwald and Westerburg. The ruling family Wied-Runkel is Protestant. *See also* Wied und Runkel

RUPPIN, now in the German Democratic Republic; former Herrschaft. The Reichstag vote was cancelled in 1524. It was a Landkreis from 1816 to 1952 in Brandenburg.

SAALFELD, now in Bezirk Gera, German Democratic Republic; former prelate nullius. Now mainly Protestant. The territory was secularized under the v. Mansfeld family; later it became Saxon, from 1735 to 1826 under Sachsen-Coburg and thereafter under Sachsen-Meiningen.

SAARBRÜCKEN, now capital of the Saar; former principality (Pfalz-Saarbrücken). The city is now 55% Catholic; the Landkreis is 52% Catholic. Fell to France in 1801 and to Prussia in 1815. *See also* Pfalz; Wetterauische Grafenkolleg (Nassau-Saarbrücken)

SAARBURG (or Sarrebourg), now in Département Moselle, France. Associated with the bishopric of Metz. *See also* Kaufmanns-Saarbrücken.

SAARWERDEN UND LAHR, former Grafschaft. Reichstag vote was cancelled in the sixteenth century.

SACHSEN (or Saxony), former electoral principality. Kursachsen (Electoral Saxony) was a leading member of the Protestant corpus at the Peace of Westphalia. Sachsen-Gotha and Sachsen-Eisenach were both represented by Sachsen-Weimar in the Protestant corpus. Sachsen-Koburg and Sachsen-Altenburg were both members of the Protestant corpus; the Ernestine line of the house of Saxony was Lutheran and Catholic; the Albertine line was Catholic. The Saxon lands were extraordinarily subdivided and consisted of many enclaves and exclaves.

SAFFENBURG, near Mayschoss, Kreis Ahrweiler, Rheinland-Pfalz; former Grafschaft. From 1424 to 1773 ruled by the counts v. Virneburg, thereafter by the house of Manderscheid and the dukes of Arenberg. The dukes of Arenburg (Ligne) are Catholic. *See also* Sassenberg

SALM, near Vielsalm, Luxembourg; former principality and Grafschaft. Represented Grafschaft Anholt in the Westfälische Grafenkolleg. The ruling Salm family (Salm Supérieur; Wild- und Rheingrafen) is Catholic. The

family originated in the Mosel region and from Luxemburg. When they lost their properties west of the Rhine at the beginning of the nineteenth century, they were given Ahaus, Bocholt, and Horstmar from the former clerical properties of the bishopric of Münster in 1803.

SALM-REIFFERSCHEID, counts von. The family of Salm-Reifferscheidt (Salm-Inférieur) is Catholic. The lords of Reifferscheid probably were a branch of the dukes of Limburg; they came into possession of Herrschaft Bedburg, Dyck, Alfter, and Hackenbroich and the Grafschaft of Salm (in Luxemburg).

SALMANNSWEILER, now Salem in Kreis Überlingen, Baden-Württemberg; former prelate nullius. The town is now 58% Catholic.

SALZBURG, now in Austria; former (and present) archbishopric. Associated territories were Berchtesgaden, Passau, Eichstädt. Salzburg was a member of the Catholic corpus at the Peace of Westphalia; city is now 88% Catholic. Many Protestants have lived in the surrounding mountains, but in 1731-1732 the archbishop forced 20,000 of them to emigrate, some to Georgia. Salzburg and Berchtesgaden were merged with Austria in 1805; in 1810 they fell to Bavaria; in 1816 Salzburg was returned to Austria, and Berchtesgaden remained Bavarian. The archbishop of Salzburg has the title of primate in Germany.

ST. ÄGIDIEN ZU NÜRNBERG, now in Bavaria; former prelate nullius. Territories taken over by the city of Nürnberg in 1567 by decision of the Reichskammergericht because the church officials were unable to prove their membership in the Reichsstandschaft by documentation.

ST. BLASIEN, now in Kreis Hochschwarzwald, Baden-Württemberg; former prince-abbot. Member of the Schwäbische Grafenkolleg. The town is now 76% Catholic. Absorbed by Austria in the fifteenth century; secularized in 1806.

ST. EMMERAN, former prelate nullius. Location unknown.

ST. GALLEN, now in Switzerland; former Reichsstadt and prelate nullius. The canton is now 64% Catholic. City bought its freedom from the bishop of St. Gallen in 1457. The bishop later moved to Rohrschach, and the monks later fled across the Rhine with their library (1798). In 1805 the cloister was dissolved.

ST. GEORGENSCHILD IM HEGAU, former *Rittergut* (knightly estate). Hegau was northwest of Lake Constance. Imperial taxes were levied on the estate, but it was not a member of the Reichsstände.

ST. JOHANN, former prelate nullius. May have

been in the Alsace or in Canton Bern (St. Johannis-Insel)

ST. JOHANN IN TURITAL, now in Canton St. Gallen, Switzerland; former prelate nullius. The Reichstag vote was apparently cancelled when the canton joined the Swiss Confederation.

ST. MAXIMIN, former prelate nullius. Taken over by Kurtrier (Electoral Trier) in the sixteenth century but sporadically able to exercise membership in the Reichsstandschaft.

ST. PETER IM SCHWARZWALD, former prelate nullius. Converted by Austria into Breisgau Landstand with no further participation in the Reichsstände.

ST. ULRICH UND AFRA IN AUGSBURG, former prelate nullius. Until 1644 the prelate did not participate in the Reichsstandschaft because of a controversy with the bishopric of Augsburg.

SARGANS, now in Canton St. Gallen, Switzerland; former Grafschaft. Now 75% Catholic. Territory merged in the Swiss Confederation.

SASSENBURG (or Saffenburg), former Grafschaft. Represented by the counts zu der Mark. *See also* Saffenburg

SAVOYEN (or Savoy), now in France; former Grafschaft and principality. The Grafschaft of Savoy became a member of the Catholic corpus at the Peace of Westphalia. The Duchy of Savoy was classified as a gefürstete Grafschaft in the Reichstag. Occupied by France in 1796 to 1814. In 1860 definitively absorbed by France in return for armaments aid during the unification of Italy.

SAYN, former Grafschaft. Associated estates were Berleburg and Wittgenstein. Member of both the Westfälische and the Wetterauische Grafenkollegien. The Sayn dynasty is from the Rhineland; the Sayn-Wittgenstein-Berleburg branch is Catholic; other branches are Catholic and Protestant. Since 1606 the Sayn estates have been controlled as follows: Sayn-Altenkirchen by Brandenburg-Ansbach, Sayn-Wittgenstein by Wittgenstein, Sayn-Hachenburg by Kirchberg.

SCHAFFHAUSEN, now in Switzerland; former Reichsstadt and prelate nullius. City is now 58% Calvinist (Reformed Church); canton is 64% Calvinist. The Reichsstadt and prelature were merged and both joined the Swiss Confederation in 1501.

SCHAUMBERG, now in Upper Austria; former Grafschaft. Reichstag vote was cancelled in 1559.

SCHAUMBURG UND GEMEN, now in Regierungsbezirk Hannover, Niedersachsen; former Grafschaft. Represented in the Westfälische Grafenkolleg by the Landgraf v. Hessen-Kassel and count zu Lippe-Bückeburg; Gemen represented by count v. Limburg-Stirum. The family Schaumburg-Lippe is Calvinist (Reformed Church). There was also a prince zu Anhalt-Bernburg-Schaumburg. In 1866 the Hessian share of the Grafschaft fell to Prussia.

SCHENKEN VON LANDSBERG, former Grafschaft. It is thought that this territory was absorbed by Saxony.

SCHENKEN VON TAUTENBERG UND VARGULA, former Grafschaft. Reichstag vote cancelled in 1640, and the territory absorbed by Saxony.

SCHLEIDEN, now in Nordrhein-Westfalen; former Grafschaft. The city is now 83% Catholic; the Landkreis is 90% Catholic. Represented by the counts zu der Mark from 1593 to 1773 and thereafter by the v. Arenberg family in 1794.

SCHLESWIG, now in Schleswig-Holstein; former duchy and bishopric. The territory has been Protestant since 1542. In accordance with a decision of the Reichskammergericht, the bishopric had been erroneously recognized as a tenancy-in-chief of the kaiser in the Reichsmatrikel of 1521 and rightly belonged to Denmark. The territory was sequestered by the Danish king during the Reformation and the ecclesiastical properties merged into the Duchy of Schleswig in 1674.

SCHLETTSTADT (or Sélestat), now in Département Bas-Rhin, France; former Reichsstadt. Pertained to the Landvogtei Hagenau and became French territory after 1648.

SCHÖNBORN, counts von. A noble family of the Rhineland; emigrated to Franconia in the seventeenth century. The family was mediatized by Bavaria in 1806-1810. The family provided a number of notable Catholic church princes. *See also* Reichsberg und Wiesentheid.

SCHÖNBURG, probably near Naumburg; former Grafschaft. Member of the Wetterauische Grafenkolleg. The family v. Schönburg-Waldenburg is Lutheran; the family Schönburg-Hartenstein is Catholic but was formerly Lutheran.

SCHÖTTERN, now in Austria; former prelate nullius. Absorbed by Austria in the fifteenth century.

SCHUSSENRIED, now in Kreis Biberach, Baden-Württemberg; former prelate nullius. The territories included eight villages; secularized in 1803.

SCHWÄBISCHE GRAFENKOLLEG. Not represented in the meetings of the Catholic corpus or in the Reichsfürstenrat at the Peace of Westphalia. Membership in the collegium is set forth below.

SCHWÄBISCH GMÜND, now in Baden-Württemberg; former Reichsstadt. Member of the Catholic corpus at the Peace of Westphalia; city is now 68% Catholic; Landkreis is 63% Catholic. The territory was absorbed by Württemberg in 1802.

SCHWÄBISCH HALL, now in Baden-Württemberg; former Reichsstadt. Represented by Esslingen in the Protestant corpus at the Peace of Westphalia; city is now 65% Protestant; Landkreis is 71% Protestant. In 1512 the patrician families were overthrown by the craftsmen and saltmakers. The territory was absorbed by Württemberg in 1802.

SCHWÄBISCH WÖRTH (now called Donauwörth), Schwaben, Bayern (Bavaria); former Reichsstadt. During the Reformation Donauwörth was Protestant, but it was occupied by Bavaria and forced to return to Catholicism; this became a grounds for the Thirty Years War. The town is now 73% Catholic; Landkreis is 84% Catholic. In 1607-1608 the city fell to Bavaria but from 1705-1714 was again an independent Reichsstadt. The imperial rights were then mortgaged to the Fugger family who sold them to the burghers of Donauwörth (1723-1724). Thereafter, Bavarian sovereignty was no longer questioned.

SCHWARZBURG, now in the German Democratic Republic; former Grafschaft and principality. There were two principalities of this name: Schwarzburg-Rudolstadt and Schwarzburg-

---

REPRESENTATION IN THE

SCHWÄBISCHE GRAFENKOLLEG

Estate	Represented by
Grafschaft Heiligenberg und Werdenberg	Princes zu Fürstenberg
Buchau abbey	Princess-abbesses zu Buchau
Comthur der Ballei Elsass und Burgund (Comthur zu Alschhausen)	Hoch- und Deutschmeister (Teutonic knights)
Grafschaft Öttingen	Princes and counts v. Öttingen
Grafschaft Menthor (Montfort)	Austria (Habsburg dynasts)
Grafschaft Helfenstein	Electoral princes of Bavaria
Landgrafschaft Klettgau and Grafschaft Sulz	Princes v. Schwarzenberg
Grafschaft Königsegg-Aulendorf	Counts v. Königsegg
Grafschaft Wolfegg, Waldsee, Zeil, und Wurzach	Truchsessen v. Waldburg
Grafschaft Eberstein	Marquises v. Baden-Baden
Grafschaft Hohen-Geroldseck	Counts von der Leyen
Grafschaft Babenhausen	Counts Fugger
Grafschaft Hohenems	Austria (Habsburg dynasts)
Herrschaft Eglof	Counts v. Traun
Gefürstete Grafschaft Bonndorf	Prince-abbots v. St. Blasien
Grafschaft Thannhausen	Counts v. Stadion
Herrschaft Eglingen	Princes and counts v. Thurn und Taxis
Personalist	Counts v. Khevenhüller
Personalist	Counts v. Kufstein
Personalist	Princes v. Colleredo
Personalist	Counts v. Harrach
Personalist	Counts v. Sternberg
Personalist	Counts v. Neipperg
Personalist (erroneous)	Counts v. Hohenzollern (erroneously admitted)

Sondershausen, both in Thuringia. Both principalities joined the Rheinbund in 1807, the German League in 1815, and the North German League in 1866-1867. In 1920 the two states were absorbed by Thuringia. The Schwarzburg dynasty is Lutheran.

SCHWARZENBERG, former gefürstete Grafschaft and principality. Associated estates were Seinsheim, the Duchy of Krumau (in Bohemia), Gimborn, Grafschaft Sulz, and the gefürstete Landgrafschaft Klettgau. Member of the Fränkische and Schwäbische Grafenkollegien. The Catholic princes v. Schwarzenberg owned much land in Austrian crown lands, especially Bohemia, Krain, and Styria.

SCHWEINFURTH, now in Unterfranken, Bayern (Bavaria); former Reichsstadt. Member of the Protestant corpus at the Peace of Westphalia; city is now 57% Catholic; Landkreis is 77% Catholic. In 1802 the Reichsstadt was absorbed by Bavaria; from 1810 to 1814 it was part of the Grandduchy of Würzburg; thereafter again Bavarian.

SCHWERIN, now in the German Democratic Republic; former bishopric. Territory was secularized in 1648 with Reichstag vote exercised by Mecklenburg-Schwerin.

SECKAU, now in Upper Styria, Austria; former bishopric. Lands were absorbed by Austria.

SEINSHEIM, now in Kreis Kitzingen, Unterfranken, Bayern (Bavaria); former Herrschaft. Member of the Fränkische Grafenkolleg. Represented by the Catholic princes v. Schwarzenberg.

SELZ, now in Département Bas-Rhin, France; former prelate nullius. Taken over by Kurpfalz (Electoral Palatinate) during the Reformation and became a member of the Palatine Ritterakademie (academy of knights) in 1575. Louis XIV of France later re-Catholicized the diocese.

SIMMERN, now Rhein-Hunsrück-Kreis, Rheinland-Pfalz; former Grafschaft. The town is now 52% Protestant. Reichstag vote was cancelled during the sixteenth century. Town was burned by the French in 1689. In 1794 the Grafschaft was made an Amt (district office) of the Kurpfalz (Electoral Palatinate), having previously been the seat of a *Teilfürstentum* (partial or successional principality) of Pfalz-Simmern. In 1814 the territory became Prussian. *See also* Anhalt

SÖFLINGEN, former prelate nullius. It is now doubtful that the territories qualified for the Reichsstand.

SOEST, now in Nordrhein-Westfalen; former Reichsstadt. From 1531 the populace has been Protestant, excepting for the cathedral and its precincts; now the city is 55% Catholic. The city was taken over by Jülich-Kleve, and sovereignty rested in Brandenburg from 1609 to 1666. The city lost its free status in 1752 and became Prussian in 1816.

SOLMS, princes and counts von. A noble family of the Lahn River region (Hessen). Associated estates were Lich, Hohensolms, Braunfels, Rödelheim, and Laubach. Members of the Wetterauische Grafenkolleg. There are several branches of this dynasty: Solms-Braunfels and Solms-Lich branches may be Protestant or Catholic; Solms-Laubach, Solms-Baruth, and Solms-Rödelheim are Lutheran. Solms-Braunfels became imperial princes in 1742 and Solms-Lich in 1792. Both lines were mediatized in 1806.

SOMERUFF (perhaps Sommerau), former Grafschaft. There is no proof that this estate was held directly of the kaiser; membership in the Reichsstände is questionable.

SONNENBERG, now part of the city of Wiesbaden, Hessen; former Herrschaft. The territory was taken over by Austria in the fifteenth century but was later owned jointly by the families of Nassau-Idstein and Nassau-Weilburg. These families are Catholic and Protestant.

SPEYER, now in Rheinland-Pfalz; former Reichsstadt and bishopric. The bishopric was represented by Kurtrier (Electoral Trier) in the Catholic corpus at the Peace of Westphalia. The Reichsstadt was represented by Strassburg in the Protestant corpus; it was Protestant from 1526 to 1689 and the seat of a Protestant government; it is now 50% Catholic. In 1689 Trier was occupied by the French who drove out the inhabitants. From 1794 to 1814 it was the seat of a French arrondisement and in 1816 it became the capital of the Bavarian Rheinkreis. The bishopric held large territories but lost most during the Reformation. Some lands fell to France, especially in 1801, and the remainder to Baden in 1802-1803.

SPIEGELBERG, former Grafschaft. Represented by Braunschweig and Kur-Braunschweig (Electoral Brunswick) since 1557. Member of the Westfälische Grafenkolleg.

STABLO (or Stavelot), now in Liège Province, Belgium; former prince-bishopric. Represented by Kurköln (Electoral Cologne) in the Catholic corpus at the Peace of Westphalia.

STADION, counts von. This Swabian noble family became Reichsgrafen in 1708 through purchase of Herrschaft Thannhausen. The family was Catholic and is now extinct. *See* Schwäbische Grafenkolleg (Thannhausen)

STARHEMBERG, counts von. The senior line of this Catholic family was listed as Personalist in the Fränkische Grafenkolleg. Most of the lands of this family were in Austria.

STAUF-EHRENFELS, former Grafschaft. Reichstag vote was cancelled in 1567.

STAUFFEN, probably in Kreis Breisgau-Hochschwarzwald, Baden-Württemberg; former Herrschaft. Reichstag vote was cancelled after 1500; the estate became Austrian in 1602; merged with Baden in 1806.

STEIN AM RHEIN, now in Canton Schaffhausen, Switzerland; former prelate nullius. Populace became Protestant during the Reformation.

STEINFURT, now in Nordrhein-Westfalen; former Grafschaft. Represented by the counts v. Bentheim in the Westfälische Grafenkolleg. Town is now 83% Catholic, but the family v. Bentheim (also referred to as the house of Guterswyk) is Reformed. In 1716 the Grafschaft included only the town and the parish of Burgsteinfurt. In 1806 the territory came to the Grandduchy of Berg and in 1811 fell to France; after 1815 it was in Prussian territory.

STERNBERG, counts von. Represented Grafschaft Blankenstein and Geroldstein in the Westfälische Grafenkolleg.

STETTIN. *See* Pommern-Stettin

STIRUM. *See* Schaumburg und Gemen

STÖFFELN UND JUSTINGEN, former Grafschaft. Represented by Württemberg since 1751.

STOLBERG, counts von. Associated estates were Gedern, Ortenberg, Wernigerode, and others. Members of the Wetterauische **Grafenkolleg**. The original Grafschaft was in the Harz Mountains. The family is divided into a number of branches:

Branches	Confession
Stolberg-Wernigerode	Lutheran
Stolberg-Wernigerode-Peterswaldau	Catholic and Lutheran
Stolberg-Wernigerode-Jannowitz	Lutheran
Stolberg-Wernigerode-Kreppelhof	Lutheran
Stolberg-Stolberg	Lutheran and Catholic sub-branch
Stolberg-Rossla	Lutheran

STRASSBURG (or Strasbourg), now in Département Bas-Rhin, France; former Reichsstadt and bishopric. The bishopric was represented by the Deutschorden (Teutonic knights) in the Catholic corpus at the Peace of Westphalia; the Reichsstadt was a member of the Protestant corpus at the Peace of Westphalia; populace became Protestant in 1522 and were leaders of the Reformation movement. When the Reichsstadt fell to the French in 1681, the cathedral became Catholic again. The bishopric owned numerous territories organized into Ämtern (local offices) and districts (Rufach, Zabern, Ettenheim, Oberkirch). All the territories west of the Rhine River were merged with France in 1681; the territories east of the Rhine were secularized in 1803 and absorbed by Baden.

SULZ (UND KLETTGAU), probably in Kreis Rottweil, Baden-Württemberg. Associated estates were Albeck and Hof Geroldseck. Member of the Schwäbische Grafenkolleg. The area is now 63% Protestant. Represented by the princes v. Schwarzenberg since 1687.

SUMMERAU. *See* Someruff

TAUTENBERG. *See* Schenken v. Tautenberg und Vargula

TECKLENBURG, now in Nordrhein-Westfalen; former Grafschaft. Associated territory was the Herrschaft Rheda. Represented in the Westfälische Grafenkolleg by Prussia since 1707. The town is 73% Protestant; the Landkreis is 51% Catholic; the former ruling family v. Bentheim-Tecklenburg is Reformed. Prussia assumed administrative control after compensating the counts v. Solms and v. Bentheim-Tecklenburg for their rights therein by transferring to them Herrschaft Rheda in 1729. Tecklenburg became a part of the Grandduchy of Berg; it was occupied by France from 1808 to 1813; thereafter, it was again Prussian territory.

TENGEN, now in Kreis Konstanz, Baden-Württemberg; former gefürstete Grafschaft. The estate was held by the Catholic princes v. Auersberg from 1663 to 1806; in the 1806-1811 period sovereignty passed to Baden.

THANNHAUSEN, former Grafschaft. Member of the Schwäbische Grafenkolleg. Represented by the Catholic v. Stadion family since 1708. The family is now extinct.

THORN (Maas), apparently on the Meuse River; former abbey for women religious.

THURN UND TAXIS, princes and counts von. Associated estates were Eglingen and the gefürstete Grafschaft Friedberg-Scheer, as well as many others. Member of the Schwäbische Grafenkolleg. This family had the inherited right to administer the postal system within the German Reich and the Spanish Netherlands. The capital generated by this business enabled them to buy many estates. They changed their headquarters from Frankfurt/Main to Regensburg in 1748. A branch of the family was also in Bohemia. The house was mediatized.

TIERSTEIN UND HOHENKÖNIGSBERG, former Grafschaft. Reichstag vote cancelled after 1500.

TÖRRING-JETTENBACH, counts von. A Catholic noble family. *See* Gronsfeld

TOUL, now in Département Meurthe-et-Moselle, France; former Reichsstadt and bishopric. Became French territory in 1552; merged with France in 1648 in accordance with the Treaty of Westphalia.

TRAUN (also called Abensperg und Traun), counts von. *See* Schwäbische Grafenkolleg (Herrschaft Eglof)

TRIENT (or Trento), now in Italy; former bishopric. Member of the Catholic corpus at the Peace of Westphalia. Austrian territory (Tirol) until 1919, when it became Italian. The ecclesiastical possessions were secularized in 1803 and merged with the Tirol.

TRIER (or Treves), now in Rheinland-Pfalz; former electoral principality (ecclesiastical). The old metropolitanate of Trier included Metz, Toul, and Verdun as suffragans until 1802. After 1821 Trier became a suffragan of Cologne. Trier was the site of the first German bishopric in the third century. There was an attempt to introduce Calvinism during the Reformation, but the movement was put down and many Calvinist (Reformed) families were forced to flee. At the Peace of Westphalia Kurtrier (Electoral Trier) was a member of the Catholic corpus. The city is now about 87% Catholic; Landkreis Trier-Saarburg is 93% Catholic. The archbishop held secular power from 843 to 1803, excepting for an interregnum period 1212-1308.

TÜBINGEN, now in Baden-Württemberg; former Grafschaft. After 1534 the city became a stronghold of the Reformation; the city is now 62% Protestant; the Landkreis is 59% Protestant. Territory belonged to Württemberg since 1342; Reichstag vote cancelled in 1631.

TÜRKHEIM, now in Département Haut-Rhin, France; former Reichsstadt. Pertained to the Landvogtei Hagenau; became French territory in 1648.

ÜBERLINGEN, now in Bodenseekreis, Baden-Württemberg; former Reichsstadt. Member of the Catholic corpus at the Peace of Westphalia; city is now 62% Catholic; former Landkreis was 73% Catholic. The city was absorbed by Baden in 1803.

ULM, now in Alb-Donau-Kreis, Baden-Württemberg; former Reichsstadt. By a vote in 1530 the burghers were overwhelmingly Protestant, but Catholics remained entrenched in outposts (Söflingen and Wiblingen) outside the city.

Member of the Protestant corpus at the Peace of Westphalia; city is now 47% Protestant and 47% Catholic; former Landkreis was 48% Protestant and 48% Catholic. Ulm came to Bavaria in 1802 and was transferred to Württemberg in 1810.

UNGNADE VON WEISSENWOLF, counts von. Admitted to the Grafenkolleg in 1654 but ejected shortly thereafter, because the family held no estates directly of the kaiser.

URSIN VON ROSENBERG, counts von. Personal members of the Fränkische Grafenkolleg. *See also* Rosenberg, counts von

URSPRING (or Ursberg), part of the town of Schelklingen, Alb-Donau-Kreis, Baden-Württemberg; former prelate nullius. Associated estate was the Herrschaft Berg. From 1343 to 1806 Urspring and Herrschaft Berg belonged to Austria. In 1806 these territories were absorbed by Württemberg.

USINGEN, now in Hochtaunuskreis, Hessen. Residence of the counts v. Nassau-Usingen until 1816. Town is 62% Protestant; Landkreis is 68% Protestant. *See also* Wetterauische Grafenkolleg (Nassau-Usingen)

UTRECHT, now in The Netherlands; former bishopric. Territory taken over by Spain and later became part of The Netherlands.

VADUZ. *See* Liechtenstein

VARGULA. *See* Schenken v. Tautenberg und Vargula

VERDEN, now in Regierungsbezirk Stade, Niedersachsen; former Reichsstadt and bishopric. Represented by Osnabrück in the Catholic corpus at the Peace of Westphalia; city is now 87% Protestant; Landkreis is mainly Protestant also. Territories were secularized in 1648 with the Reichstag vote exercised by Sweden and after 1719 by Hannover. The Reichstag was taken over by the bishopric; sovereignty assumed by Hannover in 1712-1719.

VERDUN, now in Département Meuse, France; former Reichsstadt and bishopric. Member of the Catholic corpus at the Peace of Westphalia. Territory became French in 1552, when the Protestant prince transferred it to the French king as a protectorate.

VIRNEBURG, now in Kreis Mayen-Koblenz, Rheinland-Pfalz; former Grafschaft. Member of the Westfälische Grafenkolleg. Represented by the Protestant family v. Löwenstein-Wertheim-Freudenberg [Virneburg]; another branch of the family, v. Löwenstein-Wertheim-Rochefort or Rosenberg, is Catholic.

WÄCHTERSBACH, now in Kreis Gelnhausen, Hessen; former Grafschaft. The ruling family

v. Isenburg-Büdingen-Wächtersbach is Protestant; the town is now 57% Protestant. *See also* Wetterauische Grafenkolleg (Isenburg-Büdingen-Meerholz-Wächtersbach)

WALDBURG, Reichserbtruchsessen (imperial hereditary seneschal) von. Member of the Schwäbische Grafenkolleg and Austrian *Statthalter* (governor) for properties in Württemberg. There are two branches of this Catholic family: Wolfegg-Waldsee and Zeil-Wurzach. Both branches owned numerous estates in Upper Swabia. They were named imperial princes in 1803 and mediatized, most territories falling to Bavaria, the remainder to Württemberg.

WALDECK, now in Hessen; former principality and Grafschaft. Represented the Grafschaft Pyrmont in the Westfälische Grafenkolleg. The town is now 75% Protestant; the former Landkreis was 80% Protestant; the family v. Waldeck-Limburg (Bentinck) is Reformed. Raised to the Reichsfürstenrat in 1686; sovereignty passed to Prussia in 1867. Waldeck was always closely associated historically with Hessen-Kassel.

WALDSASSEN/OBERPFALZ, now in Kreis Tirschenreuth, Oberpfalz, Bayern (Bavaria); former prelate nullius. The territory was secularized in 1571 by Kurpfalz (Electoral Palatinate) and taken over by Bavaria in 1628. The town itself was founded in 1614 by Calvinist (Reformed) refugees; it is now 89% Catholic.

WALKENRIED, now in Kreis Goslar, Niedersachsen; former prelate nullius. Town is now 83% Protestant. Secularized in 1648 and later passed to Braunschweig-Wolfenbüttel.

WALLIS (Sitten or Le Valais), now in Switzerland; former bishopric. At the time of the Reformation there were many Protestants, but they were repressed. The Valais became a member of the Swiss Confederation in 1814, after having been a republic for a short time.

WANGEN/ALLGÄU, now in Baden-Württemberg; former Reichsstadt. The town is mainly Catholic. The territory became Bavarian in 1803 and passed to Württemberg in 1810.

WARBURG, now in Nordrhein-Westfalen; former Reichsstadt. The town is now mainly Catholic; it was taken over by the bishopric of Paderborn.

WARTENBERG, counts zu. Appear to have been imperial counts only from 1707 to 1739.

WEILBURG, now in Oberlahnkreis, Hessen. The populace is now mainly Protestant. *See* Wetterauische Grafenkolleg (Nassau-Weilburg)

WEIL DER STADT, now in Kreis Leonburg, Baden-

Württemberg; former Reichsstadt. Member of the Catholic corpus at the Peace of Westphalia; the town is now mainly Catholic. The territory was absorbed by Württemberg in 1802.

WEINGARTEN, now in Kreis Ravensberg, Baden-Württemberg; former prelate nullius. The town is mainly Catholic today. Until 1805 Weingarten was the seat of the imperial Landvogtei (administrative region) for Oberschwaben (Upper Swabia). The abbey properties were secularized in 1802.

WEINSBERG, owners of; now in Kreis Heilbronn, Baden-Württemberg; former Grafschaft. The area is mainly Protestant today. The Reichstag vote was cancelled in the sixteenth century when the territory was seized by Württemberg. Weinsberg was the scene of bitter fighting during the Bauernkrieg (Peasants' War).

WEISSENAU, former prelate nullius. No longer identifiable.

WEISSENBURG (or Wissembourg), now in Département Bas-Rhin, France; former Reichsstadt and prince-bishopric. The town became Protestant in 1534 but was represented by Speyer in the Catholic corpus at the Peace of Westphalia. The town was a Reichsstadt from 1306 to 1673 when seized by the French.

WEISSENBURG/NORDGAU, now in Regierungsbezirk Mittelfranken, Bayern (Bavaria); former Reichsstadt. Member of the Protestant corpus at the Peace of Westphalia; town is now mainly Protestant. Territory absorbed by Bavaria in 1806.

WEISSENWOLF. *See* Ungnade v. Weissenwolf

WERDEN, former prelate nullius.

WERDENBERG UND HEILIGENBERG, former Grafschaft. Member of the Schwäbische Grafenkolleg. Represented by the Catholic princes v. Fürstenberg since 1530.

WERNIGERODE, now in Bezirk Magdeburg, German Democratic Republic. *See* Stolberg, counts v.; Wetterauische Grafenkolleg (Stolberg-Wernigerode)

WERTHEIM, now in Kreis Tauberbischofsheim, Baden-Württemberg; former Grafschaft. Member of the Fränkische Grafenkolleg. Town is now 50% Protestant; former ruling family, v. Löwenstein-Wertheim, is Protestant.

WESEL. *See* Niederwesel

WESTERBURG, now in Oberwesterwald-Kreis, Rheinland-Pfalz; former Grafschaft. Town is now mainly Protestant; the former ruling family,

v. Leiningen-Westerburg, is Protestant; a
"new" line v. Leiningen-Westerburg is Catholic and Lutheran.

WESTFÄLISCHE GRAFENKOLLEG. Membership in the
collegium is set forth below.

WETTENHAUSEN, possibly a former Grafschaft.
In the sixteenth century it was still a member of the Swabian Reichsritterschaft (imperial knights).

WETTERAUISCHE GRAFENKOLLEG. Members of the
collegium were represented by Kurbrandenburg (Electoral Brandenburg) in the Protestant corpus at the Peace of Westphalia. The
following princes and counts were members:

- Nassau-Usingen

- Nassau-Weilburg

- Nassau-Saarbrücken

- Solms-Lich

- Solms-Hohensolms

- Solms-Braunfels

- Solms-Rödelheim

- Solms-Laubach

- Isenburg-Birstein

- Isenburg-Büdingen-Meerholz-Wächtersbach

- Stolberg-Gedern-Ortenburg

- Stolberg-Stolberg

- Stolberg-Wernigerode

- Sayn-Wittgenstein-Berleburg

- Sayn-Wittgenstein-Wittgenstein

- Wild- und Rheingraf zu Grumbach

- Wild- und Rheingraf zu Rheingrafenstein

- Leiningen-Hartenburg

- Leiningen-Heidesheim

- Leiningen-Guntersblum

- Westerburg, Christoph. Line

- Westerburg, Georg. Line

- Reussen und Plauen

MEMBERS OF THE
WESTFÄLISCHE GRAFENKOLLEG

Estate	Represented by
Grafschaft Sayn-Altenkirchen	Marquises v. Ansbach
Grafschaft Sayn-Hachenburg	Burggrafen v. Kirchberg
Grafschaft Tecklenburg	Kings of Prussia (formerly Brandenburg)
Upper Grafschaft Wied	Princes zu Wied-Runkel
Grafschaft Wied	Princes zu Wied-Neuwied
Grafschaft Schaumburg	Landgrafen v. Hessen-Kassel and counts zu Lippe-Bückeburg
Oldenburg	Dukes zu Holstein-Gottorp-Oldenburg
Personalist?	Counts von der Lippe
Grafschaft Steinfurt	Counts v. Bentheim
Grafschaft Hoya; Grafschaft Diepholz; Grafschaft Spiegelberg	Kings of England
Grafschaft Virneburg	Princes and counts v. Löwenstein
Grafschaft Rietberg	Princes v. Kaunitz
Grafschaft Pyrmont	Princes v. Waldeck
Grafschaft Gronsfeld	Counts v. Törring
Grafschaft Reckheim (or Reckum)	Counts v. Aspremont
Grafschaft Anholt	Princes zu Salm
Herrschaft Winneburg und Beilstein	Counts v. Metternich
Grafschaft Holzappel	Princes zu Anhalt-Bernburg-Schaumburg
Grafschaft Blankenheim und Geroldstein	Counts v. Sternberg

- Schönburg

- Ortenburg

- Kriechingen

WETZLAR, now in Hessen; former Reichsstadt. Member of the Protestant corpus at the Peace of Westphalia; populace is now mainly Protestant. Became a part of the Prussian Rheinprovinz in 1815; in 1932 assigned to Province Hessen-Nassau.

WIED UND RUNKEL, now in Oberlahnkreis, Hessen; former Grafschaft. Associated estates were Kriechingen; Upper Grafschaft Wied; Wied-Neuwied. Member of the Westfälische Grafenkolleg. The former ruling family is Protestant; it was especially hospitable to dissenting religious groups, many of which later emigrated to America.

WIESENTHEID, former Grafschaft. See Schönborn, counts von; Reichsberg und Wiesentheid

WILDENFELS, former Grafschaft. Reichstag vote was cancelled in 1593.

WILD- UND RHEINGRAFEN. Members of the Wetterauische Grafenkolleg. The family v. Salm (Wild- und Rheingrafen) is Catholic; the Grumbach line thereof is Lutheran. See also Rheingrafen

WIMPFEN, now Bad Wimpfen, Kreis Heilbronn, Baden-Württemberg. Member of the Protestant corpus at the Peace of Westphalia; populace is now 67% Protestant. Town fell to Baden in 1802 and in 1803 to Hessen. In 1952, after a referendum, the town was annexed to Kreis Heilbronn.

WINDISCH-GRÄTZ, counts von. Personal members of the Fränkische Grafenkolleg. This Catholic family, which originated in Oberbayern (Upper Bavaria), held lands in Styria and Austria.

WINDSHEIM, now in Kreis Uffenheim, Regierungsbezirk Mittelfranken, Bayern (Bavaria); former Reichsstadt. Represented by Nürnberg in the Protestant corpus at the Peace of Westphalia; populace is now mainly Protestant.

WINNEBURG UND BEILSTEIN, near Cochem an der Mosel, Rheinland-Pfalz; former Herrschaft. Member of the Westfälische Grafenkolleg. The former ruling family v. Metternich-Winneburg is Catholic. In 1801 the territory fell to France and in 1815 became Prussian.

WITTEM, former Grafschaft. Represented by the counts v. Plettenberg.

WITTGENSTEIN, now in Nordrhein-Westfalen; former Grafschaft. Member of the Wetterauische Grafenkolleg.

WOLCKENSTEIN, former Grafschaft. Absorbed by Austria and lands sold in the seventeenth century.

WOLFENBÜTTEL. See Braunschweig-Wolfenbüttel; Hannover

WOLFSTEIN (allodial heirs), former Grafschaft. Member of the Fränkische Grafenkolleg represented by the princes v. Hohenlohe-Kirchberg (Neuenstein line) and the counts v. Giech; both families are Lutheran.

WOLGAST, now in Bezirk Rostock, German Democratic Republic. See Pommern-Wolgast

WORMS, now in Rheinland-Pfalz; former Reichsstadt and bishopric. The bishopric was represented by Kurmainz (Electoral Main) in the Catholic corpus at the Peace of Westphalia; the Reichsstadt was a member of the Protestant corpus; the city is now mainly Protestant. In medieval times the city had one of the most important Jewish settlements in Europe. In 1797 Worms was occupied by the French; in 1816 it was absorbed by Hessen. Territories of the bishopric were secularized in 1802-1803, mainly by Baden and Hessen. In 1814 the territories west of the Rhine River, which had been occupied by the French in 1797, were merged with the Bavarian Pfalz (Palatinate).

WÜRTTEMBERG, now in Baden-Württemberg; former Grafschaft, duchy, and kingdom. The Duchy of Württemberg was a member of the Protestant corpus at the Peace of Westphalia; the royal line v. Württemberg is Lutheran; the ducal line is Catholic. The original counts v. Württemberg had their seat at the Rotenberg bei Stuttgart. In 1801 Württemberg lost properties west of the Rhine River and was compensated by receiving church territories (Ellwangen, Schöntal, and Zwiefalten), five cloisters, and nine Reichsstädte. In 1805 it received the Austrian properties in Oberschwaben (Upper Swabia), a number of Grafschaften, and the Landvogtei Altdorf. The ensuing mediatizing of various dynasties brought in still further territories. In 1809 the territories of the Deutschorden (Teutonic knights) were also absorbed.

WÜRZBURG, now in Unterfranken, Bayern (Bavaria); former bishopric. A member of the Catholic corpus at the Peace of Westphalia; populace is now mainly Catholic. The territories were secularized under Bavaria in 1802-1803. From 1806 to 1814 territories were part of the Grandduchy of Toscana, but in 1814 they were again absorbed by Bavaria.

WUNSTORF, probably in Kreis Neustadt am Rübenberge, Niedersachsen; former Grafschaft. The Reichstag vote was cancelled in 1533.

WURMBRAND, counts von. Personal members of the Fränkische Grafenkolleg. The family v. Wurmbrand-Stuppach is Catholic and had lands in Styria (Austria) also.

WYKRADT, former Grafschaft. Represented by the Catholic family v. Quadt-Wykradt-Isny.

YSENBURG. *See* Isenburg

ZELL AM HARMERSBACH, now in Kreis Wolfach, Baden-Württemberg; former Reichsstadt. Member of the Catholic corpus at the Peace of Westphalia; populace is now mainly Catholic. The town was absorbed by Württemberg in 1803.

ZWIEFALTEN, now in Kreis Münsingen, Baden-Württemberg; former prelate nullius. Until 1750 the estate was considered to be Landstand by Württemberg; thereafter it was a member of the collegium of prelates until absorbed definitively by Württemberg in 1801.

GENEALOGY IN GERMANY

Source materials for genealogical research in Germany are richly varied, with the consequence that German genealogies often contain information rarely found in American ones. The difference has to do with the fact that Germany has had few population censuses--such as are a main source of information for American researchers--causing German researchers to rely on other types of data.

CHURCH RECORDS

The *Kirchenbücher* (church records) of Germany are similar to the parish registers of Great Britain. The principal records are the birth, marriage, and death registers for Lutheran, Reformed, and Catholic congregations. Among smaller sects, such as the Anabaptists, church records were not always kept, probably because such records would have exposed their membership to would-be persecutors.

A few *Kirchenbücher* date back to the end of the fifteenth century, but most begin during the Reformation, usually about 1550. Protestant records begin somewhat earlier than do Catholic ones. As a rule of thumb, the farther eastward one goes, the less likely it is that church records will reach back into the sixteenth century.[1] In the German Baltic settlements they begin early in the seventeenth century, but many of these early records have long been missing. In the German enclaves in southeastern Europe and Russia, church records begin even later. It frequently occurs that death registers begin later than birth and marriage registers. The death registers were often maintained by the cemetery offices, or among the town civil records, rather than by the parish minister or priest.

In general, church records are the most important sources of genealogical information available to the German researcher.[2] Most provable lineages, excepting noble ones, rarely reach further back in time than the relevant church records. Thus, genealogists will want to query any asserted lineage dating from before about 1550.

Baptismal Registers

The *Taufregister* (baptismal or christening registers) record baptismal date, sometimes the birth date, the names of the parents and the child, and the godparents (*Paten*). In all events, genealogists should give particular attention to the choice of godparents. Normally, these were relatives or close friends of one of the parents, but, in cases of Jewish or Muslim converts, blacks, or illegitimate children, one occasionally finds prominent personages acting as godparents simply as a matter of Christian piety.[3]

Church records are usually quite specific in noting illegitimacy. Such records were often separately maintained, a fact that researchers will want to keep in mind when an expected entry is not to be found in the main baptismal register. In cases of the illegitimate offspring of noble fathers, attempts were frequently made to conceal the fact in christening registers, but researchers can detect illegitimacy by considering the social position of the child's godparents. If all the godparents were not noble, it is likely that the child was illegitimate.[4]

Three subsidiary records can be used to determine birth dates: the *Patenzettel* (invitation of the godparents to attend the christening); records of the special municipal tax levied upon celebration of christenings (to be discussed below under municipal records); and the birth certificates issued when, later, the child applied to learn a trade or profession (to be discussed more fully under occupational records hereinafter). Of the three subsidiary records, the rarest is undoubtedly the *Patenzettel*, because invitations are ephemeral documents not recorded by the church or municipality and only occasionally preserved in private collections. When they exist, they are informative. They occur less frequently among the peasantry than among the bourgeoisie and nobility.

Researchers should note that births of stillborn or unbaptized children usually are not entered in the birth registers. Notice of their coming into the world appears only in the death registers.

Marriage Registers

There are two sources which ought to be consulted in the registration of each marriage—the *Trauregister* (marriage register) in the bride's church, where the nuptials actually took place, and the *Proklamationsbuch* (register of proclamation of banns) in the groom's church, if this is different from that of the bride. A final proclamation was entered on the Sunday preceding the day of marriage and is, therefore, not conclusive proof of the date or celebration of marriage. The marriage register itself ordinarily contains the name and profession of the groom, with or without the names of his parents, the name of the bride, and usually those of her parents. Widows used the surnames of their deceased husbands, so that researchers must search for her first marriage in order to determine the maiden surnames of brides in second marriages.

As in christenings, marriage celebrations were subjects of municipal taxation and such entries will be found among the municipal records.

Heydenreich[5] points out that, in the Duchies of Schleswig and Holstein until 1874, there was a special custom whereby the usual procedure of posting of banns and marriage in the church could be dispensed with by the so-called *Königsbrief* (royal permit). During the fall and winter months when travel was difficult, marriages were often performed at the bride's home, a custom especially prevalent among the upper classes. Such permits were obtained from the Duke (who was also King in Denmark) and were issued at the royal castle at Gottorp. These writers have not determined the present whereabout of records of such permits.[6]

In Austria there was the custom of the *Partezettel* (notification of marriage) which was sent to friends and relatives. Such notices often contained important genealogical data.[7] Similarly, there were wedding invitations giving more or less the same information as would be found in similar invitations in America.

Death Registers

The *Sterberegister* (death registers) give the name of the deceased person and ordinarily the profession, age, and cause of death. The age is to be given little credence, because it is so frequently inaccurate. Researchers ought to note especially the cause of death; if by disease, there may be some genetic or biological implications of interest to the researcher;[8] if by violence, there may be court or military records which will give further information.

There are a number of other records which may shed further light on the death and life of an individual. One of these is the *Totengeläutbuch* (death knell book). Where such books exist, they record the tolling of the bell which occurs during the burial, usually on the third day after death. Among Lutherans, particularly in the upper classes, it was customary from about 1550 to 1800 to have the *Leichenpredigte* (funeral sermons) printed and distributed to friends and relatives. These publications gave an account of the life of the deceased person, listing the names of his near relatives and his ancestors. They are, then, of inestimable value to the genealogist, and there are a number of large collections of such memorials extant.[9] The upper classes also issued *Ordnungen bei Begräbnisse* (orders of precedence for funerals) wherein are listed the pallbearers and other functionaries at funerals. These can have implications for genealogists, because the order by which the family members were seated in the church or marched to the grave gives an indication of relationship to the deceased person. Personages of wealth and station frequently gave property or money to churches for the saying of prayers on the anniversaries of their deaths. The records of these endowments are called *Anniversarien*. Similar records are the *Nekrologien* (necrologies) and the *Toten-Annalen* (annals of the dead). All three of these records contain material of genealogical interest.[10]

Finally, it ought to be mentioned that during the Middle Ages there were religious *Gebetsverbrüderungen* (prayer fraternities) and *Brüderschaften* (brotherhoods) with lists of members from all social classes, including the serfs. The lists, assembled in *Seelenbücher* (books of the souls), survive and are of importance to the research.[11]

Other Church Records

There are a number of other records which have genealogical value. Confirmation, communion, and confession lists, *Familienregister* (family registers), and notes on *Kirchenstrafen* (penances) exist, but they seem nowhere to have been kept with regularity over long periods of time, apparently because there was no fixed administrative regulation requiring them.

Records on Lutheran ministers are especially complete. There were five steps in the formation of a minister, and each step was likely to have been recorded:

the *Berufung* (call) under the sponsorship of a church patron;

the *Prüfung* (examination) before a consistory;

ordination, which took place at the spiritual capital of the *Land* (principality or state) wherein the General Superintendent had his residence;

the *Bestätigung* (confirmation or acceptance) on the part of the ruling prince; and the

Einführung (installation) as a parish minister or other church official.[12]

Data on ministers and priests also are to be found in the *Universitätsmatrikeln*

(university enrollment records), discussed hereinafter under academic records. There are also records of religious orders and foundations.[13] Since Lutheran ministers were often sent to congregations in America, these records are of interest to American researchers.[14]

There are also records of church *Visitationen* (inspections) containing much information of genealogical interest. These records go back a thousand years and are of particular value in determining the circumstances of heresy. Such material has been used extensively in the writing of the early history of Anabaptist *Schwärmer* (enthusiasts). Similarly, persons playing an active part in church affairs may be mentioned in *Synodalbücher* (synod records).

Military Chaplaincy Records

Garrison towns in Germany normally maintained marriage and death records for soldiers separately.[15] The birth records of the children of soldiers may be found in the ordinary christening records or among the *Militärkirchenbücher* (military chaplaincy records). For the American researcher, chaplaincy records are especially valuable, because many Germans arrived in the colonies as soldiers during the American Revolution. In the Staatsarchiv Marburg, for example, there are 24 *Militärkirchenbücher*, of which the following are directly relevant to German-American genealogical research, because the Hessen-Kassel (or Kurhessen) troop units were then serving in North America:

Leibgarde Regiment, 1765-1780

Infanterie-Regiment von Huyne, 1776-1781

Infanterie-Regiment von Bunau, 1777-1779

Infanterie (Fusilier) Regiment von Ditfurth, 1779

Landgrenadier-Regiment Marquis d'Angelelli, 1780-1783

Infanterie-Regiment von Benning, 1781-1782

Jägerkorps und Hessen-Hanau Freikorps, 1781-1783

Translations of these records ought to be published for the use of American researchers.

Among the Evangelical-Reformed church records at Malsfeld (Kreis Melsungen) there is a record of the marriages and christenings performed by Chaplain Köster (Cöster) who served with the German troops in America.[16] This record appears to be available in its entirety in the United States under the following title:

Maria Paula Dickoré, *Hessian Soldiers in the American Revolution: Records of Their*

Marriages and Baptisms of Their Children in America Performed by the Rev. G. C. Cöster, 1776-1783, Chaplain of Two Hessian Regiments. Cincinnati, Ohio? privately printed, 1959.

The foreword to this ephemeral publication, a copy of which is to be found in the Newberry Library, Chicago, does not state the provenance of her data. She has taken it either from the Malsfeld document or from a transcription in *Deutsch-Amerikanische Geschichtsblätter.*

There is also another chaplaincy record (called a *Protokoll*) of Chaplain Kümmel during his tour of duty in America. This record was in the library of the Hennebergischen Geschichtsverein (Henneberg Historical Society) in Schmalkalden in 1930, but its present whereabouts is unknown to these writers.[17]

The chaplaincy record of the Ansbach-Bayreuth troops who served in America also exists,[18] and it seems likely that a concerted effort to locate more such records pertaining to German mercenary troops serving in America would be productive. The transcription and publication of all the above-listed chaplaincy records would be a distinct service to German-American genealogical researchers.

RELIGIOUS MINORITIES

In devout Catholic areas, where Lutheran or Reformed churches were not permitted, researchers should determine whether there existed a consulate of a protestant country. Vienna, for example, had no protestant churches, so protestants in that city attended services in the Dutch consulate. In Berlin, where no Catholic churches were permitted, communicants attended Mass in the Spanish consulate. As a rule of thumb, one can say that, after 1780, such intolerance began to wane, and minority churches were permitted in towns throughout Germany. Nonetheless, ancient consular records will contain many surprises for the persevering researcher.[19]

For religious groups other than Lutheran, Reformed, and Catholic, vital records are likely to be fragmentary. Anabaptist groups, much persecuted in their formative stages, kept none. Occasionally, there were entries in Lutheran or Reformed records pertaining to Anabaptists, but more frequently the only sources of birth, marriage, and death information are to be found in family Bibles. This tradition has been carried down to modern times among Mennonite and Amish congregations in all parts of the world, including the United States and Canada.

An article dealing specifically with eighteenth and nineteenth century settlements of Jews in Germany will be found elsewhere in this Encyclopedia. The following general statements can be made regarding German-Jewish genealogical research:

¶ There have been two quite distinct groups of Jews in Germany, the Ashkenazim and the Sephardim. The Ashkenazim are descendants of Jews who settled in central Europe, principally along the Rhine River in Germany, as early as Roman times. For example, there was an organized community of Jews in Cologne by A.D. 321. These Jews eventually came to speak a special dialect of medieval German, usually referred to as *Jüdisch* (Yiddish). In the seventeenth through nineteenth centuries, the Ashkenazim were mainly centered in southwestern Germany, but they had long since formed colonies to the eastward in the Slavic countries, particularly Poland, where occupational restrictions were not severe.

The Sephardim, or Maranos, are Jews who fled Spain and Portugal at the time of the Inquisition in the late fifteenth century. About 120 families of Marano Jews settled for a time in and near Hamburg in the early sixteenth century. Their language, Ladino, is based upon medieval Spanish. Their cemetery was at Altona, then Danish territory, and they had synagogues at Altona, Hamburg, and Wandsbek.

¶ Although the Ashkenazim and the Sephardim share the same religious beliefs and similar customs, they did not usually intermarry until quite recent times.

¶ The Ashkenazim have surnames usually derived from German words or adaptations thereof; the Sephardim bear distinctly Hispanic surnames for the most part.

¶ Names were given to Jewish children according to unvarying order prescribed by religious custom: A son was given the name of a deceased grandfather; in the event that his two grandfathers were still alive, he was given the name of a deceased great-grandfather. Only if the father was dead before the birth of the son was he given his father's name. Names of children alternated between paternal and maternal lines. After 1890 this custom fell into disuetude.

¶ Surnames were not adopted by German (Ashkenazim) and Alsatian Jews until the early nineteenth century and then only as a result of governmental requirement. Previously, a typical name would have been, for example, Izak ben Schmuel (Isaac (grandfather's name), son of Samuel). This complicates the tracing of

Jewish ancestry enormously.

¶ German (*Ashkenazim*) Jews were restricted to certain towns in which they lived apart in ghettos. These communities were largely self-governing, so that researchers will find few references to them in the ordinary *Gemeinde* (village) records.

¶ Jewish vital records were kept by the local rabbis. Because so many restrictions were placed upon the number of Jews who might reside in a given town or village, rabbinical records often were purposely incomplete or inaccurate. As a consequence of the fearful events of the Third Reich period, many of these old records have been destroyed, and it becomes a special obligation of modern-day genealogists to reconstruct as much of the Jewish past as is possible from data still available. Special mention should be made of the work of Dr. Arthur Czellitzer, founder of the Gesellschaft für jüdische Familienforschung (Society for Jewish Genealogical Research) in Berlin in 1924 and publisher of *Jüdische Familienforschung* until he was killed in Holland during the second world war. His collection of research materials has disappeared.

¶ German Jews were usually the direct subjects of the kaiser or of a few princes who tolerated them for financial reasons. Thus it is that Jews will not be found evenly settled throughout Germany but were restricted to a relatively few cities and towns, mainly in southwestern Germany. Restrictions against Jews were gradually lifted during the first half of the nineteenth century, and Jews began to assume a more direct part of the national cultural life.

¶ There have been a number of censuses and special tax lists on German Jews in Baden and Württemberg prepared during the eighteenth and nineteenth centuries. A summary of this data is presented in the article entitled Jewish Settlements in Southwestern Germany in this Encyclopedia. A very rare book, entitled *Dénombrement général des Juifs qui sont tolérés en la Province l'Alsace* (General list of Jews tolerated in the Province of the Alsace), was published in Colmar, France, by Henri Decker in 1785. It listed all the Jewish families in the province; many of these people later were forced to emigrate to Basel and to other Swiss and German towns which would accept them.[20]

¶ Tombstone inscriptions were formerly a source of genealogical information for Jews in Germany; some of the tombstones were very old, the oldest dating from A.D. 1077. A great tragedy of the Third Reich period was the destruction of these tombstones and the desecration of the Jewish cemeteries.

Jewish-German genealogy is, then, an area with special problems and difficulties. It would seem a special moral obligation to assemble the data which has survived the Holocaust.

STATE VITAL RECORDS

In 1849, or shortly thereafter, the various German states began officially to record births, marriages, and deaths for all residents, regardless of religion. The new policy was caused by the fact that it had previously not been possible for persons of differing religious confessions to marry one another, because neither the protestant denominations nor the Roman Catholic Church would permit mixed marriages. For the nonconforming groups and the Jews the situation was particularly difficult. The new wave of liberalism of the 1840s caused sectarian prejudices to be swept slowly aside.

Today, a civil marriage must be performed by officials of the *Standesamt* (office of vital records); only thereafter, is a second celebration, the church marriage, permitted. The civil marriage is the only marriage legally recognized. Thus, it became possible for persons of differing confessions to marry.

For genealogical researchers, then, the year 1849 is an important one. The *Standesamtbezirke* (vital records registration districts) of Germany usually encompass a number of *Gemeinden* (communes or townships) without consideration of ancient parish boundaries. Because larger areas are now combined into one set of records, methodically kept, it is easier to locate a post-1849 marriage record than it is to find one in the parish records.

It should be noted that the princely houses of Germany were exempted from registration of their births, marriages, and deaths in the ordinary Standesamt records. Instead, they were allowed to keep their own records, duly signed by the *Familienhaupt* (head of the family) and Standesamt officials, and maintained in their private dynastic archives.

In recent years, local police authorities have maintained *Melderegister* (report registers) wherein are listed all residents and their movements into and out of the area. This makes the taking of periodic censuses unnecessary, because it is possible at all times for the authorities to determine population data from these registers. In the years immediately after the second world war, when housing was very scarce in Germany, it was possible to control undesirable population movements—as, for example, rapid population growth in an industrial area at the expense of less economically-beckoning ones—by requiring would-be migrants to obtain a *Zuzuggenehmigung* (permit to move into an area) and an *Abmeldeschein* (permit to move away from the place of former residence).[21] These records have great value to genealogists; the value of these documents will increase as future researchers seek to trace the movements of families after the second world war.

Finally, mention should be made of the *Kennkarte* (identity card) issued to all German residents. It is issued for identification purposes and contains name, a passport-size photograph, a description, and the home address. In the future these documents, too, will be of interest to genealogists.

LAND RECORDS

Modern records pertaining to land are contained in the *Grundbücher* (land books), each parcel of land being assigned a special sheet in which the description, ownership, indebtednesses, and mortgages are recorded. These books are kept by the *Amtsgericht* (lower court) of the district in which the parcel is located.

In a country as old as Germany, the chain of title to land stretches far back into the mists of time. As a consequence, there are many kinds of records which have bearing upon land ownership and usage, depending upon historical period and the *Stand* (social class) of the owners—*Güterbücher* (chattel records), *Flurbücher* (field or parcel records), *Lagerbücher* (warehouse books), and *Erbebücher* (inheritance books) are some to be found in various parts of the country. For properties owned by the church, there are the *Kirchenlagerbücher* (church property records) listing not only real property and chattels of the parish church or convent but, often, notations on property owned by parishioners; thus, such records become near equivalents of the modern *Grundbücher* (land registers).

Reaching back almost a thousand years are the *Lehnbücher* (fief records) and *Lehnbriefe* (fief certificates). Embedded in German history and thinking was the notion that all men owed fealty to an overlord who, in turn, owed a responsibility to protect his vassals and subjects. Springing from this notion it was customary for the vassals—in fact, landowners—to list their estates from time to time and to have the use of these estates reconfirmed to them by their overlords. These confirmations were recorded first in *Lehnbriefe*—lists of estates owned (also called

Reversen) and containing on the dorso the confirmation of ownership by the overlord. These letters were bound in no particular order. Out of this system the *Lehnbücher* evolved. These registers are simply more formalized, better organized confirmations of ownership rights and privileges.[22] It follows that such records are particularly valuable to researchers of noble lineages.

ACADEMIC RECORDS

For members of the bourgeoisie, particularly professors, teachers, ministers, lawyers, and physicians, there are a number of academic records which can be consulted. Records of the secondary schools often contain revealing insight into the personality of young men, for, in addition to a letter grade, instructors commented upon general conduct and industry. Most secondary schools have published *Schülerverzeichnisse* (alumni lists); some of them date back to the early seventeenth century.[23] In like manner there are records of the acceptance (*Inmatrikulation*; *Inskription*) of students into the secondary schools. These are particularly important, because the students' former places of residence and previous schooling is given, as well as his parentage.

Of even greater importance are the *Universitätsmatrikeln* (university enrollment registrations) containing date of entrance; name of student; citizenship (*Vaterland*); date and place of birth; data on oaths taken, if any; course of study; date on which the student left the university; and degree granted. Heydenreich lists several bibliographies of these *Matrikeln*.[24] In addition, there are many special publications, such as *Augsburger in Heidelberg* (students from Augsburg at Heidelberg University), *Czechen in Wittenberg* (Czech students at Wittenberg University), *Schweitzer in Köln* (Swiss students at the University of Cologne). These, too, are listed by Heydenreich.[25]

Records of the student *Korps* (corps) and *Burschenschaften* (fraternities) are also of value to the genealogical researcher. From early times university students have had broad self-governing powers in university towns, requiring internal organization of the student body. The earliest organizations were the *Korps* based upon place of origin. Students from a given principality or city banded together for social and self-help purposes. In time, the *Korps* became highly aristocratic in manner. With the stirring of liberalism in Germany in the mid-nineteenth century, new organizations, called *Burschenschaften*, came into being. The latter were, and remain, highly political. Both *Korps* and *Burschenschaften* typically wear special caps and colors and even in present times are addicted to dueling. During the National Socialist era these organizations were prohibited, but they were revived after the second world war. Heydenreich cites published lists of student organizations.[26]

OCCUPATIONAL RECORDS

Crafts have an old and venerable tradition in Germany. By the eleventh century some craftsmen were already organizing themselves into *Zunfte* (guilds) which, as they grew in importance, challenged the power of the patricians in the towns. The purpose of the guild was to provide training for apprentices, to maintain product quality, to fix prices, and otherwise to regulate craftsmen.

There were, and still are, three stages in the training of a craftsman in Germany: first, a boy was apprenticed by his father or guardian to a *Meister* (master craftsman). Apprentices (*Lehrlinge*) worked for their masters for a minimum of three years. At the end of the apprenticeship period, the young man was allowed to take a *Gesellenprüfung* (examination) and, if he passed satisfactorily, he became a *Geselle* (journeyman) and was given a *Gesellenbrief* (journeyman's certificate). It was customary thereafter for the journeyman to undertake a *Wanderschaft* (journey), traveling about the country, working for, and receiving the support of, master craftsmen and *Innungen* (guilds) in other towns. In this manner the young craftsman gathered experience and learned the tricks of his trade. At the end of his itinerancy the *Geselle* then had the right to be accepted as a *Meister* with the ability to open his own shop and to train apprentices. In some crafts a second examination was required, the *Meisterprüfung*, before acceptance as a master craftsman.

Each stage in the training of a craftsman was the occasion of a written record and, thus, the interest of genealogical researchers is engaged. For admission into a guild, the applicant had to present a *Geburtsbrief* (birth certificate) or a *Geburts- und Herkunftszeugnisse* (statement of birth and origin). Only legitimate persons were admitted into the guilds. Frequently, the apprenticeship contracts are also to be found. As a *Geselle*, the young craftsman received a *Wanderzettel*, not unlike a passport, in which his guild attested to his competence as a craftsman and to his identity. As he passed from town to town, the master craftsmen for whom he worked added notations in his *Wanderzettel* observing on the quality of his work and the satisfactoriness of his conduct. Such *Wanderzettel* survive in many collections. Those who thereafter successfully passed the master craftsman's examination were so recorded in a *Meisterbuch* (book of masters).

The records of the guilds are extensive and important. They often contain lists of members and notations on journeymen temporarily working in the town. Very little of this material has been published, despite its potential value to genealogists. It should be added, however, that some professions--the pharmacists, physicians, librarians, and protestant ministers--have published *Verzeichnisse der Berufsangehörigen* (lists of professional members).[27] These are of value to the researcher.

MILITARY RECORDS

In a country with such a strong military tradition it is surprising that so little has been done to bring order to military source materials for the purpose of genealogical research. There is, for example, no readily available listing of pension claims, such as has been prepared for American veterans of the Revolution, the War of 1812, and the Civil War. But military records in vast quantity do exist in the archives of Germany, and they hold great potential usefulness to the genealogical researcher.

A major difficulty with German military records has to do with the fact that such records are dispersed among many archival collections, reflecting the fact that, until the twentieth century, each of the principalities recruited its own troop units--much as did the thirteen rebelling colonies in the American Revolution. Another difficulty has to do with the fact that, for centuries, German principalities provided mercenary troops to any country willing to pay for them. Thus, many valuable military records pertaining to German troops are to be found in archives quite foreign to them. For example, in preparing his valuable treatise on the Ansbach and Bayreuth mercenaries leased to the British government for service in North America during the American Revolution, Professor Städtler had to rely heavily upon materials in the British Museum, rather than in the relevant German archives.[28]

Among the most plentiful of published military records are the *Offizier-Stammlisten* (lists of officers and their assignments) and regimental histories. A bibliography of such works, published in 1906, contained 869 entries.[29] It follows, of course, that such *Stammlisten* are mainly of use when researching noble families, since the majority of the officers were noblemen. Recently, the Staatsarchiv in Marburg has begun the publication of muster rolls for Hessian units serving the British in North America.[30] Herein, data on enlisted men is included, disclosing the immense amount of information which could be gleaned from extant rolls, once they have been made accessible to the researcher.

The Hessian muster rolls present a particularly good example of the dispersal of military records. The Staatsarchiv Marburg is preparing its publications partially from the "smooth copies"--the rolls which were periodically forwarded to the Hessian War Ministry by units then in North America.[31] Quite like the information forwarded to the Pentagon by an American field unit, not everything has been reported to headquarters; a deserting soldier, for example, may have been reported to the ministry as missing in action. As a consequence, researchers ought always to look for field records to supplement the "smooth copies." In the case of the Hessian units, some field records are to be found at Marburg; others are in the British Museum; and a surprising amount of additional material is in Canadian and American collections. Thus, for just one simple soldier in a Hessian mercenary unit, archives in four countries are likely to contain relevant material.

COURT RECORDS

Genealogists need to know something of the German court system in order to identify court records likely to yield data of interest. In general, the system has a trial level and two appellate levels, as shown below.

This very cursory overview of the German court system reflects the modern court system of Germany beginning in 1877. The *Schöffengericht*[32] dates back to much earlier times, and the institution of appellate jurisdiction is also very ancient. Researchers seeking court records for a period before 1877 will find them to be of many kinds and under numerous titles--*Schultheissengericht* (local or communal court), *Hofgericht* (appellate court), *Patrimonialgericht* (court on a noble estate), *Reichskammergericht* (imperial court of appeal), *Landmarschallschengericht* (appellate court), *Kirchengericht* (ecclesiastical court)--depending upon locality, time period, and *Stand* (social class). A particular complication has to do with the right of all reigning nobles to maintain courts of justice for their subjects. A necessary step in locating the court records on a particular person is the determination of jurisdiction to which he was subject. Certain nobles, for example, were not subjects of the ordinary courts; residents of a given town often were not subject to the jurisdiction of the local prince but of a neighboring one (or to none at all); Jews enjoyed special status as protégés of some princes but not of others. In general, then, the problem of jurisdiction will not be one easily solved by the researcher

THE GERMAN COURT SYSTEM

Subject Matter	Trial Level	First Appellate Level	Second Appellate Level
Estates, wills, rents, separate maintenance, money claims	Amtsgericht	Landgericht: (a) Civil branch (b) Commercial branch	Oberlandesgericht (Zivilsenat)
Trespass, small claims, misdemeanors, certain felonies (recidivism), juvenile delinquency	Amtsgericht (Schöffengericht)[32]	Landgericht: (Lesser Strafkammer)	Oberlandesgericht (Lesser Strafsenat)
Civil cases over 1000 marks, divorces, claims against the State	Landgericht (Zivilkammer)	Oberlandesgericht (Zivilsenat)	Bundesgerichthof (Zivilsenat)
Felonies, serious juvenile delinquency	Landgericht (Greater Strafkammer)	Oberlandesgericht (Greater Strafsenat)	Bundesgerichthof (Strafsenat)
Certain commercial cases	Landgericht (Commercial branch)	Oberlandesgericht (Zivilsenat)	Bundesgerichthof (Zivilsenat)
Heinous crimes (mainly death penalty)	Landgericht (Schwurgericht)	none	Bundesgerichthof (Strafsenat)
Political crimes, treason, assassinations	none	none	Bundesgerichthof (Strafsenat)

without considerable effort.

Achtbücher

The incredibly complex problems of jurisdiction made it possible for a good many alleged criminals to avoid standing trial simply by fleeing the area over which the court had jurisdiction; at one time trials in absentia were almost the rule.[33] As a consequence, it was customary to publish the names of persons tried in absentia for serious crimes in Achtbücher (proscription books), to confiscate whatever property could be found within the court's jurisdiction, and to sentence the criminals to death, if caught. Such records are numerous throughout Germany.

Schöffenbücher

Records of the Schöffengericht (court of first instance) are particularly important for the personal affairs of town dwellers. They date back to the fourteenth century and contain certifications, wills and gifts, sales notations, and mortgages.

Schuldbücher

Records of indebtednesses, secured and unsecured, began to be registered separately in the market towns by the fourteenth century and in the noble estates and principalities by the seventeenth century. These records can be particularly useful in determining heirs.

Testamente

In modern times Testamente (wills) are to be found mainly among the records of the local Amtsgerichte (lower courts), but in earlier times they are likely to be found among town records. Such records can be very ancient; those of Lübeck, for example, were reported by Heydenreich to extend almost without lacunae from A.D. 1310 into the twentieth century.[34]

MUNICIPAL RECORDS

The records of some towns in Germany begin in the eleventh century. They are likely to contain a great deal of material which, in modern times, would be found in court records. The reason is simply that many of the towns had imperial charters and conducted their affairs quite independently of the surrounding principalities. There were 83 such free cities—some no more than villages. As an automatic step in genealogical research, German municipal records should be searched along with the church records.

Ratsrechnungen

Among the municipal records likely to hold the most useful materials for genealogical researchers are the Ratsrechnungen (municipal accounting records). Herein will be found tax lists, records for welfare payments (alms) made to emigrants, and numerous payments for transporting indigents and convicts to America. The accounts are infrequently indexed, so that researchers will not find them easily accessible.

CENSUSES

There have never been regular censuses in Germany such as the federal decennial censuses of the United States. In the eighteenth and nineteenth centuries the fragmented political geography of the country made thorough census-taking impossible, and, with the institution of the Personenstandregister (registry of vital statistics) in the 1870s, censuses became unnecessary, because a continuous record of inhabitants was available. Nonetheless, lists of citizens (Bürgerlisten) and of municipal councillors were prepared, either regularly or sporadically, in many cities and towns. Heydenreich lists a number of censuses, mainly for towns and small principalities, and particularly described the censuses taken with some regularity in Mecklenburg, which were, apparently, the most thorough for a larger region of the country.[35] In Württemberg there was also a Familienregister (family register) beginning in the sixteenth century and including, in the nineteenth century, a house-to-house listing of residents.[36] Throughout Germany researchers will find Seelenregistern (lists of souls), usually prepared by parish priests or ministers.

MISCELLANEOUS RECORDS

Among German records there are an astonishing number of lists of various kinds which cannot be classified other than miscellaneous and occasional, for example:

lists of singers and musicians who have appeared in concert in Aachen from 1780 to 1832;

lists of courtiers in the entourage of Duke Ulrich von Mecklenburg in 1582;

lawyers of Geneva, Switzerland, 1712-1904;

lists of stonemasons and carpenters who took part in the construction of the castle in Meissen in 1481 and a list of stonemasons from 1488 to 1519.

Heydenreich cites a great many such occasional

lists,[37] and it seems likely that many more unpublished ones will be found in the archives of Germany. All such lists have potential value to the researcher; finding one of specific use is, however, a matter of pure chance.

Memoirs, diaries, and autobiographies, both published and unpublished, exist in great variety in Germany. German participation in the American Revolution is recorded, for the most part, by such records. The most famous diary pertinent to the American Revolution is, no doubt, that of the Baroness Riedesel who accompanied her husband General Riedesel, of the Brunswick contingent of mercenaries, to America.

Deduktionsschriften

There exists in seventeenth and eighteenth century German literature a type of publication hardly paralleled in English literature, the *Deduktionsschriften* (deductive polemics). Succession to title of nobility (and to the estates which went with them) was frequently controverted. In order to set forth their claims as rightful heirs, the writers of such publications had to trace their lineages with proofs thereof. These writings will be found only for noble families, and there are no adequate bibliographies of them.

Newspapers

German newspapers provide rich sources of genealogical data. It is customary to publish death notices listing the birth and death dates, place of burial and, occasionally, place of birth, and the members of the immediate family. Unfortunately, however, few, if any, of the newspapers of Germany have been indexed, so that research access to them is quite as difficult as it is in the United States.

MONUMENTALIA

American genealogical researchers are accustomed to the use of gravestone inscriptions in the construction of lineages; in Germany, such evidences engraved in stone are not only to be found in cemeteries but in the churches themselves, for it was formerly the custom of the wealthy to have their caskets embedded within the outer and inner walls of the churches or under their floors. The inscriptions and arms of the deceased are still to be seen in every ancient church of the land. There is a large literature on gravestone inscriptions, and researchers ought to be aware of it when studying noble and patrician lineages.[38]

The fortresses (*Burgen*) and castles (*Schlösser*) of Germany are also family monuments, for possession of such structures was legally restricted to certain families, all of the nobility. Typical of the vast literature on castles and fortresses are the following, selected at random:

Geschichte der Burg und Familie Herberstein (History of the fortress and family of Herberstein)

Schloss Kalkofen und seine Besitzer (Kalkofen castle and its owners)

Schloss Hohenaschau und seine Herren (Hohenaschau and its lords)

Note that in all cases the history of the edifice is inextricable from that of the families which owned them.[39]

The houses of patricians and burghers in the towns of Germany also have an ancient history. Frequently, the surname or nickname of the first owner was given to the house, and the name remained long after his death. Occasionally, it occurs that later owners took the name of the house as their surname, a possibility which genealogists will want to keep in mind when assuming that ownership of the house remained within the same lineage for centuries.

REQUESTING RESEARCH ASSISTANCE IN GERMANY

The volume of inquiries made by foreign genealogists to German consular and diplomatic representatives abroad regarding research in Germany has been so large that in 1972 an instruction was issued by the Auswärtige Amt (Foreign Office) in the matter.[40] According to this instruction, general inquiries of a genealogical or heraldic nature should be addressed to the

Deutsche Arbeitsgemeinschaft genealogischer
   Verbände e.V.,
D-33 Braunschweig,
Steintorwall 15 (Stadtarchiv),
West Germany

The DAGV is an umbrella organization of important regional genealogical societies charged with the task of maintaining contacts with the public and with foreign genealogical organizations. Inquiries made to the DAGV will be passed along to the appropriate regional societies for research and reply.

Foreign researchers knowing precisely where information is to be sought may address their inquiries directly to the regional societies. As of late 1974 the addresses of these regional societies were as follows:

Baden-Württemberg:

    Verein für Familien- und Wappenkunde in
      Württemberg und Baden e.V.,
    D-7 Stuttgart 1,
    Hasenbergstrasse 18,
    West Germany

Bavaria (Upper):

    Bayerische Landesverein für Familien-
      kunde e.V.,
    D-8 München 13,
    Winzererstrasse 68,
    West Germany

Bavaria (Franconia):

    Gesellschaft für Familienforschung in
      Franken e.V.,
    D-85 Nürnberg,
    Archivstrasse 17,
    West Germany

Berlin:

    Der HEROLD, Verein für Heraldik, Genealogie
      und verwandte Wissenschaften,
    D-1 Berlin 33 (Dahlem),
    Archivstrasse 12-14,
    Germany

Bremen:

    Gesellschaft für Familienkunde e.V. "Die
      Maus,"
    D-28 Bremen 1,
    Präsident-Kennedy-Platz 2, Staatsarchiv,
    West Germany

Hamburg:

    Genealogische Gesellschaft, Sitz Hamburg,
      e.V.,
    D-2 Hamburg 36,
    Postfach 239,
    West Germany

Hessen-Darmstadt:

    Hessische Familiengeschichtliche Verein-
      igung e.V.,
    D-61 Darmstadt,
    Staatsarchiv (Schloss),
    West Germany

Hessen (Nassau and Frankfurt/Main):

    Familienkundliche Gesellschaft für Nassau
      und Frankfurt e.V., Sitz Wiesbaden,
    D-637 Oberursel (Taunus),
    Hopfengarten 19,
    West Germany

Hessen (Kurhessen and Waldeck):

    Gesellschaft für Familienkunde in Kur-
      hessen und Waldeck e.V.,
    D-35 Kassel-Wilhelmshöhe,
    Postfach 128,
    West Germany

Hessen (Fulda):

    Vereinigung für Familien- und Wappen-
      kunde Fulda e.V.,
    D-6411 Edelzell,
    Taunusstrasse 4,
    West Germany

Lower Saxony:

    Niedersächsische Landesverein für Famil-
      ienkunde e.V.,
    D-3 Hannover,
    Köbelinger-Strasse 59,
    West Germany

Lower Saxony (Göttingen):

    Genealogisch-Heraldische Gesellschaft,
      Sitz Göttingen,
    D-34 Göttingen,
    Theaterplatz 5 (Stadtarchiv),
    West Germany

Lower Saxony (Oldenburg):

    Oldenburgische Gesellschaft für Familien-
      kunde e.V.,
    D-29 Oldenburg,
    Stargarder-Weg 6,
    West Germany

Lower Saxony (East Friesland):

    Arbeitsgruppe Familienkunde und Heraldik
      der Ostfriesischen Landschaft,
    D-296 Aurich,
    Bürgermeister-Müller-Platz 2,
    West Germany

Lower Saxony (Eastphalia):

    Familienkundliche Kommission für Nieder-
      sachsen und Bremen sowie angrenzende
      ostfälische Gebiete e.V.,
    D-3 Hannover,
    Appelstrasse 9,
    West Germany

Nordrhein-Westfalen (the Rhineland):

    Westdeutsche Gesellschaft für Familien-
      kunde e.V.,
    D-53 Bonn-Beuel 1,
    Rheinallee 34,
    West Germany

Nordrhein-Westfalen (Westphalia):

> Westfälische Gesellschaft für Genealogie
> und Familienforschung,
> D-44 Münster (Westf.),
> Warendorfer-Strasse 25,
> West Germany

Rheinland-Pfalz (the Palatinate):

> Arbeitsgemeinschaft für pfälzische Fam-
> ilien- und Wappenkunde e.V.,
> D-67 Ludwigshafen (Rhein),
> Carl-Bosch-Strasse 195,
> West Germany

Rheinland-Pfalz (the Rhineland):

> Westdeutsche Gesellschaft für Familien-
> kunde e.V.,
> D-53 Bonn-Beuel 1,
> Rheinallee 34,
> West Germany

Rheinland-Pfalz (Upper Rhine):

> Hessische Familiengeschichtliche Verein-
> igung e.V.,
> D-61 Darmstadt,
> Staatsarchiv (Schloss),
> West Germany

Rheinland-Pfalz (Eastern Palatinate):

> Familienkundliche Gesellschaft für Nassau
> und Frankfurt e.V., Sitz Wiesbaden,
> D-637 Oberursel (Taunus),
> Hopfengarten 19,
> West Germany

Saarland:

> Arbeitsgemeinschaft für Saarlandische
> Familienkunde im Historischen Verein
> für die Saargegend e.V.,
> D-66 Saarbrücken 2,
> Neunkircherstrasse 98,
> West Germany

Schleswig-Holstein:

> Schleswig-Holsteinische Gesellschaft für
> Familienforschung und Wappenkunde e.V.,
> D-23 Kiel 1,
> Gartenstrasse 12,
> West Germany

Middle Germany (Brandenburg, Mecklenburg, and
Saxony):

> Arbeitsgemeinschaft für mitteldeutsche
> Familienforschung e.V., Sitz Marburg,
> D-35 Kassel,
> Emilienstrasse 1,
> West Germany

Eastern Germany (Silesia, East and West Prussia, Pomerania):

> Arbeitsgemeinschaft ostdeutscher Familien-
> forscher e.V., Sitz Herne,
> D-433 Mülheim a. d. Ruhr-Saarn,
> Eibenkamp 23/25,
> West Germany

East and West Prussia:

> Verein für Familienforschung in Ost- und
> West-Preussen e.V., Sitz Marburg,
> D-2 Hamburg 62,
> Postfach 126,
> West Germany

Although not listed in the Auswärtige
Amt instruction, there are several other ad-
dresses which will be of interest to German-
American researchers:

German Democratic Republic:

> Zentralstelle für Genealogie in der
> Deutschen Demokratischen Republik,
> DDR-701 Leipzig,
> Georgi-Dimitroff-Platz 1,
> German Democratic Republic

Germans from Czechoslovakia (Sudetendeutsche):

> Vereinigung sudetendeutscher Familien-
> forscher,
> D-8416 Hemau,
> Wittelsbacherstrasse 33,
> West Germany

Dortmund area:

> Roland zu Dortmund e.V.,
> D-46 Dortmund-Wickede,
> Düttelstrasse 1,
> West Germany

Cologne (and lower Rhine River area):

> Westdeutsche Gesellschaft für Familien-
> kunde e.V., Bezirksgruppe Köln,
> D-5 Köln 1,
> Postfach 101471,
> West Germany

The Nobility (for all Germany):

> Deutsche Adelsarchiv,
> D-355 Marburg,
> Friedrichsplatz 15 (Staatsarchiv),
> West Germany

Heraldry (and the registration of newly-
adopted armorial bearings):

> HEROLD, Verein für Heraldik, Genealogie
> und verwandte Wissenschaft,
> D-1 Berlin 33 (Dahlem),
> Archivstrasse 12-14

FOOTNOTES

1. Eduard Heydenreich, *Handbuch der praktischen Genealogie* (Leipzig, 1913; reprint ed., Neustadt an der Aisch: Verlag Degener & Co., 1971), 2:33.

2. For a bibliography of extant church registers, *see* Erich Wentscher and Hermann Mitgau, *Einführung in die praktische Genealogie*, 4th ed. rev. and enl. (Limburg an der Lahn: C. A. Starke Verlag, 1966), pp. 19–23.

3. Ibid., p. 28.

4. For some interesting examples of baptismal entries for the illegitimate offspring of noblemen, *see* Heydenreich, op. cit., 2:53–55. The number of illegitimate children in Germany was, during some periods, quite high:

		Illegitimate Births
In Berlin:	1789–1798	9.3%
	1799–1803	10.8
	1804–1808	13.9
	1830–1840	16.7
In Stuttgart:	1750–1780	3.4
	1790–1799	8.0
	1831–1835	16.7
In Leipzig, Göttingen, and Jena around 1800		16.7
In Dresden, around 1800		20.0
In Munich, around 1800		25.0

Statistics adapted from Karl Biedermann, *Deutschland in 18. Jahrhundert* (Leipzig, 1880; reprint ed., Aalen: Scientia Verlag, 1969), 1:343.

5. Heydenreich, op. cit., 2:50.

6. *See* Helen Höhnk, "Königs- und Echte-Briefe," *Der deutsche Herald: Zeitschrift für Wappen-, Siegel, und Familienkunde*, 31 (1900): 90.

7. Heydenreich, op. cit., 2:50.

8. The writers suggest that, since many diseases appear to have genetic implications, genealogical researchers should find the cause of death of considerable interest. Even the ancient diagnoses of disease can, in some instances, be translated into modern medical terminology by the use of special medical glossaries, so that an educated guess can be made as to the causes of death.

9. *See* Wentscher-Mitgau, op. cit., pp. 92–93, for a list thereof. Another list will be found in Heydenreich, op. cit., 1:54–56. The published catalog of the Stolberg-Stolberg'schen *Leichenpredigte* collection of some 40,000 entries is held by the Newberry Library, Chicago.

10. For a complete description of these minor death records, *see* Heydenreich, op. cit., 2:83–85 and 2:90–92.

11. Heydenreich cites some of the published lists at 2:85–86, footnote 2.

12. For a list of such records, *see* Wentscher-Mitgau, op. cit., pp. 81–82.

13. Heydenreich gives a lengthy bibliography at 1:109–112.

14. *See also* Lutheran records listed in Clifford Neal Smith and Anna Smith *geborene* Piszczan-Czaja, *American Genealogical Resources in German Archives*, forthcoming.

15. Wentscher-Mitgau, p. 23, gives a short and very incomplete list of German chaplaincy records.

16. Location reported in *Archiv für Sippenforschung*, 7 (1930): 285. Most of the remaining chaplaincy records reported therein pertain to the period 1792–1795 and, although postdating the American Revolution, may have entries of interest to American researchers.

17. Since Schmalkalden is in the present German Democratic Republic, the record is probably inaccessible to American researchers.

18. The Ansbach chaplaincy record is cited in Erhard Städtler, *Die Ansbach-Bayreuther Truppen in Amerikanischen Unabhängigkeitskrieg, 1777-1783*. Freie Schriftenfolge der Gesellschaft für Familienforschung in Franken, Band 8 (Nurnberg: The Society, 1956), p. 173, footnote 5. Städtler used a microfilm of the St. Johannes Church chaplaincy record, Ansbach, which may be consulted in the Landeskirchliches-Archiv, Nürnberg, film no. 164.

19. *See* German-American Genealogy in this Encyclopedia for information on American consulates in Germany and the likely trove of genealogical data preserved among consular records in the National Archives, Washington, D. C.

20. Described in the article by Ludwig Kahn, "Jüdische Familienforschung," *Genealogie: Deutsche Zeitschrift für Familienkunde*, 8 (1966): 157-164.

21. Terminology used herein is that current in the German Federal Republic. In the German Democratic Republic, the terminology varies, but the principle of controlling population movement is quite similar.

22. Georg Droege, *Landrecht und Lehnrecht in hohen Mittelalter* (Bonn: Ludwig Röhrscheid, 1969) makes a distinction between *Landrecht* (land right) and *Lehnrecht* (privilege inherent in fealty). Essentially, the one pertains to the right of the *Grundherr* (landlord) to enjoy the fruits of ownership, and the other to the right of the *Grundherr* to lease parcels of the land granted him to persons (usually peasants) who would till the land.

23. For a bibliography of *Schülerverzeichnisse, see* Heydenreich, op. cit., 1:77-83.

24. Ibid., 1: 85-98.

25. Ibid., 1: 86-88.

26. Ibid., 1: 99-102.

27. *See* Ibid., 1: 72-75, for a bibliography of such professional lists and directories. A recent publication listing German mining engineers active abroad is Hans Lüert, *Deutscher Bergbau im Ausland: In der Vergangenheit, Gegenwart, Zukunft* (Cologne: G. Grote'sche Verlagsbuchhandlung, 1971).

28. Erhard Städtler, *Die Ansbach-Bayreuther Truppen in amerikanischen Unabhängigkeitskrieg 1777-1783.* Freie Schriftenfolge der Gesellschaft für Familienforschung in Franken, Band 8 (Nürnberg: Kommissionsverlag Die Egge, 1956).

29. Paul Hirsch, *Bibliographie der deutschen Regiments- und Bataillonsgeschichten* (Berlin: Mittler & Sohn, 1906). Heydenreich, op. cit., 2: 109, lists a number of titles which should also be consulted.

30. The first of of this extraordinarily valuable series is entitled *Hessische Truppen in amerikanischen Unabhängigkeitskrieg (Hetrina): Index nach Familiennamen,* Band 1. Veröffentlichungen der Archivschule Marburg, Institut fur Archivwissenschaft, No. 10 (Marburg: Staatsarchiv, 1972). A second volume, under the same title, appeared in 1974.

31. These publications of the Archivschule are described in some detail in the article German-American Genealogical Research in this Encyclopedia.

32. The *Schöffen* are non-lawyers called in to sit as judges. Today, a *Schöffengericht* is composed of one legally-trained judge and two non-lawyers.

33. Heydenreich, op. cit., 2: 125.

34. Ibid., 2: 105. It is not known to these writers whether the Lübeck records survived the bombings of the second world war, however.

35. Ibid., 2: 148-149.

36. Foreigners in Württemberg, even Germans from other principalities, were not listed in the *Familienregistern.*

37. Heydenreich, op. cit., 2: 135-146.

38. Ibid., 1: 189-197, a lengthy, but incomplete, bibliography.

39. Ibid., 1: 168-174, gives an extensive bibliography of the older literature on castles and fortresses.

40. *Gemeinsamen Ministerialblatt 1972,* p. 315, published by the Bundesministerium des Innern.

JEWS IN SOUTHWESTERN GERMANY

Emigration of Jews from Germany to
America began in the eighteenth century and
increased markedly in the nineteenth. Many
of the immigrants came from the villages of
southwestern Germany shortly after their emancipation in the early nineteenth century. In
1938, during the crescendo of hatred which led
to the Holocaust, the statistical office of
Württemberg published a survey of census data
by Helmut Kluge, "Die Siedlungen der Juden"
[settlements of the Jews] in Erwin Hölzle, *Der
deutsche Südwesten am Ende des alten Reiches*
[the German Southwest at the end of the Old

empire] Stuttgart: Württembergisches Statist-
isches Landesamt, 1938. The intent of the
article was unfriendly but no doubt statis-
tically accurate. It is reproduced here, in
revised form, as an aid to Jewish genealogical
researchers with ancestors from Germany, and
as a descriptive example of how complicated
the feudal system was, as regards to citizenship and allegiance even in a small village,
for Jews and gentiles alike. However reprehen-
sible the motives for this compilation of census data may have been, it serves the unwitting
purpose of preserving information available for
no other regions of Germany in which Jews
lived before the Ultimate Solution.

Jews have lived in Germany since Roman
times. A great deal of their culture shows the
clear imprint of their sojourn among the Germans. Through the ages their fate among the
peoples around them shifted back and forth from
toleration at best to ferocious repression and
extermination at worst. From village to village and estate to estate within the Holy Roman
Empire German Nation restrictions against Jews
varied; in some villages and estates they lived
for centuries unmolested; in others they were
not permitted even to spend the night. Generally speaking, the Jews were direct subjects of
the kaiser and had his protection, if not good-
will, but, because of the tenuousness of the
central administration within the Empire, the
kaiser often was a most ineffectual protector.
Some nobles viewed their *Schutzjuden* (protected
Jews) as definite financial resources to be
taxed at special rates—in an economy with very
little liquid funds the Jews, forced into commercial ventures by the glacial social stratification of the age, were especially useful as
sources of monetary taxation.

There were special laws, of which the
imperial *Familiantengesetz* (family law) was
one, which determined precisely the number of
Jews which might reside in a given village; until a father died his eldest son was not allowed
to marry, for this would mean an increase in the
number of families in the village. Younger sons

were, legally, unable to marry at all. Thus it was that there were many clandestine marriages concealed by the Jewish community leaders from the gentile town and district officials. Furthermore, it caused there to be a large floating population of Jews with no fixed abode, the *Betteljuden* (beggar Jews), who lived much like Gypsies from horse-trading and transporting farm produce to market.

The survey points out that Jewish settlements in villages east of the Rhine River were relatively stable until at least the 1830s. Ancient settlements west of the Rhine were set in motion by the French Revolution and the French occupation of the Rheinland-Pfalz in 1792. Thus it may be that Jewish immigration to the United States is a mirror image of the greater German immigration--first the Palatine Jews and only thereafter followed by coreligionists from east of the Rhine.

Statistical data assembled herein was taken from manuscript materials in the Württemberg Statistical Office, the Badische General Landesarchive in Karlsruhe, the Hessian State Archive in Darmstadt, and the Bavarian state archives at Nürnberg and Speyer. *Most early censuses reported numbers of families; later ones reported individuals. Hereinafter, all figures are in family units, unless followed by an asterisk denoting individuals.*

HABSBURG (AUSTRIAN) TERRITORIES
IN GERMANY

Until the beginning of the nineteenth century the Habsburg dynasty owned a number of estates and principalities in what are now the states of Baden-Württemberg and Bavaria in southern Germany. During the late middle ages a number of the towns in the Breisgau (Baden-Württemberg) and Swabia (Bavaria) controlled by the Habsburgs had Jewish residents, particularly Friedburg, Breisach, and Günzburg, as well as the free city of Konstanz (Constance). During the Reformation period antisemitism increased, and the Habsburgs began, little by little, to expel the Jews from Austrian-controlled areas. Only in Breisach and a few villages were Jews able to remain; in other areas of the Breisgau they were entirely driven out by 1574 and from the Burgau in 1617. An exception was the anciently-established Jewish populace of Grafschaft Falkenstein which came to Austria upon the marriage of Maria Theresia with Duke Franz Stephan of Lorraine in 1736. Thus, the Jewish population in Habsburg possessions in southern Germany was as follows:

Breisach/Breisgau: 1710, 30; 1809, 85; 1825, 438*

Hürben/Burgau: 1820, 80

Nordstetten/Hohenberg: 1807, 176*

Framersheim/Falkenstein: 1800, 42*; 1806, 6

Ilbesheim/Falkenstein: 1800, 22*; 1806, 3; none in 1925-1933

MARQUISATES OF ANSBACH
AND BAYREUTH (BRANDENBURG)

Jews lived in the two marquisates of Ansbach and Bayreuth from very early times. Beginning in 1609 they had a certain degree of internal autonomy and organization (the *Landjudenschaft*). At the court in Ansbach during the seventeenth and eighteenth centuries the Jewish families of Model and Fränkel were prominent. In 1667 the total number of Jews living in the Marquisate of Ansbach was about 150 families; in 1714 there were about 500 families; in 1790 there were 870 families. In the Marquisate of Bayreuth there were 139 Jewish families in 1709; 208 in 1736; and 356 in 1771. The territories of the two marquisates were later merged into the modern states of Bavaria and Baden-Württemberg. Territories with Jewish settlements which eventually merged with Württemberg had the following Jewish populations:

Oberamt Crailsheim (Ansbach)

	1714	1808	1812
Crailsheim[1]	16	20	106*
Gerabronn[1]	3	5	24*
Ingersheim[1,2]	–	5	34*
Wiesenbach[1]	3	6	35*

[1]No Jewish residents in the 1925-1938 period.

[2]Some of the Jewish residents of Ingersheim may not have been Ansbach subjects.

Oberamt Creglingen (Ansbach)

	1714	1808	1812
Craintal[1]	–[2]	2	4*
Gnodstadt[3]	1[4]	8	55*
Marktsteft[1]	2	13	?[5]
Neunkirchen[1,3]	–	44*	–
Obernbreit[3]	6[6]	30[7]	150*
Signitz[1,8]	1	–	90*
Sickershausen[1]	3	9	30*
Giebelstadt[9]	–	–	–
Gossmannsdorf[9]	–	–	–

[1]No Jewish residents in 1925-1938 period.

[2]One Jewish family lived in Craintal before 1800.

[3]Some of the Jews of Gnodstadt, Neunkirchen, and Obernbreit may have been subjects of the Bishop of Würzburg, since these villages were only partly owned by Ansbach. It is certain that in Obernbreit there lived Jewish subjects of the princes v. Schwarzenberg.

[4]An Ansbach subject.

[5]There were 75 Jews in Marktsteft in 1840.

[6]Ansbach subjects.

[7]Included 27 direct subjects and 3 indirect subjects of Bavaria.

[8]Some Jewish residents of Segnitz were subjects of the Freiherren (Barons) v. Zobel.

[9]It could not be determined whether there were any Ansbach Jews living among the Jewish subjects of the Bishop of Würzburg and the barons v. Zobel in these two villages.

Oberamt Uffenheim (Ansbach)

	1714	1808	1813	1840
Uffenheim	6	1		?
Ermetzhofen	?[1]	17[2]		80*
Hohenfeld[3,4]	4	9		48*
Mainbernheim	7	24		110*
Nenzenheim	?	10[5]	12	
Welbhausen[3]	2[6]	36	30	
Wiesenbronn[7]	8[6]	?	?	
Hüttenheim[8]	?	?	?	

[1]In 1736 there were 4 Jewish families subject to Bayreuth in Ermetzhofen.

[2]Included 6 direct subjects and 11 indirect subjects of Bavaria. Ansbach owned the village jointly with the princes v. Schwarzenberg and Niederadel (lower noble families), so that it cannot now be determined which of the Jewish residents were Ansbach subjects.

[3]No Jewish residents in 1925-1938 period.

[4]Some Jewish residents may have been subjects of the Bishop of Würzburg.

[5]Includes 6 direct subjects and 4 indirect subjects of Bavaria.

[6]Ansbach subjects.

[7]Some Jewish residents of Wiesenbronn may have been subjects of the princes v. Castell and of the Bishop of Würzburg.

[8]Hüttenheim had Jewish residents who were subjects of the princes v. Schwarzenberg and of Ritterschaftlichen (knightly) families, and perhaps of the Bishop of Würzburg; it is not certain that there were Ansbach subjects among them.

Oberamt Wassertrüdingen (Ansbach)

	1714	1808	1813
Wassertrüdingen	17	?	25
Wittelshofen	30	38	41

Bayreuth Territory (in Württemberg)[1]

	1709	1736	1771	1813
Burgbernheim	4	4	3	2

[1]The remaining territory of the former Marquisate of Bayreuth is in modern-day Bavaria.

HOHENZOLLERN

The Jewish residents of Land Hohenzollern (now in Baden-Württemberg) were confined to two of the main towns: Haigerloch (Haag) had 30 Jewish families at the end of the eighteenth century and 323* Jewish individuals in 1844; Hechingen (Friedrichstrasse) had 6 Jewish families in 1701 and 507* Jewish individuals in 1852.

PFALZBAYERN (THE BAVARIAN PALATINATE)

Although the Jews were expelled from the Duchy of Bavaria in 1551 and from the principality of Neuburg in 1671 by branches of the reigning house of Wittelsbach and the Bavarian Herrschaften (noble estates) of Illertissen and Wiesensteig were completely devoid of Jewish residents by 1789, the Rhine-Palatine lands of the Wittelsbach house remained havens for the Jews. It is said that about one-fourth or one-third of all villages in the Electoral Palatinate had Jewish residents at one time or another. The population fluctuated from decade to decade as they moved about to avoid persecution. In 1550 there were 150 Jewish families in the Pfalzgrafschaft; in 1743 the population had increased to 488 families. For those areas of the Palatinate which were in Baden-Württemberg in 1938, the Jewish population was as follows:

Oberamt Alzey

	1722	1743	1800	1806	1829
Alzheim[1]					
Alzey	9	1	139*	30	243*
Dalsheim[2]					
Eich	4	3	?	?	18*

Oberamt Alzey--Continued

	1722	1743	1800	1806	1829
Eppelsheim	1	2	?	7	?
Erbesbüdes-heim[1]					
Freinsheim[3]	2	4	?	12	?
Gauodernheim[1]					
Grosskarlbach[2]					
Gundersheim[3]	1	1	?	2	?
Hamm[3]	2	3	?	3	?
Heppenheim/ Wiese	2	1	15*		
Hessheim	?	2	32*	6	
Kriegsheim[3]	1	1	17*	12*	
Mölsheim[2]					
Mörstadt[2]					
Niederflörs-heim[3]	2	1	25*	6	
Offstein[2]					
Osthofen	4	7	?	13	
Pfeddersheim	4	2	25*	9	
Pfiffligheim[2]					
Weisenheim/Sand	?	3	20*		
Westhofen	4	4	23*	7	

[1] There were Jewish settlements in these villages, now no longer shown on German maps.

[2] In 1722 and 1743 there were Jewish settlements in these villages, but nothing further is known about them.

[3] The village had no Jewish residents in 1925-1938 period.

Oberamt Boxberg (Palatinate)

	1743	1788	1803	1825
Angeltürm[1]		?	8	2	48*
Boxberg	?	1	1	?
Sachsenflur	2	?	?	11*

[1] No Jewish residents in 1925-1938 period.

Oberamt Bretten (Palatinate)

	1722	1743	1825
Bretten	7	13	189*
Diedelsheim	?	?	89*
Eppingen	9	11	187*
Heidelsheim	4	5	149*
Mühlbach	?	?	19*

	1722	1743	1825
Weingarten	5	8	120*[1]

[1] In 1809 there were 17 Jewish families in Weingarten.

Stadt Frankental (Palatinate)

	1775	1785	1786	1800	1806
Stadt Frankental	1	8	15	93*	20

Oberamt Germersheim

	1722	1743	1800	1806	1840
Bellheim[1]	3	3	?	3	?
Billigheim	10	11	?	?	96*
Böbingen[1]	?	?	?	9	?
Germersheim[2]					
Hördt[3]					
Kleinfisch-lingen[1]	?	?	34*	9	?
Leimersheim	2	?	59*	10	?
Lingenfeld[1]	1	1	?	7	?
Offenbach[3]					
Rohrbach[3]					
Schwegenheim[3]					

[1] No Jewish residents in 1925-1938 period.

[2] Jewish families settled in Germersheim during the French occupation period.

[3] Around the middle of the eighteenth century a few Jewish families lived in this village.

Stadt Heidelberg (Palatinate)

	1689	1700	1722	1743	1809	1825
Heidelberg	35	11	20	12	36	349*

Oberamt Heidelberg (Palatinate)

	1722	1743	1825	1834
Baiertal			149*[1]	
Dossenheim[2]	2	3	14*	
Feudenheim		3		106*
Gross-Sachsen	4	3	28*	
Handschuhsheim	4	2	?	17*
Hockenheim	2	2	46*	
Ilvesheim	?	?	150*	
Leimen	7	9	36*	
Leutershausen	?	?	103*	
Lützelsachsen	?	?	97*	

Oberamt Heidelberg—*Continued*

	1722	1743	1825	1834
Meckesheim	2	3	40*	
Nussloch	?	3	51*	
Reilingen	?	1	94*	
Rohrbach	4	4	?	113*
Sandhausen	?	1	34*	
Schriesheim	6	5	101*	
Schwetzingen	3	4	50*	
Seckenheim	3	1	4*	
Walldorf	2	7	128*	
Weinheim	10	12	54*	
Wiesloch	5	5	51*	

[1]It has not been possible to determine whether these Jews were subjects of the Kurpfalz (Electoral Palatinate) or of the Deutschorden (Teutonic order).

[2]No Jewish residents in 1925–1938 period.

Oberamt Ladenburg (Palatinate)

	1722	1743	1825
Hemsbach	9	10	61*
Ladenburg	8	26	93*
Laudenbach[1]	5	5	17*

[1]No Jewish residents in 1925–1938 period.

Stadt Mannheim (Palatinate)

	1771	1784	1809	1825
Mannheim	264	274	308	1456*

Oberamt Mosbach (Palatinate)

	1722	1743	1825
Eberbach	2	1	21*
Grosseicholzheim			99*
Hilsbach[1]	3	5	46*
Horkheim (Burg)			68*[2]
Kirchardt[1]	1	1	9*
Mosbach	8	16	111*
Obergimpern[3]			67*
Richen	1		63*
Schlüchtern	1		63*
Siegelsbach			77*
Sinsheim	9	9	75*
Stebbach			75*
Steinsfurt			35*

	1722	1743	1825
Strümpfelbrunn			60*
Untergimpern[1]			40*
Zwingenberg			27*

[1]No Jewish residents in 1925–1938 period.

[2]Population as of 1807, rather than 1825.

[3]*See also* Untergimpern.

Oberamt Neustadt (Palatinate)

	1722	1743	1800	1806	1840
Alsheim[1]			37*	14	
Böchingen		21[2]		10	
Böhl[1,3]		1		3	
Dannstadt[4]					
Duttweiler[4]					
Ebenkoben	9	16	53*	17	
Eppstein[1]			35*	9	
Friedelsheim			40*	7	
Friesenheim[4]					
Grethen[1]		1	24*[5]		
Haardt[4]					
Hassloch[3]	3	9	31*	8	
Iggelheim[3]		3			31*
Lachen	1	3	31*	7	
Lambsheim	6	7	93*	16	
Meckenheim[4]					
Mussbach	5	6	62*	14	
Mutterstadt	1	1	31*	9	
Neuhofen				9	
Neustadt	8	10	115*	31	124*
Rheingönheim[4]					
Schauernheim[1]			40*		
Wachenheim	8	7	49*	12	
Winzingen bei Neustadt[4]					

[1]No Jewish residents in 1925–1938 period.

[2]There were 21 Jewish families, totaling 88 persons, in 1759.

[3]Böhl, Hassloch, and Iggelheim were jointly owned by Kurpfalz (Electoral Palatinate) and the princes v. Leiningen-Hardenburg. The Jewish residents therein could have been subjects of either sovereign.

[4]There were Jewish residents in this village in 1722 and 1743.

[5]As of 1808.

Pfaffenbeerfurth/Odenwald[1]

	1790s	1829
Village of	a few	34*

[1]Village belonged to the Heiliggeist-Hospital in Heidelberg.

DUCHY OF PFALZ-ZWEIBRÜCKEN

As in the Rheinpfalz, there were numerous villages in the Duchy of Pfalz-Zweibrücken which had Jewish inhabitants. The following village--the only one later to come under the jurisdiction of Baden-Württemberg--had the following Jewish population:

	1722	1743	1784	1840
Hagenbach	1	2	7[1]	77*

[1]Total of 42 persons.

WÜRTTEMBERG

Old Württemberg--the principality before its accretion of the estates of the mediatised princes in 1806--had only a few Jewish settlements, due less to the policies of the princes of Württemberg than to the bitter antisemitism of their subjects. Of the seven cities and villages listed hereinafter, five of them had Jewish residents before falling to Württemberg in the seventeenth and eighteenth centuries. The remaining two settlements--in Stuttgart and Ludwigsburg, both royal residence cities--owed their existence entirely to the patronage of the Württemberg princes.

	1779	1803	1807	1812
Aldingen[1]			34*	
Freudental	24[2]		204*	
Gochsheim[1]			19*	
Hochberg[1]			112*	
Ludwigsburg		4		32*
Stuttgart		5	6	109*[3]
Zaberfeld			36*	

[1]No Jewish residents in 1925-1938 period.

[2]As of 1731.

[3]In 1808 Stuttgart had 14 Jewish families, totaling 109 persons.

MARQUISATES OF BADEN

Jews have lived in Baden since ancient times. The marquises of Baden pursued a variable policy toward resident Jews in their lands; at the beginning of the seventeenth century

Marquis Georg Friedrich expelled them from the Marquisate of Baden-Durlach and thereafter from the Marquisate of Baden-Baden, which he had seized. Fifty years later, Jewish residents were again accepted in Baden but with many restrictions and high taxation. There were 42 Jewish families in the Marquisate of Baden-Baden in 1698 and 1714, and 24 families in the Marquisate of Baden-Durlach in 1710 (none in the Durlacher Oberland) and 169 families (908* individuals) in 1762. In 1801 there were in the lands of the two merged marquisates east of the Rhine a total of 405 Jewish families, totaling 2,186 persons, settled in thirty villages and towns.

Baden-Durlacher Unterland

	1709	1720	1738	1740	1801	1825
Durlach	5					4*
Ellmen-dingen[1]						
Gondels-heim						79*
Graben					16*	28*
Grötzingen	5					99*
Karlsruhe		9	282*[4]	67	530*	893*
Königsbach[2]	1		3			156*
Liedols-heim[5]	3			3	5*	17*
Mühlberg[1,3]						
Münzesheim					90*[6]	75*
Pforzheim	5	9	11		103*[7]	128*
Söllingen[1]						
Stein[5]	3		4			12*

[1]Jewish residents lived in this village during the first half of the eighteenth century but were not mentioned in 1801.

[2]Most of the Jewish residents of Königsbach were subjects of the *Niederadel* (lower noble) joint owners of the village.

[3]The Jewish residents probably moved to Karlsruhe.

[4]As of 1733.

[5]No Jewish residents during the 1925-1938 period.

[6]Nineteen Jewish families, totaling 90 persons.

[7]Seventeen Jewish families, totaling 103 persons.

Baden-Durlacher Oberland

	1716	1738	1801	1825
Eichstetten		11	142*	227*
Emmendingen	5	40	158*	204*
Fischingen[1]			5*	
Ihringen		10	83*	126*
Kirchen		4	68*	73*
Lörrach	4	3	97*	127*
Müllheim	4	8	122*	146*
Opfingen		1		
Sulzburg	4	10	133*	207*
Tumringen	2		9*	4*

[1]No Jewish residents in 1925-1938 period.

Baden-Baden

Listed hereinafter are the Jewish settlemens east of the Rhine River. There were a number of such settlements west of the Rhine, which are not listed because the territory is now in the state of Rheinland-Pfalz.

	1720s	1740s	1760s	1801	1825
Baden-Baden	2				
Bühl	17			111*	25*
Durbach				106*	38*
Ettlingen				19*	33*
Friesenheim		5		33*	49*
Gernsbach					56*[1]
Hörden			2	20*	46*
Kippenheim	7		10	70*	159*
Kuppenheim	5			53*	108*
Malsch	5			87*	108*
Muggensturm[2]			3	12*	25*
Rastatt	5			37*	61*
Schwarzach[2]					21*
Stollhofen[2]				15*	21*

[1]Jewish subjects of the Bishop of Speyer also lived at Gernsbach.

[2]No Jewish residents in 1925-1938 period.

LANDGRAFSCHAFT HESSEN-DARMSTADT

In the Landgrafschaft Hessen-Darmstadt, as well as in the Grafschaft Hanau-Lichtenberg (merged in 1736), there were many Jewish residents. They had the protection of the rulers and nobles but were opposed by the gentile burghers. In the year 1770 in the Hessen-Darmstadt area south of the Main River and excluding Hanau-Lichtenberg there were 260 Jewish households. There were also four Jewish settlements in that portion of Hanau-Lichtenberg east of the Rhine and a number more west of the Rhine in the Alsace. The latter will be listed in another place.

Hessen-Darmstadt

	1770	1800	1829
Alsbach	3		31*
Auerbach	5		79*
Bickenbach			48*
Grossrohrheim[1]	3		40*
Hähnlein[1]	3		42*
Jugenheim		2	14*
Schwanheim[1]	1	3	14*
Seeheim			48*
Zwingenberg	3		39*

[1]No Jewish residents in 1925-1938 period.

Hanau-Lichtenberg

	1825
Bodersweier	60*
Lichtenau	113*
Neufreistett	48*
Rheinbischofsheim	102*

TERRITORIES OF THE HIGHER NOBILITY (HOCHADELSGEBIETE)

The plight of the Jews in the territories of the remaining higher nobility depended entirely upon the attitudes and monetary needs of the reigning sovereigns. In 1693, for example, count v. Königsegg expelled the Jewish residents of Aulendorf; in 1717 the counts v. Stadion expelled the Jewish residents of their Grafschaft Tannhausen; so, likewise, prince Josef Ernst v. Fürstenberg expelled the old and important Jewish community in the town of Stühlingen--only to have succeeding princes reinstate them at their courts. As a consequence, most of the Swabian territories of the higher nobility were devoid of Jewish residents.

In the territories of the higher nobility of Franconia, along the Rhine and Main rivers, the situation was just the opposite. High and low nobles and the clerical princes all permitted Jews to reside within their territories. When, as it occasionally happened, expulsions occurred, the Jews usually migrated to neighboring towns. An exception was the territory of the Hohenlohe dynasty which, by reason of house decrees binding on all heirs, made it practically impossible for Jews to reside therein. The rule was only breached when, for a short time, the Herrschaft Weikersheim (Hohenlohe) with its villages of Elpersheim, Hohebach, and Hollenbach, came into the possession of the Deutschorden (Teutonic knights) resulting in the elimination of the salaries of the protestant ministers and the admission of Jewish merchants. The Jewish settlements in the territories of higher nobles were as follows:

Grafschaft Nassau-Weilburg

	1800	1806	1840
Albisheim	22*	9	37*

Grafschaft Castell

	1840
Oberaltertheim	70*
Unteraltertheim	65*
Wiesenbronn	?[1]

[1]It is not known whether the Jewish residents were subjects of Ansbach (which see) or of Castell.

Grafschaft Erbach

	1829			1829
Beerfelden	111*	Reichelsheim	172*
Kirchbrombach[1]	68*	Reichenbach	52*
König	51*	Rimbach	129*
Michelstadt	177*	Steinbach	18*

[1]Village owned jointly with the princes v. Löwenstein-Wertheim, whose subjects some of these Jewish residents may have been.

Grafschaft Hohenlohe-Weikersheim

	1807			1807
Ernsbach	141*	Hollenbach	17*
Hohebach	62*	Weikersheim	158*

Grafschaft Leiningen

	1800	1806
Asselheim[1]		9
Battenberg[1]	21*	
Bechtheim[1]	62*	18
Biedesheim[1]	38*	9
Bissersheim[1]	34*	
Bobenheim/Berg[1]	18*	
Dürkheim	199*	42
Ebertsheim[1]	21*	9
Grossbockenheim		19

	1800	1806
Grünstadt	171*	93
Hardenburg[1]	93*	
Kallstadt[1]	31*	19
Kindenheim		21
Kirchheim/Teck	57*	29
Kleinkarlbach[1]	25*	
Lautersheim[1]	19*	
Monsheim	41*	13
Obrigheim[1]	59*	10
Sausenheim[1]		7
Tiefental[1]		7
Ungstein[1]	25*	
Wachenheim/Pfrimm	47*	14
Wattenheim[1]		6
Weisenheim/Berg	39*	19

[1]No Jewish residents in 1925-1938 period.

Grafschaft Limpurg-Speckfeld

	1840
Sommershausen	108*

Grafschaft Wertheim
(owned by princes v. Löwenstein-Wertheim)

	1793	1825	1840
Dertingen		46*	
Kleinheubach			145*
Rosenberg[1]		67*	
Urphar[1,2]			
Wenkheim		105*	
Wertheim	73*[3]	98*	

[1]No Jewish residents in 1925-1938 period.

[2]At the beginning of the nineteenth century, Urphar had three or four Jewish families.

[3]Thirteen Jewish families, totaling 73 persons.

Herrschaft Schweigern
(owned by the counts v. Neipperg)

	1809	1825
Gemmingen[1]	16	122*
Massenbachhausen[2]	42*[3]	

[1]Some Jewish residents may have been subjects of the barons v. Gemmingen who were part owners of the town.

[2]No Jewish residents in 1925-1938 period.

[3]Before 1800 there had been six Jewish families in Massenbachhausen and 42* Jewish persons.

Grafschaft Oettingen
(owned by the counts v. Oettingen)

	1730s	1770s	1780s	1806	1812
Aufhausen[1]				36	204*
Deggingen[1,2]	25	35	34	40	
Ederheim[1,10]				21[3]	
Hainsfarth[4]					
Harburg		56		50	
Mönchsroth[5]					
Oberdorf bei Bopfingen[11]				56[6]	
Oettingen			385*	65[7]	
Pflaumloch[1]		18		30	181*
Regelsweiler					11*[8]
Schopfloch[9]					
Wallerstein	38	34	38	50	

[1]No Jewish residents in 1925–1938 period.

[2]In 1686 there had been 3 Jewish families, increasing to 14 families by 1717, and to 25 families in the 1720s.

[3]Increasing to 25 families by 1825.

[4]Apparently had Jewish residents, but their number is now unknown.

[5]Had 190* Jewish residents in 1840.

[6]As of 1798; village had 36 families in 1752.

[7]As of 1801.

[8]Apparently these Jews remained in the town only a short time.

[9]See Marquisate of Ansbach.

[10]Some of the Edernheim Jews were subjects of the Deutschorden (Teutonic knights).

[11]There were 26 families in Oberdorf in the 1720s. Other joint owners of the village did not tolerate Jews in houses which they owned.

Territories of the Princes v. Schwarzenberg

	1800	1808	1820s	1840
Altenstadt-Iller-aichen			74*	
Bullenheim[1,3]		5	6[2]	61*
Dornheim	8			
Ermetzhofen[3,4]				
Hüttenheim[3]				207*
Marktbreit				70*
Michelbach/Lücke	26	34[2,5]		
Nenzenheim[3]		3[4]		
Obernbreit[3]		6[4]		
Thiengen			114*	
Weigenheim		9		

[1]No Jewish residents in 1925–1938 period.

[2]Indirectly Bavarian subjects.

[3]Village jointly owned with other noble families, so that Jewish subjects of Ansbach, the lower nobility, and the Würzburg bishopric were also resident here.

[4]See also Marquisate of Ansbach.

[5]In 1812 there were 139* Jews in Michelbach.

Grafschaft Wartenberg

	1800	1806
Ellerstadt[1]	60*	7
Mettenheim[1]	57*	

[1]No Jewish residents in 1925–1938 period.

TERRITORIES OF THE
LOWER NOBILITY (*NIEDERADELSGEBIETE*)

The condition of Jews within the territories of the lower nobility was much the same as in lands of the higher nobility. There was a concentration of Jews in the Rhine, Main, and lower Neckar river areas and a considerable migration among these settlements. In territories of the *Rheinischen Ritterkreis* (Rhenish circle of knights) all subdivisions had Jewish residents around 1800. In the Kraichgau, a jointly administered district belonging to twelve noble lords, ten of these magnates permitted Jewish settlements in their areas of sovereignty. In the lands of the *Schwäbischen Ritterkreis* (Swabian circle of knights), however, there were fewer Jewish residents, probably reflecting the influence of Habsburg and Württemberg princes. Such residents as there were seem mainly to have settled there in the eighteenth century, as in Laupheim, where Jews were admitted in 1730; in Jebenhausen, where they were admitted in 1777; and in Buttenhausen, where they entered in 1787.

Franconian Circle of Knights
(Fränkische Ritterkreis)

Territory	1800s	1810s	1820s	1840s
Adelsheim (v. Adelsheim)[1]			41*	
Allersheim (v. Wolfskeel)[2]				85*
Archshofen (v. Oettingen)	16*	80*[3]		
Berlichingen (v. Berlichingen)	128*[4]			
Binau (v. Waldkirch)			113*	
Birkenau (v. Wambold)			66*	
Bödigheim (v. Rüdt)			91*	
Bullenheim (v. Hutten)[2]	3[5]			
Dörzbach (v. Eyb)[2]	75*			
Dünsbach (v. Crailsheim)	59*			
Eberstadt (v. Rüdt)			90*	
Edelfingen (v. Adelsheim and prince Hatzfeld)		108*		
Ermetzhofen (v. Seckendorff)	9*[6]			
Eubigheim (v. Bettendorf and v. Rüdt)			58*	
Fechenbach (v. Reigersberg)				70*
Fränkisch-Crumbach (v. Gemmingen and v. Prettlack)			59*	
Fuchsstadt (v. Wolfskeel)[2]				80*
Geroldshausen (v. Wolfskeel)				50*[7]
Giebelstadt (v. Zobel)				103*
Gissigheim (v. Bettendorf)[2]			98*	
Gossmannsdorf (v. Zobel)				96*
Hainstadt (v. Rüdt)[8]				
Hengstfeld (v. Holtz heirs)[2,9]	10	58*		
Hoffenheim (v. Gemmingen)[2]			200*	
Hüngheim (v. Berlichingen)[2]			45*	
Hüttenheim[10]				
Kleineichholzheim (v. Waldkirch)			35*	
Kochendorf (v. Gemmingen)	78*			
Korb (v. Berlichingen)[2]	86*			
Laibach (v. Racknitz)[2]	54*			
Laudenbach/Main (v. Fechenbach)[2]				50*
Laudenbach/Vorbach (prince Hatzfeld)	74*			
Merchingen (v. Berlichingen)			250*	
Messelhausen (v. Zobel)			35*	
Neckarzimmern (v. Gemmingen)			69*	
Nenzenheim (v. Hütten)	5*			
Neunstetten (v. Berlichingen)[2]			15*	
Niederstetten (prince Hatzfeld)	138*			
Oedheim (v. Capler)	84*[11]			
Olnhausen (v. Berlichingen)	123*			
Reichenberg (v. Wolfskeel)				125*
Rödelsee (v. Crailsheim)				120*[12]
Röllbach (v. Hoheneck)	5			
Rottenbauer (v. Wolfskeel)				60*
Segnitz (v. Zobel)[2]	8[6]			
Sennfeld (v. Adelsheim and v. Rüdt)		96*		
Sindolsheim (v. Rüdt)		53*		
Tairnbach (v. Ueberbruck)[2]		124*		

	1800s	1810s	1820s	1840s
Umpfenbach (v. Gudenus)[2]				20*
Wachbach (v. Adelsheim)		101*		
Waldhausen (v. Rüdt)[2]				5*
Waldmanns-hofen (prince Hatzfeld)		2	10*	

[1]Surname of the noble landowner shown in parentheses.

[2]No Jewish residents in 1925–1938 period.

[3]There may also have been Jewish subjects of the Marquisate of Ansbach herein; in the free-city part of the town, Jews were not permitted.

[4]Some Jewish residents may have been subjects of the Abbey of Schöntal.

[5]Other Jewish residents were subjects of the princes v. Schwarzenberg (which see).

[6]See also Marquisate of Ansbach.

[7]Jewish subjects of the Bishop of Würzburg may likewise have lived here.

[8]Village jointly owned with the Bishop of Würzburg, who may have had Jewish subjects here.

[9]No Jews lived in the portion of the village owned by the barons v. Crailsheim, but Ansbach Jewish subjects may have lived here.

[10]See Territories of the Princes v. Schwarzenberg.

[11]Includes 41* Jewish subjects directly of Württemberg who had formerly been subjects of the Deutschorden (Teutonic order).

[12]It is not certain whether these Jews were subjects of v. Crailsheim or of the Bishop of Würzburg, or of both lords jointly.

Rhenish Circle of Knights

(Rheinische Ritterkreis)

	1800	1806	1829	1840
Abenheim (v. Dallberg)[1]		56*	9	69*
Altdorf (count Degenfeld)				100*
Essingen (v. Dallberg)			31	323*

	1800	1806	1829	1840
Freisbach (count Degenfeld)[1]				30*
Fussgönheim (count Hallberg)			10	170*
Gauersheim (v. Wallbrunn)	113*	28		173*
Gommersheim (count Degenfeld)				90*
Herrnsheim (v. Dallberg)	31*	7	52*	
Hessloch (v. Dallberg)	34*	10	56*	
Heuchelheim (count Hallberg)[1]	26*			
Ruchheim (count Hallberg)	120*	13		109*

[1]No Jewish residents in 1925–1938 period.

Swabian Circle of Knights

(Schwäbische Ritterkreis)

	1700s	1807	1809	1825
Altdorf (v. Türkheim)			52	244*
Babstadt (v. Gemmingen)[1]				9*
Baisingen (v. Stauffenberg)		115*		
Berwangen (v. Helmstatt)			25	120*
Bonfeld (v. Gemmingen)		92*		
Buttenhausen (v. Liebenstein)	25[2]	146*		
Diersburg (v. Röder)			39	190*
Dühren (v. Venningen)[1]				36*
Ehrstädt (v. Degenfeld)				61*
Eichtersheim (v. Venningen)				129*
Eschenau (v. Killinger)		55*		
Fellheim (v. Reichlin-Meldegg)				76[3]
Flehingen (count Metternich)				156*
Gailingen (v. Liebenfels)	18[4]			596*
Gemmingen (v. Gemmingen)[5]				

	1700s	1807	1809	1825
Grombach (v. Venningen)				48*
Heinsheim (v. Racknitz)				100*
Hochhausen (v. Helmstatt)[1]				113*
Hüffenhardt (v. Gemmingen)				19*
Ichenhausen (v. Stain)				203*[3]
Ittlingen (v. Gemmingen)				86*
Jebenhausen (v. Liebenstein)[1]	20[6]	244*		
Königsbach (v. St. André)	15[7]			
Laupheim (v. Welden)	40[8]	270*		
Lehrensteinfeld (v. Gemmingen)		102*		
Massenbach (v. Massenbach)		51*		
Menzingen (v. Menzingen)				78*
Michelfeld (v. Gemmingen)				172*
Mühlen (v. Münch)[1]		65*		
Mühringen (v. Münch)		342*		
Neckarbischofsheim (v. Helmstatt)				187*
Neidenstein (v. Venningen)				215*
Nonnenweier (v. Rathsamhausen)			35	112*
Orschweier (v. Brandenstein)[1]			8	42*
Osterberg (v. Osterberg)				40[3]
Randegg (v. Deuring)				289*
Rappenau (v. Gemmingen)				42*
Rohrbach (v. Venningen)[1]				91*
Rust (v. Böcklin)			5	150*
Schmieheim (count Waldner et al)			57	325*
Unterdeufstetten (v. Pfeil)			24*[9]	
Unterschwandorf (v. Kechler)		23*		
Wangen und Marbach (v. Ulm)				224*
Wankheim (v. St. André)[1]		23*		
Weiler am Steinsberg (v. Venningen)[1]				106*
Wollenberg (v. Gemmingen)				108*
Worblingen (v. Liebenfels)[1]			46*[10]	63*

[1] No Jewish residents in 1925-1938 period.

[2] As of 1787.

[3] As of 1820; shown as families.

[4] As of 1734.

[5] *See* Herrschaft Schwaigern, owned by the counts v. Neipperg.

[6] As of 1777.

[7] Around 1750 twelve to fifteen Jewish families; for further statistics, *see* Baden.

[8] As of 1784   [9] As of 1812.   [10] As of 1816.

ECCLESIASTICAL TERRITORIES

Neither the Roman Catholic nor the Lutheran churches of Germany followed entirely consistent policies regarding the residence of Jews in their territories. No Jews were permitted in the territories of either the bishoprics of Augsburg or of Konstanz, but there were large numbers of Jewish residents in the ecclesiastical territories along the Rhine and Main rivers, with over 3,000 living in the territories of the bishopric of Würzburg alone. In Electoral Mainz Jews had a particularly high degree of protection from the prince-bishop in that they had the right to appeal directly to him in the event that parish priests and parishioners agitated against them. The Christian subjects of the bishops were frequently very antisemitic, however; in 1716 the town of Ettenheim (bishopric of Strassburg) tried unsuccessfully to expel Jewish residents by paying them a bonus to leave; in the bishopric of Speyer many Jewish residents were forced to leave because of the high taxation imposed upon them.

Parts of the archbishopric of Mainz, the bishoprics of Speyer, Strassburg, Worms, and Würzburg are in Baden-Württemberg:

Archbishopric of Mainz

	1803	1806	1825
Altkrautheim[1]			6*
Ballenberg[1]			20*
Bensheim		20*	
Biblis		41*	
Billigheim			85*
Buchen			125*
Bürstadt		27*	
Eschelbach[1]			55*
Gernsheim		51*	
Grossheubach	2		
Heppenheim		50*	
Hirschhorn		50*	
Hochhausen[1]			53*
Königheim			67*
Königshofen[1]			
Krautheim			57*
Külsheim			51*
Lorsch		26*	
Miltenberg			70*[2]
Nagelsberg[1]		91*	
Neudenau			36*
Osterburken		1[3]	
Röllfeld[1]	1		
Sachsenflur[4]			
Stein/Kocher			93*
Tauberbischofsheim			109*
Unterschüpf[1]			49*
Viernheim		29*	
Walldürn			23*

[1] No Jewish residents in 1925–1938 period.

[2] As of 1840.

[3] As of 1809.

[4] It is not known whether Jews lived in the part of town owned by Mainz.

Bishopric of Speyer

	1785	1806/09	1825
Arzheim	1		
Bauerbach[1]		17*	67*
Bruchsal	14[2]	20	178*
Diedesfeld[1]	2		
Diedesheim	4	6[3]	
Edesheim	3	6[4]	
Freimersheim[1]	2		
Geinsheim	6	6[5]	
Gernsbach	4[6]		
Hambach	1		
Herxheim	4		140*[7]
Jöhlingen			83*
Ketsch			24*
Kirrweiler	8	14	
Lauterberg	9		
Maikammer	1		
Malsch	6		54*
Mingolsheim	6		43*
Neckarsteinach	5		47*[8]
Obergrombach[1]	8		43*
Odenheim			75*
Oestringen	7		54*
Otterstadt		7	
Philippsburg	2	2	24*
Rülzheim	9		309*[7]
Untergrombach	10		78*
Venningen	1		
Waibstadt	3		42*

[1] No Jewish residents in 1925–1938 period.

[2] Ten Jewish families lived here in 1747.

[3] In 1800 there were 30* Jewish residents.

[4] In 1800 there were 19* Jewish residents.

[5] In 1800 there were 39* Jewish residents.

[6] Other Jewish residents were subjects of Baden (which see).

[7] As of 1840.

[8] As of 1829. Jewish subjects of Worms also lived here.

Bishopric of Strassburg[1]

	1809	1825
Ettenheim	11	72*

[1] Portion east of the Rhine River only.

Bishopric of Worms[1]

	1800	1806	1829
Beindersheim[2]	27*		
Bubenheim[2]	6*		34*[3]
Dirmstein	93*	13	
Horchheim[2]	17*	9	
Lampertheim			79*
Neckarsteinach[4]			
Neuleiningen[2]	35*	19	
Rheindürkheim		1	25*

[1] Verifiable places of residence only; there may have been other Jewish settlements in the bishopric.

[2] No Jewish residents in 1925–1938 period.

[3] As of 1840.

[4] *See* Bishopric of Speyer.

Bishopric of Würzburg

	1807	1825	1840
Acholshausen			60*
Aub			96*[1]
Böttigheim[2]			24*
Braunsbach	165*		
Bütthard			60*
Dittigheim		87*	
Freudenberg		64*	
Gaukönigshofen			100*
Geroldshausen[3]			
Gnodstadt[3]			
Gossmannsdorf			96*[4]
Grosslangheim			70*
Grunsfeld		37*	
Hainstadt		160*[5]	
Hardheim		76*	
Heidingsfeld			500*
Hohenfeld[3]			
Homburg			70*
Hüttenheim[3]			
Impfingen[2]		37*	
Kirchheim			42*
Mulfingen[2]	24*		
Neubrunn[2]			50*
Neunkirchen[3]			
Obernbreit[3]			

	1807	1825	1840
Rödelsee[2,7]			120*[6]
Steinbach bei Hall[2]	60*		
Tauberrettersheim[7]			70*
Wiesenbronn[3]			

[1] Part of these Jewish residents probably had formerly been subjects of the Deutschorden (Teutonic order).

[2] No Jewish residents during the 1925–1938 period.

[3] It is not certainly known whether Jewish subjects of the bishopric of Würzburg lived here.

[4] *See also* Franconian Circle of Knights.

[5] Jewish subjects of the v. Rüdt family also lived here.

[6] Jewish subjects of the v. Crailsheim family are thought to have lived here.

[7] It is not certainly known whether the Jewish residents were subjects of the bishopric of Würzburg or of the lower noble joint owners.

Cloisters and Other Religious Foundations

	1807	1820
Berlichingen (Abtei Schöntal)	128*[1]	
Bieringen (Abtei Schöntal)	30*	
Binswangen (Abtei Kempten)		65*
Dettensee (Abtei Muri)[2]		?
Kappel (Stift Buchau)	52*[3]	

[1] A portion of these Jewish residents were subjects of the lower noble joint-owners.

[2] No Jewish residents in the 1925–1938 period.

[3] Jews allowed to settle here in 1793.

TERRITORIES OF THE NOBLE ORDERS

(*RITTERORDENSGEBIETE*)

In the territories of the two noble orders—the Deutschorden (Teutonic order) and the Johanniterorden (Maltese order)—Jews had been allowed to reside from ancient times. The protection of the Jews of Mergentheim (now Bad Mergentheim) was transferred from the kaiser to the Deutschorden in 1495. At the end of the eighteenth century a Jew was the business agent of the Order.

Deutschorden
(Teutonic Order)

Oberamt Mergentheim. According to a census of 1812, Ailringen[1] had 25* Jewish residents, Igersheim had 53*, Markelsheim had 18*, and Mergentheim had 81*; probably subjects of the Deutschorden also lived at Aub, Edelfingen, and Wachbach, as well as the Jewish subjects of other lords.

Oberamt Horneck. According to an 1807 census, Neckarsulm had 39* Jewish residents and Sontheim 65*; in Gendelsheim[1] 8* Jews were living in 1792, and there may have been other Jewish subjects of the Deutschorden in Heinsheim and Oedheim.

Oberamt Ellingen. In Lauchheim there were 78* Jewish residents in 1807 and probably others at Ederheim.[1,2]

[1]No Jewish residents in 1925-1938 period.

[2]*See* Territories of the Higher Nobility (Oettingen).

Johanniterorden
(Maltese Order)

	1735	1769	1800	1807
Affaltrach				110*
Kleinerdlingen[1]	26	34[2]		
Lustadt/Pfalz			53*	23
Niederhochstadt				26
Rexingen				240*

[1]No Jewish residents in 1925-1938 period.

[2]The *Obristmeister* (general superintendent) of the order forced the local administrator (*Komtur*) at Kleinerdlingen, who had admitted Jews without the permission of his superior, to expel these residents.

FREE CITIES (*REICHSSTÄDTE*)

With but a few exceptions, the free cities of southwestern Germany had no Jewish residents. Ordinarily, the city administrators prohibited the entrance of Jews into these cities and forbade their citizens from all contact with them. This had not always been the case; until the middle of the fifteenth century the free cities had been the places of residence most favored by Jews. Probably, their competition with gentile businessmen and craftsmen, plus the somewhat later influence of the Reformation, caused the Jews to be generally excluded from the free cities. The following towns, having the privileges of free cities, had the following Jewish residents in the nineteenth century:

	1800	1807	1829
Buchau		345*	
Landau[1]		29	154*
Speyer[1]		80*	
Wimpfen			42*
Worms			745*

[1]Jews had been expelled from these free cities in 1689 but returned during the period of the French occupation (around 1800).

THE ALSACE AND SWITZERLAND

The following list, as of 1784, has been taken from E. Scheid, *Histoire des Juifs d'Alsace* (Strassburg, 1887). The list gives both the number of families and the number of Jewish individuals.

Batzendorf	12	54*	Minversheim	11	52*
Bergheim	67	327*	Mittelhausen		2*
Biesheim	53	256*	Mommenheim	30	167*
Bischheim	79	473*	Niederhagental	67	356*
Bösenbiesen	7	36*	Oberhagental	52	271*
Brumath	9	51*	Oberschäffolsheim	16	73*
Buschweiler	38	201*			
Diebolsheim	19	72*	Offendorf	2	13*
Eckwersheim	5	30*	Ohlungen	12	63*
Fegersheim	40	175*	Osthausen	14	63*
Fort Louis	13	55*	Plobsheim	4	20*
Gerstheim	15	74*	Riedweier	8	39*
Grussenheim	29	138*	Rixheim	50	243*
Habsheim	29	128*	Schirrhofen	27	127*
Hagenau	64	325*	Sierenz	43	217*
Hegenheim	83	409*	Sufflenheim	4	19*
Herlisheim	36	160*	Strassburg	4	68*
Hönheim	6	34*	Uffheim	26	122*
Horburg	18	92*	Uhlweiler	3	17*
Kembs	17	84*	Waltenheim	5	35*
Lauterburg	16	84*	Wingersheim	21	100*
Mackenheim	17	92*	Wittersheim	30	163*
Markelsheim	8	47*	Wolfisheim	14	80*

Switzerland

Endingen	no statistics
Lengnau	no statistics

HERALDRY

THE GERMAN NOBILITY

HERALDIC ENCYCLOPEDIAS AND OTHER WORKS

BOURGEOIS ARMS

In Germany and the countries of central Europe the use of armorial bearings appears to have been more prevalent, and perhaps to have occurred earlier, than in England. Whereas the arms of all the families of England are encompassed within the covers of two volumes,[1] those of the Holy Roman Empire German Nation fill 101 volumes.[2] In Germany, armorial bearings are not the exclusive prerogatives of noble families but are borne by burghers, even tradesmen, peasants, guilds, towns, and cities.

The first known secular seal in Germany dates from A.D. 927. By the twelfth century the noblemen began to display armorial bearings, followed a century later by the bourgeois patricians and the guilds. By the fourteenth century bearings were being used even by peasants.[3] It is customary in treatises on heraldry to associate the beginnings of armorial bearings with the Crusades. A more accurate statement might be that the Crusades--those great undertakings which, for the first time, brought together warriors from many European lands and tribes--caused the use of heraldic devices and usages to spread from one European subculture to another with a rapidity which otherwise might not have been possible. Clearly, it became necessary to determine who were knights and to be able to recognize them when in full armor. Being, for the most part, illiterates, the only means of doing so was by the use of armorial bearings.

Unlike England, where the use of armorial bearings seems to have been under the centralizing influence of the King since at least 1417,[4] there has never been a controlling force in Germany limiting the use of armorial bearings. The reason is simply that Germany was a congeries of principalities, and each of the princely dynasties had the ability to create nobles and to grant arms. In addition, the emperors issued patents of nobility and granted 83 towns and cities the right of self-governance (the *Freistädte* or *Reichsstädte*). Each such imperial favor, bargained and paid for, carried with it the right to display arms.

THE GERMAN NOBILITY

There are, in general, two types of noble families: the *Uradel* and the *Briefadel*. The *Uradel*, literally those families which have been noble from times immemorial, can show acceptance as nobles from a period before 1350. They are probably the descendants of functionaries of the late Carolingian period. Their rights as nobles are based not upon acts of ennoblement substantiated by written patents, but upon historical evidence, perhaps as holders of a fortress (*Burg*) or castle (*Schloss*) in unbroken succession from at least the reign of Kaiser Charles (Karl) IV of Luxemburg (*reg.* 1347-1378). By about 1350 the various princes and magnates of Germany began issuing written patents of nobility. Holders of these written patents are known as *Briefadel*. There has been little, if any, difference between *Uradel* and *Briefadel*, excepting in prestige; the distinction is one of ceremonial precedence.

In a period in which communication was confined to the rivers and to trails through dense forests, there was no possibility of centralizing governmental administration. It was necessary for the kaiser to appoint semi-autonomous local administrators (*Grafen*=counts) for the various regions (*Gaue*) of the Empire. Usually, the selection process was simply a matter of accepting tribal leaders already in possession. In the earliest days such tribal leaders had been elected by the tribal group mainly for military and raiding purposes.

Later, such leadership tended to become hereditary, because the tribal mentality gave great weight to tradition.

The feudal system was based upon the concept of loyalty to a superior. This principle can never be forgotten when analyzing the origins of noble lineages, their antiquity and rights. Perhaps the organization of the German state can best been seen schematically, as set forth below. It will be seen that, for the most part, counts and barons were vassals of the *Fürsten* (princes), rather than of the Kaiser himself. Thus it is that the majority of the noble families of Germany are *Landadel*, an elite based within a given country or *Land*, rather than *Reichsadel*, or vassals owing direct homage and allegiance to the Kaiser. There are, however, imperial nobles, usually *Reichsgrafen* (imperial counts), whose titles and privileges flow directly from the Kaiser.

The original organization of imperial officials was subject to modification over the centuries. Most importantly, certain of the princes and prominent bishops came to have the hereditary right to elect the Kaiser. This right was called the *Kur* and the electors *Kurfürsten*. In the earliest period all Princes of the Realm (*Reichsfürsten*) had been electors, but in 1257 the number was limited to seven. Since the prefix *Kur-* was also attached to the lands of an electoral prince--Kurpfalz, or Kurmainz, for example--and to the official documents thereof, it becomes important in the dating of documents to know during what periods each of the princes held this electoral right:

	When Made *Kurfürst*
Baden, Markgraf (Marquis) of	1803
Bavaria, Herzog (Duke) of	1623
Bohemia, King of	1217
Brandenburg, Markgraf (Marquis) of	1217
Hannover, Herzog (Duke) of	1693
Hessen-Kassel, Landgraf (Count) of	1803
Köln (Cologne), Archbishop of	1217-1803
Mainz, Archbishop of	1217-1803
Pfalzgraf bei Rhein (Count Palatine on the Rhine)	1217
Regensburg, Archbishop of	1803
Salzburg, Fürstbischof (prince bishop) of	1803-1805
Saxony, Herzog (Duke) of	1217
Trier, Archbishop of	1217-1803
Württemberg, Herzog (Duke) of	1803
Würzburg, Furstbischof (Prince bishop) of	1805

ORGANIZATION OF THE MEDIEVAL GERMAN STATE

Political Function	Secular Official	Ecclesiastical Official
Overlord	German King and Kaiser (emperor)[5]	The Pope
Central administration	Councillors--seneschal, butler, marshall, chamberlain, envoys (*missi*)	Cardinals, legates, Curia
Over-regional administration	Prince (*Fürst*),[6] usually of an ethnic group	Metropolitans, Archbishops
Regional administration (of tribal *Gaue*)	Count (*Graf*) in settled areas; Margrave or marquis (*Markgraf*) or duke (*Herzog*) in frontier areas needing military protection	Bishops
Subregional administration (for land)	Barons or free lords (*Freiherren*) as owners of estates	*Vögte* (administrators of church lands)
Subregional administration (for justice)	Counts (*Grafen*) or barons (*Freiherren*) with appointed lay judges (*Schöffen*)	Ecclesiastical court system; parish priests
Free towns and cities (*Freistädte* or *Reichsstädte*)	Burgher patricians, usually organized as a senate or council	Abbeys and cloisters administered by an abbot or abbess

HERALDIC ENCYCLOPEDIAS AND OTHER WORKS

The great work of German and central European heraldry is the series known as the *Siebmacher'schen Wappenbücher*. Johann Siebmacher (also spelled Sibmacher) was a painter and sketcher living in Nürnberg. In 1596 he published a small collection of copper etchings called the *Wappenbüchlein* (Booklet of Armorial Bearings). After his death in 1611 his wife published further *Ausgaben* (issues), a custom carried on by successors down to 1806. Certainly, this is one of the longest series of publications ever undertaken.

In 1854 it was decided by heraldry specialists that a "new Siebmacher" should be launched. That series continued down to 1961, when the last volume appeared. The analysis of the contents of the new series will be found hereinafter. A great difficulty in using the Siebmacher has been the fact that, until recent years, there has been no inclusive index to all the families whose arms appear in the 101 volumes. The Library of Congress compiled a card catalog of the families mentioned therein, but it was never published.[7] Recently, the difficulty has been remedied, in great part, by the publication of Hanns Jäger-Sunstenau's *General Index zu den Siebmacher'schen Wappenbücher*.[8] A distinguished American genealogist informs us, however, that the Jäger-Sunstenau index fails to include Siebmacher's volume 58, *Mährische Adel* (Noble Families of Moravia). These lacunae should not be forgotten by genealogical researchers when using the general index.

The *Siebmacher'schen Wappenbücher* are organized in such manner that all the ennoblements of a given princely house are listed together. Thus, for Silesia, which was a possession of the Austrian crown from 1163 to 1742, and thereafter of Prussia, Siebacher lists the Austrian ennoblements in volume 59 and the Prussian ennoblements in volumes 88, 89, and 90. Use of these volumes will not encompass all noble families with estates in Silesia, however, for many had been ennobled elsewhere and settled in Silesia only as a result of additional grants of estates or offices therein.

GERMAN ARMORIAL BEARINGS:

Subject and Geographic Divisions

of the *Siebmacher'schen Wappenbücher*

	Siebmacher Volume No.		Siebmacher Volume No.
Subject Divisions:		Municipal arms: Arms of cities and market towns in Germany and neighboring countries [formerly parts of the Holy Roman Empire German Nation]	15
Counts (*Grafen*): German counts addressed as *Erlaucht*; supplement: Families not entitled to be addressed as *Erlaucht*	11	Princely (*Fürstlich*) dynasties: The mediatized princely dynasties of Germany; supplement: Ennoblements of the Princely House of Hohenzollern	10
Ecclesiastical lordships: [German] ecclesiastical lords; supplement: English ecclesiastical lordships	16	Princely (*Fürstlich*) dynasties: Princes of the Holy Roman Empire German Nation	12
Ecclesiastical lordships: cloisters	17	Princely (*Fürstlich*) dynasties: Dynasties elevated to princely rank by the Princes of the Federated States (*Bundesstaaten*)	13
Flags	18	Princely (*Fürstlich* dynasties: European princely houses not of Roman-Reich or German-federated-state (*Bundesstaaten*) derivation	14
Imperial noble families (*Reichsadel*): Files of the imperial noble families	65		
Introduction: Principles of heraldry	1	Professions and trades: Arms of the professions [and trades]	19
Introduction: History of heraldry	2		
Introduction: Handbook of heraldic terminology in twelve languages	3		

BOURGEOIS ARMS

Although, as will have been noted, the Siebmacher collection contains thousands of armorial bearings of bourgeois families, it is by no means complete. A better record is the special compilation of Johann Josef Kenfenheuer, *Alphabetische Namenregister bürgerlicher deutscher Wappenvorkommen* (alphabetical name list of the arms of the German

---

GERMAN ARMORIAL BEARINGS:

Subject and Geographic Divisions

of the *Siebmacher'schen Wappenbücher*

bourgeoisie).[9] Few copies of this work are to be found in the United States; it is available, however, in the Library of Congress.

Since the use of armorial bearings, especially in signet rings, is still very popular in Germany, new bearings are still being devised. Two recent presidents of the

---

GERMAN ARMORIAL BEARINGS:

Subject and Geographic Divisions

of the *Siebmacher'schen Wappenbücher*

	Siebmacher Volume No.		Siebmacher Volume No.
Geographic Divisions (continued)		Rothenburg, Nördlingen, Amberg	65
Austria: Noble families of Hungary with neighboring lands of St. Stephan's crown	63, 64	Bourgeoisie: 2000 arms of burgher families [similar to volume 65]	66
Austria: Noble families of the Principality of Tirol County	47	Bourgeoisie: 2000 arms of burgher families (mainly North German, particularly Hamburg families; also from Ingolstadt and Zürich)	67
Austria: Abeyant noble families of the Tirol	83		
Austria: Seals of the German universities . . . in Austria	20	Bourgeoisie: 2000 arms of burgher families (partially from the Rhineland)	68
Baden: Noble families of Baden; supplement; Ennoblements of the Princely House of Fürstenberg	27	Bourgeoisie: 2000 arms of burgher families (from all parts of Germany); also [lists] of Hamburg *Bürger-Capitäne* and [families] from Baden	69
Baden, *see also* Bourgeoisie	69		
Baltic region: Noble families of the Russian Baltic Sea Provinces: The Knights (*Ritterschaft*)	45	Bourgeoisie: 1945 arms of burgher families, some from Augsburg	70
Baltic region: Noble families of the Russian Baltic Sea Provinces: The uncertified (*nichtinmatrikulierte*) noble families	46	Bourgeoisie: 1871 arms of burgher families; newly-adopted arms; the "Genannten" [nicknamed] families of Nürnberg; imperial certificates (*Wappenbriefe*) from the Vienna Adelsarchiv [archives of the nobility]; Swiss, mainly Zürich, families; Rhenish house signs from Enkirch	71
Basel, *see* Bourgeoisie	73, 74		
Bavaria: Noble families of the Kingdom of Bavaria	21		
Bavaria: Abeyant Bavarian noble families	79, 80, 81		
Bavaria: Additions to . . . noble families (counts and barons) of Bavaria	96	Bourgeoisie: 1528 arms of burgher families; including *Hofpfalzgrafendiplome* (diplomas of the Count Palatine); guild members at Augsburg; and arms from Münsterland.	72
Bavaria: *see also* Bourgeoisie	65, 67, 73		
Bavaria: *see also* Augsburg, Amberg			
Beiedel an der Mosel, *see* Bourgeoisie	74	Bourgeoisie: 1559 arms of burgher families, including Basel, Bavaria, Danzig, Osnabrück, Saxony; housemarks from Göttingen	73
Bohemia, *see* Austria	57		
Bourgeoisie: 2000 arms of burgher families of Germany and Switzerland (Nürnberg, Augsburg, Regensburg,			

German Federal Republic are reported to have adopted armorial bearings for the first time, and their example is not infrequently followed by other Germans. New and "revived" armorial bearings are simply registered in the Deutsche Wappenrolle (German roll of arms) maintained by the world's oldest heraldic organization:

> Verein Herold,
> D1000 Berlin 33 (Dahlem),
> Archivstrasse 12-14

GERMAN ARMORIAL BEARINGS:

Subject and Geographic Divisions

of the *Siebmacher'schen Wappenbücher*

	Siebmacher Volume No.		Siebmacher Volume No.
Geographic Divisions (continued):		Görz: Noble families of the County of Görz	48
Bourgeoisie: 1470 arms of burgher families; including Basel, the Palatinate, Wurstenerland; housemarks from Beiedel an der Mosel	74	Göttingen, *see* Bourgeoisie	73
		Gradiska: Noble families of . . . the County of Gradiska	48
Bourgeoisie: 1685 burgher arms	75	Hamburg: Noble families of the free cities of Hamburg, Bremen, and Lübeck	37
Bourgeoisie: 904 burgher arms	76	Hamburg, *see* Bourgeoisie	67, 69
Bourgeoisie: 742 burgher arms	77	Hannover: The Hannoverian noble families	30
Bourgeoisie: 575 burgher arms	78	Hessen: Noble families of the Electoral Principality (*Kurfürstentum*), Grandduchy (*Grossherzogtum*), and Landgravate (*Landgrafschaft*) of Hessen	38
Brandenburg (and Mark Brandenburg): Abeyant Prussian noble families of Province Brandenburg	99		
Brandenburg: Abeyant noble families of Mark Brandenburg	85	Hohenzollern: Ennoblements of the Princely House of Hohenzollern	10
Bremen: Noble families of the free cities of Hamburg, Bremen, and Lübeck	37	Holstein: Flourishing noble families of Schleswig, Holstein, and Lauenburg	42
Brunswick [Braunschweig]: Noble families of the Duchy of Brunswick	22	Hungary, *see* Austria	63, 64
Bukovina, *see* Austria	62	Ingolstadt, *see* Bourgeoisie	67
Carinthia, *see* Austria	56	Krain: Noble families of the Duchy of Krain . . .	48
Czechoslovakia, *see* Austria (Bohemia, Moravia)	57, 58	Lauenburg: Flourishing noble families of Schleswig, Holstein, and Lauenburg	42
Dalmatia: Noble families of the Kingdom of Dalmatia	49	Lippe and Schaumburg-Lippe: Noble families of the principalities of Lippe and Schaumburg-Lippe	44
Danzig, *see* Bourgeoisie	73		
England: English ecclesiastical lordships	16	Lodomerien (Volhynia), *see* Austria	62
Enkirch, *see* Bourgeoisie	71		
Frankfurt/Main: Noble families of the Free City of Frankfurt	29	Lorraine: Noble families of German Lorraine . . .	32
Fürstenberg: Ennoblements of the Princely House of Fürstenberg	27		
Galicia, *see* Austria	62		

FOOTNOTES

1. Arthur Charles Fox-Davies, *Armorial Families: A Directory of Gentlemen of Coat-Armour* (Rutland, Vermont: Charles E. Tuttle Co., 1970).

2. As listed in the 101 volumes of the *Siebmacher'schen Wappenkunde*.

3. Heinrich Hussmann, *Über deutsche Wappenkunst: Aufzeichnungen aus meinem Vorlesung* (Wiesbaden: Guido Pressler Verlag, 1973).

4. Henry V of England issued a proclamation in 1417 stating that "no man in future be allowed to bear arms without authority." Fox-Davies, op. cit., p. xviii.

GERMAN ARMORIAL BEARINGS:

Subject and Geographic Divisions

of the *Siebmacher'schen Wappenbücher*

5. In Merovingian and Carolingian times Germany was a kingdom ruled by an elected king. Beginning in 1152 most elections were held at Frankfurt/Main. Until 1531 the crowning of the king took place at Aachen (Aix-la-Chapelle), thereafter in Frankfurt. Beginning with Otto the Great in 962, the German kings have borne the additional title of *Römische Kaiser* (Roman Emperor) when so crowned in Rome by the Pope. After 1508 the title was assumed even without papal crowning.

6. In earlier times, over-regional magnates, frequently the leaders of ethnic groups, were called *Fürsten* (princes). In contrast, the sons and brothers of *Fürsten* are called *Prinzen* (princes) in German.

GERMAN ARMORIAL BEARINGS:

Subject and Geographic Divisions

of the *Siebmacher'schen Wappenbücher*

	Siebmacher Volume No.
Geographic Divisions (continued):	
Prussia, *see also* Austria; Silesia	
Regensburg, *see* Bourgeoisie	65
Reuss, Principalities of: Noble families of the Principalities of Reuss	25
Rhineland, *see* Bourgeoisie	68, 71
Rothenburg, *see* Bourgeoisie	65
Salzburg, *see* Austria	53
Saxony: Noble families of the Kingdom of Saxony	23
Saxony: Abeyant noble families of the Saxon duchies	94
Saxony: Additions . . . to noble families (counts and barons) of . . . Saxony	96
Saxony: Abeyant Prussian noble families of Province Saxony	101
Saxony: *see also* Bourgeoisie	73, 86
Schaumburg, *see* Lippe	
Schleswig: Flourishing noble families of the duchies of Schleswig, Holstein, and Lauenburg	42
Schwarzburg: Arms of the noble families of Schwarzburg and Waldeck	24
Schwarzburg: Extinct noble families of the duchies of Schwarzburg	95
Schwarzburg: Additions . . . to noble families (counts and barons) . . . of Schwarzburg	96
Siebenbürgen (Transylvania), *see* Austria	

	Siebmacher Volume No.
Silesia: Abeyant noble families of the Prussian province of Silesia	88, 89, 90
Silesia, *see also* Austria; Prussia	
Slovenia (Slavonien), *see* Austria	61
Styria (Steiermark), *see* Austria	54, 55
Switzerland, *see* Bourgeoisie	65, 73
Switzerland: Seals of the German universities . . . Switzerland	20
Tirol: Noble families of the Principality of Tirol County	47
Tirol: Additions . . . to noble families (counts and barons) of the Tirol	96
Tirol, *see also* Austria	83
Transylvania (Siebenbürgen), *see* Austria	60
Ukraine, Little (Galizien), *see* Austria	62
Volhynia, *see* Austria	62
Waldeck: Additions . . . to noble families (counts and barons) of . . . Waldeck	96
Waldeck, Arms of the noble families of . . . Waldeck	24
Wurstenerland, *see* Bourgeoisie	74
Württemberg: Noble families of the Kingdom of Württemberg	26, 96
Württemberg: Abeyant noble families of Württemberg	82
Zürich, *see* Bourgeoisie	67, 71

7. This card catalog is available to the public in the Local History and Genealogy Reading Room of the Library of Congress, Washington, D. C.

8. Hanns Jäger-Sunstenau, *General Index zu den Siebmacher'schen Wappenbücher* (Graz, Austria: Akademische Drück u. Verlagsanstalt, 1964).

9. Johann Josef Kenfenheuer, *Alphabetisches Namenregister bürgerlicher deutscher Wappenvorkommen* (Hoffnungsthal: E. Pilgram, 1937).

GERMAN-AMERICAN GENEALOGY

DEFINITION

DEGREES OF EVIDENCE

MANUSCRIPT SOURCES IN AMERICA

Port of Entry Records and Passenger Lists in America

Naturalization Records in America

Muster Rolls of German Mercenaries in the American Revolution Found in American Archives (Anhalt-Zerbst, Ansbach, Bayreuth, Braunschweig (Brunswick), Hessen-Hanau, Hessen-Kassel, Waldeck, Unassigned or unidentified)

United States Consular Records

United States Military and Pension Records

MANUSCRIPT SOURCES IN EUROPE

Port of Departure Records

Hamburg Emigration Lists--Direct and Indirect

Bremen Emigration Lists

Rotterdam Emigration Lists

French and Belgian Port Records

Records of Other European Ports

Records of German Shipping Companies

German Consular Records

Gemeinde (village) and Länder (state) Records in Germany

German Mercenaries in the British-American Colonies, 1620-1775

German Mercenaries Who Served with the British During the American Revolution

Hessen-Kassel and Waldeck

Braunschweig (Brunswick)

Ansbach and Bayreuth

Hessen-Hanau

Anhalt-Zerbst

German Mercenaries Serving with the French in the American Revolution

PUBLISHED SOURCE MATERIALS IN AMERICA

Pennsylvania Germans

Other Published Source Materials in America

Membership Lists and German-Language Newspapers

PUBLISHED SOURCE MATERIALS IN GERMANY

Bibliography of Published Emigration Lists

1. Austria

2. Baden

3. *Burgundy* (ship)

4. Canada and the United States

5. Czechoslovakia

6. Croats (of Yugoslavia)

7. *Elizabeth* (ship)

8. Franconia

9. General articles

10. Hessen

11. Jews

12. *Logan* (ship)

13. Lower Saxony

14. Nordrhein-Westfalen (Lower Rhineland and Westphalia)

15. North Germany

16. Northeastern Germany

17. Poland

18. Reformed Church

19. Russian Germans

20. The Palatinate

21. The Saar

22. Saxony

23. Silesia (and Moravia)

24. Southern Germany

25. Specific Immigrants

26. Thuringia

27. *Volksdeutsche* (ethnic Germans)

DEFINITION

This article is restricted to the problem of linking German immigrants to America with their European places of origin. Within the United States itself, the techniques for researching a German-American lineage are exactly the same as those used for any other American; in Germany the techniques for researching an emigrant varies in no way from those for Germans who remained in the Old Country; only in linking the immigrant in America to his birthplace in Germany are special techniques required.

DEGREES OF EVIDENCE

Establishing the European place of origin of an immigrant ancestor is a matter of marshalling evidence, and it will be seen that the evidence may be incontestable, circumstantial, or inferential, depending upon the kinds of documentation available in each individual case. Hereinafter, we discuss each of the three degrees of evidence separately.

Incontestable evidence, of the kind that every genealogical researcher seeks, is most likely to come from original documentation which has been handed down among the American descendants of the original emigrant linking him directly to a particular village or parish in Germany. There are many such documents, often beautifully preserved by descendants who cannot read a word of the original German. Such documents are most usually the emigration permits (*Auswanderungsgenehmigungen*) issued to the emigrant by the office in the village of his origin. They were absolute requirements for legal emigration. For immigrants arriving in America in the period before 1800, one might find a manumission document, though probably of great rarity, whereby a serf-emigrant was granted his freedom by his lord in Germany. In like manner an exemption from German military service obligation might still be preserved by descendants of immigrant males.

Circumstantial evidence is a more frequent, but less satisfactory, indication of an immigrant's European place of origin. As an example that comes to mind, the Louisiana French census of 1724 discloses that Jean George Poche was born near Kehl in modern-day Baden-Württemberg. Church records of the first settlers of Pointe Coupée, Louisiana, reveal that his wife Catharine Kislin was born in Dourlac (Durlach, in German).[1] There is ambiguity herein, because Durlach may refer either to the town of that name or to the principality of Baden-Durlach. Since husband and wife give places of origin within the same principality, one can say that, circumstantially, it seems likely they were married in a village in the Kehl area of Baden-Durlach. Researchers would, then, systematically search *Gemeinde* (village) and church records in this area, as well as the records of higher offices within the former principality.

Another kind of circumstantial evidence might be the appearance of the names of immigrants in a ship passenger list accompanied by a statement of the place of origin. Herein, the difficulty for the researcher is in proving that the Johann Schmidt of the passenger list, for example, is the person sought. If the passenger Johann Schmidt is accompanied by a wife and children, all named and identical with those of the ancestors sought, the evidence, though still circumstantial, approaches the incontestable.

Inferential evidence is the most tenuous of all. In it, we may include surname clues. For example, persons bearing surnames ending in -ke (as in Lemke, Wittke) are most likely to have come from Westphalia or Saxony; persons with surnames ending in -le (as in Merkle) are more likely to have originated in Swabia (Baden-Württemberg). Equally inferential would be evidence that a German mercenary during the American Revolution came from Electoral Hessen simply because he served in a military unit of this principality. In fact, many soldiers in Hessian units came from other principalities. Only by finding a Hessian muster roll setting forth the place of origin of the soldier can the researcher proceed with some confidence to reclassify his data from inferential to circumstantial. Thereafter, it would be necessary to search church and village records to accumulate conclusive evidence of the immigrant's place of origin.[2] A further example of inferential evidence is family tradition--rarely accurate, but never entirely wrong. The researcher should evaluate these traditions for even the slightest clue, but he should never accept them at face value.

MANUSCRIPT SOURCES IN AMERICA

Primary source materials on German immigrants to America are vast, but, at the time of writing, almost completely unorganized. In a sense it is a primary aim of this Encyclopedia to identify and describe them as a first step in their organization. The writers believe that, when the task of organizing and indexing these manuscripts has finally been accomplished--if it ever is--researchers will have a good deal more data on Americans of German origin than ever will be the case on Americans of British origin. The reason is simply that German immigration to the United States is mainly in the nineteenth century, with better record-keeping both in the Old Country and in the United States, whereas Anglo-Saxon movement to America, being internal within the British Empire and frequently dating from the eighteenth century, was the occasion of much less record-keeping.

As a general rule, the American researcher ought first to exhaust the archival sources in the United States and Canada before proceeding to an examination of European source materials. Excepting for cases in which the researcher has incontestable proof or strong circumstantial evidence of the exact place of origin of an immigrant, no attempt should ever be made to institute research in Germany. This basic rule is frequently overlooked, particularly in cases in which the German principality may be known from American documentation but not the exact place of origin within the principality. A common example is an inquiry made in Germany based only upon documentary evidence from an American county court naturalization record to the effect that the immigrant was born in the Kingdom of Prussia. Nineteenth-century Prussia was a conglomeration of petty territories stretching from the Russian border to that of Switzerland, and it is simply impossible for research to cover such an area. The researcher is doomed to failure from the outset.

Discussed hereinafter are the kinds of documentary materials to be found in the United States most likely to yield information on exact European birthplaces of immigrants to America. One can say at the outset that the records prepared by American officials are usually unspecific as to exact birthplace. Port of entry records are likely to give only the port of departure or the German principality from whence the immigrant came. Naturalization records of the nineteenth century nearly always give the principality of former citizenship, but little else. Only after the commencement of record-keeping by the United States Immigration and Naturalization Service in the twentieth century can one expect to find precise data on birthplace in American records.

Port of Entry Records
and Passenger Lists in America

The passenger arrival lists compiled at American ports of entry are numerous but incomplete. Some are readily accessible through indexes and soundexes, others have had very little attention given to them. These records are described in detail in

National Archives and Records Service. General Services Administration. *Guide to Genealogical Records in the National Archives* (Washington, D.C.: Government Printing Office, 1964), pp. 22-43.

We offer the following observations regarding American port of entry records:

¶ Passenger arrival lists in the National Archives pertain almost exclusively to the nineteenth and twentieth centuries. For eighteenth-century immigrants, the researcher must usually consult the published source materials listed in

Harold Lancour, *A Bibliography of Ship Passenger Lists, 1538-1825; Being a Guide to Published Lists of Early Immigrants to North America*. 3d ed. rev. and enl. by Richard J. Wolfe (New York: New York Public Library, 1963).

¶ For nineteenth-century immigrants, researchers should, if at all possible, determine ports of entry from sources other than the National Archives passenger arrival lists, in order to avoid extensive search in these lists. Here, family tradition is likely to be accurate, if it exists. Researchers ought, also, to determine as closely as possible the year of arrival. Such arrival dates can frequently be approximated from data in the decennial federal censuses. For example, if the 1860 census shows the family of Johann Schmidt with an eight-year-old child born in Germany and another, age five, born in America, it is clear that the family's arrival in America is sometime between 1852 and 1855. This reduces the searching of passenger arrival lists to manageable proportions. Parenthetically, it can be said that researchers are more likely to be able to fix the approximate date of arrival than they are to determine the port of entry.

¶ In the event that the port of arrival is unknown, one must proceed on the basis of probabilities:

The great majority of immigrants arrived through the port of New York. It follows, then, that the majority of all immigrants, particularly those settling in the upper Middle West, came through New York, and these records should be searched first for the arrivals of immigrants settling in this region.

For immigrants settling along the East Coast from Philadelphia southward, the researcher may want first to consider the ports of Baltimore and Philadelphia and, thereafter, the nearby minor ports of entry.

For immigrants settling in the South and Southwest, particularly in Louisiana and Texas, the ports of New Orleans and Galveston become important.

For immigrants settling in the Mississippi River basin, even as far north as Minnesota, New Orleans ought to be considered right after New York as the probable port of entry, because the Mississippi River afforded easy access to immigrants entering via New Orleans. For example, three of the four vessels carrying the Saxons who settled in Missouri landed at New Orleans, the fourth vessel landed at New York.

For West Coast immigrants, particularly in the period just after the 1849 gold rush, San Francisco would be an important port of entry. However, these records seem no longer to exist, no doubt the casualty of the fire.

¶ Researchers should not expect to be able to identify with certainty the immigrants from the ship arrival lists, nor their exact birthplaces in Germany. Clearly, there are likely to be a number of Johann Schmidts entering the port of New York during the 1852–1855 period. One should list all these individuals, the ships upon which they came, the dates, and the ports of departure. With such information in hand, it may be possible to enter certain German records to obtain additional information which may determine, circumstantially at least, the Johann Schmidt in question.

Naturalization Records in America

Until the twentieth century, the naturalization of foreigners was normally a function of local court officials of the county in which the immigrants lived. Usually, birthplace in Germany is not given in these records; instead, the principality of origin--Kingdom of Prussia, Duchy of Mecklenburg-Schwerin, and the like--is given. This is ordinarily insufficient information for the researcher, because it provides only a general clue as to place of origin.

We wish to point out that naturalization was never a requirement for residency in the United States, and many immigrants were never naturalized. One may hypothesize that immigrant women rarely went through the procedure--it held no benefits for them--and it may be suggested that, in remoter areas with sizable German colonies, naturalization may not have been held particularly desirable by immigrant men. The principal advantage to naturalization was to be able to vote; for groups having little interest in voting, there was probably very little incentive to taking out American citizenship. Thus it is that researchers cannot assume that a naturalization record can be found for every immigrant.

Muster Rolls of German Mercenaries
in the American Revolution
Found in American Archives

The writers have located 71 muster rolls and prisoner-of-war lists in American archives pertaining to the German mercenaries who fought with the British during the American Revolution. Among them is the only list of recruits from Anhalt-Zerbst known to be extant, either in Germany or America; a series of prisoner-of-war lists of the so-called Convention Army (British and German troopers captured at Saratoga); and lists of prisoners "farmed out" to various landowners of eastern Pennsylvania. The prisoner-of-war lists are especially important, because they give clues as to places where these men might have settled after the war, if not repatriated to Germany. Apparently, no official and complete list of Convention Army prisoners of war was ever prepared. General Washington asked for one, but General Bourgoyne refused to supply it on the grounds that the captured men were not prisoners of war, but merely pledged to remain noncombattants during the remainder of the Revolution.

All 71 of these lists have been translated, transcribed, and indexed in

Clifford Neal Smith, *Muster Rolls and Prisoner-of-War Lists in American Archives Pertaining to the German Mercenary Troops with the British Forces During the American Revolution.* German-American Genealogical Research Monograph No. 3. Thomson, Illinois: Heritage House, 1975.

These rolls are described below. Abbreviations are as follows:

Br   Braunschweig contingent

DLC   Library of Congress, Manuscript Division, Washington, D. C.

GR   The number following this designation refers to the serial number assigned to the muster roll as it

appears in the publication cited above.

HH   Hessen-Hanau contingent

HK   Hessen-Kassel contingent

ICH   Chicago Historical Society, Chicago, Illinois

ICN (BM) Newberry Library, Chicago, Illinois. The BM thereafter refers to a photostatic copy in this library made from an original document said to be among the Rainsford papers in the British Museum, London. Inspection of the Rainsford papers at the British Museum by these writers did not disclose the original document, however, and it may be that the Newberry Library photocopy is the only remains of this valuable genealogical source.

MIU-C University of Michigan Library, William L. Clement Collection, Ann Arbor, Michigan

---

GERMAN MUSTER ROLLS IN AMERICAN ARCHIVES

Regiment	Company	Description	Repository
		1. Anhalt-Zerbst	
Contingent	Unassigned	List of recruits sent over from Jevern; inspected by Wm. Porter, 20 Jul 1781, Fort Brooklyn, Long Island, 53 men	MIU-C GR-51
		2. Ansbach	
		(No muster rolls known to be extant in American repositories.)	
		3. Bayreuth	
		(No muster rolls known to be extant in American repositories.)	
		4. Braunschweig (Brunswick)	
Br Dragoons	Bartling	Inspection by Wm. Porter, 26 Jul 1781, Fort Brooklyn, Long Island, 9 men	MIU-C GR-55
Br Dragoons	Lohneisen	Inspection by Wm. Porter, 26 Jul 1781, Fort Brooklyn, Long Island, 4 men	MIU-C GR-55
Br Dragoons	Schlagenteuffel	Muster roll of recruits, 20 Jul 1781, Brooklyn, Long Island, 70 men	MIU-C GR-56
Br Dragoons	Vacant	Inspection by Wm. Porter, 26 Jul 1781, Fort Brooklyn, Long Island, 8 men	MIU-C GR-55

GERMAN MUSTER ROLLS IN AMERICAN ARCHIVES--*Continued*

Regiment	Company	Description	Repos-itory

4. Braunschweig (Brunswick)--*Continued*

Regiment	Company	Description	Repos-itory
Br Grenadier Battalion	Mengen	Inspection by Wm. Porter, 26 Jul 1781, Fort Brooklyn, Long Island, 2 men	MIU-C GR-55
Br Regiment Prinz Friedrich	Hille (detachment)	Muster roll, 20 Jul 1781, Fort Brooklyn, Long Island, 2 men	MIU-C GR-57
Br Regiment Prinz Friedrich	Leib (bodyguard)	Muster roll, 24 Jun 1782, [no place given] 2 men	MIU-C GR-58
Br Regiment Prinz Friedrich	Praetorius (detach-ment)	Muster roll, 20 Jul 1781, Fort Brooklyn, Long Island, 1 man	MIU-C GR-57
Br Regiment Prinz Friedrich	Tunderfeld (detach-ment)	Muster roll, 20 Jul 1781, Fort Brooklyn, Long Island, 1 man	MIU-C GR-57
Br Regiment Prinz Friedrich	Not stated (detach-ment)	Muster roll, 24 Jun 1782, [no place given] 28 men	MIU-C GR-58
Br Regiment v. Rhetz	Ehrenkrook (detach-ment)	Muster roll, 20 Jul 1781, Fort Brooklyn, Long Island, 2 men	MIU-C GR-59
Br Regiment v. Rhetz	Lucke	Muster roll, 20 Jul 1781, Fort Brooklyn, Long Island, 10 men	MIU-C GR-59
Br Regiment v. Rhetz	Mers (detachment)	Muster roll, 20 Jul 1781, Fort Brooklyn, Long Island, 3 men	MIU-C GR-59
Br Regiment v. Rhetz	Schlagenteuffel (de-tachment)	Muster roll, 20 Jul 1781, Fort Brooklyn, Long Island, 1 man	MIU-C GR-59
Br Regiment v. Rhetz	Colonel's Company (detachment)	Muster roll, 20 Jul 1781, Fort Brooklyn, Long Island, 1 man	MIU-C GR-59
Br Regiment v. Rhetz	Regimental Staff (detachment)	Muster roll, 20 Jul 1781, Fort Brooklyn, Long Island, 2 men	MIU-C GR-59
Br Regiment v. Rhetz	Unassigned recruits	Muster roll, 20 Jul 1781, Fort Brooklyn, Long Island, 24 men	MIU-C GR-59
Br Infantry Regiment v. Riedesel	Morgenstern (detach-ment)	Muster roll, 20 Jul 1781, Fort Brooklyn, Long Island, 7 men	MIU-C GR-60
Br Infantry Regiment v. Riedesel	Pöllnitz (detachment)	Muster roll, 20 Jul 1781, Fort Brooklyn, Long Island, 3 men	MIU-C GR-60
Br Infantry Regiment v. Riedesel	Speth (detachment)	Muster roll, 20 Jul 1781, Fort Brooklyn, Long Island, 10 men	MIU-C GR-60
Br Infantry Regiment v. Riedesel	Colonel's (detach-ment)	Muster roll, 20 Jul 1781, Fort Brooklyn, Long Island, 12 men	MIU-C GR-60
Br Infantry Regiment v. Riedesel	Regimental Staff (detachment)	Muster roll, 20 Jul 1781, Fort Brooklyn, Long Island, 6 men	MIU-C GR-60
Br Infantry Regiment v. Riedesel	Vacant (detachment)	Muster roll, 20 Jul 1781, Fort Brooklyn, Long Island, 2 men	MIU-C GR-60
Br Infantry Regiment v. Riedesel	Unassigned recruits	Muster roll, 20 Jul 1781, Fort Brooklyn, Long Island, 25 men	MIU-C GR-60

GERMAN MUSTER ROLLS IN AMERICAN ARCHIVES--*Continued*

Regiment	Company	Description	Repository

4. Braunschweig (Brunswick)--*Continued*

Regiment	Company	Description	Repository
Br Regiment v. Specht	Ehrenkrook (detachment)	Muster roll, 20 Jul 1781? Fort Brooklyn, Long Island, 4 men	MIU-C GR-61
Br Regiment v. Specht	Lützow (detachment)	Muster roll, 20 Jul 1781? Fort Brooklyn, Long Island, 6 men	MIU-C GR-61
Br Regiment v. Specht	Plessen (detachment)	Muster roll, 20 Jul 1781? Fort Brooklyn, Long Island, 2 men	MIU-C GR-61
Br Regiment v. Specht	Colonel's (detachment)	Muster roll, 20 Jul 1781? Fort Brooklyn, Long Island, 4 men	MIU-C GR-61
Br Regiment v. Specht	Regimental Staff (detachment)	Muster roll, 20 Jul 1781? Fort Brooklyn, Long Island, 4 men	MIU-C GR-61
Br Regiment v. Specht	Vacant (detachment)	Muster roll, 20 Jul 1781? Fort Brooklyn, Long Island, 26 men	MIU-C GR-61
Br Regiment v. Specht	Unassigned recruits	Muster roll, 20 Jul 1781? Fort Brooklyn, Long Island, 25 men	MIU-C GR-61
Br Jägerkorps (Chasseurs)	Barner (detachment)	Muster roll, 20 Jul 1781, Fort Brooklyn, Long Island, 2 men	MIU-C GR-53
Br Jägerkorps (Chasseurs)	Schottelius? (detachment)	Muster roll, 20 Jul 1781, Fort Brooklyn, Long Island, 3 men	MIU-C GR-53
Br General Staff	[Riedesel]	Muster roll, 20 Jul 1781, [Fort Brooklyn, Long Island] 23 men	MIU-C GR-52
Br Unidentified	Dommer (detachment)	Muster roll, 20 Jul 1781, Fort Brooklyn, Long Island, 3 men	MIU-C GR-53
Br Unidentified	Geyso [Gensau?] (detachment)	Muster roll, 20 Jul 1781, Fort Brooklyn, Long Island, 5 men	MIU-C GR-53
Br Unidentified	Thomae? (detachment)	Muster roll, 20 Jul 1781, Fort Brooklyn, Long Island, 2 men	MIU-C GR-53
Br Unidentified	Unassigned recruits	Muster roll of recruits arriving in New York on 21 Apr 1781, dated 20 Jul 1781, Fort Brooklyn, Long Island, 24 men	MIU-C GR-57
Br Unidentified	Unassigned recruits	Muster roll of recruits arriving in New York on 22 Apr 1781, dated 20 Jul 1781, Fort Brooklyn, Long Island, 20 men	MIU-C GR-53
Br Unidentified	[various]	List of paroled officers' servants [prisoners of war] 1777? 65 men	ICH GR-50
Br Unidentified	[various]	Statistical report, 26 Jun 1783 [final recapitulation]	MIU-C GR-54

GERMAN MUSTER ROLLS IN AMERICAN ARCHIVES--*Continued*

Regiment	Company	Description	Repository

5. Great Britain (associated with German mercenaries)

GB 16th Regiment	Not stated	List of captured officers for exchange, 26 Mar 1778 [Lancaster, Pennsylvania]	DLC GR-45
GB 44th Regiment	Not stated	List of captured officers for exchange, 26 Mar 1778 [Lancaster, Pennsylvania]	DLC GR-45
GB 55th Regiment	Not stated	List of captured officers for exchange, 26 Mar 1778 [Lancaster, Pennsylvania]	DLC GR-45
GB 71st Regiment	Not stated	List of captured officers for exchange, 26 Mar 1778 [Lancaster, Pennsylvania]	DLC GR-45
GB Skinner's Levies	Not stated	List of captured officers for exchange, 26 Mar 1778 [Lancaster, Pennsylvania]	DLC GR-45
Miscellaneous	*see also* Braunschweig General Staff		

6. Hessen-Hanau

HH Regiment Erbprinz (Hereditary Prince)	Artillery (Mayr)	Corps of recruits inspected by Col. Rainsford, Nymegen [Holland2 11 Mar 1777, 106 men	ICN-BM GR-9
HH Regiment Erbprinz (Hereditary Prince)	Artillery (Päusch)	Muster roll, inspection by Col. Rainsford, Nymegen [Holland] 24 May 1776, 132 men	ICN-BM GR-7
HH Regiment Erbprinz (Hereditary Prince)	Artillery (Schacht)	Transport list, 12 Nov 1777 [Nymegen, Holland?] 30 men	ICN-BM GR-2
HH Regiment Erbprinz (Hereditary Prince)	Infantry (Company Corps & Etat Major) (Germann)	Muster roll, inspection by Col. Rainsford, Nymegen [Holland] 22 Mar 1776, 128 men	ICN-BM GR-6
HH Regiment Erbprinz (Hereditary Prince)	Infantry (Gall)	Muster roll, inspection by Col. Rainsford, Nymegen [Holland] 22 Mar 1776, 113 men	ICN-BM GR-10
HH Regiment Erbprinz (Hereditary Prince)	Infantry (Lentz)	Muster roll, inspection by Col. Rainsford, Nymegen [Holland] 22 Mar 1776, 112 men	ICN-BM GR-5
HH Regiment Erbprinz (Hereditary Prince)	Infantry (Martens)	Muster roll, inspection by Col. Rainsford, Nymegen [Holland] 21 Mar 1776, 112 men	ICN-BM GR-4
HH Regiment Erbprinz (Hereditary Prince)	Infantry (Schacht, temporarily)	Transport list, 12 Nov 1777 [Nymegen, Holland?] 137 men	ICN-BM GR-1
HH Jägerkorps (Chasseurs)	Creutzburg	Muster roll, inspection by Col. Rainsford, Nymegen [Holland] 11 Apr 1777, 117 men	ICN-BM GR-13

GERMAN MUSTER ROLLS IN AMERICAN ARCHIVES--*Continued*

Regiment	*Company*	*Description*	*Repos-itory*
6. Hessen-Hanau--*Continued*			
HH Jägerkorps (Chasseurs)	Francken	Muster roll, inspection by Col. Rainsford, Nymegen [Holland] 11 Apr 1777, 117 men	ICN-BM GR-14
HH Jägerkorps (Chasseurs)	Kornrumpff	Muster roll [probably inspection by Col. Rainsford, Nymegen, Holland] 1776? 117 men	ICN-BM GR-8
HH Jägerkorps (Chasseurs)	Schacht (temporarily)	Transport list, 12 Nov 1777 [no place] 56 men	ICN-BM GR-3
HH Jägerkorps (Chasseurs)	*see also* 9. Unassigned or Unidentified		
7. Hessen-Kassel			
HK Grenadier Battalion v. Löwenstein	Biesenrodt	Muster roll, 4 Jul 1782, Camp Greenwich [New York] 134 men	MIU-C GR-66
HK Grenadier Battalion v. Löwenstein	Klingender	Muster roll, 4 Jul 1782, Camp Greenwich [New York] 134 men	MIU-C GR-67
HK Grenadier Battalion v. Löwenstein	Mondorff	Muster roll, 4 Jul 1782, New York, 134 men	MIU-C GR-68
HK Grenadier Battalion v. Löwenstein	Wachs	Muster roll, 4 Jul 1782, New York, 139 men	MIU-C GR-69
HK Fusilier Regiment v. Lossberg	Leib (bodyguard)	Prisoner-of-war list? [Lancaster, Pennsylvania?] 6 Jan 1777, 59 men	DLC GR-25
HK Fusilier Regiment v. Lossberg	Leib (bodyguard)	Prisoner-of-war list? [Lancaster, Pennsylvania?] 26 men	DLC GR-35
HK Fusilier Regiment v. Lossberg	Leib (bodyguard)	Prisoner-of-war list, 17-19 Apr 1777 [Lancaster, Pennsylvania] 3 men	DLC GR-34
HK Fusilier Regiment v. Lossberg	Leib (bodyguard)	Prisoner-of-war list? [no date or place] 58 men	DLC GR-18
HK Fusilier Regiment v. Lossberg	Altenbochum	Muster roll [6 Jan 1777] 34 men	DLC GR-20
HK Fusilier Regiment v. Lossberg	Altenbochum	Prisoner-of-war list, 27 Aug 1777, Lancaster, Pennsylvania, 22 men	DLC GR-37
HK Fusilier Regiment v. Lossberg	Altenbochum	Prisoner-of-war list? [no date or place] 34 men	DLC GR-16
HK Fusilier Regiment v. Lossberg	Hanstein	Prisoner-of-war list, Jan 1777, Lancaster, Pennsylvania, 38 men	DLC GR-22
HK Fusilier Regiment v. Lossberg	Hanstein	Prisoner-of-war list, 17-19 Apr 1777 [Lancaster, Penna.] 2 men	DLC GR-34

GERMAN MUSTER ROLLS IN AMERICAN ARCHIVES--*Continued*

Regiment	Company	Description	Repository

7.   Hessen-Kassel--*Continued*

Regiment	Company	Description	Repository
HK Fusilier Regiment v. Lossberg	Hanstein	Prisoner-of-war list, 27 Aug 1777, Lancaster, Pennsylvania, 23 men	DLC GR-38
HK Fusilier Regiment v. Lossberg	Hanstein	Prisoner-of-war list? [no date or place] 38 men	DLC GR-15
HK Fusilier Regiment v. Lossberg	Heringen, or vacant	Prisoner-of-war list, 6 Jan 1777, Lancaster, Pennsylvania, 57 men	DLC GR-23
HK Fusilier Regiment v. Lossberg	Heringen, or vacant	Prisoner-of-war list, 17-19 Apr 1777 [Lancaster, Penna.] 9 men	DLC GR-34
HK Fusilier Regiment v. Lossberg	Heringen, or vacant	Prisoner-of-war list? 27 Aug 1777, Lancaster, Pennsylvania, 27 men	DLC GR-39
HK Fusilier Regiment v. Lossberg	Heringen, or vacant	Prisoner-of-war list? [no date or place] 57 men	DLC GR-17
HK Fusilier Regiment v. Lossberg	Light infantry	Prisoner-of-war list [no place or date] 2 men	DLC GR-34
HK Fusilier Regiment v. Lossberg	Scheffer	Prisoner-of-war list, 17-19 Apr 1777 [Lancaster, Penna.] 4 men	DLC GR-34
HK Fusilier Regiment v. Lossberg	Scheffer	Prisoner-of-war list? 27 Aug 1777, Lancaster, Pennsylvania, 18 men	DLC GR-36
HK Fusilier Regiment v. Lossberg	Scheffer	Prisoner-of-war list? [no date or place] 53 men	DLC GR-19
HK Fusilier Regiment v. Lossberg	various	Prisoner-of-war list, Lebanon, Pennsylvania, 8 Oct 1777, 15 men	DLC GR-41
HK Fusilier Regiment v. Lossberg	various	Prisoner-of-war list, 12 Mar 1778, captured officers for exchange? Lancaster, Pennsylvana	DLC GR-46
HK Fusilier Regiment v. Lossberg	various	Prisoner-of-war list, 26 Mar 1778, captured officers for exchange, [no place] 6 men	DLC GR-45
HK Fusilier Regiment v. Lossberg	various	Prisoner-of-war list, 16 Jun 1778, prisoners from Middletown to Lancaster, Pennsylvania, 40 persons	DLC GR-47
HK Grenadier Battalion Vacant Graff	Hohenstein	Muster roll, 4 Jul 1782, Camp Greenwich [New York] 134 men	MIU-C GR-63
HK Grenadier Battalion Vacant Graff	Hessenmüller	Muster roll, 4 Jul 1782, Camp Greenwich [New York] 134 men	MIU-C GR-62
HK Grenadier Battalion Vacant Graff	Saltzmann	Muster roll, 4 Jul 1782, Camp Greenwich [New York] 138 men	MIU-C GR-64
HK Grenadier Battalion Vacant Graff	Sandrock	Muster roll, 4 Jul 1782, Camp Greenwich [New York] 138 men	MIU-C GR-65
HK Grenadiers & Jäger-korps (Chasseurs)	Miscellaneous	Prisoner-of-war list, 23 Jan 1777, Lancaster, Penna. 10 men	DLC GR-32

GERMAN MUSTER ROLLS IN AMERICAN ARCHIVES--*Continued*

Regiment	Company	Description	Repository

7. Hessen-Kassel--*Continued*

Regiment	Company	Description	Repository
HK Jägerkorps (Chasseurs)	Wangenheim	Muster roll of recruits, 28 Mar 1777, Scravendeel ['s Gravendael, Holland] 60 men	ICN-BM GR-12
HK Artillery Corps	[not stated]	Prisoner-of-war list? 6 Jan 1777, Lancaster, Pennsylvania, 39 men	DLC GR-29
HK Artillery Corps	[not stated]	Prisoner-of-war list, 8 Oct 1777, Lebanon, Pennsylvania, 6 men	DLC GR-41
HK Artillery Corps	[not stated]	Prisoner-of-war list? 12 Mar 1778, captured officers for exchange? Lancaster, Pennsylvania, 6 men	DLC GR-46
HK Artillery Corps	[not stated]	Prisoner-of-war list, 26 Mar 1778, captured officers for exchange [no place] 6 men	DLC GR-45
HK Artillery Corps	[not stated]	Prisoner-of-war list, 16 Jun 1778, prisoners from Middletown to Lancaster, Pennsylvania, 10 persons	DLC GR-49
HK Artillery Corps	[not stated]	Prisoner-of-war list? [no date or place2 33 men	DLC GR-44
HK Fusilier Regiment v. Knyphausen	Biesenrod	Prisoner-of-war list? 6 Jan 1777, Lancaster, Pennsylvania, 64 men	DLC GR-21
HK Fusilier Regiment v. Knyphausen	Biesenrod	Prisoner-of-war list, 17-19 Apr 1777 [Lancaster, Penna.] 4 men	DLC GR-34
HK Fusilier Regiment v. Knyphausen	Borck	Prisoner-of-war list, 17-19 Apr 1777 [Lancaster, Penna.] 6 men	DLC GR-34
HK Fusilier Regiment v. Knyphausen	Dechow	Prisoner-of-war list, 6 Jan 1777, Lancaster, Pennsylvania, 56 men	DLC GR-34
HK Fusilier Regiment v. Knyphausen	Dechow	Prisoner-of-war list, 17-19 Apr 1777, Lancaster, Pennsylvania, 2 men	DLC GR-34
HK Fusilier Regiment v. Knyphausen	Minnigerode	Prisoner-of-war list, 17-19 Apr 1777, [Lancaster, Penna.] 70 men	DLC GR-24
HK Fusilier Regiment v. Knyphausen	Minnigerode	Prisoner-of-war list, 1777? [Lancaster, Pennsylvania] 70 men	DLC GR-24
HK Fusilier Regiment v. Knyphausen	Steinrad	Prisoner-of war list, 17-19 Apr 1777 [Lancaster, Penna.] 1 man	DLC GR-34
HK Fusilier Regiment v. Knyphausen	[not stated]	Prisoner-of-war list, 8 Oct 1777, Lebanon, Pennsylvania, 7 men	DLC GR-41
HK Fusilier Regiment v. Knyphausen	[not stated]	Prisoner-of-war list? 12 Mar 1778, captured officers for exchange, Lancaster, Pennsylvania, 4 men	DLC GR-46
HK Fusilier Regiment v. Knyphausen	[not stated]	Prisoner-of-war list, 26 Mar 1778, captured officers for exchange [Lancaster, Pennsylvania] 4 men	DLC GR-45

GERMAN MUSTER ROLLS IN AMERICAN ARCHIVES--*Continued*

Regiment	Company	Description	Repos-itory
		7. Hessen-Kassel--*Continued*	
HK Fusilier Regiment v. Knyphausen	[not stated]	Prisoner-of-war list, 16 Jun 1778, prisoners from Middletown to Lancaster, Pennsylvania, 37 persons	DLC GR-48
HK Fusilier Regiment v. Knyphausen	[not stated]	Prisoner-of-war list? [no date or place] 132 men	DLC GR-43
HK Grenadier Regiment v. Rall	Biching	Prisoner-of-war list? [no date or place] 18 men	DLC GR-42
HK Grenadier Regiment v. Rall	Bigsbiy? [Bixby?]	Muster roll [no date or place] 62 men	DLC GR-27
HK Grenadier Regiment v. Rall	Brandt	Prisoner-of-war list, 17-19 Apr 1777 [Lancaster, Penna.] 2 men	DLC GR-34
HK Grenadier Regiment v. Rall	Brethauer	Prisoner-of-war list? [no date or place] 19 men	DLC GR-42
HK Grenadier Regiment v. Rall	Brethauer	Prisoner-of-war list, 7 Jan 1777, Lancaster, Pennsylvania, 59 men	DLC GR-31
HK Grenadier Regiment v. Rall	Brocking	Prisoner-of-war list, 17-19 Apr 1777 [Lancaster, Penna.] 4 men	DLC GR-34
HK Grenadier Regiment v. Rall	Hag?	Prisoner-of-war list, 17-19 Apr 1777 [Lancaster, Penna.] 4 men	DLC GR-34
HK Grenadier Regiment v. Rall	Köhler	Prisoner-of-war list, 6 Jan? 1777, Lancaster, Pennsylvania, 46 men	DLC GR-33
HK Grenadier Regiment v. Rall	Köhler	Prisoner-of-war list, 17-19 Apr 1777, Lancaster, Pennsylvania, 5 men	DLC GR-34
HK Grenadier Regiment v. Rall	Köhler	Prisoner-of-war list? [no date or place] 10 men	DLC GR-42
HK Grenadier Regiment v. Rall	Leib (bodyguard)	Prisoner-of-war list, 17-19 Apr 1777 [Lancaster, Penna.] 5 men	DLC GR-34
HK Grenadier Regiment v. Rall	Leib (bodyguard)	Prisoner-of-war list [no date or place] 56 men	DLC GR-30
HK Grenadier Regiment v. Rall	Leib (bodyguard)	Prisoner-of-war list? [no date or place] 9 men	DLC GR-42
HK Grenadier Regiment v. Rall	Mathäus (*also* Mathews)	Prisoner-of-war list [no date or place] 19 men	DLC GR-42
HK Grenadier Regiment v. Rall	Mathäus (*also* Mathews)	Prisoner-of-war list? [no date or place] 52 men	DLC GR-28
HK Grenadier Regiment v. Rall	[not stated]	Prisoner-of-war list, 8 Oct 1777, Lebanon, Pennsylvania, 7 men	DLC GR-41
HK Grenadier Regiment v. Rall	[not stated]	Prisoner-of-war list? 12 Mar 1778 [Lancaster, Penna.] captured officers for exchange, 1 man	DLC GR-46

GERMAN MUSTER ROLLS IN AMERICAN ARCHIVES--*Continued*

Regiment	Company	Description	Repository

7. Hessen-Kassel--*Continued*

Regiment	Company	Description	Repository
HK Grenadier Regiment v. Rall	[not stated]	Prisoner-of-war list, 26 Mar 1778 [no place] captured officers for exchange, 1 man	DLC GR-45
HK Grenadier Regiment Marquis d'Angelelli (formerly v. Rall)	Corps	Muster roll, 24 Jun 1782, Charleston, South Carolina, 151 men	MIU-C GR-70
HK Grenadier Regiment Marquis d'Angelelli (formerly v. Rall)	Bauer	Muster roll, 24 Jun 1782, Charleston, South Carolina, 133 men	MIU-C GR-71
HK Grenadier Regiment Marquis d'Angelelli (formerly v. Rall)	see also 9. Unassigned or Unidentified		

8. Waldeck

Regiment	Company	Description	Repository
Contingent	Delbeck	Prisoner-of-war list, 17-19 Apr 1777 [Lancaster, Penna.] 1 man	DLC GR-34
Contingent	Hanaledin	Prisoner-of-war list, 17-19 Apr 1777 [Lancaster, Penna.] 1 man	DLC GR-34
Contingent	Horn	Prisoner-of-war list, 17-19 Apr 1777 [Lancaster, Penna.] 1 man	DLC GR-34
Contingent	[not stated]	Prisoner-of-war list, 8 Oct 1777 [Lebanon, Pennsylvania] 2 men	DLC GR-41

9. Unassigned or Unidentified

Regiment	Company	Description	Repository
HK (probably)	Recruits and replacement officers temporarily under v. Benning	Muster roll [inspection by Col. Rainsford?] 28 Mar 1777, Schravendeel ['s Gravendael, Holland] 462 men	ICN-BM GR-11
Hessian	Unidentified	Prisoner-of-war list, 19 Apr 1777, Lancaster, Pennsylvania, 30 men	DLC GR-40

United States Consular Records

The records of American consuls in German towns and cities are a potential source of information on immigrants to America not systematically exploited by researchers. The National Archives has microfilmed a large number of the consular despatches, but these are mainly of a political and diplomatic nature. These microfilms contain little material of genealogical interest. However, there are quantities of post records in the National Archives which have not been photocopied and, indeed, have never even been adequately calendared. Among these materials are some of potential usefulness to genealogists. Here are some examples:

Consulate	Description of Record
Bremen	Certificates of Registration of American Citizens, July 1907 to September 1916. An extremely valuable record listing American citizens (mainly naturalized) returning to, or residing in, Germany. These certificates give birth dates and places, when coming (or returning) to Germany, when and where naturalized (if applicable), reason for being in Germany. Indexed.
Bremen	Certificate of Registration of Widow or Divorced Woman Who Acquired American Citizenship by Marriage, March 1908 to November 1916. Gives birth dates and places, when and where married to American citizens, names of children. There are only two persons listed in this register (Marie Pape and Frieda Poltmann), but similar registers in other consulates may contain more names.
Bremen	Marriage Contracts (in German and English). These contracts bear the following provision:

"That they [the emigrants] are about emigrating to the United States as man and wife and wish to have this declaration in this Consulate, provisionally to serve in lieu of a regular marriage the formalities of which shall take place after arrival in the United States."

Gives names and places of origin in Germany; witnesses. Not indexed, but there is occasionally a loose-leaf list inserted in the registers:

September 1850 to June 1851 (Register No. 36)

Consulate	Description of Record
	September 1851 to June 1852 (Register No. 37)
	June 1852 to July 1853 (Register No. 41)
	July 1853 to August 1853 (Register No. 45)
Hamburg	Certificate of Registration of American Citizens, 1909–1913. Same form as for Bremen. Indexed.
Hamburg	Certificate of Registration of Widow or Divorced Woman Who Acquired American Citizenship by Marriage, 1909–1914. Same form as for Bremen.
Hamburg	Bound volume of interrogatories on estate and business matters concerning German-Americans in all parts of the world; late nineteenth century.
Hamburg	Registrations of American Citizens, September 1907 to January 1908. Same form as for Bremen.
Hamburg	Marriage Contracts, March 1857 to June 1858, and July 1858 to January 1865. Same form as for Bremen, excepting that the statement of intent to marry varies:

". . . being desirous of entering into the state of Matrimony, and the laws of Hamburg not permitting us to do so, have, here in the Consulate of the United States . . . entered into the following Marriage Contract. . . ."

Consulate	Description of Record
Le Havre	List of Crews Book, 1824? 1826? 1828, 1837? 1838? This register lists both American and foreign seamen and often gives the names of deserters. For some foreigners, nationality or place where engaged as sailors is given. There are a number of other registers which have not been inspected by these writers.

The above description of some of the registers available is intended merely to indicate the nature and scope of genealogical material available in consular records of the United States. The National Archives has the records of the following American consulates in Germany. It seems likely that some, or all, of these consulates prepared records similar to those of Bremen and Hamburg described above.

Consulate	Record Dates	Quantity	Remarks
Aachen	1878-1917	12'	
Altona	1854-1862	3v.	
Annaberg	1879-1908	7'	
Augsburg	1867-1906	1'	
Bamberg	1890-1908	12'	
Barmen	1869-1923	33'	
Berlin	1865-1912	66'	
Brake-Nordenham	1863-1917	3'	
Bremen	1797-1917; 1921-1939	136'	
Bremerhaven	1857-1917; 1921-1932	26'	
Breslau	1874-1917	40'	
Brunswick	1858-1916	18'	
Buntscheid	1882-1926	1v.	
Chemnitz	1867-1917	33'	
Coblenz	1890-1912	31'	
Cologne	1852-1917; 1921-1939	58'	
Cuxhaven	1880-1910	2v.	
Dresden	1837-1917	20'	
Düsseldorf	1867-1921	13'	
Eibenstock	1891-1909	6'	
Emden	1914-1916	2v.	
Erfurt	1892-1917	20'	includes Weimar
Essen	1883-1905	1'	
Flensburg	1882-1909	1'	
Frankfurt/Main	1854-1917	67'	
Freiburg	1891-1916	6'	
Fürth	1872-1905	3'	
Gera	1880-1916	10'	
Glochau	1882-1908	9'	may be Glauchau
Hamburg	1821-1917; 1921-1927	60'	
Hannover	1875-1917	39'	
Karlsruhe	1857-1874	6v.	see also Mannheim
Kassel	1890-1915	3'	
Kehl	1882-1917	31'	see also Strasbourg, France
Kiel	1866-1916	2'	
Königsberg	1879-1911	2'	
Krefeld	1853-1908	12'	Aendin am Rhein
Leipzig	1837-1940	104'	
Lübeck	1837-1940	1'	
Ludwigshafen am Rhein	1862-1888	1'	includes some Mannheim
Magdeburg	1886-1916	17'	
Mainz	1869-1906	3'	
Mannheim	1857-1919	43'	includes Frankfurt/Main, Karlsruhe, Ludwigshafen
Monkneukirchen	1893-1916	5'	
Munich	1856-1912	39'	
Neustadt/Haardt	1890-1916	2v.	also called Niewenstat
Nürnberg	1846-1912	27'	
Oldenburg	1856-1869	1'	
Plauen	1887-1917	18'	
Solingen	1893-1905	2'	
Sonneberg	1851-1912	18'	
Stettin	1862-1912	18'	
Stuttgart	1851-1917	27'	
Strasbourg, France	1862-1871; 1919-1939	–	includes Kehl (1886-1900)
Swinemünde	1899-1909	3v.	
Weimar			see Erfurt
Wiesbaden	1901-1917	7'	
Zittau	1890-1908	9'	

United States Military and Pension Records

The military and pension records of German-born soldiers serving with the American forces in all the wars of the United States are likely to contain exact information on places of birth in Germany. These records are described in

National Archives and Records Service. General Services Administration. *Guide to Genealogical Records in the National Archives*. Washington, D.C.: Government Printing Office, 1964.

What is not wellknown is the fact that, during the American Civil War, there were a number of northern military units in which German-Americans predominated; in some of the units German, rather than English, was commonly spoken. These units were:

New York regiments:
  4th Cavalry, Dickel's Mounted Rifles
  Light Artillery, 2d Battery, Blenker's
  7th Infantry, Steuben Regiment
  8th Infantry, First German Rifles
  20th Infantry, United Turner Rifles
  29th Infantry, First Astor Regiment
  45th Infantry, Fifth German Rifles
  46th Infantry, Frémont Regiment
  52d Infantry, Sigel Rifles, or German Rangers
  54th Infantry, Barney Rifles, or Schwarzes-
    jäger Regiment
  86th Infantry, Steuben Rangers

Pennsylvania regiments:
  74th Infantry, First German Regiment
  75th Infantry, Second German Regiment

Ohio regiments:
  28th Infantry, First German Regiment
  37th Infantry, Second German Regiment (Col-
    onel Siber)
  67th Infantry, Third German Regiment (Col-
    onel Bürstenbinder)

Indiana regiments:
  32d Indiana, First German Regiment (com-
    manded successively by Willich, von
    Trebra, and Erdelmeyer)

Illinois regiment:
  24th Illinois, Hecker's Yäger [Jäger] Regi-
    ment

Wisconsin regiments:
  9th Wisconsin, First German Regiment
  26th Wisconsin, Second German Regiment

    At the outset of the Civil War German-
American volunteers were especially numerous
in the following Pennsylvania units:

  4th Regiment, Colonel Hartranft
  8th Regiment, from Lehigh and Northampton
    counties
  9th Regiment, under Colonel Pennypacker
  10th Regiment, from Lancaster County
  11th Regiment, from Northumberland County
  14th Regiment, from Berks County
  15th Regiment, from Luzerne County
  16th Regiment, from York County
  18th Regiment, from Philadelphia, under Col-
    onel Wilhelm
  21st Regiment, under Colonel Ballier

    German-Americans were also active in
the Unionist troops of the state of Missouri.
The complicated story of their participation
in Missouri units is set forth in

  Albert Bernhardt Faust, *The German Element
  in the United States with Special Reference
  to Its Political, Moral, Social, and Educational Influence* (Boston and New York: Hough-
  ton Mifflin Co., 1909), 1: 529-542.

    There are many manuscript sources in
Europe which can be used to establish the links
between German-Americans and their homelands.
Some of these sources, the grist of routine
genealogical research, are described in the
article Genealogy in Germany in this encyclopedia. The existence of other materials is
more difficult to predict, but such records
may contain information available in no other
place. The police records of Germany, not adequately described herein, comprise one such
manuscript category. These records would be
particularly illuminating in the cases of the
revolutionaries of 1848, many of whom emigrated to the United States. Such records
will also be found useful for the many indigents and social outcasts who received German
governmental assistance for emigration. Many
such files are listed in

  Clifford Neal Smith and Anna Smith *geborene
  Piszczan-Czaja, American Genealogical Re-
  sources in German Archives*. Littleton,
  Colorado: Libraries Unlimited, forthcoming.

No systematic effort, other than the above,
has ever been made to locate such records, and
there are likely to be many more extant than
are listed in that work.

Port of Departure Records

    It was not until about 1850 that the
Hanseatic cities--Hamburg and Bremen, in par-
ticular--perceived that German emigration to
America was a swelling tide which, since it
could not be turned back, ought to be monopol-
ized. Before that time most emigrants had
crossed into Holland or France to seek transportation to the New World. Rotterdam was the
principal port of departure. Apparently, most
eighteenth-century emigrants came to America
aboard British ships, if the Philadelphia arrival lists are to be taken as typical. After
1850, nearly all German emigrants left from
German ports, particularly Hamburg and Bremen,
aboard German flag vessels.

    Passenger lists prepared in Europe will
become the most important sources of information on German emigrants, when these sources
have been adequately indexed. At this writing,
indexing has hardly begun.

Hamburg Emigration Lists--Direct and Indirect.
Certainly, the most important source of information on German and Slavic emigrants to America are the lists prepared by the Hamburg police and port authorities from 1850 to 1913.
These lists are divided into two lengthy series, direct and indirect. The direct series

contains the names of persons (both German and eastern European) leaving for the New World from Hamburg (and minor ports controlled by Hamburg) on ships having no intermediate stops at other European ports; the indirect series contains the names of persons leaving on ships with intermediate ports of call. The direct series begins in 1850; the indirect series begins in 1855. The basic volumes of both series contain passenger lists arranged chronologically by ship departure date. For example, passengers on the ship *Attila*, leaving Hamburg on 1 January 1860, are listed with some attempt at alphabetical order. Thereafter, passengers on the *Reinbek*, leaving Hamburg on 2 January 1860, follow. This means that, unless one knows the name of the ship and its departure date, finding a given emigrant's name becomes very difficult. To remedy this, companion volumes were prepared by the Hamburg police in which the passengers' names were partially alphabetized, and the corresponding ship and date of departure given. From 1850 to 1854 the lists of direct emigrants are in alphabetical order by surname within each year. There is no list for the first six months of 1853. Beginning in 1853, in both the direct and indirect series, arrangement is in chronological succession of the departure of ships.

Two repositories in the United States hold microfilms of all, or parts, of these lengthy series of passenger lists. The Library of Congress Manuscript Division has microfilms of volumes covering the period 1850–1872 for the direct series, and 1855–1873 for the indirect series. The Genealogical Society of the Church of Jesus Christ of Latter-day Saints, Salt Lake City, has microfilms of all volumes in both series. Copies of the Library of Congress microfilm holdings may be purchased; those of the Genealogical Society are available only on loan through the LDS stake libraries. The following lists the holdings of the Library of Congress in detail; * indicates alphabetical order, ** indicates chronological order.

Direct Series		Indirect Series	
Volume Number	Date	Volume Number	Date
1*	1850	1*	1855–1865
2*	1851	2*	1866–1871
3*	1852/I	3*	1872–1873
4*	1852/II	4**	1855
5*	1853–1854	5**	1856
6*	1854/I	6**	1857
7*	1854/II	7**	1858
8*	1855–1856	8**	1859
9**	1855	9**	1860
10**	1856	10**	1861
11*	1857–1858	11**	1862
12**	1857	12**	1863
13**	1858	13**	1864
14*	1859–1861	14**	1865
15**	1859	15**	1866
16**	1860	16**	1867
17**	1861	17**	1869
18*	1862–1863	18**	1870
19**	1862	19**	1871
20**	1863	20**	1871
21*	1864–1865	21**	1872 Jan–Jul
22**	1864	22**	1872 Aug–Dec
23**	1865	23**	1873 Jan–Apr
24*	1866	24**	1873 May–Aug
25**	1866	25**	1873 Aug–Dec
26*	1867–1868		
27**	1867		
28**	1868		
29*	1868–1869		
30**	1869		
31*	1870–1871		
32**	1870		
33**	1871		
34	[not listed]		
35**	1872 Jan–Jun		
36**	1872 Jul–Dec		

Bremen Emigration Lists. The port of Bremen had emigration lists similar to those of Hamburg, but they were destroyed during the second world war as a result of Allied bombing. It may be that some of these lists have survived in photocopied form in the Library of Congress Manuscript Division; if so, they will be found on three reels of microfilm under the following description and call number:

Germany, Bremen. Archiv der Handelskammer. A.I.1 Auswanderer [Emigrants] 1841–1875.

Rotterdam Emigration Lists. There ought to be a large amount of manuscript material on eighteenth-century German emigration to America via the port of Rotterdam. Unfortunately, inquiries made by German and American investigators have not succeeded in locating these materials. Very likely, many of the passenger lists which may have accumulated at Rotterdam and Amsterdam are duplicated in British port records, because many ships carrying European emigrants stopped at British ports on their way to America. No systematic attempt has ever been made to discover what materials can still be found at British ports of call.

French and Belgian Port Records. Very little is known about French and Belgian passenger lists. Records at Antwerp are said to have been destroyed during the first world war, excepting for those of 1855 in the State Archives.[3] It has been reported in a German genealogical publication[4] that early records of the port of LeHavre are still extant in Paris in the *Generallandesarchiv*; presumably the French Archives Nationales is meant. Under the rubric *Colonies*, this archive holds the following:

Year	Serie	Location
1686–1822	F 5 B	Karton 111
1749–1770	F 5 B	Register 45
1772–1789	F 5 B	Register 46
1790–1821	F 5 B	Register 47
1822–1830	F 5 B	Register 48
Nineteenth century	F 5 B	Kartons 114, 117, 119, 121, 123, 126, 129, 135, 136, 137, 141, 142, 148

The Manuscript Division of the Library of Congress does not have microfilms of any of these cartons or registers. The Division does have among its collection of photocopies of the French Archives Nationales, *Colonies Serie F 5 B*, selected transcripts of volume 34, entitled "List of Passengers Embarking in Louisiana for France in 1732, 1733, 1737, 1748, 1749, 1752, 1754, 1758, and 1765" and of volume 37, entitled "Lists of Soldiers and Passengers Embarking in France (La Rochelle) for Louisiana from 1717 to 1720."

Records of Other European Ports. According to Strassburger's and Hinke's *Pennsylvania German Pioneers*, a few German immigrants to Pennsylvania embarked at Lisbon. This surprising detail raises the possibility that the records of still other ports in Europe should be searched for lists of German emigrants. As suggested above, the British port records certainly contain information not yet reported. What might be discovered among port records at Bordeaux, northern Spanish ports, even the Scandinavian ports, is still quite unknown and awaits investigation.

Records of German Shipping Companies

The archives of Germany contain many files pertaining to emigration agents--persons who arranged passages and expedited the departure formalities for would-be emigrants. Some of these files have been listed in

Clifford Neal Smith and Anna Smith *geborene* Piszczan-Czaja, *American Genealogical Resources in German Archives*. Littleton, Colorado: Libraries Unlimited, forthcoming. ·

It seems likely that many more records of such agencies remain undiscovered; possibly, they still remain in the hands of private individuals as business records.

No attempt has been made, to the writers' knowledge, to discover whether the business records of Hamburg and Bremen shipping companies are still extant and to assess their potential value to genealogical researchers.

German Consular Records

The records of German consulates in American cities contain much information of value to the genealogical researcher. A great many such files are described in the above-mentioned work *American Genealogical Resources in German Archives*. It is probable, however, that there remain many other registers still unlisted, particularly among the archival materials of the Auswärtige Amt, Bonn. Consular files are particularly important sources of information on wills and missing heirs.

Gemeinde (village) and *Länder* (state) Records in Germany

Village records are usually extant for at least the eighteenth through twentieth centuries in most areas of Germany. Ordinarily, the older records will be found in the Staatsarchiv for the region in which the village is located. The private collections of noble families (*Hausarchiven*) are likely also to contain village records, when these villages formerly belonged to them. *American Genealogical Resources in German Archives* contains many entries describing the available records of villages, but, since the contents of *Hausarchiven* are inadequately inventoried, it seems likely that a considerable amount of manuscript material still remains to be uncovered.

Locating village records entails considerable knowledge of local history. When, as has often been the case, a village or region has changed hands, passing from one noble house to another, it is likely that some records will be found in widely separated archives.

An even more difficult problem arises when ownership of a village was formerly divided among several noble houses or held in common by several heirs. For example, in the border area between the Duchy of Sachsen-Altenburg and the Electoral Principality (*Kurfürstentum*) of Saxony, sovereignty was so fragmented that some fields and gardens, along with the peasants who tilled them, were under the jurisdiction of Altenburg, and the neighboring fields and peasants were under the jurisdiction of Electoral Saxony. Since the fields of Germany are most often strips of land only a few yards wide and several hundred yards long and irregular in shape, the problem of defining the corresponding political jurisdiction, even within an area of one square kilometer, can often defy depicting on a map.

German Mercenaries in the British-American Colonies, 1620-1775

The British government normally had Swiss and German mercenaries among its garrison troops. It seems quite likely that individual soldiers, or small units of soldiers, may have been assigned to American forts during the 150-odd years before the American Revolution. If so, it may be that some of these soldiers eventually settled in America. In 1763, for example, the British army had contingents from Hessen-Kassel, Brunswick, Hannover, Saxe-Gotha, and Lippe-Bückeburg. There was also a unit called the Britannic Legion made up largely of foreigners,[5] as well as the King's German Cavalry. It is not known whether any of these units served in colonial America, but it is surmised that study of records in the Public Records Office, London, might uncover some foreign soldiers settling in America, either by desertion or dismissal, much before the American Revolution.

In like manner it is known that the British government, as a matter of policy, refused to hunt down the sailors of foreign merchant vessels deserting in British or colonial ports, even when requested to do so by diplomatic agents of courts to which such deserters were subjects.[6] Some of these individuals undoubtedly settled in America. The likelihood of finding a record of such desertions is not great, however.

Here, then, is a broad area for investigation by German-American genealogical researchers. Study of the extant colonial records discloses numerous references to such troops but remarkably few muster rolls. The most likely repository of such lists will probably be among the records of payment (financial papers) in the Public Records Office annex near Berkhampstead, outside London. Ship pay records, with notations on desertions, seem to be particularly complete.

German Mercenaries Who Served with the British During the American Revolution

Troops from six German principalities served under British command during the American Revolution. The principalities were Electoral Hesse (Hessen-Kassel), Waldeck, Hessen-Hanau, Braunschweig, Ansbach-Bayreuth, Anhalt-Zerbst. As might be expected, certain of the German archives have extensive collections of ministerial records on these mercenaries, supplementing the field records and prisoner-of-war lists which have found their ways into American archives. The ministerial records often reveal places of origin for the soldiers; the field records (muster rolls) rarely do.

Hessen-Kassel and Waldeck. The largest body of source materials on the troops of Hessen-Kassel and Waldeck is in the Staatsarchiv Marburg where, currently, there is an ambitious project to index the names of all the soldiers sent to America by these two principalities. At the time of writing, the project has produced two volumes of computer printout published under the title

Hessische Truppen im amerikanischen Unabhängigkeitskrieg (Hetrina) [Hessian troops in the American Revolution (Hetrina Project)]. Veröffentlichungen der Archivschule Marburg, Institut für Archivwissenschaft, Nr. 10 (Marburg/Lahn: Staatsarchiv, 1972).

Other publications in this series are expected annually. The publication can be easily used by persons not reading German, because an English-language summary has been included. Names, approximate birth dates, places of origin in Germany with their modern-day zip code number (an efficient aid in identifying obscure villages), rank, unit, when entered service, and what happened to them (killed in action, deserted, returned to Europe, etc.), and citations to archival sources are included. This series of publications is of basic importance to German-American researchers; no genealogical collection should be without it.

Volume one of the publication (8813 entries) covers the following military units:

Grenadier Battalion v. Linsingen
First company (1776, v. Eschwege; 1777, v. Plessen)
Second company (1776, v. Wurmb; 1777, v. Webern)
Third company (1776, v. Stamford; 1778, v. Dincklage)
Fourth company (1776, v. Mallet)

Grenadier Battalion Block (after 1777, v. Lengerke)
First company (1776, v. Eschwege; 1780, Vogt)
Second company (1776, v. Weitershausen; 1777, v. Gall; 1781, Gissot)
Third company (1776, d'Oreilly; 1782, Eigenbrodt)

Fourth company (1776, v. Bentheim; 1777, v. Wurmb; 1778, v. Wilmowsky)

Grenadier Battalion v. Minnigerode (after 1780, v. Löwenstein)
First company (1776, Höpfner; 1778, Wachs)
Second company (1775, Hendorf; 1783, Klingender)
Third company (1775, v. Wilmowsky; 1783, Mondorff)
Fourth company (1775, v. Dechow; 1777, v. Stein; 1777, Schimmelpfeng; 1778, v. Biesenrodt)

Grenadier Battalion Köhler (1778, Graf; 1782, Platte)
First company (1776, Bode; 1781, Saltzmann)
Second company (1776, v. Hohenstein)
Third company (1776, Neumann; 1782, Sandrock)
Fourth company (1776, Hessenmüller)

Garrison Regiment v. Huyn (after 1780, v. Benning)
First company (1776, v. Huyn; 1780, v. Mirbach; 1780, v. Benning; 1783, v. Normann)
Second company (1776, Kurtze; 1782, v. Prüschenck)
Third company (1776, Hillebrand)
Fourth company (1776, Martini)
Fifth company (1776, Wagner; 1777, v. Schallern; 1779, Sonneborn; 1783, Heilmann)

Volume two of the Hetrina project (12,311 entries) covers the following military units:

Regiment Prinz Carl
Bodyguard (Leibkompanie)
Second company (1775, Schmitt; 1780, v. Gose)
Third company (1775, v. Gose; 1776, Georg Emanuel v. Lengerke)
Fourth company (1775, Schreiber)
Fifth company (1775, Wilhelm v. Löwenstein)

Regiment v. Ditfurth
Bodyguard (Leibkompanie)
Second company (1775, v. Bose; 1777, v. Westernhagen)
Third company (1775, Heinrich v. Borck; 1776, Ernst Leopold v. Borck)
Fourth company (1775, v. Schuler)
Fifth company (1775, duBuy; 1776, v. d. Malsburg)

Regiment v. Donop; 1784, v. Knyphausen
Bodyguard (Leibkompanie)
Second company (1775, Friedrich Wilhelm v. Lossberg; 1776, v. Gose; 1781, Heymel)
Third company (1775, Bürmann; 1776, Heymel; 1777, v. Wurmb)
Fourth company (1775, Hinte)
Fifth company (1775, v. Kutzleben)

Regiment v. Lossberg; 1780, Alt [senior] v. Lossberg
Bodyguard (Leibkompanie)
Second company (1775, Scheffer)
Third company (1775, v. Fritsch; 1776, v. Altenbockum)

Fourth company (1775, Georg Emanuel v. Lengerke; 1776, v. Hanstein; 1783, Krafft)
Fifth company (1775, v. Heringen; 1776, v. Loose)

Regiment v. Mirbach; 1780, Jung [junior] v. Lossberg
Bodyguard (Leibkompanie)
Second company (1775, v. d. Malsburg; 1776, v. Loose; 1776, Block; 1778, v. Romrod)
Third company (1775, v. Schieck; 1778, v. Biesenrodt)
Fourth company (1775, v. Biesenrodt; 1777, v. Wilmowsky)
Fifth company (1775, v. Borck; 1776, Baurmeister)

Regiment v. Bose; 1778, v. Trümbach
Bodyguard (Leibkompanie)
Second company (1775, v. Bischhausen; 1781, v. Oreilly)
Third company (1775, Block; 1777, duBuy)
Fourth company (1775, v. Münchhausen)
Fifth company (1775, Scheer)

Further volumes, reflecting the research of the Hetrina Project of the archives school at the Staatsarchiv Marburg may be expected in the future.

Braunschweig (Brunswick). A list of the mercenaries from the Duchy of Braunschweig (Brunswick) is to be found in the Staatsarchiv Wolfenbüttel under catalog number 38 B Alt Nr. 260. The names of 1,700 Brunswick soldiers failing to return to Europe in 1783 have been published by Rimpau.[7] Recently, an abridged version, in English, containing only the names of soldiers remaining in North America at the end of the war, was published under the following title:

Clifford Neal Smith. *Brunswick Deserter-Immigrants of the American Revolution.* German-American Genealogical Research Monograph No. 1 (Thomson, Illinois: Heritage House, 1973).

The monograph contains the names, birthplaces, ages, and how, when, and where the soldiers left Brunswick service. This affords a clue as to probable places of settlement in the United States and Canada. The names, without ancillary information, also appear in an article of the same title in *Illinois State Genealogical Society Quarterly,* 6 (1974):77-81. It should be noted, however, that both the monograph and the article contain only the names of known deserters and settlers. It may be that some of the soldiers listed as killed in action or dying of disease could, in fact, have survived and remained in America, as well. The German princes received a special indemnification from the British government for such casualties, so there may have been a pecuniary reason for listing deserters as casualties. It follows, then, that genealogists should consider the possibility that an ancestor will be found in the casualty list of dead and wounded, rather than among the admitted deserters in America or post-1783 settlers in Canada.

Ansbach and Bayreuth. Lists of mercenaries from the marquisates of Ansbach and Bayreuth (now Bavaria) have also been published by Staedler in German.[8] Those soldiers deserting to the Americans or settling in Canada after the Revolution have been listed in an English-language publication:

> Clifford Neal Smith. *Mercenaries from Ansbach and Bayreuth, Germany, Who Remained in America after the Revolution.* German-American Genealogical Research Monograph No. 2 (Thomson, Illinois: Heritage House, 1974).

Names, military units, and usually when and where the soldier left the service of his unit are given. Although birthplace is usually missing from this list, it can often be inferred from the unit in which he served. Both the Ansbach and Bayreuth marquisates were territorially small, so that search of only a few German church records in these marquisates should disclose the birthplaces of most of these men.

Hessen-Hanau. A major lacunae in our knowledge has to do with the troops of Hessen-Hanau. Muster rolls exist at the Staatsarchiv Darmstadt pertaining to these soldiers, but they have never been published. An archivist in the Stadtarchiv Frankfurt/Main expects to publish the results of his extensive research on these soldiers in the new few years.

Anhalt-Zerbst. Little is known of the small contingent of troops from Anhalt-Zerbst. The records of this principality are now in the German Democratic Republic and inaccessible to American researchers. It may be, however, that the majority of these men came from Jever, an estate now in the Federal Republic of Germany. If so, search of local archival remains might turn up muster rolls, particularly the 1783 summary which recounted the fates of all those soldiers sent to America. One muster roll for the Anhalt-Zerbst contingent is among the writers' collection of materials found in American archives and will eventually be published in

> Clifford Neal Smith. *Muster Rolls and Prisoner-of-war Lists in American Archival Collections Pertaining to the German Mercenary Troops Who Served with the British Forces during the American Revolution.* German-American Genealogical Research Monograph No. 3 (Thomson, Illinois: Heritage House, forthcoming).

The number of soldiers from this contingent remaining in America after the Revolution is thought to be very small.

German Mercenaries Serving with the French in the American Revolution

At least one German-speaking military unit, the Regiment Royal Allemand de Deux Ponts (Royal German Zweibrücken Regiment) from the principality of Zweibrücken, served with the French during the American Revolution. A list of the soldiers of this unit killed in action has been published,[9] but no complete muster rolls have come to the writers' attention. It seems probable that some members of this unit remained in the United States after the Revolution, and it remains an unfinished task of genealogical researchers to discover who these men were. Presumably, they would have been eligible for American pensions and bounty-land grants. The leading, and only, article on the Zweibrücken regiment appears to be

> Anon. "Die deutschen Truppen im französischen Hülfsheere des amerikanischen Unabhängigkeitskrieg" [German troops in the French auxiliary army during the American revolution] *Der deutsche Pionier*, 13:317-325, 360-367, 420-441.

According to this article, there were other French military units in which Germans were numerous. These were:

¶ A battalion of Kurtrier (Electoral Trier) grenadiers in the Regiment Saar, called Detachement du regiment "La Sarre," which was later joined with the Regiment Saintonge under Colonel Adam Philipp Count von Custine;

¶ Several units of troops recruited from the Alsace and Lorraine and designated as *Jägerkompanien* (chasseur companies) in the French Bourbonnais and Soissonais regiments;

¶ A large portion of the French cavalry unit under the Duke de Lauzun, of which there is reported to be a muster roll in the Pennsylvania State Archives, Harrisburg;

¶ A 600-man regiment of troops from Anhalt in the army of Count d'Estaing. It has been suggested that this unit may have been a part of the West Indies Corps under Vicomte de Noailles which captured the British islands of St. Vincent and Grenada in 1778;

¶ It appears that the French had engaged the services of a battalion of troops from Ansbach. If so, it may be that Ansbach troops fought on both the British and French sides of the American Revolution. No document has come to light proving that the French-Ansbach battalion was sent to America, but it is reported that, when British-Ansbach troopers taken prisoners of war by the American forces were marched by the French-Zweibrücken regiment, they recognized countrymen therein, broke ranks, and embraced. Perhaps, then, as a unit in the Zweibrücken regiment, the French-Ansbach battalion reached America.

The combatants in the French forces in the American Revolution are listed in

U.S., Congress, Senate, *Les Combattants Français de la Guerre Americaine 1778-1783: Listes établiés d'apres les documents authentiques déposés aux Archives Nationales et aux Archives du Ministère de la Guerre*, 58th Congress, 1st session. Washington, D.C.: Government Printing Office, 1905.

Inspection of this lengthy document discloses very few persons with German surnames. Only the officers of the Zweibrücken regiment are listed. One is left with the impression that muster rolls for these men do not exist in French archives, or that they have been omitted intentionally. Perhaps the bitter defeat by the Germans in 1870 was still too poignant for the French government to have commemorated the German auxiliary troops who had fought in their service a century before.

PUBLISHED SOURCE MATERIALS IN AMERICA

Published literature in the United States on the origins of German-Americans consists of a few compilations and a vast number of biographies and obituaries, mainly in newspapers. Unfortunately, very little has been done systematically to abstract this information, and it remains largely undiscovered.

Pennsylvania Germans

Eighteenth-century German immigration was mainly to Pennsylvania. As available land in Pennsylvania became scarce in the areas open to settlement, and as a consequence of the French and Indian wars, many of these immigrants and the first generation of their descendants began moving southward along the eastern face of the Appalachian Mountains into Virginia and the Carolinas. Thus it is that immigration through the port of Philadelphia becomes important not only to Pennsylvania but also to the areas to the southward. The great reference work on early German immigration to Pennsylvania is

Ralph Beaver Strassburger and William John Hinke, *Pennsylvania German Pioneers: A Publication of the Original Lists of Arrivals in the Port of Philadelphia from 1727 to 1808* (Norristown, Penna.: Pennsylvania German Society, 1934; reprint ed., Baltimore: Genealogical Publishing Company, 1966).

The original work was published in three volumes; the reprint edition, in two volumes, does not include the facsimile signatures which had comprised the second volume of the original edition.

All researchers in German-American genealogy should be familiar with this work, because it lists a large portion, though not all, of the early German settlers in Pennsylvania. The following considerations should be kept in mind, however:

¶ Some of the earliest German settlers in Pennsylvania are not included in this work, because the ship lists herein begin only in 1727.

¶ A substantial number of Germans settling in Pennsylvania landed at ports other than Philadelphia (particularly at New York) and thus do not appear in *Pennsylvania German Pioneers*.

¶ The numerous German deserters and prisoners of war of the American Revolution are not included in Strassburger; therefore, a substantial portion of the German population of Pennsylvania at the time of the 1790 federal decennial census will not be found in this work. (Indeed, researchers able to trace an ancestor to Pennsylvania in the decades after the Revolution and unable to link him to any immigrant listed in *Pennsylvania German Pioneers*, should automatically suspect the possibility that the ancestor may have been a deserter from a German mercenary unit in the service of the British during the Revolution, or a settler formerly in the service of the French.)

¶ The index to *Pennsylvania German Pioneers*, though it may appear to be thorough, is utterly inadequate. A cursory and random check of the index discloses glaring deficiencies, making it exceedingly difficult for the unwary researcher to find all entries for a given surname. Because of the orthographic variations which occur in the passenger lists, the only adequate way to have provided access to the passenger lists would have been by soundexing all surnames. Here are but a few examples:

-- Czolbe should be listed under Scholbe. The Cz- herein is a Polish (or Silesian) spelling which undoubtedly was changed very early.

-- Copfirs should be listed with Küpfer and Küper.

-- Cost belongs with Kost.

-- Bogert and Pogert are probably the same surname.

-- Böhmer and Pommer may be the same surname.

-- Druckmiller (Truckin Miller) and Trockenmiller (Trookmiller) seem certainly to be the same surname, although separately indexed under D and T.

-- Dywell; Teubel (Divel; Dufel (Tewfel); and Teufel (Teuffel, Teufell) are the same surnames, though separately entered and indexed.

-- Deiss (Deis, Dise, Tice) and Theiss (Theis, Teis, Theys, Deys, Thais) are the same.

A thorough soundexing of all surnames appearing in *Pennsylvania German Pioneers* will disclose a very large number of other spelling variations not heretofore placed in juxtaposition. The consequence will be that many probable family members, heretofore hidden by an inadequate index, will be discovered.

Study of the passenger lists in *Pennsylvania German Pioneers* discloses that most emigrants left a European port in English flag vessels, and that these ships usually touched at a British port before crossing the Atlantic. A typical voyage was from Rotterdam to Cowes (Isle of Wight) to Philadelphia. Of the 506 ship lists in *Pennsylvania German Pioneers*, the following statistical data on ports of departure and of call have been derived:

European Ports of Departure and of Call of Ships Debarking Immigrants at Philadelphia, 1727-1808

	1727-1775	1785-1808
European Ports of Departure:		
Amsterdam	12	57
Bremen	-	10
Copenhagen	-	1
Friedrichstadt (Schleswig)	-	1
Hamburg	9	43
Jade River, near Bremen	-	1
Lisbon	10	-
Lübeck	-	1
Rotterdam	243	8
Tönningen, Denmark (now Tönning, Schleswig, Germany)	-	6
Unknown, or unstated	50	53
	324	181
Intermediate Ports of Call:		
Aberdeen	1	-
Berwick on Tweed	1	-
Boston	2	-
Charleston, South Carolina	1	-
Cowes	145	-
Deal	21	-
Dover	13	

	1727-1775	1785-1808
Falmouth	3	-
Gosport	4	-
Leith, Scotland	5	-
London	28	1
Orkney Islands	2	-
Plymouth	18	-
Poole, Dorsetshire	1	-
Portsmouth	35	-
St. Christopher	1	-
St. Domingo	-	1
St. Thomas	-	1
Teignmouth, Devonshire	1	-
Unknown, or unstated	42	178
	324	181

The 324 ships landing at Philadelphia before the Revolution are estimated to have debarked a total of 65,040 persons; no similar estimate has been made for the 181 ships arriving in the early Federal period.

Two details should be noted: First, no French ports of departure are shown in the above table, although it is known that large numbers of Palatine emigrants left Europe via French ports. Perhaps these are among the unknown or unstated ports in the preceding table; if so, the Philadelphia port authorities may simply have ignored British regulations and admitted immigrants on ships not having touched at a British port of call. On the other hand, it may be that vessels from France did not normally land at Philadelphia. If so, this implies a selection process operative among Pennsylvania Germans heretofore unsuspected, because many of the emigrants via France had left Germany without proper permits or were young men avoiding military service obligations. Further, since the British early rejected would-be Catholic immigrants, it may be that Germans of the Catholic faith were forced to immigrate to ports permitting the landing of French ships--Canada and Louisiana, in particular. Here, then, is an area for further research by genealogists.

Other Published Source Materials in America

There are no other published source materials comparable to Strassburger's *Pennsylvania German Pioneers*. One is left with only snippets of information--some small, some larger--nowhere systematically collected, indexed or critically evaluabled. Researchers will find many of these fragments listed in

Harold Lancour, *A Bibliography of Ship Passenger Lists, 1538-1825: Being a Guide to Published Lists of Early Immigrants to North America.* 3d. ed. rev. and enl. by Richard J. Wolfe. . . . New York: New York Public Library, 1963.

Lancour's work--one of very great value, it must be said--is chronologically bound. There is no cross-referencing to geographic areas, and one is forced to go through it page by page in search of articles likely to contain pertinent information. What is needed is a surname compilation based upon all the articles listed in this bibliography. Pending the appearance of such a reference tool, researchers will be unable to obtain full use of the vast but fragmentary evidences of early immigration to North America which are preserved for us in printed form.

Membership Lists and

German-Language Newspapers

Germans in the United States were frequently members of social clubs and fraternal organizations, particularly after 1850. Organizational records ordinarily contain the birthplaces and dates of members; as a consequence, such records are of great value to the researcher. As an example, see

Clifford Neal Smith and Anna Piszczan-Czaja Smith, "Some German-speaking Immigrants in Ohio and Kentucky, 1869," *National Genealogical Society Quarterly*, 62 (1974): 17-32.

The birthplaces of the German-Americans listed therein were recorded when they became subscribers to the magazine *Der deutsche Pionier* (Cincinnati, Ohio). Although the above-cited article lists only the subscribers to the first volume of this magazine, all seventeen of the succeeding volumes (published 1869 to 1887) contain the names and birthplaces of additional subscribers. It seems likely that, for many of these German settlers, the pages of the magazine are the only links between their Ohio and Kentucky residences and their places of origin in Germany.

It ought also to be noted that *Der deutsche Pionier* published numerous obtiuaries which give a great deal of additional information as to descendants, arrival dates, accomplishments. Lengthy and detailed obituaries were a standard feature of almost every German-language newspaper and periodical devoted to the maintenance of contacts among German speakers on the frontier. Researchers should automatically search German-language newspapers of the locality in which the ancestor lived for information on places of birth appearing in his obituary. To identify these periodicals, the following publication is useful:

Karl J. R. Arndt and May E. Olson, *German-American Newspapers and Periodicals, 1732-1955: History and Bibliography.* Heidelberg: Quelle and Meyer, 1961; distributed in the United States by Clark University Press, Worcester, Massachusetts.

PUBLISHED SOURCE MATERIALS IN GERMANY

Although it has not been the writers' intention to provide lengthy bibliographies of published materials available to researchers elsewhere, it has seemed desirable to have an inventory of German emigration lists, arranged by geographic area within Germany, so far as they have come to our attention. The purpose here is to have as complete an overview as possible to materials which might be suitable for eventual translation, editing, and republication in the *German-American Research Monograph* series and to determine which areas of Germany are in most need of further research. Investigators should note that some articles, notably those of Friedrich Krebs, have already been published in English and are available to the American and Canadian genealogist; such items are listed in Lancour's *Bibliography of Ship Passenger Lists*.

The inventory of published emigration lists which follows makes it clear that, while the Palatinate has received considerable attention, particularly from such distinguished genealogical publicists as Herr Josef Mergen, very little has been done for vast areas of the country, notably northeastern Germany, from whence a great many immigrants to America came. The inaccessibility of the records from this region, being now in the German Democratic Republic, Poland, and the Soviet Union, makes it unlikely that researchers will have much information on Prussian emigration for a long time to come. This makes the Hamburg emigration lists, described elsewhere, doubly important as a source of information otherwise unavailable.

Bibliography of

Published Emigration Lists*

1. Austria

Eferding (*Herrschaft*)   Titze, W., "Auswanderung aus d. Eferdinger Herrschaft" [Emigration from the Eferding Estate]. *Der Wegweiser* 2:34-35, 51-52, 217-218.

---

* English-language articles listed in Lancour's *Bibliography of Ship Passenger Lists* have been excluded, for the most part.

1. Austria--Cont.

General

Groeschel, K. "Exulantenforschung" [Exile research] *Der Wegweiser* 1:17.

Pfretschner, A. "Ein- und Auswanderung" [Immigration and emigration] *Zeitschriften des Vereins Adler in Wien* (1939), pp. 80-81. Also in *Die Sippe* (1937-1938), p. 204.

Goisern

v. Frank, Karl Friedrich. "Auswanderer aus Goisern nach Nordamerika, 1850 bis 1882" [Emigrants from Goisern to North America, 1850 to 1882] *Senftenegger Monatsblatt für Genealogie und Heraldik* 3 (1955-1956): 233-240.

Güssing (*Bezirk in Bürgenland*)

Graupner, Ludwig. "Der Ablauf der Amerikawanderung im Güssinger Bezirk" [Development of emigration from the Güssing district to America] *Volk und Heimat: Kultur- und Bildungsblatt für das burgenländische Volk* 9 (1956), Nr. 11, pp. 2-3.

Graupner, Ludwig. *Die Amerikawanderung im Güssinger Bezirk* [Emigration to America from Güssing district] Vienna: Ferd. Berger, 1949.

Himmelberg (*Herrschaft in Carinthia*)

v. Zenegg, E. "Evangelische Auswanderer aus Herrschaft Himmelberg in Kärnten [Evangelical emigrants from the estate of Himmelberg in Carinthia] *Zeitschriften des Vereins Adler in Wien* (1940), pp. 20-21.

Kärnten (Carinthia)

see Steiermark (Styria)

Salzburg

Oertel, E. "Salzburger Auswanderer" [Salzburger emigrants] *Familiengeschichtliche Blätter* (1914), p. 365.

Steiermark (Styria)

Hildmann, O. "Exulanten aus Steiermark und Kärnten" [Exiles from Styria and Carinthia] *Blätter für oesterreichische Familienkunde* (1933), pp. 41-45.

Gruell, G. "Auswanderer aus Steiermark" [Emigrants from Styria] *Der Wegweiser* 1-126-129.

Zillertal

Federer, Johann. *Die Auswanderer aus d. Zillertal, 1837* [Emigrants from the Zillertal, 1837] Innsbruck: Innsbrucker Buchdr. J. Winkler, 1937.

2. Baden

Asperg

Bolay, T. "Auswanderung aus Asperg im 18. und 19. Jahrhundert [Emigration from Asperg in the eighteenth and nineteenth centuries] *Ludwigsburger Geschichtsblätter* (Ludwigsburg) 16 (1964): 98-126.

Baden

Bauer, H. "Untersuchungen zur Geschichte der Auswanderung in den Jahren 1712, 1737 und 1787" [Investigations in the history of emigration in the years 1712, 1737, and 1787] *Diöcesan-Archiv* (Freiburg/Br.) N.F., 37:314-357.

Krebs, Friedrich. "Auswanderer aus Baden" [Emigration from Baden] *Archiv für Sippenforschung* (1931), p. 424.

see also Franconia, Herbolzheim

Baden-Durlach

Krebs, Friedrich. "Amerika-Auswanderer aus Baden-Durlach im Jahre 1738" [Emigrants to America from Baden-Durlach during the year 1738] *Senftenegger Monatsblatt für Genealogie und Heraldik* 4 (1956-1959): 17-18.

Krebs, Friedrich. "Einige Amerika-Auswanderer des 18. Jahrhunderts" [Some eighteenth-century emigrants to America] *Senftenegger Monatsblatt für Genealogie und Heraldik* 5 (1960-1963): 123-126.

Krebs, Friedrich. "Studien zur Amerika-Auswanderung aus Baden-Durlach für das Jahr 1751" [Studies regarding the emigration to America from Baden-Durlach in 1751] *Badische Heimat* (Freiburg/Br.) 36 (1956): 155-156.

Breisgau

Priesner, Paul. "Die Auswanderung aus dem Breisgau vor hundert Jahren" [Emigration from the Breisgau 100 years ago] *Der Lichtgang: Nebst Beilage: Nachrichtenblatt der öff. Kultur- und Heimatpflege im Reg. Bez. Südbaden* (Freiburg/Br.) 3 (1953): 4-5.

2. *Baden--Cont.*

Heidelberg *see* The Palatinate. Heidelberg

Markgräfler- Buhrin, E. "Aus dem Leben ein
land Markgräfler Auswandererfamilie"
[From the life of an emigrant
family from Markgräflerland]
Markgräfler Jahrbuch (Schopf-
heim) 3 (1954): 86-90.

3. *Burgundy* (ship)

Mahrenholtz, Hans. "Die Pas-
sagiere des an der britischen
Kuste gestrandeten Auswanderer-
schiffes *Burgundy*" [Passengers
aboard the emigrant ship *Burgundy* stranded off the coast of
Great Britain] *Norddeutsche
Familienkunde: Zeitschrift d.
Arbeitsgemeinschaft Genealogischer Verbande in Niedersachsen* (Berchtesgaden-Schellenberg) 6. J. (1957), p. 233.

4. *Canada and the United States*

California Smolka, Georg. "Auswanderung
und Kolonisationsprojekte im
Vormärz, Kalifornienplan und
Texasverein" [Emigration and
colonization projects on the
eve of the [1848] revolution,
California and the Texasverein]
*Staat und Gesellschaft: Fest-
gabe für Günther Küchenhoff zum
60. Geburtstag am 21. August
1967*. Göttingen: Franz Mayer,
1967.

Cincinnati,
Ohio *see* Lower Saxony. Blockwinkel

Illinois Hauth, W. "Deutsche Pioniere
im Land Illinois . . . 18. und
19. Jahrhundert" [German pioneers in the state of Illinois
(during) the eighteenth and
nineteenth centuries] *Familiengeschichtliche Blätter* (1935)
pp. 137, 223, 263.

Iowa Reimer, G. "Emigranten aus
Schleswig-Holstein in Land
Iowa" [Emigrants from Schles-
wig-Holstein in the state of
Iowa] *Mitteilungen der Gesell-
schaft für Schleswig-Holstein-
ische Familienforschung und
Wappenkunde* (1958), p. 121.

Hauth, W. "Deutsche Pioniere
in Land Iowa . . . 19. Jahrhundert" [German pioneers in
the state of Iowa (during the)

nineteenth century] *Familiengeschichtliche Blätter* (1933),
pp. 215, 263, 317.

Dieterichs, H. "Als Gast d.
Nachkommen Waldecker Emigranten
in Iowa" [As guest of the descendants of emigrants from Waldeck in Iowa] *Hessische Familienkunde* (1959), p. 643.

Massachusetts *see* Hessen

New Orleans Lampe, K. H. "Verzeichnis
deutsche Familien in New Orleans, Oktober 1769" [A list
of German families in New Orleans, October, 1769] *Zeitschrift für niedersächsische
Familienkunde* (1951), p. 66.

New York "Deutsche Einzelwanderer und
Familien in Neu Niederland"
[German occasional emigrants
and families in New Nether-
lands] *Jahrbuch für auslanddeutsche Sippenkunde* 1 (1936):
45-53.

New York (Hud- v. Stockhausen, Juliane. "Die
son River Teersieder vom Hudson-Tal:
valley) Deutsche Auswanderer Schicksale in Amerika" [The tar re-
finers of the Hudson River
valley: German emigrants and
their fate] *Christ und Welt*
(Stuttgart) 11. J. (1958), Nr.
48, p. 13.

New York Espenscheid, L. "Siedler in
(Wayne Wayne County, New York aus der
County) Rheinland" [Settlers in Wayne
County, New York, from the
Rhineland] *Pfälzische Familien-
und Wappenkunde: Mitteilungen
zur Wanderungsgeschichte der
Pfälzer* (1958), p. 185.

see also Württemberg. Kochertal

Nova Scotia Mahrenholtz, Hans. "Auswanderer
nach Nova Scotia" [Emigrants to
Nova Scotia] *Norddeutsche Familienkunde: Zeitschrift d.
Arbeitsgemeinschaft Genealogischer Verbände in Niedersachsen* (Berchtesgaden-Schellenberg) 11 (1962): 80-82.

Pennsylvania "Einwanderer in Pennsylvania
vor 1700" [Immigrants to Pennsylvania before 1700] *Jahrbuch
für auslanddeutsche Sippenkunde*
1 (1936): 53-54.

4. *Canada and the United States--Cont.*

Texas

Bonnet, R. "Texas and deutsche Familienforschung" [Texas and German genealogical research] *Familiengeschichtliche Blätter* (1928), pp. 48, 136.

Mueller, R. "Deutsche Dorfer in Texas" [German villages in Texas] *Familiengeschichtliche Blätter* (1937), p. 279.

Scheffel, Fritz. *Deutsche suchen den Garten der Welt: Das Schicksal deutsche Auswanderer in Texas vor 100 Jahren: Nach Berichten erzählt* [Germans seek the garden spot of the world: the fate of German emigrants in Texas 100 years ago: retold from personal accounts] Stuttgart: Union, 1943.

Winkel, Harald. "Der Texasverein: Ein Beitrag zur Geschichte der deutschen Auswanderung im 19. Jahrhundert" [The Texas Verein (association): A contribution to the history of German emigration in the nineteenth century] *Vierteljahresschrift für Sozial- und Wirtschaftsgeschichte* 55 (1968-1969): 348-372.

see also California; Hessen. Rheinhessen; Specific Immigrants (Holm)

5. *Czechoslovakia*

General

Budin, Stanislav. "Auswanderung aus der CSSR in den USA und der UdSSR" [Emigration from Czechoslovakia to the United States and the Soviet Union] *Wissenschaftlicher Dienst für Ostmitteleuropa* (Johann Gottfried Herder-Institut, Marburg/Lahn) 17 (1967): 455-458.

6. *Croats (of Yugoslavia)*

General

Prpic, Georg J. "Kroatische Auswanderung nach Amerika [Croatian emigration to America] *Der Donauraum: Zeitschrift des Forschungsinstituts für Fragen des Donauraums* 9 (1964): 167-174.

7. *Elizabeth* (ship)

Braun, F., and Krebs, F. "Auswanderer auf dem Schiff *Elizabeth,* Bremen-New York, 1832" [Emigrants on the ship *Elizabeth,* Bremen to New York, 1832] *Pfälzische Familien- und Wappenkunde: Mitteilungen zur Wanderungsgeschichte der Pfälzer* (1957), p. 61.

8. *Franconia (Franken)*

General

Pfrenzinger, A. "Mainfränkische Bauern-Auswanderung des 18. Jahrhunderts" [The emigration of Franconian farmer from the Main River area during the eighteenth century] *Der deutsche Erzieher, Gau Mainfranken* (1939), pp. 173-176; also in *Zeitschrift für bayerische Landesgeschichte* (Munich) 9:445-467.

"Auswanderung aus Franken d. 18. und 19. Jahrhunderts" [Emigration from Franconia during the eighteenth and nineteenth centuries] *Frankische Heimat* (L. Spindler, Nürnberg) 1 (1922?): 158.

Redelberger, R. "Fränkische Auswanderung vor 125 Jahren" [Franconian emigration 125 years ago] *Mainlande* (Würzburg) J. 16 (1965), Nr. 8, pp. 29-30.

see also Specific Immigrants (Gerlinger)

Herbolzheim (which of three villages of this name is not stated)

Koch, Conrad. "Die Herbolzheimer Auswandererliste [The emigration lists of Herbolzheim] *Genealogie: Deutsche Zeitschrift fur Familienkunde* (Neustadt/Aisch) J. 15 (1966), 8:167-170.

Hohentrüdingen

Bischoff, J. "Amerika-Auswanderer aus Hohentrüdingen in 18. Jahrhundert" [Emigrants to America from Hohentrüdingen in the eighteenth century] *Blätter für frankische Familienkunde* (1939), p. 203.

Spessart

see Hessen. Volgelsberg

Wertheim (*Grafschaft*)

Langguth, O. "Auswanderer aus Grafschaft Wertheim in 18. und 19. Jahrhundert" [Emigrants from the county of Wertheim

8. Franconia (Franken)--Cont.

during the eighteenth and nineteenth centuries] *Familienge-schichtliche Blätter* (1932), pp. 53, 109, 155, 206.

9. General Articles

Unidentified Location

"Auswandererverzeichnis" [Emigration list] *Familiengeschicht-liche Blätter* 23 (1925?): 175.

Dieterichs, Heinz. "Anschriften von Auswanderer in Mittel- und Nordamerika" [Addresses of emigrants in Middle and North America] *Zeitschrift für nieder-sächsische Familienkunde* (Hamburg) 34 (1959): 131-133.

General

Klüber, Karl Werner. "Indirekte Auswanderung: Deutsche wanderten über England nach New York aus" [Indirect emigration: Germans emigrated via England to New York] *Genealogie: Deutsche Zeit-schrift für Familienkunde* (Neustadt/Aisch) J. 14 (1965), 7: 774-779.

Günther, Karl. "Randbemerkungen zur 'Indirekte Auswanderung'" [Marginal notations on 'indirect emigration'] *Genealogie: Deutsche Zeitschrift für Fam-ilienkunde* (Neustadt/Aisch) J. 15 (1966), 8:40-41.

Klüber, Karl Werner. "Bericht über weitere Auswanderungs-listen" [Report on further emigration lists] *Genealogie: Deutsche Zeitschrift für Fam-ilienkunde* (Neustadt/Aisch), J. 17 (1968), 9:284-285.

Dieck, A. "Deutsche Reisender nach Amerika in 16. Jahrhundert" [German travelers to America in the sixteenth century] *Familie und Volk* (1956), p. 240.

Vowinckel, Renate. "Ursachen der Auswanderung, gezeigt an bad[ischen] Beispielen aus d. 18. und 19. Jahrhundert" [The causes of emigration as reflected by cases from Baden of the eighteenth and nineteenth centuries] *Vierteljahrs-schrift für Sozial- und Wirt-schaftsgeschichte*, Beiheft 37 (dissertation). Stuttgart: Kohlhammer, 1939.

Binder-Johnson, H. "Der deutsche Amerika-Auswanderer des 18. Jahrhunderts im zeitgenössischen Urteil" [Eighteenth century German emigrants to America in the opinion of [their] contemporaries] *Deutsche Archiv für Landes- und Volksforschung* (Leipzig) 4: 211-234.

Woltersdorf, G. "Deutsche Massenauswanderung nach Amerika im 19. Jahrhundert" [The mass emigration of Germans to America in the nineteenth century] *Jambo* (Leipzig) 15:257-264.

Schnitzer, Ewald. *Der National-gedanke und d. deutsche Auswan-derung nach den Vereinigten Staaten von Amerika in der 1. Hälfte d. 19. Jahrhunderts* [National opinion and the German emigration to the United States of America in the first half of the nineteenth century] Dresden: Risse-Verlag, 1935.

"Aufruf zur Auswanderung nach Amerika in Jahr 1848" [Call to emigrate to America in 1848] *Judaica: Zeitschrift für Ge-schichte, Literatur, Kunst und Bibliographie* (Bratislava), H. 11/12, p. 3.

Woltersdorf, G. "Das 'dolles Jahr' 1848 und d. 'Emigranten'" [That 'wonderful year' 1848 and the 'emigrants'] *Jambo* (Leip-zig) 15: 283-286.

Gelberg, Birgit. *Auswanderung nach Übersee: Soziale Probleme der Auswandererbeförderung in Hamburg und Bremen von der Mitte der 19. Jahrhunderts bis zum 1. Weltkrieg* [Overseas emigration: Social problems encountered by the emigration process at Ham-burg and Bremen from the middle of the nineteenth century to the beginning of the first world war] Hamburg: Hans Christians, 1973.

Pross, H. *Deutsche akademische Emigration nach den Vereinigten Staaten 1933-1941* [German aca-demic emigration to the United States 1933-1941] Berlin: Duncker & Humblot, 1955.

Link, Werner. *Mit dem Gesicht nach Deutschland: Eine Doku-mentation über die sozial-*

9. General Articles--Cont.

demokratische Emigration [With their faces toward Germany: Documents on the emigration of social democrats] Düsseldorf: Droste, 1968.

Zimmer, Norbert. "Auf unbekannten Spuren der deutschen Überseeauswanderer" [Heretofore unknown clues to German overseas emigration] Der Weg ins Ausland: Deutsche Monatschrift für wirtschaftliche und kulturelle Beziehungen zur Ausland (Frankfurt/Main), 3. J. (1953), N. 5, pp. 4-6; and N. 6, pp. 4-5.

Kloss, H. "100 Jahre überseedeutsche Familienkunde" [One hundred years of overseas German genealogy] Familie und Volk: Zeitschrift für Genealogie und Bevölkerungskunde (Neustadt/Aisch) 6 (1957): 284-285.

Schumann, Gert. "Die Auswanderung nach Amerika im vorigen Jahrhundert" [Emigration to America in the last century] Westfälischer Heimatkalender (Münster/Westfalen) 14 (1960): 99-103.

Monnerjohn, Engelbert. "Der St. Raphaels-Verein zum Schutze katholischer deutscher Auswanderer" [The St. Raphael Society for the protection of German Catholic emigrants] Jahrbuch für Caritaswissenschaft (Freiburg/Br.) 5 (1963): 109-115.

Richter, Franz. "Erwägungen über die Auswanderung nach Amerika" [Thoughts on emigration to America] Christ Unterwegs: Beilage: Der deutsche Katholik im Ausland (Munich) J. 17 (1963), N. 7-8, pp. 7-9.

Vagts, Alfred. Deutsch-Amerikanische Rückwanderung: Probleme, Phänomene, Statistik, Politik, Soziologie, Biographie [German-American return-migration: Problems, phenomena, statistics, politics, sociology, biography] Heidelberg: Carl Winter Universitätsverlag, 1960.

10. Hessen

Darmstadt

Wiesenthal, Georg. "Darmstädter Auswanderer aus dem Jahre 1847" [Emigration from Darmstadt in the year 1847] Der Odenwald: Heimatkundliche Zeitschrift des Breubergbundes (Darmstadt) 4 (1957): 81-82.

Dill (Wetzlar)

Laufer, H. "Auswanderer aus Dillgemeinden um 1700" [Emigrants from Dill communities around 1700] Heimatkalender des Kreises Wetzlar (Wetzlar), (1958), pp. 59-62.

Roth, E. "Auswanderung aus der Dillkreis" [Emigration from the Dill district] Volk und Scholle: Heimatblatt für beide Hessen, 20. J. (1942), H. 1-3, pp. 11-14.

Gedern

Klingelhoffer, H. "Auswanderung aus Gedern in Oberhessen" [Emigration from Gedern in Upper Hessen] Mitteilungen der hessischen familiengeschichtlichen Vereinigung in Darmstadt 2:122.

see also Hessen. Stolberg-Gedern

Gelnhausen

see Hessen. Vogelsberg

Heidelberg (Oberamt)

Krebs, Friedrich. "Auswanderung aus Kurhessen, Oberamt Heidelberg, nach Amerika, 1726-1727" [Emigration to America from Electoral Hessen, Oberamt Heidelberg, 1726-1727] Südwestdeutsche Blätter für Familien- und Wappenkunde (1958), p. 512.

Hessen (in general)

Krebs, Friedrich. "Ein Aufruf zur Auswanderung nach den amerikanischen Staat Massachusetts aus dem Jahre 1751" [An appeal for emigration to the American state of Massachusetts in 1751] Hessische Familienkunde (Frankfurt/Main) 5 (1961): 435-437.

Kurhessen (Electoral Hessen)

Gunther, Kurt. "Beiträge zum Problem der kurhessischen Auswanderung im 18. und 19. Jahrhundert insbesondere nach Nordamerika" [Contribution to the problem of emigration from Electoral Hessen in the eighteenth and nineteenth centuries, especially to North America] Zeitschrift des Vereins für

10. *Hessen--Cont.*

hessische Geschichte und Landeskunde (Kassel) 75-76 (1964-65): 489-538.

Limburg? (Bishopric of?)

Schmidt, Josef. "Auswanderung nach Amerika vor 100 Jahren" [Emigration to America 100 years ago] *Jahrbuch des Bistums Limburg* (Frankfurt/Main), (1954), pp. 26-27.

Nassau

Gerber, Adolf. *Die Nassau-Dillenburger Auswanderung nach Amerika im 18. Jahrhundert: Das Verhalten der Regierungen dazu und die späteren Schicksale der Auswanderer* [Eighteenth-century emigration to America from Nassau-Dillenburg: Governmental attitudes and the later fate of the emigrants] Flensburg: Flensburger Nachrichten, 1930.

Northern Hessen

Gunther, Kurt. "Auswanderungsquellen des 19. Jahrhunderts aus Nordhessen" [Sources of information on emigration from northern Hessen] *Hessische Familienkunde* (Frankfurt/Main) 4 (1957-58), H. 3, Sp. 185-188.

Odenwald

Huschke, Wolfgang. "Amerika-Auswanderer aus dem Odenwald 1853-1855: Hinweisen auf Quellen zur Geschichte der Auswanderung aus dem Grossherzogtum Hessen im 19. Jahrhundert" [Emigrants to America from the Odenwald 1853-1855: Direction to sources for the history of emigration from the Grandduchy of Hessen in the nineteenth century] *Genealogie: Deutsche Zeitschrift für Familienkunde* (Neustadt/Aisch), J. 18 (1969), 9: 639-643, 751-758, 823-827.

see also Specific Emigrants (Eisenhower)

Rheinhessen

Richter, H. "Texas-Auswanderung aus Rheinhessen" [Emigration to Texas from Rhine-Hessen] *Volk und Scholle: Heimatblatt für beide Hessen* 7 (1929?): 346.

Schlüchtern (*Kreis*)

Jäger, Johannes, and Glock, Heinrich. "Die Amerika-Auswanderer aus unserem Kreis vor 100 Jahren" [Emigrants to America 100 years ago] *Bergwinkel-Bote: Heimatkalender für d. Kreis Schlüchtern* (Schlüchtern) 16 (1964): 50-55.

Stolberg-Gedern

Klingelhoffer, H. "Auswanderung aus Standesherrschaft Stolberg-Gedern in 18. Jahrhundert" [Emigration from the noble estate of Stolberg-Gedern in the eighteenth century] *Mitteilungen der hessischen familiengeschichtlichen Vereinigung in Darmstadt* 1:122.

Vogelsberg

Frey, Julius. "Auswanderung nach Nordamerika aus der Landschaft zwischen Vogelsberg und Spessart im 18. Jahrhundert [Emigration to North America from the region between the Vogelsberg and the Spessart in the eighteenth century] *Heimat-Jahrbuch des Kreises Gelnhausen* (Gelnhausen), (1962), pp. 56-57.

Westerwald

see The Palatinate. Eitelborn

Wetzlar

see Hessen. Dill

11. *Jews*

Reissner, Hanns Günther. "Die jüdische Auswanderer" [The Jewish emigrant] *Judentum: Schicksal, Wesen und Gegenwart.* Herausgegeben von Franz Böhm und Walter Dirks unter Mitarbeit von Walter Gottschalk (Wiesbaden) 1 (1965): 2.

12. *Logan (ship)*

Braun, F. "Auswanderer auf d. Schiff *Logan*, LeHavre-New York, 1833" [Emigrants on the ship *Logan*, LeHavre-New York, 1833] *Pfälzische Familien- und Wappenkunde: Mitteilungen zur Wanderungsgeschichte der Pfälzer* (1959), p. 69.

13. *Lower Saxony (Niedersachsen; Braunschweig; Oldenburg)*

Ammerland

Wichmann, Hans. "Ammerländer Auswanderer nach den Vereinigten Staaten von Nordamerika aus den letzten 75 Jahren" [Emigrants from Ammerland to the United States in the last 75 years] *Der Ammerländer: Heimatkalendar* (Westerstede), (1952), pp. 21-26.

Blockwinkel

Mahrenholtz, Hans. "Dorothea Buck aus Blockwinkel ruft aus Cincinnati ihre Verwandten in ihre neue Heimat, 1831" [Dorothea Buck from Blockwinkel, in

13. *Lower Saxony*--Cont.

Cincinnati, invites her relatives to her new homeland, 1831] *Niedersachsen: Zeitschrift für Heimat und Kultur* (Hildesheim) 57 (1957): 179.

Braunschweig (Duchy)

Gruhne, Fritz. *Auswandererlisten des ehemaligen Herzogtum Braunschweig 1846 bis 1871* [Lists of emigrants from the former Duchy of Brunswick, 1846 to 1871] Quellen und Forschungen zur braunschweigischen Geschichte Nr. 20. Wolfenbüttel: Selbstverlag des Braunschweigischen Geschichtsverein, 1971.

Bruchhausen (Amt)

Mahrenholtz, Hans. "Norddeutsche in aller Welt: Auswanderungen 1860-1866 aus dem Amt Bruchhausen" [North Germans in all the world: Emigration 1860-1866 from Amt Bruchhausen] *Norddeutsche Familienkunde: Zeitschrift d. Arbeitsgemeinschaft Genealogischer Verbände in Niedersachsen* (Berchtesgaden-Schellenberg) 12 (1963): 181-184.

Catlenburg-Lindau

see Lower Saxony. Duderstadt

Damme (Amt; Oldenburg)

Ostendorf, J. "Geschichte d. Auswanderung aus d. früheren Amt Damme (Oldenburg), insbesondere nach Nordamerika, 1830-1880" [History of emigration from the former Amt Damme, Oldenburg, particularly to North America, 1830-1880] *Oldenburger Jahrbuch* (1943), p. 164.

Denkershausen, Kreis Northeim

see Specific Immigrants (Holzhausen)

Diepholz (Amt)

Mahrenholtz, Hans. "Norddeutsche in aller Welt: Auswanderer aus dem Amte Diepholz 1823-1830 und 1831-1840" [North Germans in all the world: Emigrants from Amt Diepholz 1823-1840] *Norddeutsche Familienkunde: Zeitschrift d. Arbeitsgemeinschaft Genealogischer Verbände in Niedersachsen* (Berchtesgaden-Schellenberg), 8? (1959?): 247-251.

Mahrenholtz, Hans. "Norddeutsche in aller Welt: Auswanderer aus dem Ämtern Diepholz 1841-1849 und Lauenstein 1841-1860" [North Germans in all the world: Emigrants from Amt Diepholz 1841-1849 and from Amt Lauenstein 1841-1860] *Norddeutsche Familienkunde: Zeitschrift d. Arbeitsgemeinschaft Genealogischer Verbände in Niedersachsen* (Berchtesgaden-Schellenberg), 9 (1960): 82-84.

Mahrenholtz, Hans. "Auswanderer aus dem Amte Diepholz 1841-1858" [Emigrants from Amt Diepholz, 1841-1858] *Norddeutsche Familienkunde: Zeitschrift d. Arbeitsgemeinschaft Genealogischer Verbände in Niedersachsen* (Berchtesgaden-Schellenberg) 9 (1960): 22-24.

see also Lower Saxony. Hannover

Diepholz (Grafschaft)

Fricke, Karl. "Auswanderung nach Nordamerika aus der Grafschaft Diepholz" [Emigration to North America from the county of Diepholz] *Diepholzer Heimatblätter* (Diepholz) 9. F. (1953), N. 8, p. 64.

Doepenau

see Lower Saxony. Hannover

Duderstadt (Amt)

Mahrenholtz, Hans. "Norddeutsche in aller Welt: Auswanderungen aus den Ämtern Catlenburg-Lindau, Duderstadt, und Gieboldshausen, 1831-1863 bzw. 1839-1866" [North Germans in all the world: Emigration from Amt Catlenburg-Lindau, Amt Duderstadt, and Amt Gieboldehausen, 1831-1863 or 1839-1866] *Norddeutsche Familienkunde: Zeitschrift d. Arbeitsgemeinschaft Genealogischer Verbände in Niedersachsen* (Berchtesgaden-Schellenberg) 10 (1961): 245-249.

Ehrenberg

see Lower Saxony. Hannover

Freudenberg

see Lower Saxony. Hannover

Gieboldehausen (Amt)

see Lower Saxony. Duderstadt

Göttingen

see Specific Immigrants (Schramm)

Hannover

Mahrenholtz, Hans. "Norddeutsche in aller Welt: Über Auswanderernachweise im Staatsarchiv Hannover" [North Germans in all the world: Emigration registers in Staatsarchiv Hannover (from

13. *Lower Saxony--Cont.*

Nienburg, Syke, Stolzenau, Hoya, Bruchhausen, Uchte, Ehrenburg, Freudenberg, Siedenburg, Lemförde, Doepenau, Westen-Thedinghausen, Harpstedt, Diepholz, Wölpe)] *Norddeutsche Familienkunde: Zeitschrift d. Arbeitsgemeinschaft Genealogischer Verbände in Niedersachsen* (Berchtesgaden-Schellenberg) 6 (1957): 183-186, 208-211.

Harpstedt — *see* Lower Saxony. Hannover

Harxbüttel/ Hannover — *see* Specific Immigrants (Dassel)

Hildesheim — Mahrenholtz, Hans. "Ein Zeitgenössischen Bericht über Auswanderung nach Amerika, 1831" [A contemporary report on emigration to America, 1831] *Niedersachsen: Zeitschrift für Heimat und Kultur* (Hildesheim) 58 (1958): 123.

Hildesheim (*Landdrosteibezirk*) — Mahrenholtz, Hans. "Auswanderer aus dem Landdrosteibezirk Hildesheim" [Emigration from Hildesheim administrative district] *Norddeutsche Familienkunde: Zeitschrift d. Arbeitsgemeinschaft Genealogischer Verbände in Niedersachsen* (Berchtesgaden-Schellenberg) 7 (1958): 110-115.

Mahrenholtz, Hans. "Auswandererzahlen aus der Landdrostei Hildesheim, 1866-1867" [Number of emigrants from Hildesheim administrative district, 1866-1867] *Norddeutsche Familienkunde: Zeitschrift d. Arbeitsgemeinschaft Genealogischer Verbände in Niedersachsen* (Berchtesgaden-Schellenberg) 6 (1957): 276.

Hoya — *see* Lower Saxony. Hannover

Lauenstein (*Amt*) — *see* Lower Saxony. Diepholz

Lehe (*Kreis*) — Graue, N. "Auswanderung im Kreise Lehe" [Emigration in Lehe district] *Land* 39 (1930?): 165.

Lemförde — Mahrenholtz, Hans. "Norddeutsche in aller Welt: Auswanderungen aus dem Amte Lemförde 1825-1840 und Regierungsverordnungen und

Massnahmen gegen die Auswanderungen aus dem Bezirk Stade 1727-1761" [North Germans in all the world: Emigration from Lemförde 1825-1840, and governmental regulations and measures against emigration from Stade district 1727-1761] *Norddeutsche Familienkunde: Zeitschrift d. Arbeitsgemeinschaft Genealogischer Verbände in Niedersachsen* (Berchtesgaden-Schellenberg) 9 (1960): 118-124; *and* 10 (1961): 173-178.

see also Lower Saxony. Hannover

Lüneburg (region) — Mahrenholtz, Hans. "Norddeutsche in aller Welt: Auswanderung aus dem Lüneburgischen, 1849" [North Germans in all the world: Emigration from the Luneburg region, 1849] *Norddeutsche Familienkunde: Zeitschrift d. Arbeitsgemeinschaft Genealogischer Verbände in Niedersachsen* (Berchtesgaden-Schellenberg) 7 (1958): 80-82.

Mahrenholtz, Hans. "Auswanderer aus dem Lüneburgischen, 1850" [Emigration from the Lüneburg region, 1850] *Norddeutsche Familienkunde: Zeitschrift d. Arbeitsgemeinschaft Genealogischer Verbände in Niedersachsen* (Berchtesgaden-Schellenberg) 7 (1958): 116-118.

Mahrenholtz, Hans. "Norddeutsche in aller Welt: Auswanderungen aus dem Lüneburgischen, 1851" [North Germans in all the world: Emigration from the Lüneburg region, 1851] *Norddeutsche Familienkunde: Zeitschrift d. Arbeitsgemeinschaft Genealogischer Verbände in Niedersachsen* (Berchtesgaden-Schellenberg) 7 (1958): 23.

Mahrenholtz, Hans. "Norddeutsche in aller Welt: Auswanderer aus dem Lüneburgischen, 1853" [North Germans in all the world: Emigrants from the Lüneburg region, 1853] *Norddeutsche Familienkunde: Zeitschrift d. Arbeitsgemeinschaft Genealogischer Verbände in Niedersachsen* (Berchtesgaden-Schellenberg) 8 (1959): 154, 186-188.

Penners, Theodor. "Entstehung und Ursachen der überseeischen Auswanderungsbewegung im Lande Lüneburg vor 100 Jahren" [Beginnings and causes of the

13. Lower Saxony--Cont.

overseas emigration movement in Lüneburg region 100 years ago] *Lüneburger Blätter* 4 (1952): 102–129.

Niedersachsen (Lower Saxony)

Mahrenholtz, Hans. "Norddeutsche in aller Welt: Nachweise über 1830–1848 nach Amerika ausgewandernde Niedersachsen" [North Germans in all the world: Information on Lower Saxons emigrating to America, 1830–1848] *Norddeutsche Familienkunde: Zeitschrift d. Arbeitsgemeinschaft Genealogischer Verbände in Niedersachsen* (Berchtesgaden-Schellenberg) 5 (1956): 144.

Mahrenholtz, Hans. "Norddeutsche in aller Welt: Auswanderer nach Amerika, Polen, Venezuela, Neuseeland, 1753–1882" [North Germans in all the world: Emigrants to America, Poland, Venezuela, and New Zeeland, 1753–1882] *Norddeutsche Familienkunde: Zeitschrift d. Arbeitsgemeinschaft Genealogischer Verbände in Niedersachsen* (Berchtesgaden-Schellenberg) 14 (1965): 85–88.

Mahrenholtz, Hans. "Auswanderer nach Australien, Nord- und Südamerika" [Emigrants to Australia, North and South America] *Norddeutsche Familienkunde: Zeitschrift d. Arbeitsgemeinschaft Genealogischer Verbände in Niedersachsen* (Berchtesgaden-Schellenberg) 15 (1966): 215–221.

Mahrenholtz, Hans. "Militärpflichtige und arme Auswanderer 1838–1858" [Military draftees and poor emigrants, 1838–1858] *Norddeutsche Familienkunde: Zeitschrift d. Arbeitsgemeinschaft Genealogischer Verbände in Niedersachsen* (Berchtesgaden-Schellenberg) 6 (1957): 234.

Mahrenholtz, Hans. "Über den Umfang der Auswanderung aus Niedersachsen" [Regarding the dimensions of emigration from Lower Saxony] *Norddeutsche Familienkunde: Zeitschrift d. Arbeitsgemeinschaft Genealogischer Verbände in Niedersachsen* (Berchtesgaden-Schellenberg) 7 (1958): 80–82.

Reinstorf, E. "Auswandererverzeichnisse" [Emigrant list] *Zeitschrift der Zentralstelle für niedersächsische Familienkunde* (1920), p. 16.

see also Canada and the United States. Nova Scotia

Nienburg *see* Lower Saxony. Hannover

Oldenburg Büsing, Wolfgang. "Personengeschichtliche Nachrichten aus den wochentlichen *Oldenburgischen Anzeiger*, 1746–1800" [Personal historical news from the weekly *Oldenburger Anzeiger* 1746–1800] *Oldenburger: des Oldenburger Landesvereins für Geschichte, Natur- und Heimatkunde* (Oldenburg) 55 (1956): 1, 193–232.

Bockhorst, H. "Auswanderung und Heuerleutenot [in] Oldenburger Munsterland" [Emigration and the poverty of day laborers in the Oldenburg diocese] *Heimatkalender für Oldenburg-Münsterland* (Vechta), (1959), pp. 100–105.

Osnabrück (Regierungsbezirk) Kiel, N. "Auswanderung aus d. Osnabrücker Regierungsbezirk" [Emigration from the Osnabrück governmental region] *Mitteilungen d. Verein für Geschichts- u. Landeskunde v. Osnabrück* 61 (1941): 85.

Siedenburg *see* Lower Saxony. Hannover

Stade (Bezirk) *see* Lower Saxony. Lemförde

Stolzenau *see* Lower Saxony. Hannover

Syke *see* Lower Saxony. Hannover

Thedinghausen *see* Lower Saxony. Hannover

Uchte *see* Lower Saxony. Hannover

Uelzen (Kreis) von der Ohe, Hans. "Die Auswandererforschung für d. Kreis Uelzen" [Emigrant research in the Uelzen district] *Archiv für Landes- und Volkskunde von Niedersachsen* (1942), pp. 264–267.

Westen-Thedinghausen *see* Lower Saxony. Hannover

Woelpe *see* Lower Saxony. Hannover

14. *Nordrhein-Westfalen*

(Lower Rhineland; Westphalia)

Bentheim
(*Grafschaft*)
Friedrich, W. "Sie gingen nach Amerika . . ." [They went to America . . .] *Jahrbuch des Heimatvereins der Grafschaft Bentheim* (Bentheim) 49 (1959): 231-234.

Berleburg
see Nordrhein-Westfalen. Wittgenstein

Krefeld
Nieper, Friedrich. *Die ersten deutsche Auswanderer von Krefeld nach Pennsylvanien . . .* [The first German emigrants from Krefeld to Pennsylvania . . .] Neukirchen: Buchdr. d. Erziehungsverein, 1940.

Niepoth, Wilhelm. "Die Abstammung der 13 Auswanderer von Krefeld nach Pennsylvanien in Lichte niederrheinischer Quellen" [The lineages of the 13 emigrants from Krefeld to Pennsylvania in the light of Lower Rheinish source materials] *Aus der Heimat: Naturwissenschaftliche Monatschrift* (Öhringen) 24 (1953): 2-9.

Niepoth, Wilhelm. "Krefelder Genealogie: Ist in der Erforschung der mennonitischen Familien Krefelds über das sogenannten Scheutensche Stammbuch hinaus noch weiterzukommen?" [Krefeld genealogy: Is it possible to do further research on the Mennonite families of Krefeld outside the so-called Scheuten book of lineages?] *Heimat: Zeitschrift für niederrheinische Heimatpflege* (Krefeld) 31 (1961): 116-130.

Lippe
Lohmeier, W. "Von Lippern in Amerika" [Persons from Lippe in America] *Lippischer Kalendar* (Detmold) 263 (1951): 84-85.

Gleis, P. "Einige Westfalen und Lipper der 1848er Revolutionszeit in Nordamerika" [Some Westphalians and persons from Lippe of the 1848 Revolution period in America] *Der Ravensberger: Heimatkalender für das Minden-Ravensberger Land* (Bielefeld) 25 (1953): 47-50.

Lippstadt
Lederle, M. "Aus Lippstadt nach Amerika" [From Lippstadt to

America] *Heimatblätter: Organ für die Belange der Heimatbundes* (Lippstadt) 44 (1963): 95.

Malmedy
(*Kreis*;
now in
Belgium)
Kaufmann, K. L. "Auswanderung aus d. Kreise Malmedy" [Emigration from Malmedy district] *Rheinische Heimatpflege* 12 (1940); 355.

Minden
see Nordrhein-Westfalen. Lippe

Münster (*Regierungsbezirk*)
Müller, Friedrich. "Westfälische Auswanderer in 19. Jahrhundert: Auswanderung aus dem Regierungsbezirk Münster. I: 1803-1850" [Westphalian emigrants in the nineteenth century: Emigration from the Münster governmental region. Part I: 1803-1850] *Beiträge zur Westfälischen Familienforschung* (Münster/Westfalen) 22-24 (1964-1966): 7-484. [Also listed in slightly different form under Westfalen hereinafter.]

Müller, Friedrich. "Westfälische Auswanderer im 19. Jahrhundert: Lückenlose Überlieferung für den Regierungsbezirk Münster von 1828-1850" [Westphalian emigrants in the nineteenth century: Records without gap from 1828 to 1850 for the Münster governmental region] *Auf roter Erde: Monatsblätter für Landeskunde und Volkstum Westfalens: Heimatsbeilage der "Westfälischen Nachrichten"* (Münster/Westfalen) 22 (1966), N. 90, pp. 2-3.

Tonsmeyer, N. "Die Auswanderer der Münsterländer nach Amerika" [Emigrants from the Munster region to America] *Auf roter Erde: Monatsblätter fur Landeskunde und Volkstum Westfalens* (Münster/Westfalen) 13 (1952) N. 1, pp. 5-7.

Ravensberg
see Nordrhein-Westfalen. Lippe

Rheinland
van Ham, H. "Die Stellung d. Staates und d. Regierungsbehörden im Rheinland: Zum Auswanderungsproblem im 18. und 19. Jahrhundert" [The policy of the State and governmental officials in the Rhineland regarding the emigration problem in the eighteenth and nineteenth centuries] *Deutsches Archiv für*

14. *Nordrhein-Westfalen--Cont.*

Landes- und Volksforschung 6
(1942): 261-309.

Neu, H. "Beiträge zur Ge-
schichte d. rhein. Amerika-
Auswanderung im 18. Jahrhundert"
[Contributions to the history of
Rhenish emigration to America
during the eighteenth century]
Rheinische Vierteljahrsblätter
(Bonn)(1936?): 176-185. [Cita-
tion in the *Internationale
Zeitschriften Bibliographie*,
1936/I, appears to be incom-
plete.]

see also Canada and the United
States. New York (Wayne County)

Siegkreis — Walterscheid, Josef. *Auswanderer
aus d. Siegkreis* [Emigrants from
the Sieg district] Bonn: Röhrscheid, 1939.

Westfalen — Müller, Friedrich. *Westfälische
Auswanderer. Beiträge zur westfälischen Familienforschung*,
volumes 22-24. Münster/West-
falen: Westfälische Gesellschaft
fur Genealogie und Familienforschung, 1966. [Also listed
herein under Münster Regierungsbezirk.]

Müller, Friedrich. "Auswanderungen aus Westfalen im 19. Jahrhundert" [Emigration from Westphalia in the nineteenth cen-
tury] *Auf roter Erde: Monatsblätter fur Landeskunde und
Volkstum Westfalens* (Münster/
Westfalen) 18 (1962-1963), N.F.,
Nr. 46, p. 3.

Nordhoff, Franz, and Müller,
Friedrich. "Brief eines westfälischen Aussiedlers" [Letter
from a Westphalian emigrant (to
North America)] *Westfälischer
Heimatkalendar* (Münster/West-
falen) 18 (1964): 148-150.

see also Nordrhein-Westfalen.
Lippe

Wittgenstein — Krämer, Fritz. "Wittgensteiner
(*Landkreis*) Auswanderer" [Emigrations from
Wittgenstein] *Wittgenstein: Im
Auftrag des Arbeitsausschusses
Heimatbuch* (Balve/Westfalen) 1
(1965): 344-359, 611-612.

15. *North Germany*

(*Bremen; Friesland; Hamburg; Schleswig-Holstein*)

Amrum (is- — see North Germany. Föhr (island) land)

Bremen — Spengemann, Friedrich. *Die
Reisen der Segelfregatten* Isa-
bella, Pauline, Meta, *und* Uh-
land *nach Nordamerika: Nach
Kapitän Jürgen Meyers Bordbuch*
[The voyages of the sailing
frigates *Isabella, Pauline,
Meta,* and *Uhland* to North Amer-
ica: According to the log of
Captain Jürgen Meyers] Bremen:
Buchdr. Vahland & Co., 1937.

Wehner, Gustav. "Das Schicksale
der Bremer Auswanderer-Listen"
[The fate of the Bremen emigration lists] *Norddeutsche Familienkunde: Zeitschrift d. Arbeitsgemeinschaft Genealogischer
Verbände in Niedersachsen*
(Berchtesgaden-Schellenberg) 1
(1952): 74, 96, 113.

Klüber, Karl Werner. "Wiederge-
fundene Bremer und Hamburger
Auswandererlisten" [Rediscovered
emigration lists from Bremen and
Hamburg] *Genealogie: Deutsche
Zeitschrift für Familienkunde*
(Neustadt/Aisch) 15. J. (1966)
8: 329-332.

Föhr (island) — Alander, Ursel. "Die Auswanderung von der Insel Föhr in den
Jahren 1850 bis 1875" [Emigra-
tion from the island of Föhr in
the years 1850 to 1875] *Jahrbuch
der Gesellschaft fur bildende
Kunst und vaterländische Alter-
tümer zu Emden* (Aurich) 41 (1961):
244-262; also in *Jahrbuch des
Nordfriesischen Instituts* (Husum) 7 (1961): 244-262; also in
*Jahrbuch des Nordfriesischen Ver-
eins für Heimatkunde und Heimat-
liebe* (Mönkebüll/Langenhorn,
Kreis Husum) 34 (1961): 244-265.

Hamburg — Suchan-Galow, E. "Hamburger
Quellen zur Auswandererforschung" [Source materials in Hamburg for emigration research]
*Deutsches Archiv für Landes-
und Volksforschung* (Leipzig) 7
(1943): 90-98.

Knoop, E. "Nachforschungen und
d. Auswandererlisten Hamburgs

15. *North Germany--Cont.*

und Bremens" [Research and the emigration lists of Hamburg and Bremen] *Zeitschrift der Zentralstelle fur niedersächsiche Familiengeschichte* (Hamburg), (1937), p. 10. [Also entitled *Zeitschrift für niedersächsische Familienkunde.*]

Schultze, Karl-Egbert. "Zur Bearbeitung der Hamburger Auswandererlisten, insbesondere: Kann man sie drucken? [Working with the Hamburg emigration lists, specifically: Can they be published?] *Zeitschrift für niederdeutsche Familienkunde* (Hamburg) 41 (1966): 7-9.

Ostfriesen (Eastern Friesland) "Deutsche Auswanderung nach Nordamerika" [German emigration to North America] *Ostfriesische Familienforschung* 3 (1951): 36.

Probstei (Ostholstein; area formerly under Kloster Preetz) Finke, Günter. "Auswanderer aus der Probstei (Ostholstein) [Emigrants from the Probstei (Eastern Holstein)] *Norddeutsche Familienkunde: Zeitschrift d. Arbeitsgemeinschaft Genealogischer Verbände in Niedersachsen* (Berchtesgaden-Schellenberg) 18 (1969): 223-226.

Schleswig-Holstein *see* Canada and the United States (Iowa)

16. *Northeastern Germany*

(Mecklenburg; Pomerania; East and West Prussia)

Berent (*Kreis*; West Prussia) Preuss, U. "Auswanderung aus Kreis Berent" [Emigration from Berent district] *Mitteilungen des Westpreussischen Geschichtsvereins* (1943), p. 1.

East Prussia Weinreich, A. "Ostpreussische Auswanderer 1818-1866" [East Prussian emigrants, 1818-1866] *Archiv für Sippenforschung* (1943), p. 169.

Schwetz (*Kreis*; West Prussia) Goerz, Adalbert. "Aus Mennonitischen Kirchenbücher Westpreussen: 2. Gemeinde Montau-Gruppe, Kr. Schwetz" [From the Mennonite church books of West Prussia: 2. The Montau-Gruppe congregation, Schwetz district] *Ostdeutsche Familienkunde: Zeitschrift für Familien-*

geschichtsforschung im deutschen Osten (Neustadt/Aisch) 16. J. (1968) 5:22.

Stuhm (*Kreis*; West Prussia) Goerz, Adalbert. "Aus Mennonitischen Kirchenbücher Westpreussen: 3. Gemeinde Tragheimerweide, Kr. Stuhm [From the Mennonite church books of West Prussia: 3. The Tragheimerweide congregation, Stuhm district] *Ostdeutsche Familienkunde: Zeitschrift für Familiengeschichtsforschung im deutschen Osten* (Neustadt/Aisch) 16. J. (1968) 5:85-86.

West Prussia Schwarz, F. "Ubersee-Auswanderung in fruheren Jahrhundert" [Overseas emigration in earlier centuries] *Mitteilungen des Westpreussischen Geschichtsvereins* (1942), p. 69.

Wesenberg (Mecklenburg) Hoeval, Ruth. "Auswanderer der Stadt Wesenberg in Mecklenburg" [Emigrants from the town of Wesenberg in Mecklenburg] *Mitteldeutsche Familienkunde: Beilage zu Genealogie: Deutsche Zeitschrift fur Familienkunde* (Neustadt/Aisch) 13.? J. (1972): 3: 381-382.

17. *Poland*

General Olczewski, H. "Verzeichnis polnischer Auswanderer" [A list of Polish emigrants] *Archiv für Sippenforschung* (1939), p. 89.

18. *Reformed Church*

"Westdeutsche Reformierte Pfarrer in Nordamerika in 18. Jahrhundert" [West German Reformed ministers in North America in the eighteenth century] *Norddeutsche Familienkunde* (1953), p. 202.

19. *Russian Germans*

Klüber, Karl Werner. "Aus Hamburger Schifflisten: Russlanddeutsche Auswanderer nach Nordamerika im Jahre 1874" [From the Hamburg ship lists: Russian German emigrants to North America in 1874] *Genealogie: Deutsche Zeitschrift für Familienkunde* (Neustadt/Aisch) 14. J. (1965) 7: 816-819.

20. *The Palatinate (Rheinland-Pfalz;*

Eifel; Mosel; Hunsrück; Nahe; Saarland)

Allscheid
(Eifel)

Mergen, Josef. "Was alles uber Allscheid geschrieben wurde" [What was written about Allscheid] *Mosella: Heimatbeilage des Trierischer Volksfreund* (January 1969). [Inhabitants of this village emigrated together as a group to the United States.]

Bernkastel
(*Kreis*)

Mergen, Josef. "Die Amerika-Auswanderung aus dem Kreis Bernkastel" [Emigration to America from Bernkastel district] *Mosella: Heimatbeilage des Trierischer Volksfreund* (February 1954).

see also The Palatinate. Trier; Specific Immigrants (Engel)

Birkenfeld/
Nahe

Questor, Erich. "Auswanderer aus dem Raum um Birkenfeld/ Nahe" [Emigrants from the area around Birkenfeld on the Nahe River] *Ostdeutsche Familienkunde: Zeitschrift fur Familiengeschichtsforschung im deutschen Osten: Beilage: Archiv ostdeutscher Familienforscher* (Neustadt/Aisch) 11 (1963): 161-164.

Bitburg
(*Kreis*)

Mergen, Josef. "Die Amerika-Auswanderung aus dem Kreis Bitburg im 19. Jahrhundert" [Nineteenth-century emigration to America from the Bitberg district] *Eifel: Monatschrift des Eifelvereins* (Cologne) 49 (1954): 151-152.

see also The Palatinate. Trier

Daleiden

Mergen, Josef. "Die Auswanderung aus Daleiden nach Nord-Amerika" [Emigration from Daleiden to North America] *Trierisches Landeszeitung* (28 September 1954).

Daun (*Landratsamt*)

Mergen, Josef. "Auswandererverzeichnis" [Emigration list]. Typescript, now out of print; a copy is in the Landratsamt Daun.

Duchroth

Herzog, A. "Duchroth in der Pfalz; ein klassischer Auswanderungsort" [Duchroth in the Palatinate; a classic emigration village] *Pfälzische Heimatblätter* (Neustadt) 13

(1965): N. 2-3, pp. 10-11.

Düren (*Kreis*)

Mergen, Josef. "Von der Eifel nach Nord-Amerika" [From the Eifel region to North America] *Jahrbuch des Kreises Düren* (1973).

Ehrang

Mergen, Josef. "Ehranger suchen eine neue Heimat in Nord-Amerika" [Emigrants from Ehrang search for a new home in North America] *Ehranger Heimat* (December 1964), p. 82.

Eifel

Graafen, R. "Die Aus- und Abwanderung aus der Eifel in den Jahren 1815-1955" [Emigration and wandering away from the Eifel during the years 1815-1955] *Forschungen zur deutschen Landeskunde* (Berlin) volume 27 (1961).

Kasper, J. "Eifler Auswanderer in Amerika und ihre Schicksale" [Emigrants from the Eifel to America and their fate] *Jahrbuch des Kreises Ahrweiler* (Remagen) 8 (1940?): 139-143; 9 (1941): 154.

see also The Palatinate. Düren

Eitelborn/
Westerwald

Arndt, W. "Auswanderungen aus ein Westerwalddorf [Eitelborn]" [Emigration from a village in the Westerwald (Eitelborn)] *Der deutsche Erzieher: Beilage: N.-S. Erzieher: Gau Hessen-Nassau* 6 (1938?): 311-313.

Frankenthal
(town)

Krebs, Friedrich. "Amerika-Auswanderer des 18. Jahrhunderts aus der Stadt Frankenthal" [Eighteenth-century emigrants to America from the town of Frankenthal] *Mitteilungen der westdeutschen Gesellschaft für Familienkunde e. V.* (Cologne) 47. J. (1959) 19: 577-580.

Frankenthal
(*Kreis*)

"Auswanderer aus der Kreis Frankenthal" [Emigrants from Frankenthal district] *Monatschrift der Frankenthaler Altertumsverein* 46. J. (1938), H. 5, p. 29.

Freckenfeld

Krebs, Friedrich. "Auswanderer nach den nordamerikanischen Kolonien im 18. Jahrhundert auf Grund der Einträge in lutherischen Kirchenbuch von Freckenfeld" [Eighteenth-century emigrants to the North

20. *The Palatinate--Cont.*

American colonies as reflected by the entries in the Lutheran church registers at Freckenfeld] *Blätter für pfälzische Kirchengeschichte und religiöse Volkskunde* 28. J. (1952) 19: 99-101.

Freilingen (Eifel)

Ottermann, Karl. "Zusammenbruch der Eisenindustrie und Auswanderung: Zwischen Freilingen und Lommersdorf" [The crisis in the iron idustry and emigration: Between Freilingen and Lommersdorf] *Heimatkalendar des Eifelgrenzkreises Schleiden* (Schleiden), (1956), pp. 117-119.

Friedelsheim

Braun, Fritz. *Auswanderer aus der Mennonitengemeinde Friedelsheim im 19. Jahrhundert* [Emigrants from the Mennonite congregation at Friedelsheim in the nineteenth century] Ludwigshafen/Rhein: R. Louis, 1956; also in *Mitteilungen zur Wanderungsgeschichte der Pfälzer* (1955) F. 1-2, pp. 1-16.

Gemünden (*Amt*; Hunsrück)

Diener, W. "Der Auswanderung aus der Amte Gemünden [Hunsrück] im 19. Jahrhundert" [Nineteenth-century emigration from Amt Gemünden in the Hunsrück region] *Rheinische Vierteljahrsblätter* (Bonn) 5 (1935): 191-222. [Pagination may vary; part of this article at pp. 215-222.]

Hambach

Becker, A. "Vom Hambach nach Amerika: Geschichte d. Pfälzer Auswanderungsbewegung vor 100 Jahren" [From Hambach to America: History of the Palatine emigration movement a century ago] *Auslandsdeutsche* (Stuttgart) 16 (1933?): 72-75.

Hartenburg bei [Bad?] Dürckheim/ Haardt

see Specific Immigrants (Windbiegler)

Heidelberg (*Oberamt*)

Krebs, Friedrich. "Amerika-Auswanderer aus den kurpfälzischen Oberämtern Heidelberg und Mosbach für die Jahre 1749-1750" [Emigrants to America from the Electoral Palatine offices of Heidelberg and Mosbach, 1749-1750] *Badische Heimat* (Freiburg/Breisgau) 33 (1953): 76-77.

Krebs, Friedrich. "Die Amerika-Auswanderung aus dem kurpfalzischen Oberamt Heidelberg in den Jahren 1737, 1738, 1751, 1753 und 1754" [Emigration to America from the Electoral Palatine office of Heidelberg in the years 1737, 1738, 1751, 1753, 1754] *Badische Heimat* 38 (1958): 303-304.

"Zur Amerika-Auswanderung aus dem kurpfälzischen Oberamt Heidelberg 1741-1748" [Regarding the emigration to America from the Electoral Palatine district of Heidelberg, 1741-1748] *Zeitschrift für des Oberrheins* (Karlsruhe) 106 (1958): 485-486.

see also Hessen. Heidelberg

Homburg/Pfalz

Fischer, Karl. "Homburger Handwerker wandern nach Amerika aus: Ein Beitrag zur pfälzischen Auswanderung im 19. Jahrhundert" [Homburger craftsmen emigrate to America: A contribution to Palatine emigration (history) in the nineteenth century] *Pfälzer Heimat* (Speyer) 10 (1959): 101-106.

Hunsrück and Nahe (region)

Krebs, Friedrich. "Amerika-Auswanderer des 18. Jahrhunderts aus der heutigen Pfalz und der Nahe- und Hunsrückgegend" [Eighteenth-century emigrations to America from modern-day Palatinate and the Nahe and Hunsrück region] *Pfälzische Familien- und Wappenkunde (nebst Beilage: Pfälzische Genealogie)* (Ludwigshafen/Rhein) (1954) F. 11-12, pp. 62-66.

[Another source gives this reference as *Pfälzische Familien- und Wappenkunde: Mitteilungen zur Wanderungsgeschichte der Pfälzer* (1954), p. 71.]

Krebs, Friedrich. "Amerika-Auswanderer des 18. Jahrhunderts aus der Hunsrück- und Nahegegend" [Eighteenth-century emigrants to America from the Hunsrück and Nahe region] *Rheinische Vierteljahrsblätter: Mitteilungen des Instituts für geschichtliche Landeskunde der Rheinlande an der Universität Bonn* (Bonn) 19 (1954): 240-241.

Kell

Mergen, Josef. "Die Auswanderer von Kell nach Amerika" [The

20. The Palatinate--Cont.

emigrants from Kell to America] *Trierischen Landeszeitung* (15 July 1956).

Kurpfalz (Electoral Palatinate)

Männer, E. "Zur Auswanderung aus der Kurpfalz im 18. Jahrhundert" [Emigration from the Electoral Palatinate in the eighteenth century] *Unter d. Dorflinde im Odenwald* (Darmstadt) 24 (1940?): 8.

Häberle, N. "Auswanderung aus der Kurpfalz zu Karl Theodors Zeiten" [Emigration from the Electoral Palatinate in the time of Karl Theodor] *Pfälzische Museum* [50 (1933)]: 19.

Leiwen (near Trittenheim)

Mergen, Josef. "Von Leiwen nach Nord-Amerika" [From Leiwen to North America] *Mosella: Heimatbeilage des Trierischer Volksfreund* (September 1969).

Lettweiler

see The Palatinate. Ransweiler

Lommersdorf/ Eifel

see The Palatinate. Freilingen

Ludwigshafen/ Rhein

Braun, Fritz. "Auswanderung aus dem heutigen Stadtgebiet von Ludwigshafen am Rhein im 18. Jahrhundert" [Eighteenth-century emigration from the present city of Ludwigshafen/Rhein] *Pfälzische Familien- und Wappenkunde (nebst Beilage: Landsleute drinnen und draussen)*, (1953), F. 5, pp. 26-32.

Braun, Fritz. *Auswanderer aus der Umgebung von Ludwigshafen am Rhein auf dem Schiff "Thistle of Glascow" 1730* [Emigrants from the neighborhood of Ludwigshafen on the Rhine on the ship *Thistle of Glascow*, 1730] Schriften zur Wanderungsgeschichte der Pfälzer 8. Kaiserslautern: Heimatstelle Pfalz, 1959.

Eyselein, H. "Auswandererschicksale 1816-1817" [Emigrant fate, 1816-1817] *Heimatblätter für Ludwigshafen am Rhein* 25 (1937?): 17.

Mannheim

see Specific Immigrants (Stoll)

Mosbach (*Oberamt*)

see The Palatinate. Heidelberg

Mosel (region)

Mergen, Josef. "Die Auswanderung aus dem Moselland nach Nord-Amerika im 19. Jahrhundert" [Emigration from the Mosel region to North America in the nineteenth century] *Kurtrierisches Jahrbuch* (1964), pp. 70-84.

Milz, H. "Auswanderer aus Moselland" [Emigrants from the Mosel region] *Mitteilungen der westdeutschen Gesellschaft für Familienkunde* 10: 167.

Mergen, Josef. "Als die Mosel- und Saarschiffer auswanderten" [When the Mosel and Saar boatmen emigrated] *Die Brücke (Porta): Heimatbeilage der Trierischen Landeszeitung* (1970) Nr. 12.

Mergen, Josef. "Lehrer und Lehrersöhne ziehen in die Neue Welt" [Teachers and teachers' sons move to the New World] *Mosella: Heimatbeilage des Trierischer Volksfreund* (November 1967).

Mergen, Josef. "Auswandererbriefe berichten" [As told in the letters of emigrants] *Mosella: Heimatbeilage des Trierischer Volksfreund* (February 1964; March 1964).

Mergen, Josef. "Auswandererwelle im 19. Jahrhundert" [The nineteenth-century emigrant wave] *Mosella: Heimatbeilage des Trierischer Volksfreund* (June 1963).

Neumagen (*Amt*; Kreis Bernkastel)

Mergen, Josef. "Die Amerika-Auswanderung aus dem Amt Neumagen" [Emigration to America from Amt Neumagen] *Heimatkalendar für den Kreis Bernkastel* (1956), pp. 56, *et. seq.* [Published by the Kreisverwaltung Bernkastel]

Neu-Mehring

Mergen, Josef. "Neu-Mehring, ein verfehlte Dorfgründung [New Mehring, an unsuccessful founding of a village] *Porta: Heimatbeilage der Trierischen Landeszeitung* (13 November 1952). [According to a letter from the author, nearly all of the unhappy inhabitants of this village emigrated to Boston, Massachusetts.]

20. *The Palatinate--Cont.*

Niederheimbach (Kreis St. Goar)	Scheiffarth, Engelbert. "Übersee-Auswanderer aus Niederheimbach, Kreis St. Goar" [Overseas emigrants from Niederheimbach . . .] *Genealogie: Deutsche Zeitschrift für Familienkunde* (Neustadt/Aisch) 18. J. (1969) 9: 644-645.
Obereichsfeld	Goldmann, L. "Obereichsfeld Auswanderung nach Amerika in d. 2. Hälfte d. 19. Jahrhunderts" [Emigration from Obereichsfeld to America in the second half of the nineteenth century] *Unser Eichsfeld* 23 (1927): 257.
Orenhofen	Mergen, Josef. "Die Auswanderung aus Orenhofen nach Nord-Amerika" [Emigration to North America from Orenhofen] *Trierisches Landeszeitung* (26 November 1954).
Odernheim/Glan	Braun, Fritz. "Amerika-Auswanderer aus Odernheim an Glan" [Emigrants to America from Odernheim on the Glan River] *Nordpfälzischer Geschichtsverein* (Rockenhausen) 40 (1960): 438-439.
Oppenheim (*Oberamt*)	Krebs, Friedrich. "Amerika-Auswanderer aus dem Oberamt Oppenheim, 1742-1749" [Emigrants to America from Oppenheim, 1742-1749] *Hessische Familienkunde* (Frankfurt/Main) 3 (1954-1955), H. 6, Sp. 341-342.
Otterberg	Krebs, Friedrich. "Einige Amerika-Auswanderer des 18. Jahrhunderts aus Otterberg" [Some eighteenth-century emigrants from Otterberg] *Nordpfälzischer Geschichtsverein* (Rockenhausen) 38 (1958): 236.
Otterstadt	Zink, Albert. "Die grosse Otterstädter Auswanderung: Behördlich geforderte Auswanderung gegen Bevölkerungsüberschuss [The great emigration from Otterstadt: Officially promoted emigration as a measure against overpopulation] *Pfälzische Heimatblätter* (Neustadt) 3. J. (1955), N. 6, pp. 45-46.
Pfalz (The Palatinate)	Jung, Otto. "Der Trieb zur Auswanderung in die Neue Welt" [The compulsion to emigrate to the New World] *Pfälzische*

Heimatblätter (Neustadt) 5. J. (1957), N. 5, pp. 36-37.

Christmann, E. "Von d. Ursachen d. Auswanderung aus d. Pfalz u. ihre Nachbarschaft im 18. Jahrhundert" [Regarding the reasons for emigration from the Palatinate and neighboring regions during the eighteenth century] *Deutsche Monatshefte in Polen* (Posen), N. F., 4: 385-389.

Lohr, Otto. "Erste Pfälzer in Nordamerika: Mit dem Hollandern in die Neue Welt" [The first Palatine in North America: With the Dutch in the New World] *Pfälzische Heimatblatter* (Neustadt) 2. J. (1954), N. 1, p. 7.

Lohr, Otto. "Erste grosse Überseewanderung deutscher Bauern [1709-1756]" [The first large overseas migration of German peasants, 1709-1756] *Auslandische Volksforschung* (Stuttgart) [n.d.] pp. 26-44. [Citation appears in *Internationale Bibliographie der Zeitschriftenliteratur* (1937) volume 30.]

Krebs, Friedrich. "Einige Amerika-Auswanderer des 18. Jahrhunderts" [Some eighteenth-century emigrants to America] *Senftenegger Monatsblätter für Genealogie und Heraldik* (Senftenegg, Austria) 6 (1966): 60-64.

Krebs, Friedrich. "Pfälzer Amerika-Auswanderer des 18. Jahrhunderts. Teil I" [Eighteenth-century Palatine emigrants to America, Part I] *Familie und Volk: Zeitschrift für Genealogie und Bevölkerungskunde* (Neustadt/Aisch) 5 (1956): 60-62.

Krebs, Friedrich. "Pfälzische Auswanderer nach Amerika" [Palatine emigrants to America] *Familie und Volk: Zeitschrift für Genealogie und Bevölkerungskunde* (Neustadt/Aisch) 5 (1956): 154, 176-179.

Braun, Fritz, and Krebs, Friedrich. "Amerika-Auswanderer des 18. Jahrhunderts aus Süd-Pfälzischen Gemeinden" [Eighteenth-century emigrants to America from southern Palatine communities] *Pfälzische Familien- und*

20. *The Palatinate*--Cont.

Wappenkunde (Nebst Beilage: Pfälzische Genealogie): Mitteilungen zur Wanderungsgeschichte der Pfälzer (1956) F. 5, pp. 29-37, *and* (1957) [F. 6?] p. 83.

Braun, Fritz, and Krebs, Friedrich. *Amerika-Auswanderer des 18. Jahrhunderts aus Süd-Pfälzischen Gemeinden* [Eighteenth-century emigrants to America from southern Palatine communities] Schriften zur Wanderungsgeschichte der Pfälzer, Nr. 2. Ludwigshafen/Rhein: R. Louis, 1956.

Huber, Armin O. "Dokumente zur Pfälzischen Auswanderung des 18. Jahrhunderts nach Amerika" [Documents on eighteenth-century Palatine emigration to America] *Pfälzer Heimat* (Speyer) 13 (1962): 22-23, 54-55, 94, 137-138.

Trautz, Fritz. "Die pfälzische Auswanderung nach Nordamerika im 18. Jahrhundert" [Eighteenth century Palatine emigration to North America] *Pfälzische Heimatblätter* 8. J. (1960), N. 11-12, pp. 83-84; and *Ruperto-Carola: Mitteilungsblatt der Vereinigung der Freunde der Studentenschaft der Universität Heidelberg* (Heidelberg) 11. J. (1959), N. 25, pp. 161-169.

Trautz, Fritz. *Die pfälzische Auswanderung nach Nordamerika im 18. Jahrhundert.* Heidelberg: Carl-Winter Universitätsverlag, 1959. [A small historical summary from secondary source materials.]

Bartholomäus, E. "Amerika-Auswanderer aus der Pfalz im 18. Jahrhundert" [Eighteenth-century Palatine emigrants to America] *Familie und Volk: Zeitschrift für Genealogie und Bevölkerungskunde* (Neustadt/Aisch) 5? (1956): 239.

Keller-Huschemenger, Max. *Pfälzische Emigrantengemeinde in Irland* [Palatine emigrant community in Ireland] Kiel: Lutherisches Verlagshaus, 1973?

Zink, Albert. "Die pfälzische Auswanderung des 19. Jahrhundert im Lichte des pfälzischen Wirtschaftsleben" [Nineteenth-century Palatine emigration in the light of Palatine economic conditions] *Pfälzer Heimat* (Speyer) 5 (1954): 56-60.

see also Specific Immigrants (Kreischer) (Windbiegler)

Pirmasens   Siegel, W. "Die Pirmasenser Auswanderung: Im Jahre 1816 drohte der Westrich zu entvölkern" [The emigration from Pirmasens: The Westrich threatened by depopulation in 1816] *Pfälzische Heimatblätter* (Neustadt) 3. J. (1958), N. 2, p. 15.

Prüm (*Kreis*)   Mergen, Josef. "Die Amerika-Auswanderung aus dem Kreis Prüm" [Emigration to America from Kreis Prüm" [Emigration to America from Kreis Prüm] *Eifel: Monatschrift des Eifelvereins* (Cologne) 48 (1953): 99-101.

see also The Palatinate. Trier

Ransweiler   Krebs, Friedrich. "Amerika-Auswanderer des 18. Jahrhunderts aus der Nordpfalz (Ransweiler, Lettweiler, mit Auswandererbrief)" [Eighteenth-century emigrants to America from the northern Palatine (Ransweiler, Lettweiler, with emigration permits)] *Nordpfälzischer Geschichtsverein* (Rockenhausen) 41 (1961): 556-557.

Remagen   *see* The Palatinate. Eifel

Saarburg   *see* The Palatinate. Trier

Schleiden (*Kreis*)   *see* The Palatinate. Freilingen/Eifel

Staudernheim/ Nahe   Frohlich, Hugo. "Auswanderer im lutherischen Kirchenbuch von Staudernheim an der Nahe" [Emigrants recorded in the Lutheran church book of Staudernheim/Nahe] *Pfälzische Familien- und Wappenkunde (nebst Beilage: Pfälzische Genealogie): Mitteilungen zur Wanderungsgeschichte der Pfälzer* (Ludwigshafen/Rhein), (1954) F. 10, pp. 55-62.

20. The Palatinate--Cont.

Thaleisch-
weiler
(parish)

Sigel, Walter. "Auswanderungen im 18. Jahrhundert aus dem Kirchspiel Thaleischweiler" [Eighteenth-century emigration from the parish of Thaleischweiler] *Pfalzische Heimatblatter* 8. J. (1960) N. 7, p. 55.

Thalesch-
weiler

Krebs, Friedrich. "Auswanderer nach den nordamerikanischen Kolonien im lutherischen Kirchenbuch von Thaleschweiler" [Emigrants to the North American colonies as recorded in the Lutheran church book of Thaleschweiler] *Pfälzische Familien- und Wappenkunde (nebst Beilage: Pfälzische Genealogie): Landsleute drinnen und drausen* (1952) F. 3-4, pp. 21-24.

Trier (*Regier-
ungsbezirk*)

Mergen, Josef. *Die Amerika-Auswanderung aus dem Regierungsbezirk Trier im 19. Jahrhundert* [Nineteenth-century emigration to America from the Trier governmental region] A series as follows:

1. Trier-Land   5. Bitburg
2. Saarburg   6. Wittlich
3. Prüm   7. Trier-Stadt
4. Bernkastel

Saarkreise:

8. Merzig   11. Saarlouis
9. Ottweiler   12. St. Wendel
10. Saarbrücken

[This is a major series of publications to be published as time and funds permit. So far, only the Stadt Trier volume (number 7 above) has been published. It may be obtained through the Stadtbibliothek Trier, 55 Trier, Weberbachstrasse, for DM 10. The volumes for Bernkastel, Daun, and Wittlich have been mimeographed by the respective Landratsämter but are now out of print. For information from the other projected volumes, writer directly to the compiler, Herr Josef Mergen, Trier-Ehrang, Hochstrasse 8, West Germany. In addition to the above, Herr Mergen has published *Die Auswanderung aus den ehemals preussischen Teilen des Saarlandes im 19. Jahrhundert. I: Voraussetzungen und Grundmerkmale* [Nineteenth-century emigration from the former Prussian portions of the Saar. Part I: General conditions and principles] Saarbrücken: Institut für Landeskunde des Saarlandes an der Universität Saarbrucken, n.d. [This volume may be obtained from the Institut, 66 Saarbrücken, Universität, Bau 35, West Germany. The names of the emigrants from the Saar districts are to be published in three volumes, the first in 1975.]

Mergen, Josef. "Trierer beerben Amerikaner" [American heirs of estates in Trier] *Mosella: Heimatbeilage des Trierischer Volksfreund* (October 1956).

Mergen, Josef. "Trierer Handwerker zogen vor 100 Jahren nach Amerika" [Craftsmen from Trier moved to America a century ago] *Mosella: Heimatbeilage des Trierischer Volksfreund* (November 1954).

Mergen, Josef. "Trierer Amerika-Auswanderer, 1855-1856" [Emigrants from Trier to America, 1855-1856] *Porta: Heimatbeilage der Trierischen Landeszeitung* (12 December 1950).

Mergen, Josef. "Auswanderung im 19. Jahrhundert: Beitrage zur Alt-Trierer Familiengeschichte" [Nineteenth-century emigration: Contributions to the family history of Old Trier] *Mosella: Heimatbeilage des Trierischer Volksfreund* (April 1969).

Mergen, Josef. "Über Meere in ferne Lander" [Over the seas to far-away countries] *Mosella: Heimatbeilage des Trierischer Volksfreund* (November 1963; December 1963; January 1964).

Trittenheim/
Mosel

Mergen, Josef. "Trittenheimer wandern nach Amerika aus" [Trittenheim residents move to America] *Mosella: Heimatbeilage des Trierischer Volksfreund* (March 1966).

Wittlich
(*Kreis*)

Mergen, Josef. "Sie sogen aus Not übers Meer" [They moved overseas because of poverty]

20. *The Palatinate--Cont.*   21. *The Saar*

Von den Maaren bis zur Mosel:
Der Kreis Wittlich in Vergangen-
heit und Gegenwart. Wittlich:
Kreisverwaltung, 1966.

see also The Palatinate. Trier

Zweibrücken   Jost, Karl. "Die Auswanderung
aus Zweibrücken im Spiegel der
herzöglichen Verordnungen"
[Emigration from Zweibrücken
as reflected by the ducal
regulations] *Pfälzische Heimat-*
blätter (Neustadt) 7 (1959):
5-6.

Krebs, Friedrich. "Verzeichnis
deutsche Auswanderer nach d.
amerikanischen Kolonien aus
Zweibrücken, 1750-1771" [A
list of German emigrants to
the American colonies from
Zweibrücken, 1750-1771] *Fam-*
ilie und Volk: Zeitschrift für
Genealogie und Bevölkerungs-
kunde (Neustadt/Aisch) 1 (1952):
29-32.

Krebs, Friedrich. "Amerika-Aus-
wanderer des 18. Jahrhunderts
aus dem Gebiet des Herzogtums
Zweibrücken: Aus den Akten des
Staatsarchives Speyer" [Eigh-
teenth-century emigrants to
America from the region of the
Duchy of Zweibrücken: From the
files of the State Archives at
Speyer] *Genealogie: Deutsche*
Zeitschrift für Familienkunde
(Neustadt/Aisch) 19. J. (1970),
10: 50-53.

Schmidt, Erwin Friedrich.
"Fremde in lutherischen Kirchenbuch Zweibrücken" [Foreigners
in the Lutheran church register at Zweibrücken] *Genealogie:*
Deutsche Zeitschrift für Famil-
ienkunde (Neustadt/Aisch) 18.
J. (1969) 9: 758-760.

Wilms, R. "Auswanderungssucht
in der Westpfalz, 1816: Darge-
stellt an Regierungsverordnung-
nungen in *Zweibrücker Wochen-*
blatt" [The emigration fever
in the western Palatinate, 1816:
Reconstructed from the regulations appearing in the *Zwei-*
brücker Wochenblatt (weekly
newspaper)] *Pfälzische Heimat-*
blätter (Neustadt) 4 (1956): 7.

Haustadt (*Bür-*   Kell, H. "Auswanderungen aus d.
germeisterei)   Bürgermeistereien Haustadt und
Hilbringen im 18. Jahrhundert"
[Eighteenth-century emigration
from the Haustadt and Hilbringen
mayoral offices] *Abhandlungen*
zur Saarpfälzischen Landes- und
Volksforschung (Kaiserslautern)
2 (1938): 432-456. [Now entitled *Westmärkische Abhand-*
lungen zur Landes- und Volks-
forschung.]

Hilbringen
(*Bürger-*
meisterei)   *see* The Saar. Haustadt

Illingen   Engel, Johann. "Auswanderungen
(*Bürger-*   aus der Bürgermeisterei Ill-
meisterei)   ingen" [Emigration from the
Illingen mayoral office] *Saar-*
heimat: Zeitschrift zur Pflege
von Volkstum, Landschaft und
Kultur (Saarbrucken), (1960),
N. 8-9, pp. 27-28.

Merzig   *see* The Palatinate. Trier

Ottweiler   Mergen, Josef. "Die Nord-Amer-
ika-Auswanderungen im 19. Jahrhundert" [Nineteenth-century
emigration to North America]
Land und Gruben und Wälder, der
Landkreis Ottweiler im Saar-
land: Veröffentlichung d. Land-
kreis Ottweiler zur 150-Jahr-
feier des Kreises im Jahre 1964,
p. 45, *et seq.*

see also The Palatinate. Trier

Remmesweiler Becker, Wilhelm, and Weber, Wilhelm. "Remmesweiler Auswanderer
im 18. und 19. Jahrhundert"
[Eighteenth and nineteenth-
century emigrants from Remmes-
weiler] *Heimatbuch des Kreises*
St. Wendel (St. Wendel) 6. Aus-
gabe (1955-1956), pp. 77-84.

Saar, The   Mergen, Josef. "Umfang und
Gründe der Amerika-Auswanderung
aus dem Saarland in der ersten
Hälfte des 19. Jahrhunderts"
[Magnitude and reasons for the
emigration from the Saar to
America during the first half
of the nineteenth century] *Saar-*
brücker Hefte (Saarbrücken),
(1960), N. 12, pp. 68-78.

Mergen, Josef. "Die Folgen der
Amerika-Auswanderung (Saar)"

21. *The Saar--Cont.*

[Consequences of the emigration from the Saar to America] *Neues Trierisches Jahrbuch* (1968), pp. 89-99.

Mergen, Josef. "Als die Mosel- und Saarschiffer auswanderten" [When the Mosel and Saar boatmen emigrated] *Die Brücke (Porta): Die Heimatbeilage der Trierischen Landeszeitung,* Nr. 12 (1970).

see also The Palatinate. Trier

Saarbrücken *see also* The Palatinate. Trier

Saarlouis *see also* The Palatinate. Trier

St. Wendel Braun, Fritz. "Auswanderer aus St. Wendel" [Emigrants from St. Wendel] *Heimatbuch des Kreises St. Wendel* 9 (1961-1962): 96-97.

Mergen, Josef. "Er wollte wieder Preusse werden" [He wanted to become Prussian again] *Mosella: Heimatbeilage des Trierischer Volksfreund* (July 1968). [An emigrant from St. Wendel returned from the United States and petitioned to regain his Prussian citizenship, because he wished to reside again in St. Wendel. His application was rejected, and he was deported.]

see also The Palatinate. Trier; The Saar. Remmesweiler

22. *Saxony*

Cottbus (*Kreis*) Krüger, G. "Auswanderung aus Kreis Cottbus um d. Mitte d. 19. Jahrhundert" [Emigration from Kreis Cottbus around the middle of the nineteenth century] *Ekkehard: Mitteilungsblatt deutschen genealogischer Abende* (1938), pp. 284, 301.

Krüger, G. *Auswanderer nach Übersee aus der Landkreise Cottbus im 19. Jahrhundert* [Nineteenth-century overseas emigrants from Landkreis Cottbus] *Familienkundl. Hefte für d. Niederlausitz,* Nr. 5. Cottbus? Striemann, 1936.

Dresden Boer, E. "Auswanderer aus Dresden, 1852-1857" [Emigrants from Dresden, 1852-1857] *Mitteilungen des Roland* (1933), p. 11.

Klüber, Karl Werner. "Dresdener Auswanderer nach Übersee 1850-1903" [Overseas emigrants from Dresden, 1850-1903] *Mitteldeutsche Familienkunde: Beilage zu Genealogie: Deutsche Zeitschrift für Familienkunde* (Neustadt/Aisch) 12. J. (1971) 3: 199-205.

Leipzig Klüber, Karl Werner. "Leipziger Auswanderer nach Übersee 1850-1855" [Overseas emigrants from Leipzig, 1850-1855] *Mitteldeutsche Familienkunde: Beilage zu Genealogie: Deutsche Zeitschrift für Familienkunde* (Neustadt/Aisch) 10. J. (1969) 2: 273-281.

Reitzengeschwenda (**Kreis Ziegenrück**) Birkfeld, F. "Auswanderschicksale: Reitzengeschwendaer Bauern in Amerika" [Emigrant fate: Peasants from Reitzengeschwenda in America] *Heimatbuch Kreis Ziegenrück* (Pössneck), pp. 163-168. [Cited in *Internationale Bibliographie d. Zeitschriftenliteratur,* volume 83 (1938).]

Saxony Ulbrich, Harald. "Auswanderer aus Sachsen nach USA" [Saxon emigrants to the USA] *Archiv für Sippenforschung und alle verwandten Gebiete . . .* (Limburg/Lahn) 28 (1962): 394-395.

Seeberg-Elverfeldt, Roland. "Auswanderer aus Thuringen und Sachsen nach Übersee" [Overseas emigrants from Thuringia and Saxony] *Mitteldeutsche Familienkunde: Beilage zu Genealogie: Deutsche Zeitschrift für Familienkunde* (Neustadt/Aisch) 12. J. (1971) 3: 219-221.

Rosenthal, Hildegard. *Die Auswanderung aus Sachsen im 19. Jahrhundert (1815-1871)* [Emigration from Saxony in the nineteenth century (1815-1871)] Kulturhistorische Reihe, Nr. 30. Stuttgart: Deutsche Auslands-Institut, 1931.

see also Thuringia

22. Saxony--Cont.

Saxony-Weimar
Koch, Herbert. "Achthundert Auswanderer aus Sachsen-Weimar [1854]" [Eight hundred emigrants from Saxony-Weimar, 1854] *Archiv für Sippenforschung und alle verwandten Gebiete* . . . (Limburg/Lahn) 27 (1961): 131-136.

Ziegenrück
(*Kreis*)
see Saxony. Reitzengeschwenda

23. Silesia (and Moravia)

Freiwaldau
Zuber, Rudolph. "Die Auswanderung aus dem Freiwaldauer Bezirk um die Mitte des 19. Jahrhunderts" [Emigration from the district of Freiwaldau around the middle of the nineteenth century] *Schlesien: Ein Vierteljahresschrift für Kunst, Wissenschaft und Volkstum* (Nürnberg) 14 (1969): 100-106.

Freudenberg
Wolf, K. "Freudenberger Auswanderer von 1738" [Emigrants from Freudenberg in 1738] *Oberschlesische Heimat* 3 (1942?): 42.

Odergebirge
(Moravia)
Röder, J. "Wohin der Odergebirgler vor hundert Jahren wanderten" [Where emigrants from the Odergebirge went a century ago] *Heimatblätter für d. Olmützer Sprachinsel und d. Odergebirge* 2 (1939?), H. 4, pp. 13-18.

Schutter-
wald
Schott, P. "Deutsche Auswanderung in Schutterwald in d. letzten 100 Jahren" [German emigration from the Schutterwald during the last century] *C. V. Zeitung: Blätter fur Deutschtum und Judentum: Organisation d. Centralverein d. Staatsbürg. jüd. Glaubens* 16. J. (1937?) Nr. 16? pp. 40-44.

Silesia
(Schlesien)
Riegel, Gerhard. "Schlesische Auswanderer im 19. Jahrhundert" [Silesian emigrants in the nineteenth century] *Schlesische Rundschau* (Wangen/Allgäu) 8. J. (1956), Nr. 20, p. 7.

Prowe, M. "Schlesische Auswanderer" [Silesian emigrants] *Familiengeschichtliche Blätter* (1921), p. 131.

Alter, H. "Auswanderung aus Schlesien nach europaischen und überseeischen Ländern" [Silesian emigration to European and overseas countries] *Schlesien: Zeitschrift d. gesamt schles. Raumes* (Breslau) 1 (1939?): 303.

Iwan, Wilhelm. *Die altlutherische Auswanderung um die Mitte des 19. Jahrhunderts.* Ludwigsburg: Eichhornverlag für Johann-Hess-Institut, 1943.

24. Southern Germany
(*Allgäu, Bavaria, Swabia, Württemberg*)

Bavaria
"Auswandererverzeichnisse" [Emigration list] *Blätter des bayerischen Landesverein für Familienkunde* (1931), p. 34.

Beihingen/
Neckar
Ritz, Albrecht. "Auswanderung" [Emigration] in *Gestalten und Ereignisse aus Beihingen am Neckar.* Ludwigsburg: Buchdr. Otto Eichhorn, 1939.

Dilsberg/
Neckar
Kassbacher, M. "Amerika-Auswanderer aus Dilsberg" [Emigrants from Dilsberg to America] *Der Familienforscher* (1928), pp. 75, 212.

Friedberg/
Scheer
(Upper
Swabia)
Stail, G. "Auswanderer aus der oberschwäbische gefürstete Grafschaft Friedberg-Scheer" [Emigration from the Upper Swabian principality of Friedberg-Scheer] *Deutsch-Ungarische Heimatblätter* (Budapest) 2 (1931?): 131-136, 231-240.

Heidenheim/
Brenz
"Vor der Auswanderer aus dem Heidenheimer Gebiet" [Before the emigration from the Heidenheim area] in Ritz, Albert, *Nattheim und Oggenheim im Kranz der Nachbargemeinden.* Heidenheim/Brenz: Heidenheimer Verlag, 1951.

Leintal
Ruland, Fritz. "Die Auswanderung im 19. Jahrhundert: Leintal" [Nineteenth-century emigration: Leintal] *Unser Leintal: Ein Heimatbuch aus dem württembergischer Unterland* (Heilbronn), (1951), pp. 173-189.

24. *Southern Germany--Cont.*

Markgröningen
(Kreis Lud-
wigsburg)

Roemer, Hermann. *Die Auswanderung aus Markgröningen, Kreis
Ludwigsburg, in Zusammenhang
der württembergischen Auswanderung sippenkundlich darge-
stellt* [Emigration from Markgröningen, Kreis Ludwigsburg,
Württemberg, arranged for genealogical purposes] Ludwigsburg: Eichhorn Verlag L. Kal-
lenberg, 1941.

Oberdorf
(Allgäu)

Dertsch, Richard. *Abwanderung
aus der Pflege Oberdorf 1576-
1802* [Emigration from Oberdorf,
1576-1802] Alte Allgäuer Geschlechter, Nr. 21. Kempten:
Oechslhäuser, 1940. [Appar-
ently, only one person emigrated to America: Fleischhut,
Joh. Peter, 1764, from village
of Oberdorf.]

Oberschwaben

Brauns, N. "Ursachen und Ziele
der Auswanderung aus Oberschwaben im 18. und im Anfang des
19. Jahrhunderts" [Causes and
goals of the emigration from
Upper Swabia in the eighteenth
and early nineteenth centuries]
*Hohenzollerische Heimat: Vier-
teljahresblätter herausgegeben
von Verein für Geschichte, Kultur und Landeskunde in Hohenzollern* (Gammertingen) 2 (1952):
18-19.

Odenwald

see Hessen. Odenwald

Rettenberg
(Allgäu)

Huber, Heinrich. *Einwanderungen
und Auswanderungen im Gebiet d.
ehemal. Pflegeamt Rettenberg
von 15. bis 18. Jahrhundert* [Im-
migration and emigration from
the region of the former Rettenberg administrative office] Alter Allgäuer Geschlechter, Nr.
8. Kempten/Allgäu: Oechslhäuser
Verlag, 1939.

Swabia

see Specific Immigrants (Herter; Schopf)

Urach (*Ober-
amt*)

Krebs, Friedrich. "Zur Amerika-
Auswanderung des 18. Jahrhunderts aus Altwürttemberg haupt-
sächlich aus dem ehemaligen
Oberamt Urach" [Eighteenth-cen-
tury emigration to America from
Old Württemberg, particularly
from the former region of the
Oberamt Urach] *Südwestdeutsche
Blätter für Familien- und Wappenkunde* (Stuttgart) 9 (1957):
464-465.

Wangen/Allgäu

Klüber, K. "Auswandererliste
aus Wangen" [List of emigrants
from Wangen] *C. V. Zeitung:
Blätter für Deutschtum und Judentum: Organisation d. Centralverein d. Staatsbürg. jüd. Glaubens*
16. J. (1937?) Nr. 16? p. 45.

Klüber, K. W. "Auswanderer aus
ein südwestdeutschen Dorf nach
Ungarn und Amerika" [Emigrants
from a southwest German village
(Wangen) to Hungary and America]
Archiv für Sippenforschung
(1939), p. 141.

Württemberg
(Altwürt-
temberg)

Krebs, Friedrich. "Beiträge zur
Amerika-Auswanderung des 18.
Jahrhunderts aus Altwürttemberg"
[Contributions to eighteenth-
century emigration from Old
Württemberg to America] *Südwestdeutsche Blätter für Familien-
und Wappenkunde* (Stuttgart) 12
(1961): 186-189.

Gerber, Adolf. *Beiträge zur Auswanderung nach Amerika im 18.
Jahrhundert aus Altwürttemberg-
ischen Kirchenbücher* [Contribu-
tions to the eighteenth-century
emigration to America extracted
from Old Württemberg church reg-
isters] Stuttgart: Dr. Adolf
Gerber, 1928.

Gerber, Adolf. *Neue Beiträge
zur Auswanderung nach Amerika
im 18. Jahrhundert aus Altwürt-
tembergischen Kirchenbücher
unter Hinzuziehung anderer
Quellen* [Further contributions
to the eighteenth-century emigration to America extracted
from Old Württemberg church
registers and with reference
to other sources] Stuttgart:
Dr. Adolf Gerber, 1928.

Krebs, Friedrich. "Einige Amerika-Auswanderer aus Württemberg
in 18. Jahrhundert" [Some emigrants to America from Württemberg in the eighteenth century]
*Südwestdeutsche Blätter für
Familien- und Wappenkunde* (1957)
p. 442.

Marchtaler, K. "Auswanderer aus
Württemberg" [Emigrants from
Württemberg] *Zeitschriften des
Vereins Adler Wien* (1943), p.
189.

Bihl, Wolfdieter. "Zur Amerika-
Auswanderung im 19. Jahrhundert

24. *Southern Germany*--Cont.

am Beispiel einer Württembergischen Bürgersfamilie" [Re-
garding emigration to America
as exemplified by a Württemberg bourgeois family] *Adler:
Zeitschrift für Genealogie und
Heraldik* (Wien) 86 (1968) H. 4,
pp. 60-61.

Büttner, Karl. *Die Auswanderung aus Württemberg: Beitrag
zur Bevölkerungsgeographie*
[The emigration from Württemberg: Contributions to human
geography] Stuttgart: Fleischhauer & Spohn, 1938. [A dis-
sertation]

Prokopowitsch, Erich. "Dokumente württembergischer Auswanderer aus dem Jahren 1782-
1786 im Wiener Haus- Hof- und
Staatsarchiv" [Documents on
Württemberg emigration during
the years 1782-1786 in the
Vienna Haus- Hof- und Staats-
archiv] *Südostdeutsches Archiv*
(Munich) 5 (1962): 129-135.

see also Southern Germany.
Urach

25. *Specific Immigrants*

Astor family   Schuchmann, H. "Astor Familie"
Familiengeschichtliche Blätter
1: 117.

Dassel family   von Dassel, O. "Werner Ludwig
Dassel aus Hannover . . ."
[Werner Ludwig Dassel of Hannover, the oldest known ancestor of the Dassel family, of
Harxbüttel/Hannover] *Familiengeschichtliche Blätter* 2: 172.

Dern family   Friedrichs, H. F. "Amerikan-
ische Kriegsminister George
Henry Dern von deutschen Herkunft" [U.S. Secretary of War
George Henry Dern of German
ancestry] *Familie und Volk*
(1956), p. 34; see also [The
Dern family] in Ibid. (1955),
p. 122.

Engel, ____   Mergen, Josef. "Lebensgeschichte
(born in   eines Bernkasteler Auswanderers"
Bernkastel/   [Life history of an emigrant
Pfalz; lived   from Bernkastel] *Neues Trier-
in Albany,   isches Jahrbuch* (1962), pp. 52-
New York)   59.

Falk, Johann
Ludwig (of   see Specific Immigrants (Wind-
Zweibrücken)   biegler, Johann G.)

Fleischhut,
Joh. Peter   see Southern Germany. Oberdorf

Gerlinger, Joh-
ann Michael
(born in Creg-
lingen 27.10.
1752; lived
in Buffalo
Township,   Gerlinger, H. "Schicksal
Northumber-   eines Soldats aus Franken im
land County,   amerikanischen Unabhangig-
Pennsylvania,   keitskrieg" [The fate of a
in 1801; son   soldier from Franconia dur-
of Andreas and   ing the American Revolution]
Anna Maria Ger-   *Familie und Volk* (1957), p.
linger   396.

Herter, Christian   [A note on his Swabian an-
(U.S. Secretary   cestry] *Familie und Volk*
of State)   (1959), p. 363.

Heymann family   "Nassauer Familie in den Vereinigten Staaten" [A Nassau
family in the United States]
*Der Uhrturm: Mitteilungen der
nassauischen Familienge-
schichtlichen Vereinigung
Wiesbaden* (1940), p. 553.

Holm family   Holst, E. "Familie Holm in
Texas" [The Holm family in
Texas] *Familiengeschichtliche
Blatter* (1942), p. 1.

Holzhausen, Joh.   Jörns, E., and Dieck, A.
Diedrich (from   "Auswanderung nach Amerika"
Denkershausen,   [Emigration to America] *Nord-
Kreis Northeim)   deutsche Familienkunde* (1956),
p. 146.

Kaufmann family   Hofmann, M. "Kaufmann Erb-
schaft in America" [The Kauf-
mann estate in America] *Archiv für Sippenforschung*
(1944), p. 36.

Kreischer, Bal-   Rau, K. "Almanach pfälzischer
thasar   Familien: Der Pfalzer Balthasar Kreischer in Amerika"
[Almanac of Palatine families: The Palatine Balthasar
Kreischer in America] *Pfälzische Familien- und Wappenkunde* (1953), p. 63.

Morning family   Frank, B. H. W. "Die 'eng-
lische' Herkunft der Familie
Morning" [The "English" origins of the Morning family]
Familiengeschichtliche Blätter
(1936), p. 152.

25. *Specific Immigrants*--Cont.

Reinhart family Mergen, Josef. "Amtliches Dokument uber die Millionenerbschaft Reinhart" [Official document regarding the multimillion-dollar Reinhart estate] *Trierischer Volksfreund* (14 February 1954).

Rockefeller family von Stradonitz, K. "Herkunft der Familie Rockefeller . . ." [Ancestry of the Rockefeller family . . .] *Familiengeschichtliche Blätter* (1924), p. 45.

Schopf, Eugen "Eugen Schopf, J. K. Weiser . . . schwäbische Bauern machen Geschichte in Nord-Amerika" [Eugen Schopf, J. K. Weiser, Senior and Junior, Swabian peasants make history in North America] *Blätter für württembergische Familienkunde* (1938), p. 80.

Schramm family Schramm, A. "Deutsche in Nordamerika" [Germans in North America: Six generations of the Schramm family] *Göttinger Mitteilungen* (1949), pp. 78, 81.

Schuler, Christina (from Zweibrücken) *see* Specific Immigrants (Windbiegler, Johann G.)

Stoll, Karl Ludwig (doctor; born Mannheim, 17.12.1875; died Cincinnati, 17.12.1951) Stoll, A. "Dr. K. L. Stoll . . ." *Pfälzische Familien- und Wappenkunde* (1952), p. 9.

Weiser, J. K., Senior and Junior *see* Specific Immigrants (Schopf, Eugen)

Windbiegler, Johann Georg (of Hartenburg bei [Bad?] Dürkheim/Haardt) [An entry in the Evangelical Lutheran church register at Wiesbaden-Biebrich notes the birth of a son Johann to Maria Elisabeth, wife of Johann Georg Windbiegler, on 22 May 1750. The family was en route to Pennsylvania aboard a vessel at Biebrich. Godparents were Johann Ludwig Falk and Christina Schuler, both from Zweibrucken, who were also passengers. Falk was apparently the only one to reach Pennsylvania. He arrived aboard the *Sally*, Captain William Hassleton, from London, reaching Pennsylvania on 17 September 1750] *Familie und Volk* (1956), p. 236.

26. *Thuringia*

Lauscha Greiner, W. "Auswanderer aus Lauscha" [Emigrants from Lauscha] *Archiv für Sippenforschung und alle verwandten Gebiete* . . . (Limburg/Lahn) 32. J. (1966) H. 22, pp. 527-528.

Schwarzburg-Rudolstadt (Duchy) Ruhe, R. "Zur Geschichte der Überseeischen Auswanderung aus der Oberherrschaft des ehemaligen Fürstentums Schwarzburg-Rudolstadt im 19. Jahrhundert" [On the history of overseas emigration from the former Duchy of Schwarzburg-Rudolstadt, Upper Herrschaft, in the nineteenth century] *Rudolstädter Heimathefte: Beiträge zur Heimatkunde des Kreises Rudolstadt* (Rudolstadt) 4 (1958): 214-219, 244-251.

Ruhe, R. "Die deutsche Auswanderung im 19. Jahrhundert im Spiegel der Gesetzgebung des ehemaligen Fürstentum Schwarzburg-Rudolstadt" [Nineteenth-century German emigration as reflected by the laws of the former Duchy of Schwarzburg-Rudolstadt] *Rudolstädter Heimathefte: Beiträge zur Heimatkunde des Kreises Rudolstadt* 7 (1961): 278-284.

Thuringia Loeber, N. "Die sogenannte Stephans-Auswanderung, 1839 . . ." [The so-called Stephan's emigration, 1839, with particular emphasis on personal, economic, and social questions] *Die thüringer Sippe* (1939), p. 120.

Klüber, Karl Werner. "Die Hamburger Schiffslisten: Ein wertvolles Quelle zur Mitteldeutschen Übersee-Auswanderung im 19. und 20. Jahrhundert: Mit einer Liste ausgewanderter Thüringer aus dem Jahre 1850" [The Hamburg ship lists: A valuable source for Middle German overseas emigration in the nineteenth and twentieth centuries: With a list of Thuringian emigrants during the year 1850] *Mitteldeutsche Familienkunde: Beilage zu Genealogie: Deutsche Zeitschrift für Familienkunde* (Neustadt/Aisch) J. 6 (1965) 1:289-294.

Loeber, N. "Auswanderung thüringischer Lutheraner nach

26. *Thuringia--Cont.*

Nordamerika vor 100 Jahren" [Lutheran emigrants from Thuringia to North America a century ago] *Das thüringer Fähnlein* 7 (1938?): 291-293.

Seeberg-Elverfeldt, Roland. "Auswanderer aus Thüringen und Sachsen nach Übersee" [Overseas emigrants from Thuringia and Saxony] *Mitteldeutsche Familienkunde: Beilage zu Genealogie: Deutsche Zeitschrift für Familienkunde* (Neustadt/Aisch) J. 12 (1971) 3: 219-221.

see also Saxony

27. *Volksdeutsche*

Russia

"Auswanderung aus dem Bundesgebiet und West-Berlin nach den überseeischen Staaten" [Overseas emigration from Germany and West Berlin] *Heimatbuch der Deutschen aus Russland* (Stuttgart), (1963), pp. 76-80.

Slovakia

Klosz, H. "Erfassung der deutschen und nicht-deutschen Amerika-Wanderer aus Südosteuropa: Mit berücksichtigung der Slowakei . . ." [Identification of the German and non-German emigrants to America from southeastern Europe: With special reference to Slovakia and the Germans of Slovakia] *Karpathenland* (Reichenberg) 12 (1941-1942): 314-317.

Southeastern Europe

Klosz, H. "Amerikawanderer aus d. Südosten" [Southeastern European emigrants to America] *Volkstum im Südosten: Volkspolitische Monatschrift* (Vienna) 19 (1942?): 47-52. [Formerly entitled *Grenzland*]

FOOTNOTES

1. The earliest French censuses for Louisiana are published in J. Hanno Deiler, *The Settlement of the German Coast of Louisiana and the Creoles of German Descent* (Philadelphia: Americana Germanica Press, 1909; reprint ed., San Francisco: R & E Research Associates, 1968). For the church records, see Winston DeVille, *Early Settlers of Point Coupée: A Study Based upon Early Louisiana Church Records, 1737-1750* (New Orleans: Polyanthos, Inc., 1974). See also reference to early French ship-passenger lists in this chapter under the heading "French and Belgian Port Records" and also Clifford Neal Smith, "Lost Germans in French Louisiana: An Addendum to Winston DeVille's *Early Settlers of Pointe Coupée*," *Illinois State Genealogical Society Quarterly* 6 (1974): 164-165.

2. Discussion of manuscript source materials on German mercenary troops will be found in two sections within this article: "Muster Rolls of German Mercenaries in the American Revolution Found in American Archives" and in "German Mercenaries Who Served with the British During the American Revolution."

3. *Genealogie: Deutsche Zeitschrift für Familienkunde* 9 (1968): 224.

4. Ibid., 9 (1968): 284.

5. See item 799, dated 31 January 1763, in *Calendar of Home Office Papers of the Reign of George III, 1760 (25 Oct.)-1765.* (London: 1878; reprint ed., Nendeln, Liechtenstein: Kraus Repreint Ltd., 1967).

6. See item 334 (1761) in Ibid.

7. Hans Helmuth Rimpau, "'The Brunswickers' in Nordamerika 1776-1783" [The Brunswick (mercenaries) in North America, 1776-1783] *Archiv für Sippenforschung* 37 (1971): 204-219, 293-308; and 38 (1972): 346-355.

8. Erhardt Staedtler, *Die Ansbach-Bayreuth Truppen in amerikanischen Unabhängigkeitskrieg 1777-1783.* Freie Schriftenfolge der Gesellschaft für Familienforschung in Franken, Band 8 (Nürnberg: Kommissionsverlag Die Egge, 1956).

9. Francis Warrington Dawson, *Les Français morts pour l'Independance Americaine* (Paris: L'Oeuvre Latine, 1931).

INDEX

In the interest of space-saving, this index does not include the following:

1. Names of American towns and cities in which German-language newspapers have been published. These are shown alphabetically by state on pages 3-7 of the text. However, the states in which these places of publication were located are indexed herein.

2. Names of German towns and villages with primary source materials on German-Americans, as indexed in AGRIGA, which appear alphabetically by *Land* on pages 9-10.

3. German genealogical periodicals, indexed in *Der Schlüssel*, pages 12-18. The subject matter covered by these periodicals is indexed herein.

4. Locations, by county, of German-speaking congregations in the United States, pages 57-89. However, the states in which these congregations were located are indexed.

5. The alphabetical listing of German surname particles on pages 93-98.

A certain number of recurring descriptors have been abbreviated in this index, as follows:

A	America, American
bibl	bibliography (-ies)
cong	congregation(s)
G	German, Germany
GA	German-American
Gl	German-language
Gs	German-speaking
J	Jew(s), Jewish
NA	North America
pub	publication(s)

In addition, two conventions common to American indexes have been contravened:

1. Surname prefixes, such as *von* and *zu* are shown preceding the surnames, but are not indexed. For example, von Zinzendorf will be found under Z, rather than v.

2. Umlauted German vowels are alphabetized as if the the vowels were followed by an e. For example, Müller is alphabetized as Mueller, Päusch as Paeusch, Österreich as Oesterreich.